Praise for

AMERICAN GUN

• • • • • • • • • • • • • • • •

"Riveting . . . This book is not to be missed."

—Adrienne Westenfeld, *Esquire*

"The authors are meticulous in the details they recount . . . *American Gun* is a fascinating social history." —*The Economist*

"Reading the second half of *American Gun* is like watching a Shakespearean tragedy . . . The book is heartbreaking . . . A lucid, straightforward, and well-researched and -reported work."

—Colin Dickey, *The New Republic*

"[McWhirter and Elinson] have done a masterful and damning job tracing the birth and development, and rampant misuse, of the AR-15, and there are heartbreaking stories elegantly told of the destruction this weapon has wrought on families and towns across the nation . . . Poignant."

—*Air Mail*

"McWhirter and Elinson offer a comprehensive, even-handed look at the AR-15's history and the debate over gun violence . . . [Their] well-reported book is vital for anyone who wants to understand how Stoner's creation transformed over time into what the authors call the 'fulcrum of America's great gun divide.'" —Andrew Demillo, Associated Press

"[A] superb history . . . [*American Gun*] is a meticulously researched and impressively informed book . . . A riveting exploration of the cost of the nation's fascination with an iconic weapon."

—*Kirkus Reviews* (starred review)

Joann Vitelli

© Joanna Eldredge Morrissey

Cameron McWhirter and Zusha Elinson

AMERICAN GUN

Cameron McWhirter is a national reporter for *The Wall Street Journal* based in Atlanta. He has covered mass shootings, violent protests, and natural disasters across the South. He is also the author of *Red Summer: The Summer of 1919 and the Awakening of Black America*. Previously, he reported for other publications in the United States, as well as in Bosnia, Iraq, and Ethiopia.

Zusha Elinson is a national reporter writing about guns and violence for *The Wall Street Journal*. Based in California, he has also written for the Center for Investigative Reporting and the *New York Times* Bay Area section.

The authors received a MacDowell Fellowship to complete this book.

ALSO BY CAMERON McWHIRTER

Red Summer: The Summer of 1919 and the Awakening of Black America

AMERICAN GUN

AMERICAN GUN

THE
TRUE STORY
OF THE
AR-15

Cameron McWhirter and Zusha Elinson

PICADOR

FARRAR, STRAUS AND GIROUX

New York

Picador
120 Broadway, New York 10271

Library of Congress Control Number: 2023008699
Paperback ISBN: 978-1-250-33800-6

Our books may be purchased in bulk for promotional, educational, or business use.
Please contact your local bookseller or the Macmillan Corporate and Premium
Sales Department at 1-800-221-7945, extension 5442, or by email at
MacmillanSpecialMarkets@macmillan.com.

Picador® is a U.S. registered trademark and is used by Macmillan Publishing Group,
LLC, under license from Pan Books Limited.

For book club information, please email marketing@picadorusa.com.

picadorusa.com • Follow us on social media at @picador or @picadorusa

1 3 5 7 9 10 8 6 4 2

To our families

When you see something that is technically sweet, you go
ahead and do it and you argue about what to do about it only
after you have had your technical success.

—J. ROBERT OPPENHEIMER, who led the effort to make the first atomic bomb

Guns, like everything else, have their social history.

—JOHN ELLIS, *The Social History of the Machine Gun*

Contents

A photographic insert follows page 250.

A Note About Names

The AR-15

Over the decades, various individuals, companies, and government entities have given the AR-15 rifle different names, and following the many labels can get confusing. For this book, we have tried to streamline nomenclature while remaining historically accurate. The AR-15 rifle was the fifteenth weapon developed by ArmaLite, a subsidiary of Fairchild Engine and Airplane Corporation. AR-15 stood for the name of the company and a model number. Once the military adopted the gun, it assigned the rifle the designation M16, for its sixteenth model of an infantry rifle. Military bureaucracy assigned various designations to different versions of the gun, including XM16E1 (an early adopted version) and, later, M16A1. Various versions followed, all with updates, but the guns were fundamentally versions of the AR-15 invented by Eugene Stoner and his colleagues at ArmaLite that permitted automatic as well as semiautomatic firing. Commercial versions of the gun, which were limited to semiautomatic fire, were commonly called AR-15s. In the interest of clarity, we will refer to Eugene Stoner's rifle prior to its military adoption as the AR-15. In discussing military versions of the rifle, we use the designation M16, unless referring to later variants such as the M4. We have not altered quotes in which officials may have referred to the AR-15 when discussing the military version of the gun. We will call the civilian version of the rifle the AR-15 instead of the oft-used journalistic phrase "AR-15-style rifle" for simplicity's sake. Proper military usage regarding rifle designation has no hyphen between the M and the model number, for example, M16 as opposed to M-16. However, the two versions often have been used interchangeably in official reports, private correspondence, academic papers, books, newspaper accounts, and various other records from the 1960s to the present day. In the interest of uniformity, we have corrected all references to M-16 to read M16.

Colt

The gunmaker Colt purchased the manufacturing rights to the AR-15 from ArmaLite's parent company, Fairchild Engine and Airplane Corporation, in 1959. Colt used different names over the decades, including, in the 1950s, Colt's. To reduce confusion, we have simply referred to the company in this book as Colt.

Automatic, Semiautomatic, Select-Fire

An automatic rifle allows the shooter to fire a stream of bullets by holding down the trigger. A semiautomatic rifle allows the shooter to fire one shot per trigger pull. The gun automatically loads the next round using the energy from the previous shot. All the shooter has to do is pull the trigger. The distinction is important in the story of the AR-15. The military version of the gun, the M16, was designed so that soldiers could fire it on full automatic or semiautomatic with the flip of a switch. This type of gun is called select-fire. The AR-15s sold to civilians on the commercial market are semiautomatic.

Bullets, Cartridges, Rounds, and Caliber

A bullet is a metal projectile that flies out of the barrel of a gun. A cartridge, also known as a round, is made up of the bullet and a metal casing that contains propellant. A bullet's caliber is generally a measurement of its diameter. The AR-15 rifle uses a relatively small round that is called a .223, though it actually measures .224 inches, or a 5.56 round in metric nomenclature. The 5.56 round, developed for adoption by forces of the North Atlantic Treaty Organization, is loaded at a higher pressure than a .223 round.

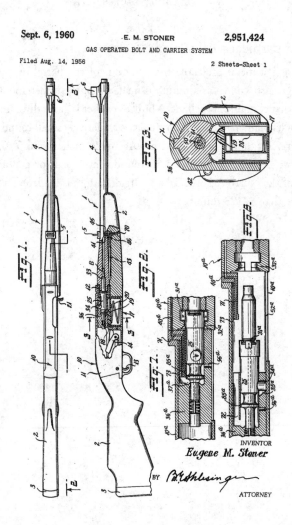

Sept. 6, 1960   E. M. STONER   2,951,424

GAS OPERATED BOLT AND CARRIER SYSTEM

Filed Aug. 14, 1956   2 Sheets—Sheet 1

FIG. 3.

FIG. 1.

FIG. 2.

FIG. 2A.

FIG. 7.

INVENTOR

Eugene M. Stoner

BY *B.E.Schlesinger*

ATTORNEY

Eugene Stoner filed for a patent in 1956 that would change firearms history and American culture. These diagrams, included with his patent, show his revolutionary gas system. Using this gas system in combination with modern materials like aluminum and plastic and other design features, Stoner created his most famous invention, the AR-15. The lightweight, rapid-fire rifle was easy to shoot and keep on target. It was used by U.S. soldiers to fight America's wars from Vietnam to Afghanistan. But a civilian version of the rifle later became an attractive weapon for mass shooters to attack fellow Americans.

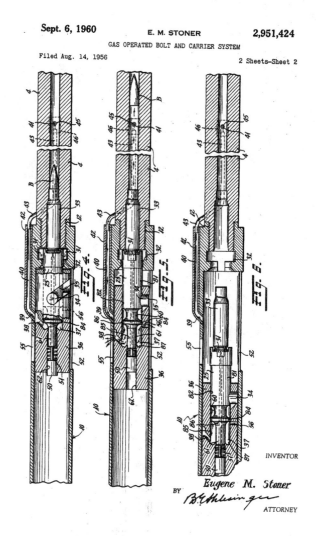

INVENTOR

Eugene M. Stoner

BY *B.E. Thiesinger*

ATTORNEY

Stoner's patented "gas operated bolt and carrier system" allowed him to use lightweight gas instead of the heavy metal parts long used in the internal operating systems of semiautomatic and automatic rifles. Stoner made a thin tube that channeled the gas from each shot into the heart of the gun to move mechanisms that ejected spent casings and loaded new rounds. Some gunsmiths compare the gas operation to blowing a paper wrapper off a straw.

AMERICAN GUN

PROLOGUE: TEN MINUTES, 1,057 BULLETS

He wandered the windowless casino floor from about three thirty to seven thirty that morning, stopping to play video poker, his favorite game. The sixty-four-year-old was a hunched six feet, pudgy and balding with sunken brown eyes and a spotty growth of white whiskers—a pasty, sullen man more comfortable with statistical probabilities than with people. He didn't stand out on that Sunday, October 1, 2017. It wasn't strange to see a disheveled man shuffling alone past rows of the bright baby-blue, ruby-pink, and neon-green machines that produced a cacophony of pings, bings, and cha-chings. This was Vegas, and he was just another lost soul. Video poker was his game because he felt he had mastered the machines. Stephen Paddock believed he was better than other video poker players because he had studied the probabilities of winning and losing. That morning he played out of habit. He no longer cared whether he won. It didn't matter anymore.

Paddock returned to his suite in the Mandalay Bay hotel. Elevators carried him thirty-two floors above the city. The upper-floor suites commanded grand views, from the south end of the famous Strip out to the desert mountains ringing the city. Paddock's multiple rooms, called a

"Vista Suite" by the hotel, looked down on Las Vegas Boulevard and beyond to the black-glass pyramid of the Luxor hotel and casino. Across the boulevard's six lanes was a large venue for concerts and festivals called Las Vegas Village.

For days, Paddock had driven his black 2017 Chrysler Pacifica minivan back and forth between his home in nearby Mesquite, Nevada, and the Mandalay Bay. Each time, he had brought more suitcases and bags. Sometimes bellboys helped him, wheeling carts stacked with his bags to the larger service elevators. They chatted and laughed, and Paddock tipped them. Early in the afternoon on October 1, Paddock brought two rolling suitcases and a bag to his suite, riding in an elevator alone. He called for room service, then set up a small video camera on a room-service cart out in the hallway to monitor any movement from a laptop in his suite. He used power tools to install a metal bracket that blocked the stairwell door in the hallway. He had a hammer to break window glass when the time came. He brought a scuba mask to help him deal with smoke or tear gas when police responded.

Paddock unzipped his bags and took out fourteen AR-15 semiautomatic rifles and eight similar guns called AR-10s. He had dozens of fully loaded hundred-round magazines. The rifles were civilian versions of guns invented in the 1950s by a tiny company in Hollywood, California. The company created a revolutionary rifle for the U.S. military. It was a light, easy-to-use weapon to help soldiers fight Communist insurgencies in the developing world. The futuristic rifles were designed to achieve a simple goal: fire a lot of bullets fast to kill or maim as many enemy soldiers as possible. The design was shaped by a military adage: whoever shoots the most lead wins.

By nighttime, Paddock arrayed the guns so he could pick them up in succession from the beds and the purple and white furniture near two floor-to-ceiling windows. To most of the rifles he attached bump stocks, devices allowing the semiautomatic guns to mimic automatic fire. Down below, a country music festival was taking place at Las Vegas Village. About twenty-two thousand people crowded before a large stage to hear the musician Jason Aldean. Paddock likely couldn't hear it. He'd stuffed tissue into his ears to drown out the loud noises he was about to make.

At 10:05 p.m., Paddock, dressed in a brown shirt and black pants, lifted an AR-15 to his shoulder. He aimed downward. Aldean was playing a slow love song called "When She Says Baby." Fans swaying to the music thought they heard fireworks, far off. Then they saw people falling. Everyone started running but no one knew where to hide. The bullets rained down in the darkness. In about ten minutes, Paddock fired 1,057 bullets. He killed 58 people that night and wounded 413 others. Another 456 were injured trying to escape the mayhem. An aging, overweight gambler who found sex exhausting killed more people in a mass shooting than any other individual in U.S. history. The AR-15 rifles had made the ghoulish feat easy. No one could explain why he wanted to kill so many people—not his girlfriend, not his brothers, not the Federal Bureau of Investigation. Paddock, who had become wealthy by investing in real estate, spent nearly $95,000 on guns, ammo, and accessories in the year leading up to the massacre. In addition to his semiautomatic rifles, Paddock brought along two other guns but fired only one of them, a Smith & Wesson .38 revolver. He used it to shoot himself in the head. Near his body, police found a lined sheet of paper on which Paddock had scribbled calculations of how much a bullet fired from an AR-15 would drop in its arc after five hundred yards. He wanted to make sure his shots would hit concertgoers. Statistical probabilities to the end.

Stephen Paddock, who grew up in Los Angeles, was born in 1953. A year later a company called ArmaLite with just a handful of employees began operations about fifteen miles away in a one-story brick building on Santa Monica Boulevard in Hollywood. The brain of this tiny outfit was Eugene Stoner, a soft-spoken, persistent, and brilliant man in his thirties. Some called him Gene, but most people, even his wife and children, called him Stoner. One of his inventions, ArmaLite's fifteenth creation, hence its designation AR-15, would make him one of the most famous gun designers of the twentieth century, perhaps any century.

American Gun is the history of how a unique rifle invented by a family man pursuing an obsessive hobby became the most popular and divisive rifle in U.S. history. The consequences of the AR-15's creation have coursed through our society and politics for generations in ways the weapon's inventor and promoters never foresaw. The gun has been used in conflicts far beyond U.S. borders, first and foremost when the select-fire version, the M16, was carried by U.S. troops and allies in Southeast Asia. The gun has played a key role in other conflicts as well, including the Troubles in Northern Ireland, the civil war in Colombia, and the drug wars in Mexico. Terrorists, death squads, and drug traffickers continue to use the weapon with deadly effect in Latin America and elsewhere. Those important stories need to be told, but this book centers on what happened in the United States. Handguns, far more pervasive in American society, are used in the vast majority of murders and suicides. That subject deserves its own careful exploration. This book is about a rifle that has become the lightning rod for the nation's gun debate: the AR-15.

How did the weapon American soldiers carried in Vietnam become best known for killing schoolchildren? *American Gun* is about how that happened and what we can learn from the story.

Americans know the horror of where we are now, with people going about their daily lives—at school, at the movies, at the store, at a concert—and suddenly finding themselves running for their lives as a disturbed person or extremist opens fire with an AR-15. And yet few of the participants in America's perpetual gun debate have known the true, complicated history of this consequential invention. The inventor created the gun with a simple goal: build a better rifle for the U.S. military and its allies during the Cold War. He wanted to protect the country he loved. But now, his invention is more well-known as a tool to kill innocent Americans.

This story involves presidents from Eisenhower to Biden, bickering generals, schmoozy businessmen, exploding watermelons, a renegade spy, desperate soldiers, cop-killing gang members, bullet-riddled goats, cult leaders, partisan senators, a tap dancer turned gunmaker, a gun-obsessed hedge-fund king, mercenary admen, a brigade of lobbyists, political extremists, disturbed killers, and victims—those who've died and those who must spend their lives wounded and struggling.

Americans no longer feel safe. Everyday activities such as going to school and clocking in to work are informed by the fear of mass shootings. Kindergartners are drilled on how to avoid being shot by attackers armed with AR-15s. Companies have tightened security and beefed up mass-shooter training. Jittery movie- and concertgoers scan for exits. Police departments from the largest cities to the smallest towns issue military-grade body armor able to withstand the high-velocity rounds from an AR-15.

Something has to change, and true change has to focus on the core issue: How do we as a society keep this weapon out of the hands of people who shouldn't have such a gun? Solutions will require trial-and-error efforts, patience, compromise, and abandonment of fiercely held positions. And they will require an understanding of how we got here.

This is the extraordinary story of the AR-15 rifle, the American gun.

PART I

1.

THE BOY WHO LIKED EXPLOSIONS

It's amazing he didn't hurt himself
or anyone else in those days.
—Eugene Stoner's daughter

The July 13, 1953, issue of *Life* magazine featured a photo essay capturing Los Angeles's extraordinary growth. It opened with a photo of tract homes and moving vans extending down a street as far as the eye could see. "Every day, including Saturdays and Sundays, is moving day in Los Angeles," the article declared.

Hollywood, from Frank Sinatra to Elizabeth Taylor, got a lot of attention. But the industry drawing the most people to Los Angeles was aviation. Tens of thousands worked designing and building airplanes. Aerospace multimillionaire executives such as Howard Hughes held out the prospect that average Joes—war veterans, factory workers, anybody willing to move to L.A.—could make it big if they had a good idea. The area exuded an aura of the new. Disneyland opened in 1955. The Dodgers, stolen from Brooklyn, started playing in L.A. in 1958. Religion got a pseudoscience makeover in Southern California: L. Ron Hubbard started the Church of Scientology in 1954. No city better captured America's muscular belief in itself.

Here the idea for what would become the AR-15 rifle took shape in the garage of an amateur tinkerer. Eugene Stoner was a man obsessed with engineering problems. He thought about them all the time. When an idea came to him, he scribbled it down, sketching ideas on anything he could find—pads of paper, napkins, restaurant tablecloths. He had no formal training in engineering or gun design and this lack of education, instead of limiting him, gave him the freedom to try out ideas that others wouldn't consider. He wore glasses and had a fondness for bow ties. His figure was slightly round and his colleagues called him a teddy bear. He refused to swear or spank his children. "Boy that frosts me," he said when he was upset. He liked to tweak self-important people with a dry sense of humor. He admired smarts, no matter the person's formal education. He hated attention. When later in life he was asked about his career as one of the most well-known firearms inventors of the twentieth century, he said, "It was kind of a hobby that got out of hand."

Eugene Morrison Stoner was born on November 22, 1922, near Gosport, Indiana, population seven hundred. His father, thirty-year-old Lloyd Lester Stoner, was working on a farm near his boyhood home. A few years earlier, Lloyd, tall with a square jaw, had traveled from Indiana's cornfields to fight in France during World War I. His lungs were scarred by a German mustard gas attack. After the war, Lloyd married Britannia "Billie" Morrison, a woman with a soft chin and a far-off look in her eyes. Life was difficult for the couple. Lloyd eked out a living as a farmer, but midwestern winters were hard on his damaged lungs. He often came down with colds and coughs. In 1925, Lloyd, his wife, and their toddler, Eugene, joined throngs of farmers abandoning homesteads in America's heartland for California, where jobs were plentiful and winters were mild. The Stoners settled in the Coachella Valley, a desert area east of Los Angeles where farmers grew dates, oranges, grapes, and cotton. The dry air soothed Lloyd's lungs. He started his own business, delivering gas and oil to farmers.

Young Gene Stoner spent his youth in the valley. He played in the dirt with toy trucks and airplanes. He pedaled along the dusty roads on his tricycle and ran through orchards with the family's Boston terrier. Gene's father often took him hunting, then a common pastime for

American boys. Little Gene had a gentle smile and a far-off look like his mom's. He wore knickers or overalls and a little cap. On special occasions, he wore a white sailor's outfit complete with insignia and neckerchief. The boy loved Flash Gordon, a popular comic strip, radio show, and movie serial featuring a muscular hero who used ray guns to battle alien foes.

Gene was fascinated with launching projectiles of all kinds. As a boy of six, he filled a pipe with gunpowder, took it into the desert, and lit it. His first pipe bomb exploded, raising a massive dust cloud. At seven, he built his own cannon. He went to a friend's father who owned a machine shop, begged for a metal pipe, and persuaded the man to drill holes in it. He got some magnesium from another friend's father who owned the local drugstore. With these ingredients, he built the primitive cannon and pointed it at a friend's house across the street. Before Gene could open fire, his father ran to stop him. "I told you to do this at the city dump," he scolded. At ten years old, Gene was building rockets, also with magnesium. He made mistakes but learned each time. Once he set up a rocket in the middle of the street. Other boys in the neighborhood cheered and counted down as he lit the fuse. The rocket flew up, then veered and slammed into his own house, blowing a hole in the wall.

"It's amazing he didn't hurt himself or anyone else in those days," his daughter Susan said years later.

When the Great Depression hit, Lloyd's oil and gas business failed and his marriage with Billie fell apart. Gene's family decided to send the teen to live in a boardinghouse by himself in Long Beach to attend Long Beach Polytechnic High School. He met a cute and feisty girl named Jean who went to a Catholic girls' school nearby. She loved hunting and shooting. She wanted to be a pilot like Amelia Earhart. Gene and Jean bonded over their shared interests. He was attracted to her verve, and she was drawn to his unconventional smarts.

"He received average grades, but he was very interested in anything mechanical and there was this curiosity; he was a genius. He was brilliant," Jean later recalled.

Their names, Gene and Jean, caused confusion, so Jean took to just calling her beau "Stoner." When Stoner graduated from high school, he had no money for college. So at age eighteen he went to work for Vega Aircraft Corporation, installing weaponry on warplanes. On weekends, the couple drove out into the desert to hunt doves, then drove back to L.A. to see a big band at the Hollywood Bowl. They owned rifles and bows and were good shots. Once they reenacted the famous William Tell legend with Jean placing an apple on her head while Stoner pointed his bow and arrow. Stoner split the apple, and Jean was untouched. "He, we, had a devil-may-care nature—we did a lot of things while looking for enjoyment," she later wrote.

After Pearl Harbor, Southern California was in a perpetual state of anxiety over a possible Japanese invasion. Stoner's factory went into overdrive, producing B-17 Flying Fortresses and other aircraft. Stoner installed machine guns on the planes, learning firsthand how the gun's parts fit together as a system. At home, Stoner and Jean began to build a life together. On July 4, 1942, the couple eloped to Las Vegas. Stoner made an intricate wedding band for Jean. Because she was allergic to gold, he crafted it out of platinum. Both wanted a family, but first Stoner wanted to be a pilot.

He tried to sign up for the army air force. He hoped—as the recruiting posters promised—to "fly and fight with the greatest team in the world." But the greatest team wasn't interested, due to Stoner's poor eyesight. His second choice was the navy, where his uncle had promised to find him a stateside post. Moments after he enlisted in February 1944, a Marine Corps recruiter walked into the room and pointed to several men, including Stoner. Stoner used a pay phone near the recruitment office to deliver the news to his wife, then pregnant with their first child. The Marines assigned Stoner to work in Aviation Ordnance, maintaining large-caliber machine guns on the planes as well as anti-aircraft guns. His first assignment was the Marine Corps Air Station in El Toro, California. "He was in heaven," his daughter Susan recalled. "Imagine being twenty years old, obsessed with guns, cannons, and then being able to work with the big stuff during a war."

In June 1945, Stoner shipped off for the Philippines. The couple devised a code that Stoner used in his letters to let her know where he was and what he was doing even though it was prohibited under military protocol. Jean used it too for important news. "Our second child was due and I wanted to let him know as quickly as I could," she recalled.

Stoner never saw battle. He spent his time repairing guns and doing "a certain amount of experimenting on different types of machine guns," he said later. On his own time, the compulsive inventor designed two different .30-caliber rifles that were similar to the standard U.S. military rifle at the time, the dependable if heavy M1. Stoner studied the inner workings of that rifle extensively, trying to figure out ways to improve it. Stoner was excited by such engineering challenges, but he had mixed feelings about the military. He wasn't an "Oorah!" kind of Marine. When he repaired military weapons or worked on his own guns, Stoner sought out the most efficient solution to whatever mechanical problem faced him. But he felt that the military didn't favor efficiency. Bureaucratic inertia usually won the day.

A few months after Stoner went overseas, the war in the Pacific ended. Troops came home as conquering heroes, but Stoner was one of many who stayed behind after the fighting stopped. Stationed in China, he continued to experiment with firearms. When he came back in February 1946, he brought a special gift for his wife: gun parts from the Far East. He used them to build her a homemade rifle. Jean loved it.

He found a job repairing slot machines and another making false teeth. The young father needed money to support his family. In February 1947, he took a job at Whittaker Corporation, which manufactured aircraft valves. He worked in the machine shop but spent much of his time fixing designs that came down from the engineering department. His intelligence caught the attention of Bob Wilson, who ran both the shop and the engineering department. After a few years, Wilson brought Stoner upstairs to work with the engineers, even though Stoner had no engineering degree. He received a cold welcome. "What do you mean taking him up here? He's not a graduate engineer," the head design engineer said in front of Stoner.

But the head design engineer also had a nurturing side and spent hours showing Stoner how to solve engineering problems. By 1951, Stoner and Wilson decided to strike out on their own as consultants, designing valves and other parts for aviation corporations. He found success in spite of his lack of formal education, teaching himself the principles of engineering, physics, and materials science. "Once I got established in that thing, nobody asked me whether I graduated from engineering school or not," Stoner recalled. Stoner had an ability to dream up new creations and to visualize mechanical systems. "I'm not sure if I had been a graduate engineer that I would've tried all the ideas I had because some of the ideas from an engineering standpoint did not look to be feasible," he recalled.

The Stoners—Jean, Gene, Patty, and Michael—had moved to a small white stucco house on a corner lot in Westchester, a neighborhood adjacent to Los Angeles International Airport. Westchester had wide streets, palm trees, and ranch-style homes. Stoner spent a lot of his time in the detached garage behind the house. The Stoner family car was never parked inside. The little building was Stoner's gun lab. Inside, he stored tooling machines to cut, bore, and grind parts. He refused, despite his wife's pleading, to move closer to the beach because he worried sand and salty air would ruin them. His daughter Patty remembered seeing prototypes of guns alongside piles of mechanical drawings when she wandered into the garage.

"He was a very quiet person," Jean said. "But if you talked about guns, cars, or planes, he'd talk all night."

In many ways, Stoner was a quintessential American male. The 1950s was the decade of the hobbyist inventor. *Popular Mechanics* magazine found lots of readers like Stoner who wanted to know about the latest advances in technology. They believed they could move the country forward with the power of their ingenuity—and strike it rich in the process. Every day after returning home from work, Stoner would eat the dinner that Jean had prepared (beef Stroganoff was his favorite), take a quick nap, and then walk to the garage to work on his guns.

"We were like *the* 1950s family. It was California. It was booming after the war. All the aerospace was booming," said daughter Susan, who was born in 1954. "I knew from my dad, I felt from him, the future was wide open."

2.

MEN AGAINST FIRE

It should be a nice project for the younger generations to
tackle and furnish our infantry with the best rifle in the world.
—John C. Garand

On the early morning of June 25, 1950, Communist North Korean troops crossed the thirty-eighth parallel and invaded U.S.-backed South Korea. In three days, they captured Seoul and pressed south. U.S. diplomats secured a United Nations resolution authorizing member states to send forces and aid to South Korea, but the whole world knew that America would do the bulk of the fighting. The U.S. Far East Command, then led by World War II hero General Douglas MacArthur, shuttled troops and materiel from Japan to the rapidly shrinking territory still under South Korean control. American commanders believed that even a modest show of force by U.S. troops would halt the invasion. Most Americans assumed their country was more than equipped to handle an army of poorly trained peasants.

An advance contingent of several hundred U.S. soldiers flew to Korea. In the early morning hours of July 5, the unit, led by Lieutenant Colonel Brad Smith, dug in along a ridge above a dirt road near Osan, a small community south of Seoul. When dawn arrived, it rained; the men ate cold rations in freshly dug foxholes. The force had a battery of artillery near the lines, heavy machine guns on tripods, some outdated mortars, and a few bazookas. But the bulk of Smith's unit—two companies of about 540 men—were infantry: grunts with rifles.

Most of the men were armed with the standard-issue rifle from World War II, the semiautomatic M1 Garand. Made of wood and steel, it weighed about 9.5 pounds unloaded, and it fired a big bullet, giving the shooter's shoulder a good kick when fired. M1s had been sturdy and successful weapons for GIs as they slogged their way across the Pacific and Europe against the Axis forces. By 1950, many officers in the army had concluded that American soldiers needed a light, rapid-fire rifle to meet the demands of modern warfare. But because of research cutbacks and dithering bureaucrats, no such rifle existed.

At 7:00 a.m. on that July morning, thirty-three Soviet-made tanks followed by five thousand North Korean soldiers in trucks approached the position. Around 8:15 a.m., Smith gave the order to fire. Americans fired recoilless rifles and scored direct hits, but the shells bounced off enemy tanks. The men fired their M1s, but the rifles didn't fire fast enough to make up for the overwhelming numerical advantage of the North Koreans. In the battle that unfolded, the small band of Americans fought as best they could, but the North Koreans outflanked them. Running low on ammunition, the Americans pulled back. The withdrawal became a rout, with U.S. infantry running down the ridge, abandoning wounded and dead. As they fled through the rice paddies, soldiers tossed their heavy M1 rifles into the mud.

The battle revealed a glaring problem to U.S. commanders. "American equipment was below par at Osan," according to a classified army report. A day after the defeat, James S. Lay Jr., executive secretary of President Harry Truman's National Security Council, wrote a classified memorandum. Lay called for the U.S. military to revamp its armament development and production from top to bottom. "[N]obody knows what to make, or how much to make, or when, or why," he complained. The four-page document conveyed panic: "Our national survival is now paramount over all other considerations."

The Korean crisis brought to a head tensions that had been festering in Washington over U.S. military preparedness as the Cold War escalated. "We may find—with overnight suddenness—that total war is upon us and we are woefully unprepared," declared an editorial in the influential *Washington Evening Star*. The same edition carried a front-page political cartoon showing an apprehensive Uncle Sam trying to make a plowshare back into a sword.

The crisis forced the U.S. military to reexamine the design, cost, and function of almost everything in its arsenal, and it solidified a consensus in Washington that U.S. troops and their allies needed a new model of their most basic weapon: the rifle. "All of the talk about push-button warfare—the generally popular concept of atomic warfare and super weapons—all of this to the contrary, *the rifleman is more important than ever*," wrote the American military journalist Bill Shadel in 1951.

Gun designers and military officials debated about the characteristics of a new infantry rifle. What was more important in a weapon: how accurately and far it fired or how rapidly? Rifle designers had to balance trade-offs over the heft and strength of materials used for the guns and the ammunition; the energy of the explosives used to propel objects; and the mechanics of how quickly and safely a weapon could be reloaded and fired. These weren't abstract concepts. They were practical considerations that determined on a battlefield who won and who lost, who lived and who died.

Gun designers had wrangled over these issues for centuries. The saga of firearms development is a complex, overlapping tale, with generations of gunmakers taking elements from previous devices and casting other elements aside to forge new, synthesized concepts. Some advancements—such as rifled barrels and bullets and gunpowder encased in metal shells—revolutionized firearms and were universally adopted. Promising ideas considered by a gunmaker in one era could be dropped because metals weren't strong enough, ammunition was too unreliable, or some other problem. Gun designers decades later would take up those ideas when metals were strengthened or ammunition could be manufactured more precisely.

Historians believe Chinese alchemists accidentally invented an early version of what would come to be known as gunpowder around 850 CE while trying to find an elixir that would grant immortality. Weapons makers soon used gunpowder to create weapons for Chinese imperial armies. These early cannons and guns had three core features: a barrel, a propellant, and a projectile that fit tightly into the barrel. When the propellant ignited, the expanding gases drove the object out at a target. When the powder came to Europe, new, faster-burning versions were developed, and firearms makers produced guns that were superior to Chinese versions. Why Chinese empires didn't devise advanced guns in this epoch is a subject of academic debate, but by the 1400s, European armies were using versions of muskets in major battles on their continent and beyond. Muskets proved critical in European expansion to other parts of the world, including the American colonies.

Gunmakers in Europe and the Americas worked to improve these long guns in a host of ways, and the issue of accuracy versus rapid-fire was a constant tension in their designs. In Europe, where armies moved in large formations over open land, military strategists tended to train troops for mass volley firing. In the Americas, frontiersmen prized marksmanship both in hunting and in their warfare with Native Americans, so American gunmakers tended to place more importance on accuracy. After the slaughter of the Civil War, many Union leaders felt their troops had been poor shots and a group of former military officials founded the National Rifle Association (NRA) in 1871 to train citizens to become better marksmen.

Gunmakers on both continents made changes to weapons and ammunition to improve accuracy. They added rifling, etching curved grooves inside a gun barrel that gave bullets a twist to stabilize them as they flew through the air (hence the term "rifle"). Gunmakers also worked to find ways for weapons to fire more rapidly.

With muskets, soldiers had to load gunpowder down the barrel, then add the lead ball and pack it down with a ramrod—a time-consuming process. The faster soldiers could reload, the more lead they could pour at the enemy. The carnage of the Napoleonic Wars in Europe and the Civil War in the United States showed that armies that fired more often had an advantage. Gunmakers started making cartridges with bullets and gunpowder together in one packet. Later they encapsulated the powder with a bullet and metal casing. By the late 1830s, European inventors created breech-loading guns, whereby a shooter could load from the back end of the barrel. Gunmakers added bolts to pop spent bullet shells out and lock fresh ammunition in place. As soon as an improvement came along, competitors adopted it—and the race was back on to find a way to shoot even faster or more accurately.

Rifles such as the AR-15 were an offshoot of gun designers' pursuit of a self-loading, rapid-fire weapon—what gunmakers came to call a machine gun. As far back as ancient China, inventors had created propellant weapons that launched multiple projectiles at once. In Europe, inventors worked on multibarrel guns and similar devices. The Renaissance artist and inventor Leonardo da Vinci sketched out plans for guns that fired volleys of projectiles. In 1718, the British inventor James Puckle filed a patent in London for a rotating gun—considered by many to be the very first machine gun—that sat on a tripod and fired multiple rounds by turning a crank. But none of these efforts got very far.

Beginning in earnest in the 1800s, gun designers used tools, metals, and designs of the industrial revolution to create guns that could fire and reload rapidly. The three leading innovators, all born in the United States, focused much of their efforts on selling weapons to European powers. All three men had no formal education in engineering or metallurgy. Two had no gunsmithing backgrounds.

The first successful machine-gun inventor was Richard Jordan Gatling, who conceived his invention during the Civil War and believed it would reduce killing in future wars.

"It occurred to me that if I could invent a machine—a gun—which could by its rapidity of fire enable one man to do as much battle duty as a hundred, that it would to a great extent supersede the necessity of large armies, and consequently exposure to battle and disease [would] be greatly diminished," he wrote.

Gatling urged Abraham Lincoln to purchase his weapon, which he called an act of Providence to end the Southern rebellion. U.S. forces, as well as state and local authorities, used the gun during a few battles in the Civil War, and later against Native Americans, rioters, strikers, and the Spanish in Cuba. The gun, based in part on the operation of a mechanical seed planter that Gatling designed, made him wealthy. Over years he came up with improved versions, but the core mechanics of the devices were rotating barrels set on cylinders. A shooter turned a crank, spinning the barrels around. After a round fired, the turning of the crank mechanically expelled the spent shell and loaded in a new round. Gatling solved the significant engineering problem of overheating barrels with the cylinder's rotation. As each barrel fired, it then rotated and cooled, while a new barrel moved into place. The gun had to be mounted on a large frame, often made of wood with wagon wheels, or it could be mounted on a large metal tripod. The Gatling gun was heavy and unwieldy, usually requiring four-man teams to operate it.

A self-promoter, Gatling once said his weapon "bears the same relation to other firearms that McCormick's Reaper does to the sickle, or the sewing machine to the common needle."

Hiram Maxim, born in 1840, was a compulsive inventor who dropped out of school in Maine at the age of fourteen. Working in Europe for an electric company, he found inventors there trying to create a more reliable machine gun. An American friend urged Maxim to give it a try, telling him, "Hang your chemistry and electricity! If you want to make a pile of money, invent something that will enable these Europeans to cut each other's throats with greater facility."

Maxim's eureka moment regarding guns came one day when he shot a military service rifle. The gun's kickback was so severe it left his shoulder bruised. That experience struck him, literally, as wasted energy.

"Cannot this great force, at present merely an inconvenience, be harnessed to a useful purpose?" he wrote. His gun recycled the "great force," using recoil to keep loading the weapon—an automatically self-loading gun. Fed with a canvas belt of bullets, the squat gun on small wheels or a tripod only needed one barrel and could fire 550 to 600 rounds a minute, an astounding rate considering most soldiers still used bolt-action rifles.

Maxim guns were put into service around the globe as British colonial troops used them in imperial expansion. Battlefield reports recounted how British soldiers with Maxim guns destroyed larger forces armed with inferior weapons. Though labeled battles, these events were massacres. During an incursion into Tibet in 1903 and 1904, a small British force armed with two Maxim guns was attacked by a Tibetan army brandishing old muskets and swords. A British officer reported his troops "with the quick-firing Maxims, mowed down the Tibetans in a few minutes with terrific slaughter . . . It was all over in about ten minutes." The officer's casualty tally: three hundred Tibetans killed, two hundred wounded, and two hundred taken prisoner. British losses were thirteen wounded. At the Battle of Omdurman in Sudan in 1898, British and Egyptian forces made heavy use of their Maxim guns against the Mahdi rebellion, with spent shells piled in heaps by the guns as the battle raged. The British and their Egyptian and Sudanese allies suffered fewer than fifty killed. The Mahdist army was destroyed, with thousands dead.

John Moses Browning, the son of a Mormon gunsmith, was the third American in the pantheon of machine-gun developers. Born in 1855, Browning never attended school, going to work at his father's shop at the age of six. He fashioned his first gun at the age of ten. After his father died, Browning formed a successful business with his brother that developed weapons for gun manufacturers around the world. Though he had worked on developing machine guns for years, he claimed that one of his major innovations arose from an experience he had in 1899, while he was shooting with friends at a rifle club in Utah. He noticed that when a friend fired his gun, the gas expelled blew down tall reeds nearby. Browning left the rifle range and got his brother. In their horse and buggy, they rushed back to the family gun shop. Within two days, Browning figured out a way to use that expelled gas to reload a rifle. Instead of pulling a lever or a bolt to reload, a shooter could just pull the trigger. Soon he had a prototype of a gas-powered, automatic rapid-fire gun.

During World War I, heavy machine guns—Gatlings, Maxims, and similar weapons—proved highly effective as defensive guns in trench warfare. The use of these weapons in World War I "negated all the old human virtues—pluck, fortitude, patriotism, honour—and made them as nothing in the face of a deadly stream of bullets, a quite unassailable mechanical barrier," the historian John Ellis wrote in his 1975 work *The Social History of the Machine Gun.* In response, Allied gunmakers designed rapid-fire guns that soldiers could carry as they charged enemy trenches. The fire would force the enemy to keep their heads down as the men crossed open land. The British and French built what they called "walking fire" automatic guns, which soldiers fired from the hip as they attacked. The strategy didn't work that well, in part because the British Lewis guns were too heavy and the French Chauchat rifle was unreliable, prone to jamming.

When the United States joined the war in 1917, the military turned to Browning to create such a "walking fire" weapon. His answer was the .30 caliber Browning Machine Rifle (later renamed the Browning Automatic Rifle, or BAR). It was an air-cooled, gas-powered, steel and wood rifle, weighing about fifteen and a half pounds and fed usually with a twenty-round magazine. Browning's rifle was made with three select settings: safety, single shot, and automatic. The military began issuing Browning's gun to the troops by the summer of 1918, but the war was over by November. His "machine rifle," a refinement of the work of Maxim, Gatling, and others, had not been extensively tested in combat. But it pointed the way to a new type of war. World War I had shown how devastating stationary heavy machine guns could be. A future war, with legions of individual soldiers carrying their own "machine rifles," would be even bloodier.

By the time America entered World War II, U.S. soldiers and Marines carried the innovative M1 Garand. It was not a "machine rifle," but instead a rapid-fire semiautomatic that served a similar function. With an eight-round disposable clip, the M1 fired large .30–06 bullets in quick succession. After eight shots the metal clip would flip out and the soldier just had to pop in another to keep firing. The sturdiness of the gun and its ability to rapidly pour out bullets gave American soldiers a distinct advantage on the battlefield against Axis enemies, who often carried bolt-action rifles.

The gun was highlighted in war reels and Hollywood propaganda movies. A government poster urging factory workers to increase ammunition production showed a tough, grimy soldier holding his battle-worn Garand in one hand and bullets in the palm of the other. "The M1 does MY Talking! . . . with your cartridges," it read. About 4 million M1s were made by the end of the war.

The inventor John Cantius Garand was a soft-spoken civilian gun designer for the Army Ordnance Department at Springfield Armory in Massachusetts. Born in Quebec in 1888, Garand moved to Connecticut when he was eleven. He first was exposed to guns while helping out at his brother's shooting gallery, and by 1916, he was making his own prototype. Garand took up a full-time job designing weapons at the government-run Springfield Armory as the U.S. military began looking for a new infantry rifle after World War I. Two factions, one interested in accuracy and the other more interested in rapid-fire, squared off over what such a gun should look like. What would eventually become the M1, a military designation just meaning "Model 1," was a compromise of the two views. The rifle was heavy for accuracy and its gas-powered piston system gave it the ability to fire faster than previous infantry rifles. Garand started working in earnest on the rifle that would become the M1 in the 1920s, but the Depression and interarmy wrangling delayed the rifle's adoption as the standard infantry rifle until January 1936. One reason why the army chose Garand's rifle: the civil servant refused to accept royalty payments for his design and signed the patent rights over to the government.

Garand's rifle was praised for its role in U.S. victories against the Axis powers. He was awarded civilian medals and honors for his work. All this attention for his rifle made the mild-mannered Garand a celebrity, with news accounts emphasizing the fact that he had refused to accept royalties. "She is a pretty good gun, I think," he said when asked about the weapon's performance.

The Germans also developed new weapons throughout the war. As Nazi troops invaded the Soviet Union in the summer of 1941, their officers pleaded for a gun that soldiers could use in close-range, urban warfare and that could be quickly produced in armaments factories. The Nazi gunmaker Hugo Schmeisser designed a rifle that was lighter than a traditional military rifle and fired rapidly, but not at far distances. One of its key innovations was the gun was made mostly from stamped, metal parts, so it could be produced cheaply and quickly. The gun was slightly lighter than other rifles and select-fire, able to shoot single rounds or automatically. Its ammunition was lighter than those of most other combat rifles, making it easier for soldiers to carry more bullets into battle. None of the Allies had anything like it.

But Adolf Hitler rejected multiple requests to mass-produce the gun, despite glowing reports from German troops using early versions of the weapon. Hitler favored more accurate, heavier rifles to keep troops from wasting precious bullets. But in 1944, Nazi commanders grew desperate for a "machine rifle" they could give their forces as the war turned against them. With German armies in retreat, Hitler finally agreed and ordered production of thirty thousand such rifles a month.

Hitler's office gave an evocative name to the new combat rifle, calling it *Sturmgewehr*, literally translated as "storm rifle." The muscular phrase echoed other Nazi labels, including the *Sturmabteilung*, or "Storm Division," the Nazi paramilitary organization. *Sturm* carried aggressive military connotations, as in the storming of an enemy position. When the U.S. military discovered the *Sturmgewehr*, arms experts translated the name of the gun as "Assault Rifle." The phrase they chose would have a profound impact on American gun debates decades later.

One of the earliest uses of the term "assault rifle" came in an article by the U.S. Military Intelligence Service in 1945. "To bolster troop and civilian morale, the German High Command is now widely advertising the general issue of an automatic small arm which . . . Hitler has personally designated the 'Assault Rifle 44,'" the article read. "[I]ntroduction of the title *Sturmgewehr*, together with the accompanying blast of propaganda concerning the weapon, is but another example of German efforts to exploit the propaganda value inherent in weapons with impressive-sounding titles, such as *Panzer*, *Tiger*, *Panther*, and *Flak 88*."

The Nazis announced the *Sturmgewehr* as a glorious new weapon. A Nazi propaganda reel for moviegoers showed *Volkssturm*, "People's storm," a Nazi militia of old men and young boys, unloading the new rifles from a truck somewhere in eastern Germany. "Men of the *Volkssturm* are being equipped with the most modern equipment," the announcer declared.

The weapons played no significant role in the war as the collapsing Third Reich faced its reckoning. The *Sturmgewehr*, however, was to have a strange postwar life. The gun's innovations—stamped parts, large magazines, close-range rapid-fire—influenced Russian and American gun designers. Russian soldiers captured *Sturmgewehrs*, and the rifles found their way back to Soviet armament factories where gun designers reverse-engineered the weapons. They also brought Schmeisser back to the U.S.S.R. after the war, pressing him to work at Factory No. 74, a major gun plant. At the same factory was a Russian gun designer who had been wounded fighting the Nazis. Mikhail Kalashnikov studied the *Sturmgewehr* as he designed his own rifles, including what would become the AK-47.

In the aftermath of the war, gun developers in Europe and the United States realized that new handheld "machine rifles"—akin to but better than the M1 or the *Sturmgewehr*—were the weapons with which future battles would be fought. The Soviets put the AK-47 into mass production. The M1 had served American troops well, but future rifles would have to be lighter and fire more than eight-round clips. The United States and its allies launched into yearslong, heated squabbles over what characteristics such a weapon should have, from its weight to how rapidly it fired to the size of the bullet.

Military officials who pushed for a lighter, rapid-fire gun that used smaller-caliber rounds at shorter distances found support from influential researchers after the war. S.L.A. Marshall's 1947 book *Men Against Fire* claimed that during World War II few American soldiers fired their weapons effectively in combat. Contrary to the public perception of soldiers as coolheaded marksmen, many fighters in battle were frightened young men pouring lead not at specific targets but in the general direction of the enemy. Combat was often at fairly close range—several hundred yards. Though statistical support for his assertions was criticized in later years, Marshall held great sway with the Pentagon. His message: whoever fired the most lead at the enemy in a battle won.

With the outbreak of the Korean War, this debate over rifle design and function took on urgency. A top-secret army study found that most soldiers interviewed felt "the M1 has not always been dependable in combat," with at least two-thirds saying they had experienced malfunctions while fighting.

In 1952, a study funded by the Defense Department analyzed data from Korean battles and came to a conclusion that echoed Marshall's: good marksmanship hadn't mattered. The researchers found that most battles took place at close range with wound patterns showing that flustered soldiers tended to fire without precision. Weapons focused on accuracy at long distances were "valueless," and the army needed a rifle with "new operational characteristics" to spray more bullets, the researchers wrote.

By the early 1950s, the Army Ordnance Department launched Project SALVO—a broad exploration into new types of rifles and ammunition that focused in part on high-velocity, small-caliber weapons.

Garand himself favored a new gun that fired a smaller-caliber bullet. In a U.S. Army film about rifle training produced a year after he retired, he spoke about how his rifle worked. With gray, thinning hair and a modest suit, Garand looked like a professor from one of the era's science fiction movies.

"For the future, we should develop a lighter rifle with the available lighter ammunition that we have now," he said. "And alloys, steels, better knowledge. It should be a nice project for the younger generations to tackle and furnish our infantry with the best rifle in the world."

Despite the consensus that a new infantry rifle was needed, the U.S. military had done little to develop such a gun by the early 1950s.

The Truman administration shrank the military as U.S. fighters came home to join a swelling domestic economy. At the end of World War II, about 12 million men and women served in the armed forces. By 1948, only 1.5 million were in uniform. The military budget—about $557 billion in 1946—dropped to $141.2 billion in 1950. When General Omar Bradley became chairman of the Joint Chiefs of Staff, he was appalled. "[T]he Army of 1948 could not fight its way out of a paper bag," he wrote.

The cutbacks came as Communism, a menacing red blob on American schoolroom maps, was on the march across the globe.

"If one of the camps does not capitulate to the other, armed conflict between them, sooner or later, will be absolutely inevitable," Stalin told his politburo in 1948.

Truman and his advisors agonized over how to respond. After the Korean War broke out, Truman pushed Congress to sharply increase the military budget. The crisis fueled the rhetoric of politicians such as Wisconsin Republican senator Joseph McCarthy and a young Republican from California, representative Richard Nixon. They claimed that the administration's flatfooted response to China and now Korea was the intentional work of spies in the government who were seeking to undermine American preparedness. Anxiety about the Communist threat rippled through American society. Schools promoted science and engineering. America, the birthplace of Thomas Edison, the Wright brothers, and Henry Ford, needed bold inventors to save it from the "Red Menace."

As the presidential election year of 1952 arrived, most Americans considered Truman ineffectual in the face of the Communist threat. In March, he made a surprise announcement that he would not seek reelection. Deflated Democrats picked a dark horse candidate, Illinois governor Adlai Stevenson. The erudite Stevenson had little international or military experience. The GOP, which hadn't held the White House since Herbert Hoover, turned to a war hero, Dwight D. Eisenhower, who had commanded Allied forces in liberating North Africa and Europe. Eisenhower promised voters that he would contain military spending but would make American defenses stronger with new strategies and weapons. He won in a landslide.

Eisenhower's approach, which his press handlers labeled "the New Look" and which politicos in Washington called "the Eisenhower shift," was an attempt to cut costs. Ike's strategy was simple: rely on nuclear weapons to offset Communist numerical advantages. That meant beefing up the air force but slashing the expensive and large army. Ike saw conflicts such as Korea as "brushfire wars" that sapped the nation's limited resources—so the United States should try to avoid sending troops to fight them. Under the New Look, Ike wanted weapons development—long the domain of military bureaucrats—to shift to the private sector under the guidance, not control, of the Pentagon. Ike chose as his first defense secretary Charles E. Wilson, president of General Motors, who famously said at his confirmation hearing, "[W]hat was good for our country was good for General Motors and vice versa." Wilson launched the shift, but instead of a smooth transition, it set off interservice battles over funding and projects. The development of weapons systems—from intercontinental ballistic missiles to rifles—became, instead of an orderly, cost-efficient process, a struggle among lobbyists, corporate executives, military bureaucrats, and members of Congress. Ike would warn the nation about "the military-industrial complex" when he left office, but he appeared powerless to control it during his presidency—and in many respects his policies fueled the infighting. Military bureaucrats dithered over the selection of a new battle rifle for American soldiers and only reluctantly allowed private companies to enter their firearms into competition with army guns. As Ike opened the door for competition from private companies and cut the army's budget, powerful generals saw their branch of the service—the branch where Eisenhower had served—becoming a stepchild. Ike saw the air force as the future and often criticized the army for being out-of-date.

General Matthew Bunker Ridgway, army chief of staff from 1953 to 1955, was furious about the delays in getting U.S. troops new rifles. Ridgway saw combat soldiers as the backbone of U.S. defense—and insisted that these fighters required new military technologies and training. Ridgway, nicknamed by his men "Old Iron Tits" because of his habit of wearing a grenade attached to his vest, had commanded the 82nd Airborne Division during World War II, and the commander even jumped into combat with his troops in Europe. He believed in troop mobility as essential in military strategy, and lighter weapons were crucial to reach that goal. As army chief of staff, he battled budget cuts and lobbied Congress to restore funding. The army wanted "to fight tomorrow's wars with tomorrow's weapons and techniques," he insisted. He retired from the army in 1955 in frustration and joined the board of directors at the gunmaker Colt.

In 1956, Ridgway published a memoir that included a scathing critique of the "New Look" Pentagon. He argued that the army was the military branch best positioned to "put out big fires or little ones wherever the Communists might set them." New missiles, bombers, nuclear warheads, and battleships couldn't win wars that were "still fought for little bits of bloody earth," he wrote. Defending American interests was "the role of the foot soldier, the man with the rifle."

3.

THE RIFLEMAN

The United States and the rifle are inseparable.
—Philip B. Sharpe

American men for generations had considered rifles to be an extension of themselves. Learning to shoot rifles had long been a rite of passage for young boys. Even into the 1950s, it wasn't odd for students to bring guns to school and leave them in their lockers so they could hunt rabbits or squirrels on their way home. Children learned how farmers gathered with their muskets at Lexington and Concord to battle the British; how pioneers with long guns headed into the wild forests; how men from the North and South marched with rifles to battle over slavery and disunion; how cowboys with Winchesters defeated Native American warriors; and how American doughboys and GIs fought the Central and Axis powers.

"This country was born with a rifle in its hand," wrote the gun expert Philip B. Sharpe in the eight-hundred-page 1953 edition of his encyclopedic book *The Rifle in America*. "As a matter of fact the rifle brought about the birth of these United States. The United States and the rifle are inseparable."

During the decade, popular fascination with the "Old West," where every rugged man carried a gun and knew how to use it, reached a zenith. The Cold War "inaugurated the Golden Age of the Western,"

Richard Slotkin wrote in *Gunfighter Nation: The Myth of the Frontier in Twentieth-Century America*. The myth of the heroic gunfighter paralleled the ethos of "counterinsurgency" promoted by a faction of American military strategists in response to the spread of Communism. This faction, which grew in influence in the late 1950s and into the 1960s, advocated for clandestine missions and rapid-strike attacks by small mobile groups or individuals with light, powerful weapons—the modern version of gunslingers and cavalry battling Indians on the frontier.

Television programs such as *The Rifleman*, starring Chuck Connors, linked rifles with masculinity. Each episode, the square-jawed Connors opened the show by staring steely-eyed into the camera as he walked a Wild West street, firing his Winchester. In the popular 1956 Western movie *The Searchers*, John Wayne and several white men fended off an attack by Native Americans. While the other defenders crouched behind logs, Wayne stood tall, steadily aiming and firing. Moviegoers knew Wayne couldn't be hit: he was an American man with a rifle.

But if John Wayne movies represented the rifle-gripping masculinity to which many American men aspired, popular science fiction films such as *The Day the Earth Stood Still* (1951) captured a growing fear of emasculation by new technology. In the movie, an alien named Klaatu lands his spaceship near the White House and announces that a galactic federation considers humanity a threat to other planets. A nervous soldier, part of a contingent of troops surrounding the spaceship, shoots and wounds the alien. In response, Klaatu's silent robot guardian disintegrates all of the soldiers' rifles, cannons, and tanks in an instant. Guns could do nothing against the dangers of advanced technology.

The experience of shooting a rifle—hefting a weapon, aiming and firing, feeling the kick as it jolted one's shoulder—was less common than for previous generations. America's population was 64 percent urban and suburban by 1950 and almost 70 percent by 1960. Fields where a few years earlier farmers hunted deer now were overtaken by tract housing, shopping malls, and parking lots. When Chuck Connors appeared on *The Steve Allen Show* in 1959, he brought his trademark Winchester as a prop. He twirled the firearm with ease. Allen, an urbane foil to Connors's strapping cowboy, fidgeted next to the gun and when Connors fired it (with blanks), Allen mocked fainting. The joke was clear: to Allen, an archetypal citified nebbish, the rifle was a foreign object.

The 1950s were an age of male dominance, but the American man's sense of self was also becoming unmoored. The sociologists David Riesman, Reuel Denney, and Nathan Glazer published their influential *The Lonely Crowd: A Study of the Changing American Character* in 1950, asserting that the structure of modern work had removed American men from the muscular customs of earlier generations. The changes extended to every facet of American masculinity, including weaponry. Was the rifle a tool that he still needed to master to protect his new-found wealth and success, or was it an anachronism rendered pointless by ever-advancing technology? Where did the wood-and-steel rifle fit in an age of shiny plastic and aluminum?

In 1951, Paul Cardinal, a writer for the NRA's *American Rifleman* magazine, interviewed troops returning from Korea. Officers told him, "Good shooting was the exception." Men in battle were often afraid to shoot because it would draw fire from the enemy, the officers said. "The old pride in being a first-class marksman is a thing of the past," Cardinal wrote in disgust. The NRA found the nation's cultural move away from familiarity with rifles alarming. By 1955, it had close to three hundred thousand members. Yet the group found itself on the defensive throughout the 1950s. Suburban and urban areas took less interest in forming shooting clubs and the group's members faced a host of proposed laws on the local and state level that would limit or prohibit gun ownership and use. NRA promotional material in the 1950s became more political, declaring, "Your first line of defense against BAD GUN LAWS begins here." The NRA's political efforts were led by retired Marine Corps Major General Merritt "Red Mike" Edson. He was the NRA's president in 1949 and 1950, and became the group's executive director in 1951. Edson was one of the most decorated officers in Marine history. In World War II, he was awarded the congressional Medal of Honor. "[I]t is more important than ever that every man know how to handle a rifle," he wrote in one of his many *American Rifleman* editorials. "Even the home front may, overnight, become the battle front. Rifle training and preparedness are synonymous. This nation must again become a nation of marksmen. The times in which we live demand it."

In August 1955, Edson went to his garage, closed the door, and turned on his automobile. His family found his body lying in the car, the air thick with carbon monoxide. Why he killed himself was unknown, but a strong voice for the notion that traditional rifles were intrinsic to American society was gone.

As anxiety grew over where the rifle fit in American culture, one unknown gun designer—Eugene Stoner—was convinced the rifle could be modernized to meet the myriad challenges of the Atomic Age. Working alone in his garage, Stoner believed he was the guy to do it.

4.

HOLLYWOOD MOON SHOT

Tomorrow's Rifle Today!
—ArmaLite brochure for the AR-10 rifle

Eugene Stoner had worked with aluminum for years. He was intrigued by the metal that was one-third the weight of steel. During World War II, the United States built its warplanes with new aluminum alloys; production of the material rose more than 600 percent between 1939 and 1943. Stoner saw its uses working at an airplane factory and later as a Marine maintaining weapons on aircraft in the Pacific. He worked with it as a machinist and as a designer in the aerospace industry when he returned stateside. Stoner figured out that aluminum could revolutionize gun making too. If humans were soaring into the atmosphere in hollow tubes made of the lightweight metal, couldn't aluminum tolerate the pressures caused by firing a gun?

After the war, companies applied aluminum to all kinds of commercial products. In *Aluminum on the March*, a Reynolds Metals Company promotional film from the period, animated aluminum figures strode across the screen as an announcer declared they would be transformed into "hundreds of thousands of useful things from washing machines to airplane wings." Foil, siding, containers for TV dinners—all were made from the miracle metal. Colt made the first mass-produced pistol with an aluminum frame in 1950, though the semiautomatic handgun wasn't popular because Americans preferred revolvers at the time.

Stoner snuck time on machines at work to make aluminum gun parts that he assembled in his garage at night. By June 1952, he figured out how to replace one of the heaviest steel components of a rifle with aluminum. Called the receiver, it was the rifle's heart. It housed the most important parts of a gun: the mechanisms that after the trigger was pulled ignited the contained explosion that sent a bullet speeding down the barrel. It was also the frame at the center of the gun to which the other parts were attached. The receiver had to be sturdy. Stoner called his first aluminum gun the M5.

"There was nothing particularly new to what I'd been doing all along in the aircraft equipment," Stoner recalled. "They were more or less materials that I'd been using all along."

Jean often caught her husband staring at guns.

"When he would pick up a hunting rifle, he would look at everything and say to himself, how can I make this better?" Jean recalled.

Stoner's early focus was the M1 Garand, the rifle he carried as a Marine. In the 1930s, a young Marine reservist named Melvin Johnson Jr. developed an alternative to the M1. In congressional testimony, Johnson said that the M1's internal system to eject spent casings and load in new rounds was prone to break down over time. Garand had used the force of the gas that's expelled when the gun fires to set in motion a piston connected to a metal operating rod that ran the length of the barrel. The rod curved near the receiver, so it could unlock the bolt and push it back to eject a spent casing. A spring then pushed all the metal pieces forward, loading a new round. The constant movement of these parts after each shot meant they could wear down, Johnson claimed. But Johnson's gun was rejected and soon his criticism was largely forgotten. Stoner picked up the issue in the 1950s.

"One of the things against the Garand rifle was the bent operating rod," Stoner recalled. It added weight to the gun and put "high eccentric loading on some of the parts it was trying to operate." By "eccentric loading" Stoner meant that some of the driving forces were being wasted, putting unnecessary pressure on key metal parts.

He set about trying to invent a new, simpler system—a quest that became an obsession. Out to dinner with his family, he scribbled designs in pen on white tablecloths, ignoring conversation and restaurant decorum.

"They launder them. It'll come out," Stoner would answer when asked by his wife to stop.

At night, he would wake up to sketch ideas on brown butcher paper at a draft table he set up in the couple's bedroom. Pads of paper were everywhere in the house, in case Stoner had a gun-related epiphany. He also carried around a smaller drawing board.

"The drawing board was a family joke," Jean recalled. "He always had a drawing board on his lap, trying to prove something new or to fix something old."

When he was thinking, he could adopt a stern expression. "Some felt he was difficult to get to know, for he seemed to wear a perpetual frown," a longtime acquaintance wrote. "That frown did not mean he was displeased; it simply meant he was concentrating on a design problem."

Stoner's first great revelation was to eliminate the M1's piston and rod, and instead use the force that set them in motion: hot gas. In place of the long, bent operating rod, he created a thin metal tube that channeled gas from the barrel back to the receiver. The gas pushed the bolt carrier backward, which in turn unlocked and moved the bolt backward, ejecting the spent casing. A spring sent them forward again, loading a fresh cartridge and locking the bolt behind it. Some gunsmiths compared the operation to blowing a paper wrapper off a straw. There were no parts to wear down, no parts to add to the weapon's weight, and much less wasted energy. "I was trying to come up with some gas operation method where you could actually keep all the driving forces in line," he recalled.

His first attempts didn't go well. An early prototype, a "kind of far-out approach," as Stoner called it, worked but had an unfortunate side effect: it blew hot gas right into his face every time he fired it.

"It was rather obnoxious because you got gas in your eyes and nose and everything," Stoner said.

He added a little nozzle to guide the gas with greater precision so it wouldn't blow into the shooter's face. Stoner was seeking a Holy Grail that gun designers had pursued for generations: how to use the energy released from the exploding gunpowder as efficiently as possible to reload the weapon. No one had made anything quite like Stoner's gas system before and it would form the basis of his first and most famous patent.

"It is amazing that anyone would think that would work," said C. Reed Knight Jr., a weapons maker who worked closely with Stoner in the inventor's later years.

U.S. Patent 2951424 for a "gas operated bolt and carrier system" described Stoner's invention. One of its purposes was "to provide a gas system which is lighter and less expensive to produce because of its simplicity than the present gas systems now used in automatic rifle mechanisms." The patent highlighted Stoner's devotion to efficiency, including having parts that performed a "double function." Fewer parts meant the gun would be smoother to operate and last longer, according to the patent. The accompanying diagrams showed a conventional rifle with the innovative gas system set inside.

Stoner's elimination of heavy metal parts and use of lightweight materials were a great engineering advance, but it created a new puzzle. A lighter gun would be harder for a shooter to aim, because it would buck and jerk with each shot, especially when firing in fully automatic mode. With a lighter gun, "you'd need every available means and crutch, if you want to call it that, to control the thing," Stoner later said.

On butcher paper, he sketched a solution, designing a rifle that looked like it came from the space adventure movies he loved as a boy. He made the rifle stock straight back instead of sloping down at an angle, like traditional rifles such as the M1. Gunmakers had angled the stock down and away for centuries because it was the easiest way to line up the aiming sights with the shooter's eye. This design was no problem with a single-shot rifle, but if you wanted to fire bullets like a machine gun, especially with a lightweight gun like Stoner was imagining, the recoil would cause the muzzle to rise and the bullets to miss their target. With a stock that went straight back, the recoil energy from each shot would go directly into the shooter's shoulder and keep the gun from climbing. To make sure that the shooter's eye would still line up with the aiming sights, Stoner raised the sights above the rifle. He designed a pistol grip for the shooter's trigger hand, something he had seen on the Nazi *Sturmgewehr*. The pistol grip would give the shooter another "crutch" to steady the gun. His gas system also made it easier to keep on target because all the driving forces were transmitted right down the center line of the rifle.

Stoner worked on a prototype of his new rifle in the early 1950s. The metal skeleton with a few pieces of wood attached looked like a closed umbrella. It combined his gas system with a number of features that he'd borrowed from other gun designers. He called it the M8. It was the foundation upon which the AR-15 would be built.

Historians of gun design liken Stoner's innovations to a symphony by Wolfgang Amadeus Mozart. Patrick Sweeney, a gunsmith and author of numerous books on firearms, said that the pantheon of gun designers was composed of people who invented something wholly new and people who combined past innovations in new ways, just like in music. Stoner was both a synthesizer and a creator in the style of Mozart, according to Sweeney: "He did new and he combined old in ways no one had thought of before."

Unlike Mozart, however, Stoner had no wealthy patrons. The Stoners were raising two children and Jean was pregnant with a third. In his early thirties, Stoner was spending hours of his free time dreaming up new inventions but earning nothing for the effort. By default, Jean did everything else. She took care of the children, cooked, mowed the lawn, repaired anything that was broken. She handled the family's finances. It was hard to raise a family on Stoner's $800-to-$1,000-a-month salary. Stoner's hobby needed to start bringing in money.

"They wanted two children, a boy and a girl and that was great, and then I was a surprise," said the third child, Susan. "That's when he said, 'I better do something serious. I've got three kids. I better concentrate on this gun thing.'"

Stoner's big break came in the spring of 1954 with an accidental meeting between the amateur gun designer and a smooth-talking entrepreneur named George C. Sullivan. The chance meeting of the two men has taken on a mythic status among fans of the AR-15 rifle. The story often told by Stoner and others was that Stoner was at a range in Topanga Canyon near Los Angeles one day, shooting homemade rifles. Impressed with the guns, Sullivan introduced himself as the head of a new weapons development unit of the Fairchild Engine and Airplane Corporation, an aircraft company and military contractor.

"I had met George kind of accidentally at a rifle range one day and I was firing some of these prototypes and he got interested and said he was starting the division with the help of Fairchild," Stoner said later.

Stoner's wife, Jean, remembered it differently. In an unpublished interview years after Stoner's death, she said that Sullivan and Stoner first met at a gun store in Hollywood. Stoner had gone to the shop to look for parts and he'd taken along one of his aluminum receivers.

"When Sullivan talked with Stoner, he was very impressed with the aluminum receiver Stoner had created," Jean said. "Anything with lightweight materials was what everyone was going for."

Wherever they met, Sullivan offered Stoner a dream job on the spot: designing guns for an as-yet-unnamed Fairchild subsidiary. Stoner, who had invented in isolation for years, didn't need convincing. Sullivan wanted to bring Stoner on as chief engineer. Stoner recalled thinking that he had arrived: "This is where your vocation and avocation can kind of meet."

Sullivan, in his forties with bulging eyes, close-cropped hair, and the beginnings of a double chin, was a patent counsel at Lockheed Aircraft Company. Sullivan—almost always in a suit and tie—was a born salesman and the chief product he peddled was himself. He visited various companies, urging them to subsidize his dream of creating and selling guns made of aluminum and other new lightweight materials such as fiberglass and plastic. Sullivan thought he could sell such guns to hunters.

Sullivan talked to everyone he could about his schemes, including a Fairchild executive. The executive thought that Fairchild's president, Richard Boutelle, an avid gun collector, would be intrigued and set up a meeting. Sullivan had never run a company, let alone a gun-making operation, but he persuaded Boutelle to fund an idea factory for futuristic weapons. Boutelle, eager to land more military contracts for Fairchild, pushed the new subsidiary in that direction. Fairchild depended on military contracts, though much of its production was not in weapons but in logistical air transport. Supplying new firearms and other weapons to the Pentagon could be a lucrative side business.

When Sullivan met Stoner, the new Fairchild gun venture was still in the planning stages, but Sullivan talked about his big plans and stressed that Fairchild had deep pockets. Both Stoner and Sullivan had hit on the idea of using aluminum parts for guns. Sullivan had another idea that Stoner hadn't yet tried: replace wooden shoulder stocks with another modern miracle: foam-filled fiberglass.

In July 1954, Stoner signed a deal with Sullivan, giving the lawyer exclusive rights to his novel gas system, which was not yet patented. Under the agreement, Stoner was to receive 2 percent of net sales for the first five hundred guns sold, 1.5 percent of the next two thousand sold, and 1 percent thereafter. Stoner signed the deal without consulting a lawyer.

Stoner's employment application with Fairchild revealed his wit. Asked to list hobbies in which he was an expert, Stoner wrote one word: "Guns." Sullivan and Stoner negotiated his starting salary at $700 a month, about $300 less than Stoner had been making at his own design company.

At first, Jean Stoner was thrilled about her husband's new job. All his hours in the garage appeared to be paying off. But when she heard about the patent agreements and the pay, she grew suspicious of Sullivan and worried about her naive husband.

On October 1, 1954, Fairchild announced the launch of a firearms subsidiary called ArmaLite. Like Silicon Valley "moon shot" labs that would come years later, ArmaLite's marching orders were broad: design off-the-wall stuff that Fairchild could sell to the U.S.

or other governments. The new venture's name was a combination of the words "armament" and "light"—underscoring the company's interest in using lighter materials. The company's logo, like that of its parent company, Fairchild, was Pegasus, the winged stallion from Greek mythology, a nod to Fairchild's primary product lines: aircraft. But ArmaLite's logo had a twist; the mythical creature was in a gun's crosshairs.

To foster ArmaLite's sense of itself as an idea lab, the company's offices were set up in Hollywood, far from Fairchild's headquarters in Maryland. All the small company needed was a workshop where Stoner, Sullivan, and others would tinker and talk. Sullivan rented a brick industrial building on Santa Monica Boulevard. Golden hills loomed behind the office, with the enormous white letters of the Hollywood sign visible from the neighborhood. The ornate Bronson gate that served as an entrance to the sprawling studios of Paramount Pictures was nearby.

ArmaLite's new office quickly filled with rifle prototypes as Stoner and others got to work. Tables for drawing plans stood like islands in the middle of the floor. A machine shop for building parts was attached to the room. A metal tube three feet across and ten yards long stood in a corner of the office for test firing. But in the chaos of the new venture, no one had thought to ask permission to test-fire guns in the shop. Neighbors raised concerns about the gunfire and city officials paid ArmaLite a visit.

Sullivan was in charge of the operation on paper but his title, duties, and financial interest in the venture were vague. He still technically worked for Lockheed. "No doubt in anybody's mind that he was the person in charge in the ArmaLite Division, but we all knew that he was employed full time by Lockheed Aircraft," Stoner later said. Some in the office believed Sullivan had a financial stake in ArmaLite; Stoner's wife, Jean, later said that Fairchild was paying him $40,000 a year, about five times what Stoner earned.

Sullivan was ArmaLite's public face. But around the office, he became the butt of jokes among Stoner's brainy group of five or six workers on the weapons-design team. Sullivan claimed credit for inventions that he didn't invent. The group mocked Sullivan for trying to name an aluminum alloy after himself. "I think he put a drop of bat's blood in it and called it Sulliloy," said Jim Sullivan, a draftsman at ArmaLite and no relation to George.

For day-to-day office management, Sullivan put Chuck Dorchester in charge with the title "superintendent." Dorchester had worked with Sullivan for about a year trying to design guns before the launch of ArmaLite, but he had little experience in the field. Dorchester looked more like a Hollywood character actor with a head full of thick, black hair, a sagging face, and stooped shoulders. He paid much more attention to women than to guns. Later, Stoner learned that Dorchester was Sullivan's brother-in-law.

Though George Sullivan and Dorchester were in charge, Stoner gave the tiny company its ethos: be smart, take chances, and don't be too serious, said Jim Sullivan, who was hired in 1957. Stoner wanted ArmaLite to be an inventors' lab, exploring ideas and solving technical problems. He didn't care for business protocol and allowed ArmaLite workers to come and go as they pleased and wear whatever they liked. Nobody wore a suit. Outsiders, even those bankrolling the company, found the group brilliant but strange.

One day, Dick Boutelle, Fairchild's imposing and hard-charging president, toured the shop. As he chatted with employees, he suggested that a way to lighten guns even further would be to use a magnet to hold the bolt solidly in place when firing. But the idea was ludicrous. A little magnet couldn't withstand the force of such an explosion, as Stoner and everyone else in the room knew.

Chuck Dorchester politely sought to move past the suggestion without insulting the boss, but Boutelle wouldn't give up. After an awkward silence, Stoner spoke up.

"You'd need beaucoup magnetism, enough to suck your wristwatch inside out from forty feet away," he said flatly.

His colleagues burst into laughter. Boutelle stormed out.

The small team designed guns at a quick pace. The designers gave each invention a name beginning with the letters AR, followed by a sequential number. To this day, some think this label stood for "assault rifle." Others, even gun aficionados, think it stood for ArmaLite Rifle. The designation stood for the first two letters of the company's name, according to Jim Sullivan. Stoner's daughter and son-in-law said it stood for "ArmaLite Research."

The company's first weapon, the AR-1, was a lightweight military sniper rifle that Sullivan pitched as the Parasniper. The AR-3 was a lightweight semiautomatic rifle that Sullivan called the Autoriflite. Neither went anywhere. The AR-5 was the first weapon to have any success. Sullivan called the two-and-half-pound rifle that could float the "New Survival Rifle" in his sales pitches. The .22 caliber rifle was made of aluminum parts that could be disassembled and stored in its fiberglass shoulder stock. The idea was that if an airman crashed, he could assemble the rifle and use it for killing "small game such as rabbits, weasels, birds and the like," Sullivan wrote in a 1956 press release. "It has been tested on game as large as antelope."

The idea for the survival rifle had come from a man who later proved pivotal in the development of the AR-15: Curtis LeMay, a cigar-chomping air force general and head of Strategic Air Command. LeMay suggested that ArmaLite build a survival rifle lighter than five pounds for pilots. Sullivan used the survival rifle as the centerpiece of public relations efforts for ArmaLite, coaxing newspapers and magazines to write about the company with photos of the tiny gun floating in a swimming pool. LeMay's interest led the air force to tentatively agree to adopt it. Though it ultimately didn't lead to a military contract, it got ArmaLite attention.

ArmaLite had been in existence for about a year and had no contracts, but Sullivan sensed opportunity. The Eisenhower administration's "New Look" opened a door for contractors to pitch new weapon systems and other products to the military. Sullivan knew the army had been searching for a new rifle and some in the Pentagon grumbled about the gun the military itself had been developing. The outsiders decided to take on Springfield Armory, the military's citadel of gun making. Nearly three thousand miles away from Hollywood in western Massachusetts, the federal arms development and manufacturing center had equipped American soldiers since the revolution. In this imposing redbrick complex, gun designers with U.S. Army Ordnance saw themselves as upholders of rifle tradition. Springfield put weapons into production only after rigorous and lengthy testing. The career military bureaucrats had little tolerance for those who challenged their expertise.

George Washington founded the armory on a bluff above the Connecticut River as an arms depot in 1777. From the early days of the republic, Congress considered it vital for national security to have the government, not private industry, develop and produce basic weapons for its armies. Springfield Armory had designed and produced guns for Lincoln's troops in the Civil War, doughboys in World War I, and the victorious GIs in World War II.

In the mid-1940s, the army tasked the Ordnance Corps with developing a new standard infantry rifle, and the engineers at Springfield worked for years to invent an heir to the M1. But even as Garand retired in 1953, the weapon that took shape, the M14, looked a lot like the M1 with a twenty-round magazine attached. It weighed almost as much, fired bullets that were almost as large, and it was made of many of the same materials Springfield had been using since the dawn of America: steel and the wood from the American black walnut tree. Springfield's craftsmen first used the wood in the 1790s as they carved muskets by hand. It was dark, dense, and hard with fine and tight grains, sought after by woodworkers for its strength and durability. They used heart grain of the black walnut cut down in nearby forests. By the time of the Civil War, the wood came from the mid-Atlantic states, and by World War II, it was harvested from forests in the Midwest. Insisting on black walnut or in fact any wood stock in the 1950s underscored how Springfield's engineers were wedded to old ways of doing things. If Los Angeles and Stoner's aluminum gun were America's future, Springfield was its past.

Sullivan believed that if Stoner could come up with a gun to challenge Springfield Armory, he could sell the story of a modern David versus a lumbering Goliath. Working long hours at his drafting table and in the machine shop, Stoner transformed his skeletal gas-operated rifle into something that looked much more like Flash Gordon's ray gun. Stoner's new version was sleek and spare, made of aluminum, fiberglass, and plastic. It had no wood and only a few steel parts. It was powered by Stoner's revolutionary gas system and it fired 7.62 caliber bullets. It could fire like a fully automatic machine gun or a semiautomatic rifle with the flip of a switch. It had a straight in-line stock and a pistol grip. The forty-inch-long rifle—which they called the AR-10—weighed just 6.65 pounds, a triumph of space-age materials and something that would have been impossible for gun designers just a decade earlier. The actual weight fluctuated by a few ounces depending on how it was measured and by whom. But it still weighed almost three pounds less than the wood-and-steel M1 Garand, and about two pounds less than Springfield Armory's best attempt at a lightweight gun of the future.

"Tomorrow's Rifle Today! Lightest Weight! Finest Workmanship!" ArmaLite boasted on the cover of its AR-10 brochure.

"A break-through has been recorded in the quest for lighter shoulder guns that still pack a killing wallop," read a Fairchild-ArmaLite ad in *Time* magazine. "Departing radically from old thinking, old techniques and old materials, Fairchild designers have evolved a whole family of sturdy, lightweight guns."

Stoner's early versions of this weapon are preserved at a private museum at the Florida offices of the arms maker C. Reed Knight Jr. On one wall of a room that re-creates Stoner's workshop, his early versions of the AR-10 hang in sequence, presenting the clear progression of Stoner's thinking. The first models looked similar to a traditional rifle.

Later versions evolved to have a straight-line shape, with first attempts looking angular and roughly made, with crude sights, metal butts, and a small, brown fiberglass stock. Down the wall the guns took on a thicker shape, with stronger stocks, better sights, and a carrying handle. The final versions of the AR-10 were stamped with ArmaLite's Pegasus-in-the-crosshairs logo. It was a larger version of what would become the AR-15.

One part of the AR-10 that Sullivan and Stoner could not agree upon was the gun's barrel. George Sullivan wanted the gun to have a lighter, steel-lined aluminum barrel. Stoner disagreed. That might work on a hunting rifle but it would melt on an automatic military rifle with bullets whizzing down the barrel. The heat and pressure would be too great. Stoner urged Sullivan to make the barrel out of steel. George Sullivan rejected the criticism, saying the company wasn't named Arma*Lite* for nothing. The company tested the AR-10 in the machine shop, firing rounds down a tube and into a metal plate. The gun performed well in early tests and it looked as if Stoner was wrong.

Sullivan believed the AR-10 had a chance of hitting it big. The agreement he'd signed with Stoner had lapsed, so he came up with a new one. In exchange for granting an exclusive license to Sullivan, Stoner would get 1 percent of the net sales price of the first five hundred guns, three-quarters of 1 percent of the net sales of the next two thousand guns, and one-half of 1 percent of any sold after that—a less lucrative deal for Stoner than the first one. Stoner asked for a better deal.

"Entirely out of the question," Stoner recalled Sullivan saying. "This is a small operation and we're putting a lot of money into the thing."

On August 6, 1956, Stoner agreed to give away his exclusive rights, signing his name at the bottom of the letter next to Sullivan's and that of the witness, Dorchester. The agreement made no mention of Fairchild or ArmaLite.

When Stoner came home and told his wife, she was upset. Jean's distrust of Sullivan had intensified after she learned he had hired his brother-in-law to run the shop. She'd told her husband not to sign anything else without talking to a lawyer first.

"It's only one page," Stoner told his wife. "It really doesn't make a difference."

In the fall, Sullivan and Stoner got word that Springfield Armory would begin testing their AR-10 in December. As Stoner fine-tuned the gun, Sullivan launched a public relations campaign. The December 3, 1956, issue of *Time* carried a short item titled "The Aluminum Rifle." It heralded ArmaLite as the savior for the army that "last week was still marching earnestly forward in search of a weapon it has been unable to perfect through ten years of research and testing." The military had spent $12 million on Springfield Armory's rifle, while ArmaLite's AR-10 was developed "(at no cost to the taxpayer) in a Los Angeles machine shop by George Sullivan, 46, a Lockheed Aircraft Corp. patent attorney and engineer, whose hobby is guns."

A photograph accompanying the story showed a beaming Sullivan in suit and tie, gripping the new weapon. The caption read: "Inventor Sullivan & ArmaLite: Dead aim at an old market." Executives at Fairchild were thrilled that its little subsidiary had landed the free national publicity, but Stoner was glum that Sullivan was labeled the gun's inventor. Jean was furious. Stoner tried to calm her, but to no avail.

An excited Boutelle asked to see the gun demonstrated at Fairchild's headquarters in Maryland. Sullivan planned to handle the demonstration, but he didn't know how to break down and reassemble the rifle. The "inventor" didn't even know his invention. Stoner had to go out to the demonstration to handle the gun's operation while Sullivan glad-handed with Fairchild executives. Stoner brought Jean along.

When Stoner's wife saw Sullivan at a dinner, she stared at him, seething. Then she erupted. "You're a liar and a thief," she said to Sullivan, according to her children. A frazzled Sullivan, with tears in his eyes, apologized and promised to rectify things in the future, she told her family.

Jean's blowup appeared to have some effect. The next big magazine spread about ArmaLite, which appeared in the March 1957 issue of *Guns* magazine, included a large photograph of Stoner with his black-rimmed glasses, wearing his signature bow tie. He wore a clip-on bow tie because it was more efficient than a normal bow tie and wouldn't get caught in the machinery. His crew cut and button-down shirt completed the look: he was a 1950s inventor straight from central casting. Stoner stood with his arms folded in the photograph, smiling next to a wall of AR-10 prototypes.

But the story, "Is This the Next G.I. Rifle?," was still centered on Sullivan. "For eight years, California hunters have been unnerved by the sudden appearance of George Sullivan in the field," it began. "There is nothing peculiar about Sullivan himself when he's out hunting. It is just his weapons that prompt a fast double-take. Most guns just don't have light, silvery barrels, bright red breech actions, and Kelly-green stocks."

Sullivan claimed to the magazine that he captured the imagination of the Pentagon with a gun so light and controllable that each soldier could "advance at a run firing up to 500 shots, *continuously*" and that this "bullet shield would allow attackers to advance behind a leaden umbrella during the most dangerous phase of assault." His claims were fantastic, but the reporter didn't press for details, instead lauding Sullivan's steel-lined aluminum barrel. "Whether or not the Army buys the AR-10 for the next basic infantry weapon . . . there is no doubt that the light gun is going to be with us for the future," the article read.

The gun, however, didn't hold up to Sullivan's grandiose claims—it wasn't ready for grueling military use. Tests at Springfield Armory in December 1956 found that parts broke, spent shell casings got stuck in the chamber, and the gas tube warped after repeated firing.

Stoner rushed back to Hollywood, where he fixed up two AR-10s with stronger gas tubes and flew back to Massachusetts in January 1957 for more tests at Springfield. The guns worked better, but during a live-fire test one of the gun's barrels—the steel-lined barrel that Sullivan insisted be made of aluminum—exploded. A bullet erupted from the side of the barrel, just missing the hand of the soldier firing the weapon.

"Naturally this stopped the test," noted Lieutenant Colonel Roy Rayle, the head of research and development at Springfield Armory. To the doubters at Springfield Armory, the exploded barrel was evidence that ArmaLite's space gun was not a serious competitor.

Crestfallen, Stoner headed back to Hollywood with the shattered rifle. The ArmaLite crew needed to create a weapon that could withstand the rigors of war. It was unclear whether the small company would ever get another chance to prove itself.

5

SPRINGFIELD'S RIFLE

They labored mightily and brought forth a mouse.
—Vernon McGee, a retired Marine general

On May 1, 1957, the army announced that it had chosen Springfield Armory's rifle to be the weapon that American soldiers would carry into battle. Secretary of the Army Wilber Brucker praised the gun as a great advancement in the field of armaments. "It gives the modern Army a better lighter rifle and a lighter machine gun to give forward infantry units greater firepower," he said. Brucker touted its improvements: it was a pound lighter, it could fire fully automatic, and it had a twenty-round detachable magazine. But after more than a decade of work by the government's foremost gun designers in Springfield, Massachusetts, the rifle, which the army called the M14, looked very much like the one that GIs used in World War II. It was made of the same steel and black walnut. Inside, the firing system had been improved, but it still required the use of a metal piston and operating rod to eject and load rounds. Beyond officials such as Brucker, the gun was mocked, even in military circles.

"This is nothing more than the M1 Garand with a semi-automatic position and an uncontrollable fully automatic position," the editor of *Army Times* wrote. Many chided Springfield Armory for spending so long on something that showed little improvement. "They labored mightily and brought forth a mouse," said Vernon McGee, a retired four-star Marine general.

Springfield's designers didn't just suffer from a profound lack of imagination; they were hobbled by the brass's various demands for the new weapon. The army wanted the new gun to weigh seven pounds and be capable of automatic fire. They also wanted to use a big bullet like they had with the M1 Garand. Any rifle firing such a large caliber on automatic would be hard to control, the designers knew. But the army was torn between past and future. They still wanted a gun that could fire accurately at great distances (hence the big bullet) even as they demanded a lightweight rifle that could fire like a machine gun. Springfield's designers struggled to meet the competing demands, trying and discarding a string of prototypes. Yet throughout the process, they never doubted their weapons would be chosen, no matter what modern marvels were being designed outside the Springfield Armory's redbrick walls. In the early 1950s, when it seemed that the army might choose a rifle designed by a Belgian company, Ordnance Corps officials concocted a rifle test at an army base in Alaska to knock out the competition. The Belgian gun had never tested in such cold temperatures before, and the freezing weather caused its firing system to gum up. The M14 prototype performed fine. It was a clever, if desperate, tactic by Springfield gun designers and it worked.

Bureaucratic machinations and inertia made the M14's adoption as the standard combat rifle seem inevitable. But within the Pentagon, a cabal of high-ranking officers set out to search for something better. The leader of this group of officers was General Willard Gordon Wyman, then the influential commander of the Continental Army Command. Wyman oversaw army operations in the continental United States and was in charge of making sure new weapons were suitable for American soldiers. Wyman's command included the influential Infantry Board, based at Georgia's Fort Benning, which was testing all potential new infantry rifles. Wyman had closely watched the development of Springfield's M14 for years and concluded the rifle didn't cut it.

A West Point graduate, Wyman was—at least on paper—old-school army. He had served in World War I and was a cavalry officer afterward. His advanced education in small-arms combat came during World War II, when he saw jungle fighting firsthand while commanding U.S. forces battling the Japanese in China, Burma, and India. Later attached to high command, Wyman could have sat behind a desk for the rest of the war. Instead, at age forty-six, he joined the D-Day invasion at Omaha Beach as an assistant commander of the First Infantry Division. As Nazis pounded American positions, Wyman—then a brigadier general—moved up and down the beach, directing soldiers to attack enemy positions. He was awarded the Distinguished Service Cross for his bravery. After the war, Wyman played a critical role in establishing the Central Intelligence Agency, serving as assistant director of the agency's Office of Special Operations. He then rejoined the army and was assigned to the Far East, where he commanded troops in Korea and developed U.S. military strategies for battling Communist insurgencies. Because he'd seen U.S. forces and their allies often outnumbered in combat, he knew they needed better firepower as the Cold War flashed hot. Vietnamese nationalists defeated French forces in 1954 at Dien Bien Phu, leading to the creation of North Vietnam and the retreat of the French from Southeast Asia. Less than two years later, guerrillas, backed by North Vietnam, started operating in South Vietnam. In 1956, the Egyptian leader Gamal Nasser, friendly with Soviet leaders, announced the nationalization of the Suez Canal, sparking an international crisis. Fidel Castro's guerrillas in Cuba made headway against the U.S.-backed Batista regime. Wyman knew more troops and insurgents hostile to the United States were being armed with AK-47s. The Soviets and other Communist countries had made millions of them.

Ordnance staff were initially dismissive of the AK-47, even as fighters across the planet took up the gun. By 1954, Ordnance produced a manual on Soviet rifles and didn't even mention the AK-47. It was a shocking oversight. The army's Aberdeen Proving Ground in Maryland didn't test the weapon until 1956. But the Soviet rifle was durable and reliable. Even if it didn't fire that accurately, it fired quickly. As C. J. Chivers noted in his comprehensive history of the Kalashnikov and its worldwide impact, *The Gun*, the weapon and its derivations would become "the most important series of infantry small arms of our time." By 1958, the rifle was being used by the Soviet military, intelligence, and police, and being distributed to Warsaw Pact allies. The United States needed something to meet the technological challenge that the AK presented.

Wyman believed American soldiers needed to be trained and equipped for close-quarters combat. Intense, short firefights were the norm in guerilla warfare. In a lengthy article in the army periodical *Infantry*, Wyman outlined the army's new rifle training program that downplayed long-distance marksmanship. The new training replicated real combat conditions and taught basic shooting skills for average soldiers fighting at close range. He stressed, "[T]he range of battlefield targets will rarely exceed 300 meters."

Wyman sponsored experiments in 1955 at Fort Benning that came to the counterintuitive conclusion that .22 caliber bullets, similar to the ones that boys used to hunt squirrels, could do just as much damage to the human body as the big bullets, maybe even more if they were fired at high enough speeds. "It was found that the high velocity, small caliber principle possesses these desirable characteristics over the heavier, slower-moving bullet: lighter weight of ammunition, less recoil, better accuracy from flatter trajectory and greater lethality," Wyman's researchers wrote. A gun using smaller bullets would allow soldiers to carry more ammunition, exactly what modern soldiers needed against numerically superior foes.

Convinced the M14 was a tragic mistake, Wyman launched a back-channel effort to stop Springfield's rifle from becoming the U.S. military's next rifle. In 1956, he wrote letters to army chief of staff General Maxwell Taylor, outlining what he called the "lightweight rifle problem." Wyman heard about ArmaLite's new designs from the retired General Jacob Devers, who had become a consultant for Fairchild. The two men were friendly as members of an exclusive club of four-star U.S. generals. Devers proved to be a key hire for Fairchild, with close ties to Pentagon leaders. When Devers suggested his company's guns, Wyman was all ears.

"Jackie Devers, in his work with the ArmaLite rifle, has shown that revolutionary changes in the shoulder weapon are feasible," Wyman wrote to Taylor. "These projects lead me to the conclusion that rather than just another rifle on our atomic battlefield we need a truly lightweight ultra-high-velocity small-caliber rifle weighing in the order of 6 pounds, one which the soldier will treasure and use."

If the military could build missile systems armed with nuclear warheads in just a few years, "there must be those in our country who could do as well or better with a comparatively simple rifle," Wyman wrote. Taylor, the army's highest-ranking officer, shared Wyman's concerns, writing back "that the light rifle project had really become a heavy rifle project."

But Taylor bowed to internal political pressures and rejected Wyman's suggestion. He recommended that Springfield's rifle be adopted by the army. Key in his decision: the M14 would be quicker to get into production. Wyman was appalled. Without telling Taylor, he flew to Los Angeles and drove straight to Hollywood. The general and his entourage stunned Stoner and his team when he strode into the ArmaLite office unannounced.

"How would you like to get in on a rifle program for me?" Stoner recalled the general asking him.

Wyman told Stoner he had been impressed with the AR-10 design, but he wanted "something in a smaller caliber." He wanted Stoner to fly to Fort Benning to meet with the Infantry Board, which was under Wyman's command.

"They'll tell you all about what they want and then . . . I want you to get back with me and tell me what you can do for me," Stoner recalled Wyman saying.

Stoner was flabbergasted and thrilled.

"This was a complete shortcut to the system because the benefactor on the thing was General Wyman, who had four stars and a lot to say about what was going on in the Army," Stoner recalled.

Just days after the army officially adopted the M14 as its standard rifle in May 1957, Stoner demonstrated a smaller version of his AR-10 model—it didn't even have a name yet—for Wyman and other officers at Fort Benning. They were impressed. The gun would soon be named the AR-15.

Even the slim chance for ArmaLite to land a military contract was welcome news. The small company had been foundering. The group had come up with a number of new, strange-looking weapons, but the output took on an air of desperation. One was the AR-13, or the "Light weight, Hyper-Velocity, Airborne Weapons System," a hexagonal device that could be attached to an airplane and loaded with missiles. It was a fusion of a shotgun and a beehive. This imaginative design was highlighted in ArmaLite's report to Fairchild titled "Outline of proposed activity for 1957." Other projects included the AR-9 autoloading shotgun, the AR-10 infantry rifle, and the AR-14, a commercial version of the AR-10 designed to look like a traditional hunting rifle. ArmaLite called it the "autoloading sporter."

ArmaLite stressed to Fairchild that it would continue to pursue military contracts, but it also urged Fairchild to back a move into the commercial gun market, an area that Sullivan had wanted to focus on from the beginning.

"We believe it necessary to get into business before the costs of research and development reach such proportions as to make recovery too difficult," the presentation noted. ArmaLite should begin production of up to five thousand of its AR-5 survival rifles for the commercial market, the presentation urged. The AR-5 was part of Sullivan's scheme to sell novel, futuristic firearms to hunters. ArmaLite launched the collapsible semiautomatic rifle as the AR-7 Explorer in 1959, but civilian sales were marginal.

The weak financial situation stressed everyone working at the small company. At the Stoner home, Jean fretted. George Sullivan had given Stoner a small raise after one year at the company, increasing his monthly salary from $700 to $725 for being a "capable and valuable employee." The Stoners, with three young children, were living paycheck to paycheck. The family had moved into a larger house in the same neighborhood. Though he didn't need it for building guns anymore, Stoner set up the garage as his workshop, creating various oddities, including a fiberglass canoe.

Little Susie Stoner wandered into the garage one day and began playing with the fiberglass cloth, which is made up of tiny slivers of glass that can pierce skin. The panicked father raised his voice when he saw her and then launched into a detailed explanation of fiberglass.

"That was the last time I went into the garage," she recalled.

Stoner would only speak sternly when it involved the children's immediate safety, but he was too gentle and distracted to be a disciplinarian, according to his daughter. Once, when the family was at her aunt's home in Northern California, Susie wandered off to the grocery store by herself. When the family finally located her, Jean was furious. "My mother said, 'Stoner, you got to spank her,'" she recalled. Stoner took his daughter into the bedroom to receive her punishment and solemnly shut the door. But he didn't lay a hand on her. "Just tell them I spanked you," she remembered her father saying.

6.

THE SPACE-AGE GUN IS BORN

It looked a little far out for that time in history.

—Eugene Stoner

Military officials briefed Stoner at Fort Benning on the battle rifle of the future that Wyman wanted. It should fire small-caliber bullets, they said, but the bullets should have enough power to penetrate a steel helmet at five hundred yards. The rifle should weigh six pounds, fully loaded with a twenty-round detachable magazine, but it should look like a conventional rifle and not like one of the inventor's strange weapons, they insisted. Stoner had doubts as he flew back to California. He knew from previous attempts that using a traditional rifle design with its sloping stock wouldn't work because the gun tended to go off target when firing rapidly. Shooters needed a stock that went straight back into their shoulder. With his first attempt, Stoner tried to satisfy the military's contradictory demands but it didn't work. "When the weapon was all together and firing, everybody decided it wasn't as easy to control as they expected," Stoner recalled years later. The solution was simply: reject the army's meddling. Just take the AR-10 and make it smaller. "That became the AR-15," Stoner said.

Stoner turned to the company's young draftsman, Jim Sullivan. This Sullivan was a kindred soul to Stoner. Sullivan was born in Alaska and raised in Washington State. His father wanted him to attend college, but Sullivan, wanting adventure, signed up for the army as a diver during the Korean War. After the war, he took a job at Boeing in Seattle while pursuing his own inventions after work hours. One invention, inspired by his diving days, was a contraption that could be used to communicate underwater. To test it, he would submerge himself in the bathtub and try to speak through it while his soon-to-be wife, Kaye, pressed her ear to the other end of the device. He also invented guns and gun parts. One was a little semiautomatic .22 caliber rifle. Another was a design for a mechanism to automatically eject a gun's magazine. When Sullivan read the short piece on ArmaLite in *Time*, "I just had to get there," he recalled. He spent hours on a job application and included his own designs for the magazine ejector, offering ArmaLite the design for free. Sullivan's energy interested Stoner, who valued inventiveness over pedigree. Sullivan remembered jumping into his convertible and driving south in June 1957. He didn't get far. His car broke down in Oregon. Sullivan gave the dead convertible to a farmer and hitchhiked the rest of the way. His fiancée followed soon after. The couple found Hollywood grimy, a far cry from the glamorous city depicted in the movies, but Sullivan loved his job. Inside ArmaLite's garage-like space on Santa Monica Boulevard, he worked with the brightest men he had ever met. "Magical," he said when asked to describe the office decades later.

"Most of the day was spent drawing with a little break for shooting," Sullivan recalled. Stoner had a corner office, but he spent much of his time in the main room, offering suggestions and listening to ideas. Meetings were impromptu and could be called by anyone no matter their status in the company.

Sullivan spent months sketching out the smaller version of the AR-10 on his drafting board. The work was challenging. It was not as simple as just making everything smaller. A draftsman couldn't simply scale down each rifle part in equal proportion. The mechanisms and pieces in the gun that loaded, fired, ejected, and surrounded the smaller ammunition had to shrink, but others, such as the trigger mechanism, couldn't.

"You can't scale that down because the human hand has to fit," Sullivan said. Some internal pieces could not be reduced too much because they would be too weak to withstand the high pressure of a rapid-fire gun. A few design decisions were personal. Stoner told Sullivan to make the distance between the trigger and the end of the buttstock a short fourteen inches. "Stoner was kind of small so he liked a fourteen-inch pull," said Sullivan.

With the creation of the AR-15, Flash Gordon's space gun became something you could hold. Stoner's design was an ode to simplicity, efficiency, and ease of use. The gun bore no trace of craftsmanship and included no polished wood. The rifle was modern and spare, made of aluminum, fiberglass, and plastic. Stoner's gas system eliminated many moving metal parts. The deft combination of modern materials and the gas system made the rifle unbelievably light. Early versions of the AR-15 weighed just over five pounds unloaded, less than hedge trimmers and handheld vacuums of the era.

"There was a real effort to make the gun as light as possible," Sullivan remembered.

With all of Stoner's innovations—lighter material, fewer parts, the gas system, the in-line stock, and the pistol grip—Sullivan found shooting the prototype AR-15 easy, even after he flipped the selector switch from semiautomatic to automatic. "That made it so well handling," he remembered. "If you're firing full auto, you don't want a gun that lifts." Sullivan found the rifle's recoil to be minimal because of its design and the small bullets, making follow-up shots quick when pulling the trigger in semiautomatic mode.

The rifle seemed to be the solution to the problem raised in troubling studies after World War II. With the AR-15, a soldier could fire lots of bullets quickly with a gun that was easy to keep on target. In close quarters, the AR-15 could transform anyone into a lethal marksman.

Stoner and his colleagues at ArmaLite focused on engineering specifics: angles, alloys, pressures, parts, and how they all came together to send lots of pieces of metal down a tube. They wanted to build a rifle that met Wyman's specifications and land a government contract. But Stoner's creation proved to be much greater than the sum of these many parts and requirements. It was a critical nexus in the evolution of firearms. A little-known but tireless inventor, an aging general determined to overcome a retrograde bureaucracy, and an idea lab with grand ambitions came together in an age of new lightweight materials to produce a weapon that went far beyond the exigencies of the moment. The AR-15 shed traditions that had long burdened gun design, such as the reliance on heavy wood and steel and the bias toward large-caliber bullets for an infantry rifle. Though they didn't know it, the men at ArmaLite were about to blow away these weighted legacies with a puff of light gas and a few pieces of plastic and aluminum.

Asked about his creation years later, Stoner said, "It looked a little far out for that time in history."

Stoner's process of designing his revolutionary weapon was a striking contrast to the way that most military armaments had been created. The vast bureaucracy of the Manhattan Project that developed the atomic bomb was comparable in size to the entire auto industry, according to Richard Rhodes, author of *The Making of the Atomic Bomb*. "There weren't just those guys down in Los Alamos tinkering to build bombs," Rhodes said. "There were six hundred thousand employed in the Manhattan Project." Some of the most brilliant minds of the era, including Enrico Fermi and Niels Bohr, worked together on the concepts behind the bomb. "They were the scientists who had pioneered physics in the twentieth century," he said. Missile systems and other advanced weapons led to similar coordination across different scientific disciplines and required extensive and prolonged government funding. Tens of thousands of people worked for years in military research centers and university labs across the United States on these projects.

In contrast, making guns by the 1950s and 1960s was a much more modest affair. An inventor with a machine shop and a good idea had a chance. The relatively simple mechanics of firearms still allowed for humble tinkerers—without fancy degrees or hefty R & D grants—to succeed. The individual still mattered, but they needed persistence and luck.

In the fall of 1957, ArmaLite moved its offices to Costa Mesa, forty miles south of Los Angeles. The new ArmaLite headquarters was much like the old one, except it had an area outside to test guns. The gun range was set up in the parking lot, with a large sandpile at the far end. The ArmaLite team didn't make the new gun public as they readied it for Wyman. The first person to shoot the gun outside of ArmaLite wasn't a reporter or a military official. Jim Sullivan remembered one day he was firing an AR-15 prototype into the sandpile when he looked up to see a tall man stroll into the offices, surrounded by excited ArmaLite employees. Sullivan did a double take: it was John Wayne, the actor, who was also an avid gun collector. Wayne had been at a nearby shipyard for repairs to his boat when the proprietors mentioned that their new neighbors made guns. Intrigued, Wayne came over to ArmaLite and introduced himself.

"He didn't need to introduce himself; we knew who the hell he was," Sullivan recalled.

Wayne asked about the gun Sullivan was holding.

"Why don't you try it out for yourself?" said Sullivan, his heart pounding.

Wayne shouldered the rifle, aiming at the sandpile. He squeezed off a flurry of shots, spraying sand into the air. Sullivan sputtered out to Wayne, "You're the first person outside of ArmaLite that's fired an AR-15." It was a fact that Wayne would boast about for years to come.

As the ArmaLite team fine-tuned their new rifle, their secret preparations also included a new type of ammunition, slightly larger than a .22 caliber bullet. Wyman wanted lighter bullets to allow soldiers to carry more ammunition, but the bullets needed to be effective on the battlefield. The answer to this riddle was speed.

Unlike Stoner's radical gun concepts, the counterintuitive notion that small bullets fired at high speeds could cause large wounds was not foreign to military researchers. In 1928, the U.S. military created a committee of officers from various branches to "recommend a specific caliber for the future development of the semiautomatic shoulder rifle." The board would become known as "the Pig Board," because it oversaw the shooting of a passel of pigs to study their corpses and assess how much damage differently sized bullets would inflict. The Pig Board determined that high-velocity, small-caliber bullets produced less recoil, had a flatter trajectory, and caused "the most severe wounds in all parts of the animal," from a distance of three hundred yards.

When they cut open the pigs, the researchers discovered that the tiny bullet didn't punch straight through the pork like the big bullet did. Instead it became unstable when it hit the hogs, spiraling through the animal's insides, ripping through organs, and shattering bones. "In practically every wound, the point at which the bullet became unstable can be demonstrated by the increased diameter of the wound and the sudden increase in the amount of trauma," the Pig Board concluded.

Decades later, as Stoner worked on his AR-15, the army once again tested a tiny bullet against a bigger one. Project SALVO used even smaller bullets than the Pig Board and it didn't use pigs. This time tests were conducted on a herd of goats. Researchers found that at 140 yards away, the "smaller bullets, because of their superior tumbling abilities . . . are able to transfer more of their kinetic energies to the targets." At five hundred yards, they noticed that "the increased tissue damage was especially noticeable after the passage of bullet through bone." The bullet that did the most damage was a .22 caliber that weighed less than two dimes, was less than an inch long, and exploded out of the barrel at about three times the speed of sound. The wounds caused by the army's preferred 7.62 caliber bullet—which was twice as heavy and about one-third of an inch longer, and traveled slower—"were not as destructive as those made by the .22 cal.," they found. The larger bullet tended to stay relatively stable as it passed through the goats, they observed.

The way to make a small bullet fly faster was to add more propellant, Stoner knew. He took a standard hunting round called the .222 Remington and redesigned it so he could add more powder. He sent drawings to Remington, which built a cartridge that would later become known as the .223 Remington "so it wouldn't get mixed up with somebody in the marketplace, though they had no intentions of ever commercially building it," Stoner said. Today, .223 ammunition is one of the most widely sold for rifles on the commercial market.

Stoner, Jim Sullivan, and another employee named Bob Fremont tried to figure out how to test Stoner's new bullet with the AR-15. Their first thought: live animals to stand in for humans, just like the military's goat and pig tests. They called around but shooting animals cost money. Then someone suggested calling the local Spam plant for animal parts. Jim Sullivan and Fremont came back from the plant with plastic bags full of something squishy and smelly. The offal would be perfect for testing, they thought.

"Just all the junk that they wouldn't put in like intestines with poop in it. Real juicy stuff," Sullivan recalled.

Sullivan and Fremont searched for a place to shoot the bags of pig viscera, driving inland from Costa Mesa until they found a field that abutted some woods, far from any houses. The men set up an ad hoc 350-yard shooting range by hanging a sturdy clothesline between two trees. Jim Sullivan remembered the feeling of holding the world's most advanced rifle and taking aim at the sloshing black bags of pig guts. He fired. Pig guts flew into the air. The smell was horrendous.

Back at the office, the two men proudly announced the results of their pig-guts test, but then realized it was a lot of work for nothing. Their messy test didn't show their gun was better than any other. It just demonstrated the gun could rip open a bag of pig intestines. What they needed were scientific controls and measurable results. They searched around the office and found their control: two five-gallon metal jerry cans that were used to carry water in the military. They could shoot one with the new small bullet and the other with the larger bullet, then measure differences. At the office's makeshift range, Sullivan and Fremont set up the box-shaped cans filled with water. They fired first with a large-caliber bullet and "knocked the can over and put a bullet through both sides," Sullivan recalled.

Then, they fired the AR-15 with the smaller-caliber bullet.

"It blew the can up," Sullivan remembered. "The jerry can is split in two places and the lid is blown off and the handles are kind of crumpled."

They rushed to tell Stoner.

"Everyone was thrilled," Sullivan said. "It was better than what we had expected."

The bullets that would become standard for both the military and civilian versions of Stoner's rifle remained small—most weighed about 3.5 grams, a gram more than a penny. They looked like miniature missile tips, measuring less than a quarter inch in diameter, .224 inches to be exact. They sat atop casings filled with powder that were large relative to the bullet's size. They flew out of the barrel at about three times the speed of sound to maximize the damage caused by the small projectile. Larger bullets tended to punch straight through a human body, but "the small bullet will go unstable faster, and therefore create a larger wound cavity than you would normally expect," Stoner said.

Over the decades, researchers came to understand how this bullet's unique combination of mass, velocity, shape, and material created such large wounds. Velocity and mass determined the energy of any bullet and "thus the maximal injury potential," said Beat Kneubuehl, a Swiss ballistics scientist who authored the definitive work on the subject. By increasing the velocity of the tiny bullet, Stoner gave it more injury potential. When the bullet hit the human body, it slowed down and released its energy. "The energy that the projectile loses through deceleration (loss of velocity) is converted into work, i.e., into damage to the tissue," Kneubuehl said. The bullets of the AR-15 maximized this effect because they went unstable so quickly. They had less energy than larger rifle rounds but they transferred more of their energy to the human body.

A bullet fired from an AR-15 flew nose first through the air. But when it hit the human body it became unstable. Once unstable, the bullet tore through the body like a tornado, spiraling and tipping as it obliterated organs, blood vessels, and bones. In the early days, researchers described this motion as "tumbling," but such a description implied that the bullet flipped rapidly head over heels like a gymnast.

Instead, the bullet "moves like a spinning top," Kneubuehl said. "Its axis constantly forms an angle with the direction of flight."

Even without the benefit of decades of later research, Stoner was correct in his description of the tiny bullet's power. "It is *not the caliber* that causes particularly severe injuries," Kneubuehl said. "The stability of a bullet is decisive for the course of injury."

Researchers like the military surgeon Dr. Martin Fackler would later discover that some bullets fired from AR-15s had a tendency to break apart when they went unstable inside the body. A bullet that fragmented was far more devastating than one that did not, the little pieces widening its deadly reach. "Velocity often dominates discussions of wound ballistics; however, a bullet can inflict more lethal damage to tissue by fragmentation," Dr. Fackler wrote.

When ArmaLite moved to Costa Mesa, the Stoners decided to move too, but Jean and Stoner argued about where. Jean wanted to live near the ocean on Balboa Island, but Stoner liked the dry air and suggested Tustin, a small town inland from his new office. As a compromise, they settled on a new development in Newport Beach a couple of miles from the ocean. Their new house was a big, one-story ranch-style home with a facade made of wood and faux stone. The kidney-shaped pool in the backyard delighted the three Stoner children. There was a garage—but Stoner didn't need to use it for his inventions anymore. "We actually kept cars in there for the first time," said daughter Susan.

On the weekends, the Stoners would go to eat as a family at one of the first International House of Pancakes restaurants there. Michael and Patty, now in their early teens, and four-year-old Susie spent their time playing in the neighborhood or going with their mother to the beach.

It was an idyllic time for the Stoner children, but as with many other Americans in the 1950s, anxiety lurked below a surface of ease and abundance. The Stoner children learned at school what to do in the event of Soviet nuclear attack. Sirens and bells went off regularly and teachers ordered kids to hide under their desks and cover their heads, Sue recalled.

At his office a few miles away, Sue's father was working to build a gun to help America defeat those Communists. Stoner knew his gun could help U.S. troops counter the durable AK-47s used by insurgents around the globe. In Stoner's and Jim Sullivan's minds, their work was engaging but also noble. For them, the task of making the best rifle for the U.S. military wasn't burdened with a moral quandary. "I think about the mechanisms," Jim Sullivan said. "I assume the U.S. is generally on the side of right."

7.

THE BUREAUCRACY STRIKES BACK

They really didn't think that this new little rifle
would have a chance. Well, it did.
—Eugene Stoner

When ArmaLite's guns arrived at Fort Benning for testing, soldiers were fascinated by the weapons they took out of the crates. The five AR-15s didn't look like any rifle the men had seen before.

"It's so lightweight. It looked different. It doesn't look like a United States rifle," recalled David Carson, a private who helped design and administer the tests.

He recalled how he and the other men marveled at the strange-looking weapons and they couldn't wait to shoot them.

"To fire a test weapon with a serial number 0000001 is a real rush," he recalled.

These rifles were about to go up against the M14 in a crucial contest that could determine whether the military would embrace Stoner's new approach to firearms or disregard his innovations for more traditional weapons. For ArmaLite, the stakes were high: the company could not survive another rejection.

The tests, held in the spring of 1958, would be the first time the AR-15 and the M14 faced off.

The men at Ordnance and Springfield Armory were certain that wars had always been—and would always be—won with good aim. It was an American creed as old as the frontier days, making sharpshooters from Davy Crockett to Audie Murphy icons. "When it came to rifles, the department's Springfield Armory seemed as attached to developing and producing a marksman's rifle as the infantry was to using it," wrote Thomas McNaugher, a military historian. The M14 with its large bullet was accurate at great distances and was "the last in a long line of marksman's rifles," he wrote. Springfield and Ordnance jealously guarded their monopoly on military weapons. They believed that any firearm issued to U.S. soldiers should be developed by the military's own gun designers and rigorously tested for years.

"Springfield had this attitude that we've been doing this a hundred years and we know what to do," Carson recalled thinking. "But they were just doing the same thing over and over again."

The traditionalists also had a key practical consideration on their side: the M14 had been designed to use the same ammunition as America's allies around the globe in the fight against Communism, while the AR-15 had not.

Yet the faction led by General Wyman feared that U.S. troops armed with M14s would be overwhelmed by Communists with superior numbers and firepower. They were certain that future wars would be won by firing large volumes of bullets over short distances and they believed that private industry was the only place that American soldiers were going to get the weapons they needed. It was why Wyman, just months from retirement, orchestrated the showdown at Fort Benning. Before he left the service, he wanted to make sure the M14, which he considered a failure, was replaced by a better weapon. In a letter before the tests to army chief of staff General Taylor, he wrote, "Should these rifles be found superior to the M14, as I am almost certain they will be, it would be most unfortunate if the Army had committed itself before Congress to irrevocable support of the M14 rifle." Though the army had already selected the M14 as its standard-issue rifle, Wyman hoped that the trials would persuade leaders to change course before the gun was issued to every soldier.

The tests were so secretive that Carson couldn't write his parents to tell them what he was doing. "Everything was need-to-know," he said. "You got it laid on pretty heavily that if you revealed anything that was classified, it was a criminal offense."

Carson, a draftee, was put on the secret tests because he had studied actuarial tables at the University of Michigan and was considered good at statistics. The young man found himself designing trials that would determine future combat rifles for the most powerful army in the free world.

The official purpose of the test was "to determine the potential of the ArmaLite (AR-15) Small Caliber Rifle to replace the M14" and a modified version of the M14 called the M15, according to a confidential Infantry Board report on the trials. But Carson and other men assigned to the project also wanted to answer another question: How would it do in jungle fighting? One of the three test officers was a major who had just returned from being an observer in South Vietnam. The men in the secret testing unit "all wanted to know what was happening in this strange country called Vietnam," recalled Carson. "Being army types, they sat around and bullshitted about all this." Carson and others working in a classified section of Fort Benning assumed the major's reassignment there meant the rifle testing had a practical and ominous purpose. "Everybody understood what the message was that was being sent," Carson said. "We need to be ready for jungle warfare."

The low red-clay hills of Georgia were not the jungles of Southeast Asia, but the army constructed tests to replicate conditions the gun might encounter there. In one test, soldiers fired the guns into a farm crib stuffed with underbrush, branches, and leaves. The goal was to "see what comes out the other side," recalled Carson. "None of them did very well," with the bullets deflecting everywhere. The soldiers also tested how long the guns could shoot before their barrels melted. Carson was one of those tasked with sitting with a rifle and firing round after round after round. As Carson fired the weapons, he began to notice differences. All the guns had some problems, and at one point an AR barrel cracked. But to Carson, the AR-15 was the clear winner. It was lighter, easier to shoot, and easy to aim. "I thought this is what you need if you are going out in the field and you have a sixty-pound backpack and you need enough ammunition to keep the enemy at bay," he said. Carson saw that other soldiers, "a mixture of southern regular army guys and draftees from the northeast," favored the AR-15 too. "When the first guys started firing it, they loved it. They could get a nice close grouping. At three hundred yards it was just as accurate as the M14, but a lot less heavy."

Stoner traveled to Fort Benning so he could show soldiers how to use his gun, in part because the AR-15 was so new that ArmaLite hadn't yet created an instruction manual. He watched anxiously from an observation area as soldiers, many of them not career army but enlisted under the peacetime draft, put his invention through test after test under a sweltering southern sun. The men dragged the rifles through mud puddles and sandpiles. They crawled with the weapons under barbed wire strung a few inches off the ground. At the end of punishing courses, the men lined up in an open field and fired at targets. Officers and observers monitored how the different guns—now covered in grit and muck—performed.

But testing results could be influenced by something as trivial as a glass of lemonade or a shady tree. If a rifle malfunctioned, a soldier checked the gun in, then officers ordered them to wait under nearby trees. The soldiers with broken guns got to rest and drink lemonade, while those with working guns continued to fire at targets in the searing heat. One day, Stoner noticed that a soldier had figured out how to spend more time in the shade. Stoner watched the young man closely: every time the soldier would take a fresh magazine out to load his rifle, he would stumble and scoop sand or mud into the magazine. Then he would hold his rifle upside down to shake it so that grime would be knocked into the internal workings of the gun. Stoner flagged down a beefy sergeant who chewed the soldier out, but Stoner learned a hard lesson about military testing: testers could mess with results in myriad ways and for a host of reasons.

After each of the many tests, Carson tabulated the results using a mechanical calculator in a barracks office. After hours of meticulous work, Carson had to go work on KP duty, peeling potatoes or washing dishes. The head of the testing unit would laugh over the fact that Carson's reports were given top-secret status—and Carson didn't have clearance to read what he had just written. Carson and the test officers felt that the AR-15 had done so well it should get a preferred status in their final report. The status wasn't just bragging rights; it would secure funding for ArmaLite to improve the gun's reliability and make other changes. Although the final report stated the AR-15 had performed well in many categories, it wasn't granted preferred status. Carson was told Springfield had blocked such a move.

The Infantry Board's confidential report on Stoner's AR-15 versus the M14 was completed on May 27, 1958. The AR-15 was superior to the M14 in lightness, ease of assembly and disassembly, reliability under simulated combat conditions, and ease of handling, the board concluded. The M14 was better for penetrating a target. On the firing line, the AR-15 scored well. Stoner's gun had just 6.5 malfunctions per hundred rounds fired on semiautomatic compared to the M14's 14.6. When spraying on full automatic, the AR-15 was also better. Stoner had been working on the AR-15 for less than a year, while Springfield had been struggling with its design for more than a decade. Yet Stoner's gun was more than twice as reliable according to the trials. The AR-15 also edged out the M14 in accuracy on some tests, and the report described the two guns as "comparable" in this category. The board's shocking conclusion: the AR-15 should be considered as "a potential replacement for the M-14."

"They really didn't think that this new little rifle would have a chance," Stoner recalled. "Well, it did. It did perform and it performed very well."

As Stoner and colleagues celebrated in Los Angeles, Springfield and Army Ordnance officials fumed. A small private company from California was threatening to upset military tradition. These officials launched a surreptitious effort to undermine the outside challenger. Back at Fort Benning, Carson saw the moves on his last day in the army. As he packed up in his barracks to move back to New York, he called over to the testing office to talk to his commander about coming over to say goodbye. His commanding officer told him not to come. A congressional delegation had shown up because Springfield had persuaded them to push for the M14, despite its poor showing. "You don't want to get involved with this at this point," the officer told Carson, adding that the two shouldn't correspond about the tests or results. They never spoke again.

The Ordnance bureaucracy used the same playbook of manipulating reports and tests it had used to torpedo challengers in the past. The mastermind of this campaign was Dr. Frederick Howard Carten, head of research and development at the Ordnance Corps. Carten, a civilian who had earned a Ph.D. from MIT, was a career military bureaucrat who was described as the "father of the M14" by the firearms historian Edward Ezell. He rose in the ranks at the Ordnance Corps because he was a master of the Pentagon's byzantine politics. Carten was "above all, a consummate pragmatist in matters of policy; he believed very sincerely that the attainment of a worthy goal would justify whatever means might be necessary to attain it," according to William Davis, who worked with Carten.

For years, Carten insisted that the M14 was "the finest rifle in production in the world today." The balding bureaucrat, who wore bifocals, admitted he wasn't a good shot but he dismissed civilian critics.

"The American public has a tremendous interest in this particular field—and it can be a most emotional subject because virtually half the population has fired a pistol or rifle or carbine or something, so they are all experts!" he said in a slight Boston accent.

That summer, Ordnance Corps officers announced to Wyman that they had discovered problems with the AR-15. Two AR-15 rifles had been damaged during separate "rain tests" at Aberdeen Proving Ground in Maryland, they said. It was a standard test to see how the rifle would fare in wet conditions, but the results had been disastrous. The gun was unsafe, they wrote. In August 1958, the Infantry Board issued an addendum—kept from the public—to its initial glowing report that declared the rain problem was a major deficiency for the AR-15.

From an engineering perspective, the AR-15's problems during the rain test were easy to solve. But Stoner and his team were no longer operating in the confines of their office, where problems had centered on material strengths, gas pressures, and bullet trajectories. The men now were caught up in the murky world of Pentagon political intrigue, where bureaucratic fiefdoms jealously held on to power; funding for projects was often capricious and fleeting; and whom you knew above you or in Congress was often the trump card in any debate over policy or procurement. Stoner thought the army's dismissal of the AR-10 had been abrupt. He had no idea what was in store for the AR-15. The rain test was just "one of several ploys of Ordnance to attempt to head off the AR-15 rifle which was threatening procurement of the M14," army Colonel Richard Hallock, a later military advocate for the AR-15, wrote in a history of the weapon.

The ArmaLite draftsman Jim Sullivan and others at the company saw the problem clearly. "Dr. Carten wanted to kill off the AR-15," he said.

William Davis, the Ordnance Corps veteran, confirmed Sullivan's suspicions years later. Ordnance had made extensive plans for mass production of the M14 and Carten didn't want that work to be derailed. Carten knew that if Congress heard about ArmaLite's promising new rifle, they would demand that the army drop the M14, he said. But if Carten could make it seem like the AR-15 was failing in supposedly objective tests, he wouldn't face any uncomfortable questions about whether the M14 was suitable.

Ordnance officers who worked for Carten had fended off a serious challenge to the M14 years earlier with shooting tests in subzero temperatures. Now it was the AR-15's turn to face the cold. About ten days before Christmas 1958, Stoner received an unexpected telegram from Alaska. It came from Fort Greely, an army base about 220 miles northeast of Anchorage and one of the coldest places in the world, which was why the army chose it for its Cold Regions Test Center.

The telegram stated cryptically that officers at the base were having trouble with AR-15s they were testing. That telegram was the first Stoner heard that his gun was being tested there at all. He flew to Alaska immediately with a crate of AR-15 parts. When he got to the base, it was freezing. Standing at Fort Greely's shooting range on the tundra, Stoner watched bundled-up soldiers firing AR-15s. A dismayed Stoner saw that none of the soldiers were hitting their targets. He asked a sergeant to order a cease-fire and then rushed over to inspect the guns. He noticed that temperature wasn't the problem. Someone had tampered with the guns' sights. The critical devices used to aim at a target had been removed and replaced with bits of metal welding. The sights were so misaligned that no matter how much a shooter tried to aim, they couldn't hit anything. Stoner complained to the officer running the tests. The man was evasive.

Stoner found a base machine shop where he was able to install proper sights that he brought from California. Shooting resumed and the guns worked well, even in the cold. Stoner trudged to the base commander's office. He started to speak, but the officer cut him off midsentence.

"'You're doing a great disservice to the United States Army,' and he says by bringing along one of these small-caliber weapons, that is going to be a danger to every American soldier that carries one," Stoner recalled the officer saying. "'I can't wait to get your ass off this base.'"

Before Stoner flew home from Alaska, he received another unexpected message. The army ordered him to fly to Fort Monroe in Virginia. Though Stoner didn't know it, a review of the army's rifle program was under way at Fort Monroe, and they wanted Stoner's testimony. The secret hearings were instigated by Wyman, alarmed by Carten's attempts to undermine Stoner's gun. It was one of Wyman's last acts before he retired. Led by Lieutenant General Herbert Powell, the hearings laid bare the increasing anxiety among many officers that Springfield Armory's M14 was no match for Soviet rifles. In a dramatic moment, recorded in confidential transcripts, a military expert in Soviet arms held Kalashnikov's invention aloft for generals and others at the meeting.

"This is the AK submachine gun . . . the Avtomat Kalashnikova," he said. "This weapon became available in 1949 and it is estimated that there have been 2,500,000 made as of 1 January 1959." He praised the Soviet weapon as "simple, rugged and effective." Another officer trashed Springfield's M14 as "marginally better" than the M1, and another gave a talk praising Stoner's AR-10. One officer wondered aloud why there were "some rather hard feelings between ArmaLite and Ordnance."

When Stoner arrived, he was met by Dorchester and Devers. They whisked him into a hearing room where the generals were waiting. Stoner launched into the technical intricacies of rifle mechanisms and wound ballistics. Stoner said that the AR-15 had "a better killing cartridge with a higher velocity" than the Soviet AK-47. Large-caliber rifles like Springfield's were not built for modern war, he insisted. "What is the point of giving a man a thousand-yard killing cartridge when he can only hit at three hundred yards?" Stoner said. The generals asked Stoner how a smaller bullet fired from his rifle could do so much damage.

"The wound capability is extremely high," Stoner answered. "It blows up on contact rather than drilling a nice neat hole." A slower .30 caliber round, similar to the one used by Springfield's rifles, "will go right through flesh leaving a neat hole," but the faster, smaller bullet from the AR-15 "will tumble and tear," he explained.

Ordnance Corps gave testimony as well, but that appears not to have been preserved in military files. A confidential letter from the office of the army's chief of research and development to the board captured Ordnance's bitterness toward Stoner and his backers. Tests of ArmaLite's AR-10 showed that it was "unsuitable for military use," the letter said. The AR-15 also was full of problems, the letter claimed. The gun's bullet was too puny, and the gun was a safety hazard as the rain tests had shown, the chief said. The chief's recommendation was to stick with the M14 but work to make it lighter. He added that the army could continue developing a lightweight rifle, but only if it was made to fire a larger bullet.

In their final secret report, Powell and the other generals dismissed the M14 as "at best, only a marginal improvement over the M1" and recommended keeping the old M1 Garands until a better gun came along. At the same time, they ordered seven hundred rifles from ArmaLite. Following Ordnance's recommendation, those rifles would be redesigned to fire a slightly larger round. All told, these developments seemed positive for ArmaLite. Stoner headed back to California with his spirits lifted.

Three days after he testified, however, Stoner received bad news: the Arctic tests sent to the Pentagon brass were the ones completed *before* Stoner arrived to repair the rifles. His frantic trip to Alaska had been for naught.

"They'd already run their tests," Stoner recalled. "They'd fouled up the weapons completely with these homemade parts, complained about the accuracy, complained about the performance and reliability, and written their report."

In the Arctic Test Board's report, they even complained about the AR-15's unique pistol grip, citing "insufficient space for arctic mittens."

To make the guns the Powell Board had ordered, Stoner contacted the Olin Mathieson Chemical Corporation, the company that was going to make the bigger cartridge, to get specifications. The company sent him a drawing and Stoner began to redesign the AR-15. Then a few days later the company sent him a second drawing that was different from the first. Two weeks after that, a third drawing arrived. Also slightly different. They seemed like needless delays.

"I guess being a little bit dense, I didn't realize what the routine really was until I read in the paper about a month later announcing that selection of the M14 rifle into production," Stoner said.

Then Stoner got a call from one of the men at Ordnance.

"Our ploy worked pretty good, didn't it?" Stoner recalled the man saying.

Stoner and ArmaLite had been played—again. The rain tests, the Arctic tests, and now the nonexistent larger bullet were all tactics to undermine his invention and buy time for the M14 to get into production. Carten had given the Hollywood upstarts a master class in bureaucratic warfare. Even the final report from the Powell Board that praised the AR-15 and bashed the M14 was buried. Just ten copies were made, and army staff later collected most to be shredded. With great bureaucratic flourish and an air of finality, Carten concluded that Stoner's rifle should no longer be considered by the army. Stoner's great invention appeared DOA.

Jim Sullivan had never seen Stoner so down. He took to calling Springfield Armory "the enemy" and muttering about how everything would have been fine if the army had used the right sights. He was so upset that he even cursed Carten. "He had some pretty foulmouthed things to say about him and Stoner generally didn't swear," recalled Jim Sullivan.

In less than one year, the AR-15's stunning victory over Springfield's M14 in Georgia had been manipulated by bureaucratic maneuvers into its reverse: clear victory now looked like defeat. The ArmaLite team had never doubted the AR-15's superiority over the M14 or its ultimate success as a military weapon. They were convinced that their radical gun would be judged on its merits. They couldn't imagine that elements in the military bureaucracy would use underhanded means to maintain the status quo—even if it meant arming U.S. troops with inferior weapons. "None of us, including Stoner, had gone through the antipathy that the military and Springfield had against any competition," said Jim Sullivan.

With the AR-15's future now in doubt, intrigue in ArmaLite's small office deepened between George Sullivan and Stoner. Several instances of scheming behavior by George Sullivan were uncovered in an investigation by a Fairchild attorney. One deposition recounted an alleged conversation between George Sullivan and Dorchester that occurred in the ArmaLite office when they thought no one else was around. Another employee was standing on a balcony above Sullivan's office and overheard the two men plotting to take over ArmaLite and its patents.

"Sullivan was telling Dorchester that eventually he felt that the Fairchild people would give up on this thing and that he would buy it real cheap and that he was happy to death to see them spend every bit of money they could to simply prepare an ultimate purchase on his part at a real bargain price," the man said. The Stoners were stunned to learn of this conversation. Sullivan wanted to run ArmaLite into the ground and then buy it, along with all of its intellectual property, for pennies on the dollar.

As the Stoners' distrust of George Sullivan grew, they sought help from an attorney. Thomas Patrick Mahoney was an engineer who had passed the difficult California bar exam without ever attending law school. He had worked with Stoner since 1956 to patent the inventor's gas system, which the U.S. Patent and Trademark Office granted in 1960. In the late 1950s, Mahoney went to work for ArmaLite's parent company, Fairchild. This move presented a conflict of interest for Mahoney, who was representing both Stoner and the company where he worked. Nonetheless, the Stoners showed the lawyer the questionable agreements that Sullivan had persuaded Stoner to sign. The lawyer took them to Fairchild's president, Richard Boutelle, who said he never knew they had existed. Boutelle was livid and tore up the recent agreement that Sullivan had gotten Stoner to sign and voided all past side deals that Sullivan had contrived. Fairchild gave Stoner the recognition and royalties he wanted and rewrote Sullivan's contract too. There is no record of George Sullivan's defense. Jean was thrilled with Mahoney's work. She called Mahoney the "only honest attorney I ever met" and insisted that he advise her husband on all future contracts that he signed.

8.

HUNTING BIG GAME

Hell, no; let's eat it.
—General Curtis LeMay, U.S. Air Force

The AR-15 never would have risen to be a contender for the infantry's next rifle without the financial backing, frenetic showmanship, and relentless hobnobbing of Richard "Dick" Boutelle, president of the Fairchild Engine and Airplane Corporation from 1949 to 1959. ArmaLite was his baby, and he was convinced that it was going to bring huge profits from contracts with the U.S. government and its allies. ArmaLite was only one of several major bets that Boutelle placed during the decade. To make those bets pay off, Boutelle needed important people in Washington to secure hefty government contracts, and he set out to court key leaders in the military, media, and entertainment. He dined at the White House, met with royalty, even hunted with celebrities and Pentagon top brass. He appeared to be an exemplar of the decade's successful American business executive: hard-charging, chummy with the powerful, adroit at trading favors, and eager to grab new business in an age of intense competition and rapid technological advances.

Born on July 4, 1898, in Vincennes, Indiana, Richard Schley Boutelle spent his life around the military but never saw any fighting. Boutelle claimed later in life that he was offered a position at West Point, but he turned it down and instead trained for the newly formed Aeronautical

Corps of the U.S. Army Signal Corps, a predecessor to the air force. During World War II, Boutelle became an assistant manager at the Fairchild airplane factory in Hagerstown, a small city in rural Maryland about sixty-five miles northwest of Washington. Boutelle thrived at the company, which made airplanes and parts. The workforce swelled from two hundred employees in 1939 to about eight thousand in 1943.

When his boss at Fairchild died of an acute embolism, Boutelle took over as plant manager. The burly, jowly Boutelle, with his slicked-back black hair and broad smile, was popular with workers and other managers. Boutelle met production deadlines, gaining a decent reputation at the Pentagon. Boutelle wanted Fairchild to land big government contracts after the war, but his aspirations faced blunt realities. Fairchild was at a clear disadvantage with its main plant in rural Maryland, far from the aircraft-making hubs of Long Island and Los Angeles or industrial centers such as Detroit and Chicago. Becoming a major player at the Pentagon would require luck and strong connections with power brokers.

Boutelle's greatest success was the development of Fairchild's C-119 transport plane, first flown in 1947. The "Flying Boxcar," as it was called, earned substantial profits for the company. Boutelle's career advanced further after a boardroom battle between top management and the company's founder, the inventor and businessman Sherman Fairchild. Boutelle sided with Fairchild and when Fairchild won a proxy fight in 1949, he installed the fifty-one-year-old Boutelle as the company's new president.

The company had a record year in 1950, with sales totaling $60.2 million, thanks in large part to orders driven by the Korean War. With Eisenhower's election in 1952, Boutelle launched hyperactive campaigns of self-promotion and lobbying in Washington. His efforts worked. By 1953, the company's sales reached almost $129 million in just the first nine months of the year. Boutelle used the cash influx in part to expand company operations into new airplanes, aluminum, plastics, boats, electronics, and guided missile systems. The next year, he also funded his pet project, ArmaLite. As one aviation historian put it, "Boutelle was interested in any product that would make a profit."

Even as Stoner was working on army tests of his AR-10 and AR-15 for the U.S. military, ArmaLite licensed manufacturing rights for the AR-10 rifle, signing a deal with the Dutch arms maker Artillerie-Inrichtingen. The company produced the rifles for the militaries of Holland, NATO allies, and other countries. Fairchild's main efforts, however, focused on landing military aircraft and commercial contracts. Beginning in 1952, the company devoted substantial resources on development of its XSM-73 guided-missile system, which attempted to launch guided missiles to simulate U.S. bombers, confusing the enemy. Research and development costs on the project were high. By 1957, however, the company was ready to test prototypes and had hopes of a major payoff in military contracts worth hundreds of millions of dollars. Fairchild also signed an agreement with the Dutch aircraft maker Fokker to make a commercial airplane, the F-27.

Fairchild's president became a regular in Washington circles. He served on military and aviation commissions, and attended private dinners at the White House hosted by President Eisenhower. Boutelle launched various publicity stunts, raising the company's profile and ingratiating Boutelle with military hawks. In March 1953, Boutelle and others at Fairchild put up seventy-five hundred dollars to pay spies in Poland to get a pilot to defect to Denmark in a Soviet-made MiG-15 jet. Boutelle and the others, who said they were acting as private citizens, refused to explain the mission's purpose.

Boutelle loved to hunt and shoot, and he used that interest to cultivate friendships with two powerful men: the Air Force General Curtis LeMay and the entertainer Arthur Godfrey. The three men bonded over rifles, hunting, and fishing. Boutelle's home was adorned with animal trophies, rifles, and pistols. A friend told Boutelle's first wife that she should buy a gun cabinet for all of her husband's weapons. "We keep house in one," she replied. Boutelle met LeMay while seeking contracts from the air force. The head of Strategic Air Command since 1948, Le-May oversaw the air force's nuclear bombers and, later, its intercontinental ballistic missiles. As the Eisenhower military shifted priorities, no officer in the Pentagon was more central to the effort, or had more say on how funding was doled out.

The newest branch of the armed forces had emerged as triumphant from the Pentagon infighting of the period. Air power had played a critical role in crushing Germany and Japan and the air force had unleashed the first atomic bombs. In Eisenhower's "New Look" strategy, the air force was seen as the essential service to keep the Communists in check—from 1952 to 1960, it would receive an average of 46 percent of the entire defense budget. And within the air force, no section was more important than Strategic Air Command.

Born in Columbus, Ohio, in 1906, Curtis Emerson LeMay joined the air corps after dropping out of Ohio State University. He initially wanted to join the regular army because of his love of firearms, but he chose the air corps instead, rising to the rank of major by World War II. During the war, LeMay's mastery of strategic bombing earned him rapid promotions in Europe and later Asia. His mantra to commanders was "get the bombs on the targets." Not only was he ruthless toward the enemy, he demanded—for the sake of accuracy—that his own men not deviate from their course to evade enemy aircraft fire, making their bombing runs much more dangerous. LeMay even led a raid himself to prove the point.

On March 9 and 10, 1945, LeMay, by then a general, oversaw the firebombing of Tokyo. Those air raids killed an estimated 105,000 civilians and left about a million homeless. It was the deadliest aerial bombing up to that point in world history. He directed five more such attacks on the city through May of that year, eventually burning more than fifty-six miles of the capital. The general, nicknamed by his men "Bombs Away LeMay" and "Old Iron Pants," later said he was disappointed he couldn't have gone on those Tokyo raids.

"I'll tell you what war is about," LeMay once remarked. "You've got to kill people, and when you've killed enough they stop fighting." Using overwhelming force and technological advantage was always the right answer in war, LeMay argued throughout his career. "[I]t's more immoral to use *less* force than necessary, than it is to use *more*," he wrote in his memoirs. "If you use less force, you kill off more of humanity in the long run, because you are merely protracting the struggle." He dismissed charges that the bombing killed innocents. "[T]o worry about the morality of what we were doing—Nuts," he later wrote. "A soldier has to fight. We fought."

By the 1950s, LeMay focused on a new enemy: Communists. Famous for always having a cigar in his mouth, the hawk-faced LeMay became the ultimate Cold War American hero—a commander eager to develop and employ new weapons to stay ahead of the enemy. LeMay promoted his macho image every chance he could. In 1954, *Life* wrote a glowing profile of "the Toughest Cop of the Western World," and relayed an anecdote of LeMay going on a mission with one of his bombing crews. When the pilot asked the general to put out his lit cigar because it could cause the plane to explode, LeMay purportedly replied, "It wouldn't dare!" Many liberals loathed LeMay's gargantuan bravado. In Stanley Kubrick's 1964 film *Dr. Strangelove*, the crazed Air Force Brigadier General Jack D. Ripper, modeled on LeMay, set off a nuclear war.

Boutelle couldn't have connected with a better insider at the air force. He worked the connection often, arranging dinners and trips with the general, including a Louisiana fishing expedition. Those also invited included Vice President Richard Nixon and James Shepley, chief of Time-Life's influential Washington Bureau.

Though Arthur Godfrey wasn't on that trip, he was a regular member of Boutelle's glad-handing threesome. Throughout the 1950s, Arthur Morton Godfrey was a ubiquitous radio and television celebrity and pitchman. The New York–born Godfrey became popular nationally in the late 1940s, and gained recognition with the puzzling 1947 hit song "Too Fat Polka (She's Too Fat for Me)." Godfrey's languid style made him popular with radio listeners and television viewers in the 1950s. His willingness to shill for any product made him a favorite with advertisers. Godfrey, often strumming a ukulele, was on CBS television multiple times a day as the medium became widespread. His evening program, *Arthur Godfrey's Talent Scouts*, was more popular than Ed Sullivan's show. By the end of the decade, *Variety* would declare Godfrey the number one television personality of all time by advertising revenue. Godfrey loved flying airplanes as a hobby and met LeMay through the U.S. Air Force General Hoyt Vandenberg. LeMay saw Godfrey as a useful media ally in promoting the air force as it battled with other military branches for funding. LeMay recalled how he impressed Godfrey by showing him U.S. bases, "and later I took him on a trip to some of the overseas places where I was going, and really gave him an indoctrination tour." At some point, LeMay introduced Godfrey and Boutelle.

By the early 1950s, the three men had formed a mutual admiration society. The relationship between Boutelle, LeMay, and Godfrey—with other influential men joining the group on numerous trips—was intense. The aircraft and armaments executive, the air force general, and the top entertainer exchanged wristwatches, hunting licenses, guns, gun magazine subscriptions, spark plugs, cigars, ammunition, show tickets, cakes, socks, books on fishing, fishing tackle, flowers, invitations to black-tie dinners, and other items. Godfrey sent a framed, signed photograph of himself for LeMay's desk. LeMay sent back a portrait of himself. In September 1954, Boutelle sent photographs of him and LeMay to the general after a recent trip. "We both seem to shine like a couple of celebrities!" LeMay gushed. The men's correspondence was a flurry of mutual praise as well as requests for aid and support on various issues. LeMay pressed Godfrey to promote a 1955 pro-LeMay film, *Strategic Air Command*, starring Jimmy Stewart, on his shows. Godfrey willingly obliged. To promote the need for an increased defense budget, LeMay sent Godfrey data on Russian nuclear strength, which Godfrey used on his programs and in speeches. Godfrey asked LeMay for help accessing bases to film and for flights around the country. Boutelle sent copies of Fairchild's promotional material, including bound annual editions of *Pegasus* magazine, to both men. Boutelle talked to LeMay and Godfrey about ArmaLite and sent them material on the company's various guns. In 1955, LeMay wrote to Boutelle: "I just received a letter from George Sullivan on the rifle. I will get off an answer to him.

I think something can be done and will give him my ideas." Boutelle also tapped Godfrey for publicity, bringing him to tour Fairchild's plant in September 1955, according to the Hagerstown *Daily Mail*. On his national radio show Godfrey told listeners that he'd had a wonderful visit.

The incessant bonding over hunting and guns culminated in a three-week trip in March 1957 to hunt big game in French Equatorial Africa, which the men turned into an opportunity for fraternal self-promotion. LeMay and a French hunter organized the trip and invited Godfrey, Boutelle, and Shepley of Time-Life. Godfrey brought along equipment to broadcast his radio show. Boutelle's friendships with the head of U.S. Strategic Air Command and a leading entertainment figure were broadcast for days to tens of millions of listeners. Shepley turned the adventure into a multipage spread in the large-circulation *Life* magazine. The article was a publicity agent's dream come true. Shepley wrote of the fifty-year-old General LeMay: "In perfect physical condition, he took to the bush like a professional hunter, trailing buffalo and elephant for hours or even days. His guns were always carefully oiled. And his famed cigar almost never left his lips." Shepley portrayed a balding and flabby fifty-eight-year-old Boutelle as rugged, comparing him to Ernest Hemingway. Suffering a bum hip from a car accident years earlier, Godfrey insisted the men hunt by helicopter. The helicopter made it much easier to bag elephants, warthogs, a lion, a leopard, a hartebeest, a water buffalo, and many other animals. The hunters brought home tusks and hooves as trophies. The trip was a clear signal to Washington circles that Boutelle had arrived. LeMay, the tough-as-nails Cold War warrior, went hunting with him, not with officials from Boeing or General Motors or other corporate giants. It could lead to good things for Fairchild and in turn ArmaLite.

Social critics such as C. Wright Mills hated Washington's fraternity of political, military, business, and entertainment leaders. "In America, this system is carried to the point where a man who can knock a small white ball into a series of holes in the ground with more efficiency and skill than anyone else thereby gains access to the President of the United

States," Mills complained. "It is carried to the point where a chattering radio and television entertainer becomes the hunting chum of leading industrial executives, cabinet members and the higher military . . . This world is at once the pinnacle of the prestige system and a big-scale business." He wrote that government operations and democracy had been subverted by wealth, power, celebrity and the "American system of organized irresponsibility." It didn't matter whether Boutelle had good products to sell or Godfrey knew anything about weapon systems or LeMay understood anything about showbiz—they were pals, and pals did favors for each other.

In Congress, some questioned the cozy relationships between defense contractors and Pentagon officials during the Eisenhower administration. The problem was considered so extensive that, in 1956, the House Armed Services Committee set up a special subcommittee to look into military aircraft production and costs. Fairchild executives were called to testify, but Boutelle declined, saying he was sick with the flu. Instead, the company's secretary, Paul Cleaveland, was grilled by the subcommittee's chairman, Democratic representative Felix Hébert, about how Fairchild hired former military muckety-mucks. Cleaveland tried to argue that the company just hired the most knowledgeable experts it could.

"I am sure if Joe Blow would go down there and be a great expert, he wouldn't have as much chance to get a job as General Jake Devers who knows everybody in the Defense Department," Hébert said, referring to the retired army general hired as a consultant for Fairchild and ArmaLite.

Boutelle likely found such criticism and concern baffling; he just was pressing advantage for his company. But by the late 1950s, his efforts began to unravel for the simple reason that Fairchild failed to deliver on all the projects that Boutelle had promised. Boutelle's repeated declarations that Fairchild was just about to present amazing and profitable innovations in commercial flight, missiles, and guns had worn thin. Extensive delays in production of the commercial F-27, which Fairchild blamed on its Dutch partner, Fokker, cost millions. The guided-missile system never worked, and the Defense Department pulled the plug in 1958. At ArmaLite, the AR-15 was stuck in a quagmire of testing, and AR-10 production in the Netherlands was slow, with international sales weak. As early as April 1956, Boutelle warned shareholders that research and development, which he argued was essential for company growth, had reduced profits. A year later at Fairchild's annual shareholder meeting in New York's Biltmore Hotel, Boutelle said research costs were again biting into profits, so no dividends were being paid. He insisted, however, that the R & D would pay off in the long run. "His explanation satisfied few of the stockholders at the session," *The Wall Street Journal* reported. The article described "a barrage of criticism from stockholders" and one "demanded a change in top management."

Boutelle's personal life also became complicated. Boutelle had married in 1935. Sometime in the mid-1950s, he met Ellen Bishop, the wife of a sales employee. The young mother, who was more than twenty years Boutelle's junior, had more children while the sales employee was working in Europe. In late 1957, Bishop divorced her husband and Boutelle divorced his first wife. Boutelle married Bishop and he later adopted her younger children, but not the older children.

Sherman Fairchild stepped in to stanch the flow of red ink at the aircraft company in June 1958, making himself chairman of the board and initiating deep cost cutting. Everything was on the table, including Boutelle's special projects, such as ArmaLite. In November 1958, as his enterprises fell apart, Boutelle fed an aphorism to a Washington columnist. It was presented as a droll turn of phrase, but in context proved more of an epitaph for Boutelle's high-flying expansion plans, now crashing to earth. "The last thing I want is money—Also the FIRST," it read. Shortly before Christmas, Fairchild took the presidency away from Boutelle, giving him an empty job as board vice chairman. In January 1959, Boutelle resigned that post and his directorship, ending his almost two decades in Fairchild management. "It wasn't Sherman's fault," Boutelle said. "We made some mistakes, and somebody had to go."

Floating in the wreckage bobbed ArmaLite, now an orphan that Fairchild wanted to unload. As early as September 1958, Fairchild opened negotiations with the famed Hartford-based arms maker Colt about selling the patent rights to the AR-15. The man who brokered the deal was Robert Macdonald, a Baltimore-based arms dealer. He had contracted with Colt for years to sell its guns overseas and was friendly with Boutelle.

Macdonald drove out to Boutelle's farm in western Maryland to shoot an AR-15. "The more I shot it, the better I liked it," Macdonald said later. Macdonald was convinced the gun, with its light recoil, would sell well in South Asia because, as he later said, "these little people" could handle the gun easily. But Boutelle had a problem: Fairchild refused to sink any more money into ArmaLite. "The board would not give the company the money to do the manufacturing, and Mr. Boutelle asked me to go out and find somebody to manufacture the rifle," Macdonald recalled.

On January 7, 1959, the deal was signed: Colt acquired manufacturing and sublicensing rights to the AR-15 and AR-10's gas system— Stoner's great firearms innovation. Colt agreed to pay Fairchild $75,000 plus 4.5 percent of royalties on any sales to the military and a sliding scale on royalties for commercial sales. Fairchild, acknowledging Stoner's contribution to the gun's creation, agreed to give half of its earnings for the guns' sales to the inventor. Macdonald was paid $25,000 up front from Colt to market the gun to the U.S. and other governments, as well as 1 percent of the selling price of each gun. Macdonald also received a portion of Fairchild's royalties. The agreement was set to last for the life of the patent, which would expire in the late 1970s.

In March and April 1959, Macdonald, Stoner, and William E. Mullen, an associate at Macdonald's firm of Cooper-Macdonald Inc., toured the Philippines, Singapore, Thailand, Malaya, Burma, and India. The men held firing demonstrations in the sweltering heat, shooting one-gallon tins, tin cans, and coconuts. In Burma, "[t]he tin cans burst in spectacular fashion, but the coconuts did not disintegrate as they had every place else. The Burmese jokingly attributed this to the inherent toughness of Burma coconuts. But actually, the fruit was a bit too dry, with not enough milk inside to produce the desired results," Mullen wrote, noting that the AR-15's .223 caliber round left a much larger exit hole in the coconuts than the AR-10's larger-caliber round.

"The Asiatic people being small stature and everything loved the small gun," Stoner recalled. "They could handle it, they could fire it. We were giving them thirty-caliber weapons like M1s and so forth to try to fight with and they were just too large for them."

Macdonald cabled Colt to stop manufacturing AR-10s and focus solely on AR-15s. Many government officials in Asia pressed for a semiautomatic version of the gun only, with no option for full automatic because it would waste bullets. Macdonald, Stoner, and Mullen found the trip frustrating because government officials were reluctant to commit to large AR-15 purchases. The U.S. military hadn't approved the weapon, and without that approval, it couldn't authorize buying the guns for military aid packages. By the fall of 1959, Macdonald had landed a few sales: Indonesia wanted 1,250; Malaya wanted 25; India 23; Singapore police just a few.

A Colt brochure for the AR-15 promised "controlled firepower" and stated, "The AR-15 cannot malfunction under any conditions including rain, snow and mud." The brochure stated the rifle could fire 750 rounds per minute.

During this period, Stoner left the troubled ArmaLite. Anyone who could do so jumped to other jobs as the little company unraveled. Stoner did some consulting work for Colt in addition to the Asian trip and took a job consulting for Cadillac Gage, a suburban Detroit defense contractor. The company allowed Stoner to set up an office in Costa Mesa. It was a stressful and deflating time for Stoner and his wife. For three intense years, Stoner had traveled across the United States and Asia to promote his rifle, hoping for a big payout and some modicum of recognition. But the AR-15 seemed doomed to the invention dustbin. He resigned himself to the fact that the gun wouldn't amount to much. He pressed on, trying to invent other weapons for his new employer.

By January 1960, Colt announced to the public that it had begun mass-producing AR-15s at its Connecticut plant, but the Associated

Press reported, "It is not likely to be used by the U.S. Army, which is beginning to distribute a new automatic rifle, the M14, for use as its basic infantry weapon."

In June of that year, Colt requested that the army look at its version of the AR-15 again, but officials refused.

"We were up against the NIH Factor—Not Invented Here," George Strichman, later president at Colt, recalled. "The rifle's basic problem was that it hadn't been invented by Army arsenal personnel."

In a last-ditch attempt to save the AR-15's prospects with the military, Macdonald wrote to LeMay in May 1960, urging him to test the rifle for himself. He dropped Boutelle's name. Though Boutelle was out at Fairchild, he still wanted ArmaLite, his creation, to succeed and had suggested LeMay as a contact to Macdonald. It was a Hail Mary because LeMay didn't oversee small firearms development. "My calendar is rather crowded for the end of this month. However, I would like to shoot the rifle if time permits," LeMay wrote back, adding, "[P]erhaps we can get together with Dick Boutelle some afternoon."

The obvious option soon presented itself. Every July 4, both the nation's and Boutelle's birthday, Boutelle would throw a large bash at Pleasant Valley Retreat, his home and horse farm about twelve miles west of Hagerstown. Invitations announcing the afternoon party "for adults only" were sent out to friends with the plea "GOSH WE HOPE YOU CAN COME!" The farm was set up for skeet shooting and trap shooting, and included pistol and rifle ranges. "It was beautifully equipped from a shooting angle," recalled Macdonald. LeMay was a party regular. Sometime during the July 4, 1960, festivities, Macdonald brought out an AR-15, as well as three watermelons from his car. He set up two of the watermelons in a field, one fifty yards away and the other 150 yards. Then he handed LeMay the gun. "He shot both of them and put his hand down in there and picked this stuff up, and I won't say what he said, but it was quite impressive—he was impressed," Macdonald recalled of LeMay's watermelon massacre. "So I asked him, 'Do you want to shoot the other one?' He said, 'Hell, no; let's eat it.' So that's the way we did."

LeMay told Macdonald on the spot that he wanted the gun to be tested for military purchase. After the party, Macdonald sent a follow-up letter with data on the AR-15. Macdonald, LeMay, and another Pentagon official met the next week to plan testing. LeMay wrote to Macdonald on August 17, 1960, "We are working with the Army now on possible full scale testing of this gun."

Macdonald never heard about test results and wondered what was going on; then he received incredible news: the air force wanted to buy 8,500 of the guns for its security teams. After beating on the Pentagon's door for years, the AR-15 was being given a real chance.

Boutelle and Macdonald's watermelon shootout had worked. Boutelle's long friendship with LeMay had paid off. But the victory proved to be Boutelle's last hurrah. After his ouster from Fairchild, Boutelle took an executive job for a spark plug subsidiary of General Motors. It was a knockdown for a man who had worked on jets, guided missiles, and futuristic firearms, who had dined with Dwight Eisenhower, and who had appeared in *Life*, shooting big game with the rich and famous.

Boutelle died on January 15, 1962, a day after he suffered a stroke at his home. He was buried in Arlington National Cemetery. The honorary pallbearers at his funeral included Jacob Devers, Sherman Fairchild, Arthur Godfrey, and Curtis LeMay.

9.

THE SPY WHO SAVED STONER'S RIFLE

Its killing power is terrific.
—U.S. Army advisor in Vietnam

South Vietnamese army rangers were patrolling in June 1962 when they spotted three Viet Cong guerrillas in the jungle. One of the rangers raised a sleek, strange-looking rifle to his shoulder. He fired, hitting one of the insurgents, according to a confidential report for the Pentagon written by a secret U.S.-led operation based in Saigon. "One round in the head—took it completely off," the report read. "Another in the right arm, took it completely off, too. One round hit him in the right side, causing a hole about five inches in diameter. It cannot be determined which round killed the VC but it can be assumed that any one of the three would have caused death. The other 2 VC ran . . ."

From February to July 1962, South Vietnamese army rangers and special forces secretly tested the AR-15 on combat missions in Vietnam's Central Highlands and the Mekong Delta. Vietnamese officers and U.S. advisors gave gory, glowing accounts of the gun's early, limited use in battle. A ranger platoon ambushed a Viet Cong company on June 9, killing five, all with AR-15 fire. After the shootout, the rangers inspected the corpses and reported the bullets exploded one man's chest and another's stomach. They shredded another guerrilla's buttocks. Yet another man died when he was struck in the heel and the wound split

open to his hip, according to the report. All the men died instanta-
neously, except for the man shot in the buttocks, who died about five
minutes after being hit. In another incident, special forces raided a Viet
Cong–controlled village on April 13, killing seven insurgents, two of
whom were hit by AR-15 fire.

"One man was hit in the head; it looked like it exploded. A second
man was hit in the chest; his back was one big hole," according to the
report. Stoner had designed his rifle to fight Communists; now his invention was getting a chance to prove itself.

One man, William Godel, was responsible for the secret project that
supplied Stoner's rifles to those South Vietnamese troops. Some dismissed the confidential report he wrote as exaggerated and many in
the military later tried to forget Godel ever existed. But like Stoner and
LeMay, Godel played a crucial role in getting the American military to
embrace the AR-15. The rifle was shunned in the early 1960s by most
of the armed forces. By the middle of the decade, the military had accepted the gun as its future, and the public viewed it as an emblem—
along with helicopters and napalm—of the nation's growing involvement
in a bloody quagmire halfway across the world. Godel was a key player in
that transformation.

Godel was an enigmatic man whose adult life was rife with intrigue
and enemies, both foreign and domestic. He devoted much of his life to
the defense of the United States, but he spent his career butting heads
with military officers, bureaucrats, and spies. He circumvented protocol
and honed evasion into an art form. In the end, his lack of scruples
landed him in prison.

Godel was born in Denver on June 29, 1921, to German immigrants
and christened Hermann Adolph Herbert Buhl. His father died when
he was young and his mother remarried another German American, the
owner of an insurance business who served as Denver consul for the
Third Reich in the 1930s. The stepfather adopted the boy, giving him
the legal name William Hermann Godel. Godel disliked his stepfather
so much that while growing up he built a shack in the family's backyard to live away from him. As a teen, Godel attended the New Mexico

Military Institute in Roswell and later enrolled in Georgetown University's School of Foreign Service. After school he worked for military intelligence, but joined the Marines as a commissioned lieutenant when the United States entered World War II. He was wounded twice in combat, including a severe leg injury. He received a Purple Heart and had a slight limp for the rest of his life. After the war, he tried to stay in the Marines, but in 1947 he was found unfit to serve because of his injury. In 1948, he joined army intelligence as a civilian consultant on the U.S.S.R. In 1950, he was attached to the U.S. military assistance program in Southeast Asia. That summer, Godel was part of a joint Pentagon–State Department mission to the region. The trip included a three-week visit to Vietnam, where the war between French colonial forces and Ho Chi Minh's Viet Minh had escalated. While the mission was ostensibly a diplomatic one concerning aid packages, the staff set about gathering intelligence about French efforts to combat the Viet Minh. They accompanied Vietnamese colonial troops on a raid of an insurgent village. French officers ordered their Vietnamese troops to bring back prisoners for questioning. Instead, the men decapitated them. For Godel, the message was clear: normal rules of war didn't apply. Godel said decades later that on that trip he realized U.S. military strategists needed "to learn to fight a war that doesn't have nuclear weapons, doesn't have the North German plain, and doesn't necessarily have Americans." Godel "earned a reputation in Washington as the go-to guy for special assignments, particularly those that combined intelligence with science," according to the author Sharon Weinberger. He became known as an expert on global politics, especially Southeast Asia, and by 1955, he was working for the National Security Agency. But he battled with other intelligence officials over tactics and strategy; he made enemies quickly. He argued so often with CIA officials that they eventually banned him from meetings. Pentagon security officials questioned Godel about his father being a Nazi sympathizer.

Godel devoted himself to the government's clandestine Cold War projects. He joined the Advanced Research Projects Agency, created in 1958 in response to the Soviet launch of the Sputnik satellite. The agency's vague and secretive mission suited Godel perfectly. Godel focused in his first years at the agency on outer space, trying to convince the world that American technology was superior to Russian. He conceived of and oversaw Project SCORE, a mission to launch a large Atlas rocket into space to deliver a tiny payload—a hundred-pound communications satellite that would broadcast a Christmas message from Eisenhower. The United States could then announce it had launched a heavy satellite into space, more advanced than what the Soviets had done with Sputnik. It wasn't true, but the world didn't know that and the Russians couldn't prove otherwise. Eisenhower approved the launch, though he demanded it be kept secret until he knew the satellite and broadcast had worked. "Technically, it was all a stunt," an official history of the agency declared later. Godel continued space race deceptions with the launch of a series of rockets. They were ostensibly sent on science missions, such as transporting small animals into orbit. In fact, those were cover stories for some of the world's first spy satellites. But Godel grew tired of the work and wanted to fight Communist insurgencies on earth, not send objects floating into space. With the change of presidential administrations in 1961, he got his chance.

John F. Kennedy, the dashing forty-three-year-old war hero, was sworn in on January 20 and brought in forty-four-year-old Robert Strange McNamara, the president of Ford Motor Company, as defense secretary. Kennedy gave McNamara a mandate to shake things up at the enormous bureaucracy. McNamara was educated at the University of California, Berkeley, in economics and philosophy and then at Harvard Business School. During World War II, he served in the U.S. Army Air Force's Office of Statistical Control, rising to the rank of lieutenant colonel. Toward the end of the war, McNamara worked with LeMay, assessing the efficiency of bombers under LeMay's command as they targeted Japanese cities.

When he joined the Kennedy administration, McNamara brought to the Pentagon a group of young academics and executives who believed quantitative analysis, testing, and science could improve military effectiveness. For this group—labeled the "Whiz Kids" by

Washington insiders, journalists, and Pentagon cynics—it was data, not hunches or inertial opinion, that should guide policy and budget decisions. The young administration faced an immediate challenge from the Soviet leader Nikita Khrushchev, who announced his government would start backing "national liberation" efforts, a signal that it would increase support for guerrilla wars everywhere, including Indochina. Eisenhower had warned that Communist insurgencies could spread in Southeast Asia and that countries in the region would fall like dominoes. Kennedy, McNamara, and their advisors feared Eisenhower's prediction was coming true. Guerrilla conflicts were also underway in the Middle East, Africa, and Latin America. In Cuba, Fidel Castro, who seized power in 1959, talked of exporting revolution throughout the region.

A crisis erupted in mid-April 1961, just three months into Kennedy's presidency, when he authorized an invasion of Cuba by an army of exiles trained and equipped by the United States. The Bay of Pigs was a humiliating failure, in part because of equipment and supply problems. The president ordered staff to search for new technologies and strategies to address Communism's spread. Godel had been obsessed with the same notions and spoke up to his superiors. He argued that the U.S. military needed to focus its weapons research on projects that would aid struggling allies such as South Vietnam. He proposed that ARPA set up a special research center in the field. At a National Security Council meeting at the White House, Kennedy approved Godel's plan to set up "a Combat Development and Test Center in South Vietnam to develop, with the help of modern technology, new techniques for use against the Viet Cong forces." The ARPA effort in Saigon—one of its Project AGILE field units focused on developing new technologies—was launched with Godel at the helm. He showed up in South Vietnam with $18,000 in cash—$5,000 of his own money and $13,000 from ARPA—to hire staff and buy office space and equipment, he said later. "Godel was very much an operator," William Bundy, deputy assistant secretary for international security affairs in Kennedy's State Department, said years later. Though Godel had a "rather legendary reputation for effectiveness in some situations overseas," Bundy considered him "a pushy, self-promoting guy."

Despite hostility within and without ARPA, Godel grew AGILE operations in Vietnam, launching field tests for new equipment and strategies. The AGILE Saigon budget swelled to millions of dollars annually. Godel became an important, if anxiety-inducing, visitor to South Vietnam president Ngô Đình Diệm's office. Godel later recalled that Diệm told him during one discussion, "The only way we lose is if the Americans come in here." Godel took the words to heart, seeing AGILE's role in Vietnam as a weapons incubator for the South Vietnamese Army, not for American forces. "I know President Diệm appreciated Mr. Godel but he was afraid of Mr. Godel," a former Diệm official said later. AGILE, with main offices near the Saigon River, developed weapons ranging from mines shaped to look like rocks to a device to generate "sustained, very high sound power levels for weapon application." AGILE created the strategy of "strategic hamlets"—forcing villagers into barbed-wire enclosures to reduce contact with guerrillas. Godel's office helped create the chemical defoliant Agent Orange.

And AGILE Saigon would champion Stoner's AR-15. Godel brought ten of the guns to Saigon in July 1961. The staff held target tests with Vietnamese soldiers on shooting ranges the next month. Godel pushed to buy more. AGILE Saigon estimated the average South Vietnamese soldier weighed ninety pounds; they needed a rapid-fire gun with light recoil.

"The idea was to give a little guy a rifle he can use, not necessarily a *better* one," Godel said later, adding, "I neither know, nor give a damn, what the U.S. soldier needs."

Godel pressed the Pentagon to issue AR-15s to South Vietnamese troops, then mostly using older, heavier rifles. But key military figures opposed the request, including Admiral Harry Felt, commander of U.S. forces in the Pacific, and Lyman Lemnitzer of the army, then chairman of the Joint Chiefs of Staff. Both men, who had seen Army Ordnance reports, initially felt the AR-15 had too many problems.

Frustrated U.S. officials in Vietnam sent their plea directly to McNamara, and on December 4, 1961, the Pentagon approved the purchase of a thousand AR-15s from Colt to test with South Vietnamese troops. Macdonald handled the sale to ARPA, which paid just under $367,000 for the shipment, including rifles, ammunition, and spare parts. The first shipment arrived in Vietnam on January 27, 1962.

Stoner heard that the tests were taking place, but "it was rather a hush-hush thing. I mean, they were trying to keep it undercover and we really didn't get much feedback on what was happening with those weapons once they were delivered over there."

McNamara watched Godel's tests closely, hoping the AR-15 could be used to oust the M14, in part as a knock against the army establishment that he wanted to bring to heel. On May 21, as the tests were under way, the ARPA director, Jack Ruina, wrote, "The Secretary of Defense personally has expressed his desire that these tests be expedited."

The reaction from Vietnamese officers and American advisors was extremely positive, according to AGILE's secret "Report of Task No. 13A," which was sent to McNamara's office in July and dispersed to others at the Pentagon and the White House in August. Troops found the gun easy to use, clean, carry, and shoot, according to the report. Vietnamese soldiers considered it much more effective in jungle fighting than any of the other guns they had been using.

"[T]he violent short clashes at close ranges which are characteristic of guerrilla warfare in Vietnam make it highly desirable to have a dependable weapon capable of producing a high rate of accurate and lethal full automatic fire," the report said.

Skeptics in the U.S. Army questioned the report's unbridled enthusiasm. Many didn't trust Godel and saw the report's findings as exaggerated at best, mendacious at worst. Every guerrilla shot with an AR died? One was killed after he was shot in the heel?

But other positive reviews for the gun made their way to the Pentagon. U.S. advisors wrote to higher-ups, praising Stoner's rifle. "Its killing power is terrific," U.S. Army Infantry Colonel James H. Moore wrote to his friend General Earle Wheeler, newly appointed as chief of staff for the army. "I know of no Viet Cong who was hit who was not an instant casualty."

Around this time, a key group of McNamara's Whiz Kids tested the rifle for themselves at "a secret CIA rifle range" in the Washington area, recalled Alain Enthoven, who was deputy assistant secretary of defense under McNamara. Enthoven, a former RAND economist in his early thirties who had been educated at Stanford, Oxford, and MIT, was intrigued with developing new ways for the U.S. military to respond to Communist aggression. Enthoven's mission was to use data to make decisions rather than rely on tradition. At the range, Enthoven and the others fired M14s, AK-47s, and AR-15s. Enthoven, who weighed about two hundred pounds and was in good shape, fired the M14 on automatic and no matter how hard he tried, he couldn't keep the second shot on the target, he recalled. The rifle would jerk away. The average soldier at the time weighed about 150 pounds, so he knew managing such a gun would be difficult.

"With the army's M14, there was just terrible recoil," Enthoven recalled. "Presenting this to the average soldier would be just disastrous." Next Enthoven fired an AK-47, and "the bullets went right in the target."

"I was worried, deeply worried, that we were going to send our soldiers into jungle combat against the AK-47 with just a clumsy difficult rifle," he said. He felt much better once he picked and fired the AR-15, as the bullets all went into the target. "It was vastly superior to the M14," said Enthoven. "We went to McNamara with all of our material and said, 'Bob, you've got a terrible problem.'"

McNamara seized on the issue to assert control over the army. The Whiz Kids pressed for the AR-15, using the AGILE report to show that it was superior to the weapon being foisted upon U.S. soldiers by the slow-moving bureaucracy. An internal Pentagon history of the M16 later declared, "By May 1962, the AR-15 rifle was a common item of discussion at high-level meetings throughout the Department of Defense." The ground shifted: the AR-15's fortunes were resurrected. McNamara asked his comptroller, Charles Hitch, to review the M14 purchase program in September 1962. Hitch, a slight man who had difficulty filling out a suit, had been the chief economist of the RAND Corporation. There, he coauthored a book on modern defense spending, *The Economics of Defense in the Nuclear Age*. Hitch's office in the Pentagon was just down the hall from McNamara's.

Hitch's assessment was a blistering rebuke of the M14. "The AR-15 is decidedly superior," the report said. It was less expensive, fired more bullets, and was more accurate. In one pointed barb, the report declared the M14 "appears somewhat inferior to the M1 rifle of WW II." The AR-15 would aid soldiers fighting against the Communists. "U.S. forces armed with the AR-15 rifle would have a marked firepower advantage over Soviet forces armed with the AK assault rifle," it said. While Godel and the earlier AGILE report had argued for the adoption of the AR-15 for South Vietnamese forces, Hitch's report went even further, making a critical leap: the gun would be great for American troops. Within the Pentagon, the report was viewed as a clear attack on the military bureaucracy and its beloved M14.

Eisenhower had shaken up the armed forces with his "New Look" and the focus on the air force and nuclear arsenal. He had turned to a Detroit auto executive to rethink military operations, including weapons development. But Charles Wilson, Ike's first defense secretary, had struggled to control infighting among the branches and lobbyists. He left office deflated early in Eisenhower's second term. Kennedy, who saw himself as a youthful, bold reformer, had brought in McNamara, another auto executive, to achieve what Ike had failed to do: bring the military bureaucrats under the control of the defense secretary. McNamara, eager to impress his boss, embraced the AR-15 early in his fight against the military's old way of doing things.

McNamara embraced the comptroller report's conclusions to hammer the army. On October 12 he sent a short memo to Secretary of the Army Cyrus Vance.

> I have seen certain evidence which appears to indicate that:
>
> 1. With the M-14 rifle in 1962, we are equipping our forces with a weapon definitely inferior in firepower and combat effectiveness to the assault rifle with which the Soviets have equipped their own and their satellite forces worldwide since 1950.

2. The AR-15 is markedly superior to the M-14 rifle in every respect of importance to military operations. For example, it is said that in overall squad firepower effectiveness it is 4 to 5 times as effective as the M-14. Further, it is stated that careful evaluation has not indicated any area where the M-14 is superior to the AR-15.

He ended his note, "If either the Soviet rifle or the AR-15 appears to be superior to the M-14, what action do you recommend?" He signed the note in his cramped, fierce handwriting: RMcN.

With the brief note to Vance, McNamara doomed a gun that the military had been developing since the 1940s. Millions of dollars and countless hours had been spent on the M14. Hundreds of thousands of soldiers and Marines trained to fight with the weapon. Now the future of the Springfield Armory creation was uncertain.

President Kennedy reviewed the Hitch report in early November and his special assistant Kenneth O'Donnell sent a memo to McNamara, noting that the president "is quite concerned about the differences of opinion." McNamara responded to Kennedy with a memorandum, announcing that he had ordered the army to reevaluate the AR-15 and the M14.

"The Army will complete its tests and evaluation in January 1963. And I shall submit to you my definitive recommendations on the Army Rifle Program by January 31, 1963," he wrote.

It was clear from McNamara's official correspondence what he thought: the army had screwed up.

"The army, some of them almost had tears in their eyes like they were being humiliated or something because their weapon wasn't chosen," Enthoven recalled.

Positive news about Stoner's gun made its way into the press. *Newsweek* published a piece about AGILE's Vietnam operations, which by late 1962 had grown to a budget of $18 million, with about 115 engineers and scientists at the office. *Newsweek* listed weapons and other devices being tested by "a little-known Pentagon brain trust," including plastic shields for helicopters, a steel crossbow for secret operations, and "the Armalite [*sic*] high-velocity rifle" that had tested well and was "easily handled by small Vietnamese soldiers."

Curtis LeMay, who had been trying to obtain 8,500 AR-15s (his initial request was for 80,000) for the air force, was elated by the shift. LeMay "was absolutely adamant that they wanted the AR-15," Enthoven said. "He was widely respected for his expertise in small arms and, well, he was a pretty forceful guy." In one account, LeMay was so demanding in his insistence that McNamara authorize purchase of the rifle that President Kennedy counseled LeMay to back off.

Robert Macdonald and William Mullen, the men marketing the AR-15, arranged demonstrations for military officials, members of Congress, foreign governments, and law enforcement agencies. Their efforts led to a handful of sales, notably including special military units and the Secret Service, which purchased several to guard Kennedy. The president commandeered one of the guns for himself, according to Mullen. On a visit to the Navy's SEAL Team Two in Virginia, Kennedy asked a seaman what weapon he preferred. The man held up an AR-15 and declared, "This one. You can stick the rest of them up your ass, sir." Kennedy reportedly laughed.

Stoner credited McNamara and "the so-called Whiz Kid bunch from universities and whatever" with reviving the AR-15's prospects. The inventor was earning good money at Cadillac Gage, but he had given up on dreams of making it rich from the AR-15. At home, his family life continued to fray. Stoner's long hours and constant travel to promote the AR-15 strained his marriage with Jean. In 1959, for example, Stoner returned from a work trip and informed his family that he was embarking on a two-month sojourn with Macdonald to Southeast Asia the following Monday, Susan recalled.

As the couple grew apart, the Stoners had their fourth child, Deirdre, in 1962. Their oldest, Patty, was eighteen at the time. Stoner's daughter Susan believed that Stoner's constant travel became too much for her mother. "He was just gone," she said.

Jean grew close to Thomas Patrick Mahoney, the lawyer who wrote the patent for Stoner's gas system and who derailed George Sullivan's plans to steal Stoner's patents. Mahoney offered things to Jean that the inventor did not. Mahoney had a big house with a pool. He was versed in art and culture. He was outgoing and enjoyed parties. He pursued Jean, showering her with attention. In 1963, Stoner and Jean divorced after nineteen years of marriage. In the divorce arrangement, Jean Stoner received half of everything, including the royalties from his patents. Stoner didn't express much bitterness about the split beyond occasionally referring to the lawyer as "Phony Mahoney," said Jim Sullivan, the draftsman. "He didn't ask for sympathy or make a fuss." Jean moved to Malibu with Sue and little Deedee. Finally, Jean could live by the ocean. Three years later, she married Mahoney.

Stoner stayed in the Costa Mesa house with the two older children, Patty and Michael. Some weekends, Susie would take a helicopter from Los Angeles International Airport to a heliport in Newport Beach to spend time with her dad. Since he worked on weekends, Susie went with him to the office, made coffee for the workers, and clipped the ammunition into belts for test firing. For dinner, Stoner and Susie would eat out at a steakhouse with white tablecloths and performers who sang Frank Sinatra tunes. "I would fall asleep and he would draw [inventions] on the tablecloth," she said.

Stoner had moved on from the AR-15 just as its chances were reviving. In October 1962, the army's General Paul Harkins, head of U.S. Military Assistance Command in Vietnam, requested twenty thousand rifles for South Vietnamese units, a decision influenced by Godel's work. The Pentagon rejected that request; but it was clear that Stoner's gun was back in play. A later official ARPA history declared the AR-15—which the military soon would designate the M16 for "Model 16"—"would almost certainly not have come about without the existence of ARPA as an alternative source of funding and a vehicle for objective testing."

Godel had no chance to relish any glory over his successes in setting up AGILE in Saigon or promoting the AR-15. He found himself under federal investigation for embezzlement after someone in his clandestine world informed authorities of questionable transactions. In August 1964, he was forced out of ARPA. He returned to Washington and lobbied briefly for Cadillac Gage, promoting Stoner inventions. In December 1964, a federal grand jury in Washington indicted Godel along with two other federal officials of embezzling more than $57,000. The government charged Godel with submitting a false voucher for $10,000 "for certain confidential projects in Vietnam." Godel, who earned a federal salary of about $20,000, pleaded not guilty, but he was convicted of one charge of conspiracy to embezzle and another of making a false statement. He was sentenced to five years in prison, which he served as American military involvement in Vietnam reached its bloody apex.

Godel envisioned Stoner's guns flooding Vietnam, but being used by Vietnamese soldiers. Instead, the gun would be carried by hundreds of thousands of American soldiers and Marines in the region—exactly what Godel believed shouldn't happen. His career long over and his reputation stained, a bitter Godel was asked by an interviewer years later to name AGILE Saigon's successes. "None," he said.

10.

"BRAVE SOLDIERS AND THE M16"

It's so good, in fact, nobody can understand
how the Army ever developed it.
—Anonymous U.S. soldier on the M16

The choppers came in low over the trees on the bright morning of November 14, 1965. Their rotating blades made a thuk-thuk-thuk sound that carried for miles. Pilots guided the machines down to a flat piece of land about the size of a football field surrounded by thigh-tall elephant grass. Howitzers far away had just pounded the area for twenty minutes to create the landing zone, or LZ in army jargon. The reddish dusty ground, dotted with termite mounds, was still smoking. Soldiers of the First Battalion of the U.S. Army's Seventh Cavalry Regiment poured out six at a time with weapons and supplies. Sixteen helicopters ferried hundreds of men from a staging area miles away to this instant base of operations, south of the Ia Drang River and not far from the Cambodian border. They called it LZ X-Ray. The operation in the Central Highlands of South Vietnam was part of a new strategy developed by the U.S. Army—air mobility. Specially trained army units were being ferried by helicopter and backed by artillery and jets. In the escalating war, the Vietnamese Communists often took the initiative, deciding when and where battles would be fought. Now the United States was going to take back the element of surprise with these "air cav" units, dropping from the skies to hit the enemy where they thought they were safe.

The Seventh Cavalry Regiment first was formed after the Civil War to battle Native American tribes. The regiment's song was "Garryowen," an Irish tune about toughs who liked to drink and fight. One of the Seventh's early commanders, Lieutenant Colonel George Custer, led the regiment into its worst defeat: the massacre at Little Bighorn. The revamped Seventh no longer rode horses; they now flew in helicopters. But the goal was the same: swiftness. In the summer of 1965, President Lyndon Johnson announced that he was increasing the number of U.S. troops in Vietnam from 75,000 to 125,000 at the request of General William Westmoreland, then commanding American forces in the country. The call-up included the Seventh. Before the men left Fort Benning, they were ordered to trade in their M14 rifles for M16s, then being issued to some special army units. The lighter black rifles allowed men to carry more ammunition, some hauling as many as sixteen magazines—up to 320 rounds—in their pouches and packs. In August, most of the Seventh Cavalry embarked on a monthlong journey by merchant marine ship that carried them through the Panama Canal and across the Pacific. On board the men cleaned their rifles every day, and spent time shooting floating targets set up off the stern to become familiar with their new weapons. They arrived in Vietnam in late September. Stationed in the Central Highlands, the men conducted patrols looking for Viet Cong but initially encountered few enemies.

Then came LZ X-Ray. That morning, the First Battalion, headed by the Korean War veteran Lieutenant Colonel Hal Moore, set up a temporary command center and a perimeter as helicopters dropped to the LZ. Soon a couple of hundred soldiers from the Seventh were at the landing zone; by the end of the day there would be about 450. Officers sent out patrols to search the immediate area. Within minutes the patrols brought back a handful of prisoners. One prisoner they captured, an unarmed draftee from North Vietnam, delivered chilling information to interrogators through an interpreter. When asked where he came from, he told them he had marched down from the north as part of two regiments, about 2,400 men. The men were not guerrillas but well-trained North Vietnamese soldiers, many armed with AK-47 rifles. Asked where the regiments were encamped, he pointed to a mountain very close to the LZ.

"The mission became quickly: defend the landing zone because without the landing zone, we will all die," recalled then Captain Ramon Antonio "Tony" Nadal II, a company commander at the battle. "They had big numbers on us."

The Americans had only a few minutes to prepare before gunfire erupted all around them in what would become U.S. ground forces' first full-scale battle against North Vietnamese troops. The struggle also would be history's first major battle in which troops with M16s fought those with AK-47s. Stoner's gun was about to be put to the test against Kalashnikov's, not on a rifle range or in an engineer's lab but in combat. North Vietnamese fighters tried to get as close as they could to U.S. troops to reduce the chance of being bombed by American planes or artillery. Fighting was so intense that men often saw the faces of those they killed. Nadal at one point gave his men the order, extraordinary in modern warfare, "Fix bayonets!" The Americans were in such danger of being overrun that Colonel Moore ordered his radio man to send the distress call "Broken Arrow," alerting all U.S. aircraft in Vietnam to come to the battalion's aid.

Second Lieutenant Walter Joseph "Joe" Marm Jr., a twenty-three-year-old platoon leader, had about thirty to thirty-five men under his command that day. Aside from machine gunners and mortar men, everyone else—including Marm—carried M16s. Marm used his M16 to kill four enemy soldiers. Then he and his men came upon a large termite mound where eight North Vietnamese soldiers were firing with a machine gun and AKs. Marm fired an antitank weapon at the mound, but that didn't stop the fire. He then signaled for one of his men to throw a grenade; the man missed. Marm grabbed his M16 and a grenade and charged. He threw his grenade and ran around the mound, firing his rifle until all the Vietnamese there were dead. Moments after the daring assault, Marm looked up and a bullet shattered his jaw. "I had to feel my mouth to see if I had any teeth left in there," recalled Marm, who never lost consciousness despite the intense pain. The M16 "was an excellent weapon. It would really stop the enemy," said Marm, who was awarded a congressional Medal of Honor for his actions at LZ X-Ray.

Both sides suffered heavy casualties and later both claimed victory. Moore wrote in his after-action report that of the 450 soldiers under his command, 79 were killed and 121 were wounded. When the North Vietnamese left the field, Moore's troops found 634 North Vietnamese corpses, and Moore estimated the actual number of enemy dead and wounded was 1,215.

The U.S. war in Vietnam was on. Which side would win the unfolding struggle was uncertain, but a clear winner arising from the LZ X-Ray fight was the M16. The battle proved to be a public relations triumph for Stoner's gun after its yearslong struggle against the M14. McNamara and his administration highlighted the battle as proof that Stoner's gun was superior to the M14 and perfect for American troops fighting in Southeast Asia. Moore choked back tears as he told reporters touring the battlefield that the gun had been crucial to victory.

"Brave soldiers and the M16 brought this victory," Moore said as he held one of the rifles over his head during a meeting with his superiors. He told Westmoreland that it was "the best individual infantry rifle ever made, clearly the American answer to the enemy's AK-47." On December 6, 1965, Westmoreland asked McNamara "as a matter of urgency" to equip all U.S. fighting units in Vietnam, as well as South Vietnamese and South Korean units, with M16s. The next day, McNamara issued a contract to Colt for 100,000 more M16s—68,000 for the army and 32,000 for the Marines. The request mentioned a possible future purchase of 400,000 more. When the contract was finalized in June 1966, it was for 403,905 rifles.

In the years before LZ X-Ray, M14 supporters within Army Ordnance had waged an intense, duplicitous campaign to derail the M16's adoption. They had flooded the Pentagon with reports that did little to clarify which gun was better. A unit of the army's Chemical and Development Laboratories at the Edgewood Arsenal in Maryland tested

M14s, M16s, and one Polish-made AK-47 on live goats and the legs and skulls of human corpses. The testers fired their weapons at "Texas angora castrated male goats (wethers) with the hair clipped off," which were tethered at different distances on a range, according to the report. The animals that didn't die from the gunshots were electrocuted, so their wounds could be examined. Testers shot "[h]uman legs, frozen shortly after amputation from cadavers," and "unbleached, undefatted human skulls" that "probably came from India." The 321-page report was replete with X-rays of shattered goat bones and photos of punctured goat organs, mangled cadaver feet, and exploding skulls. But it was inconclusive: the M14 and the AR-15 were equally lethal against goats and did a lot of damage to cadaver parts, and both did a better job than the AK-47.

The M16's backers knew that the army wasn't evenhanded in its tests. A top-secret inspector general's report found numerous examples of unfair testing of the AR-15. In one "FOR EYES ONLY" memorandum for Vance, a staffer found that "[b]eyond any question, the reports available are biased and the bias is anti-AR-15." The author concluded, however, that "they do not in a strictly legal sense 'prove' dishonesty. Incompetence perhaps."

M14 backers felt the fix was in for the M16. McNamara wanted to force the rifle down the army's throat, and was looking for any excuse to do so, they felt.

This infighting spilled into the press. In an *American Rifleman* article, a retired army colonel and an NRA staffer reviewed the gun, calling it "a fine little weapon," but noting that "there were and still are serious doubts as to the performance of a small bore round as a military cartridge for general use." To counter any bad press, Colt executives, Cooper-Macdonald salesmen, and the Pentagon Whiz Kids fed reporters pro-M16 information. The gun expert John Tompkins slammed the M14 in an article in a men's magazine called *True*, with a headline calling the rifle "The Army's Blunderbuss Bungle That Fattened Your Taxes." Tompkins labeled the army's rifle testing as a "boondoggle during which 10 rifles were tested, but the Army's own Springfield Armory design always seemed to come out on top. The doubtful objectivity of these so-called 'tests' makes you wonder why the Army even asked for outside designs. It was like playing poker with a stacked deck, and of course the house won the game." *Army* magazine conceded the inevitable defeat of the M14: "The AR-15, used in South Vietnam fighting for several months, came out smelling like a rose."

The public had little idea of the Pentagon infighting over the rifles.

At a 1963 Senate Appropriations Committee hearing, the M16/M14 factions presented to the public that discussions within the Pentagon over the best infantry rifle had led to an informed consensus. McNamara and Joint Chiefs chairman Wheeler displayed strained cordiality when asked about rifles at the meeting. McNamara praised the M14, but in the next sentence he announced—shockingly—that the Pentagon wasn't going to order any more. The gun that the Pentagon had spent at least $135 million developing, producing, and purchasing over two decades would be phased out.

The cordiality was a lie. That abrupt announcement was the result of a secret agreement between McNamara's office and the army to try to repair strained relations, later described in a private letter by Colonel Richard Hallock, a strong advocate for the M16 in the Pentagon, to the Army Lieutenant General Lionel McGarr, then head of U.S. forces in Vietnam. Hallock asked McGarr to burn the letter after he read it. Under the secret deal, Wheeler agreed to buy tens of thousands of Stoner's guns, but he got to save face by pushing off a final decision on the army's standard rifle and secured funding for research into other firearms, Hallock wrote. Hallock wrote that he knew his own support of the M16 had ruined his army career—and M14 backers had it in for him. He wrote that he considered resigning because of "the possibility of vindictive action by the highest ranking Army personnel." Hallock soon was rotated out of Enthoven's office and sent off to an honorific stint at the Army War College. The commanding officer there sent a blistering assessment of Hallock to the Pentagon that Enthoven considered "character assassination." Enthoven was convinced the report was retribution by Army Ordnance for Hallock's work on behalf of Stoner's gun.

During these years, the rifle was seen more and more in public, being carried by soldiers and government agents. John F. Kennedy had been photographed inspecting the gun, and Secret Service agents carried the weapon. On November 22, 1963, Kennedy was assassinated in Dallas. Secret Service Special Agent George W. Hickey Jr., in the car directly behind the president, rose to his feet with his agency-issued AR-15 after hearing the first shot. Hickey's proximity to the president and confusion over the number of shots fired that day gave rise to speculation, lasting decades, that Hickey accidentally fired his rifle one time, delivering the shot that actually killed JFK. Hickey and another agent both said Hickey did not fire his rifle and official investigations found no evidence or witnesses to show that he did.

Vice President Lyndon Johnson, sworn in as president, made no changes in his Pentagon team. He kept McNamara in charge and relied on his advice regarding U.S. involvement in Vietnam, including the rifles used by American soldiers. As the war Johnson inherited intensified, U.S. combat advisors clamored to get more M16s. American soldiers near Saigon told a reporter about a firefight in which eleven guerrillas were killed while six U.S. soldiers using M16s were unharmed.

"It's the greatest individual rifle I've ever seen," an anonymous soldier said. "It's so good, in fact, nobody can understand how the Army ever developed it. They ain't famous for some of their brilliant technological decisions."

In the United States, army recruiters started bringing the guns to county fairs to entice young men to sign up. A *Dallas Morning News* reporter visited air force rifle instructors in early 1966 in San Antonio and saw them demonstrate M16s. "Killing people is what it is built for, and what it does with great efficiency," the reporter wrote. "To those 'Humanitarians' who think enemy soldiers should be killed neatly and politely, the M16 is a ghastly weapon. For the American soldier in Viet Nam [sic], regardless of his branch of service, it has been a godsend." McNamara told a congressional committee that regarding M16s, "We are shipping everything we can possibly get."

Some top Pentagon officials were worried that they didn't have enough M16s as more U.S. troops were sent to Vietnam. "Looks like our rifle situation is getting very bad," wrote army chief of staff General Harold K. Johnson after returning from a visit to the country.

Colt, the sole company with rights to manufacture the rifle, had the Pentagon over a barrel.

"They had really no production military weapon at the time and they were getting involved in a shooting war," Stoner recalled later. By the middle of 1965, Colt reported the most profitable second quarter in its history, much of it due to the M16. The company ran a large ad in *The Wall Street Journal* showing a drawing of American soldiers in camouflage, holding M16s. "The best-equipped fighting men in the world are equipped with the most advanced rifle in the world . . . ours," the copy read.

But as production ramped up, the new rifle being mass-produced by Colt was not exactly the one that Stoner created. The alterations were made by a Pentagon group created by McNamara in 1963 called the Technical Coordinating Committee—an attempt by the defense secretary to mollify army elements angry about being forced to accept the M16. The committee included representatives of all four military branches and its job was to suggest any changes it felt necessary to the gun for use by U.S. servicemen.

Army Lieutenant Colonel Howard Yount, chosen by Army Material Command to be chief of the Office of Project Manager for AR-15 Activities, oversaw the new committee. He worked closely with Hallock and others in the pro-M16 faction, and was friendly with Stoner, who respected him. But he also had worked for years in Army Ordnance, where many had long supported the M14. The committee considered more than 130 modifications, and the branches argued about the various proposals. As the gun expert J. David McFarland later wrote, "Many of the M16's problems are like the proverbial camel which is a horse designed by committee."

The army, for example, insisted that bullets fired from an AR-15 accurately hit targets in temperatures as low as minus sixty-five degrees Fahrenheit, even though combat in such temperature was extremely unlikely, if not impossible. Other debates over technical modifications erupted—with bad ideas being adopted and good ideas being sidelined depending on the political sway of the participants. One change proposed by the army, adding chrome plating inside the chamber and barrel of the rifle, later proved prescient, but was refused because it added additional cost. Chrome plating was more expensive, but it was stronger metal and reduced chances of corrosion inside a rifle's chamber after a lot of firing. As guns are fired repeatedly, especially in dusty or muddy environments, bits of sand or grit in the chamber can make tiny scrapes and marks, which can cause rifles to jam. If the gun was going to be used in conditions such as those that existed in Vietnam, corrosion would be a major concern, so strong materials, proper cleaning equipment, and extensive training in rifle maintenance would be crucial.

What would become the most disastrous change made by the committee had to do with the gun's ammunition. Stoner had designed his rifle to work with rounds made by Remington that used a version of improved military rifle propellant, or IMR, made by DuPont. The key ingredient of IMR was nitrocellulose, a highly flammable wood product soaked in nitric acid. Nitrocellulose first was developed in the 1830s, and was used in all kinds of ammunition because it was extremely combustible and fast-burning and could create a relatively smokeless charge to send a bullet down a barrel. IMR 4475—the specific type of propellant used for ammunition for the AR-15—was extruded like other IMR propellants in strips, looking somewhat like miniature strands or logs, not in pellets or spheres like other types of propellant. At all major tests of Stoner's gun from the 1950s into the early 1960s, shooters used ammunition with this commercially available IMR.

Ammunition needs to be more than the right size to fit in the gun's chamber; it also has to have the right propellant packed in the proper amount to create the necessary pressure to send the bullet down the barrel and out of the muzzle at the required velocity. The firearm's various parts, mechanisms, springs, the bullet, the cartridge casing, and the propellant have to work in sync.

Early in its meetings, the Technical Coordination Committee discussed concerns about whether the AR-15's ammunition reliably delivered the right pressure levels. The committee asked the army's Frankford Arsenal to look for possible alternatives. The arsenal tested several and favored one type of propellant made by the Olin Mathieson Chemical Corporation. Olin Mathieson's propellant, which had the formal name WC 846, was known commonly as "ball powder," because its grains were spherical. It also was made from nitrocellulose but cost less to produce than IMR, with scrap and other materials added. It burned more slowly than IMR 4475. It produced more smoke and left more soot residue in the gun. But the arsenal concluded that ball powder "should not be significantly inferior to IMR 4475."

At the time, some in the military argued that key parts of Stoner's gun could be modified to allow for pressure variations. But the fact remained that ball powder was dirtier. Also, the propellant's shape and composition critically altered the gas-powered system that Stoner had created. Some tests showed the cyclic rate—the rate at which the gun fired and reloaded—rose from 750 rounds per minute with IMR to 1,000 rounds per minute with ball powder. That could cause a slight hiccup in the rifle's operation, especially during intense use in combat. Army testers seemed unconcerned and sanctioned the switch after limited examination of the issue.

Despite many concerns, the committee approved ball powder propellant for M16 ammunition. Engineers and historians have debated the committee's motives, the rifle's pressure levels and tolerances, and other issues ever since. The bottom line was simple and tragic: the army hadn't done enough testing on the ammunition switch to see what impact it might have on the rifle's performance, especially in the harsh conditions of jungle warfare.

Urgent logistical issues played a major role. After the army authorized purchase of tens of thousands of M16s, it tried to secure more ammunition. But in January 1964, DuPont notified the army that it could not make enough IMR 4475 at the military's specifications to meet the army's demand. The army rushed out a request for bids but found that only the Olin Mathieson Chemical Corporation could produce enough propellant—and it was ball powder. Some critics of this switch have argued the decision was capricious or meant to favor the long-standing army supplier Olin Mathieson, but it appears to have been more an act of desperation—the army needed lots of propellant quickly as war approached.

The committee classified the army version of Stoner's gun at first as the XM16E1, considering it a weapon for limited production for use in the escalating Southeast Asian war. The *X* signified the rifle was in development, the *E* noted it was experimental, and the *1* meant it was the military's first experimental version. Most troops simply called the M16 the black rifle. To the average grunt, the changes made to Stoner's rifle probably seemed minor, and they did little to change the appearance of the gun. But as Stoner and every gun engineer since ancient China had learned, any change to an energy system had consequences. As Stoner later would say of the modifications made to his rifle by the committee, "Timing is everything and Murphy's Law prevails."

General Harold K. Johnson, army chief of staff, didn't understand the ramifications of these changes. He just wanted to get his fighting men modern weapons as the Vietnam conflict ramped up. Johnson was known as a commander who cared about the well-being of his troops. As a young officer, Johnson endured the horrors of the Bataan Death March in the Philippines, suffering starvation and witnessing daily mistreatment of American prisoners. The experience left him deeply religious, committed to the army, and determined to help the average soldier with everything from pay to supplies. As he rose in the ranks, including a stint as a commander in Korea, he gained a reputation for making sure his men had the equipment that they needed, whether in combat or back on base. "The Army means people" was a phrase he often repeated.

But staff overseeing M16 production and ammunition for Johnson compounded possible problems caused by the propellant change by issuing special acceptance testing waivers for Colt so it could ship the contracted amount of M16s to the military. Colt had warned the army that if it tested the guns with ammunition containing ball-powder propellant, as many as half would fail because they would jam and the company wouldn't be able to deliver the rifles needed for Vietnam. In response, the army waived standard rifle testing and allowed hundreds of thousands of Colt M16s to be issued to U.S. troops without its normal testing procedures. The historians Blake Stevens and Edward Ezell laid the blame for the waivers on Howard Yount's office trying to meet demands for more guns at the expense of safety. Yount would claim that he did not make decisions about ammunition. Whoever made the waiver decisions, Colt got its testing exceptions and production of guns continued apace. The decision would soon cost American lives in Vietnam.

Some military tests at the time pointed to serious problems with the altered M16s. One report from the Small Arms Weapons Systems (SAWS) study, led by none other than Colonel Richard Hallock, showed the altered M16s had a propensity to jam. Hallock warned higher-ups that something was going wrong with the new guns, but they ignored him. Pierre Sprey, one of McNamara's "Whiz Kids" in the 1960s who worked closely with Hallock, recalled that Hallock was convinced the rifle and ammunition changes were made by anti-Stoner factions that wanted the gun to fail. Hallock's boss, Enthoven, also blamed bureaucratic meddling. "The army, out of pique, was ruining this great rifle," he said decades later.

Some key Pentagon officials at the time sounded the alarm over malfunctions caused by the replacement ammunition propellant. Wilbur Payne, a military operations expert in Vance's office, wrote a secret memorandum on the subject just a week after the Battle of LZ X-Ray, when the M16 had been praised. He noted that Stoner had called him just days earlier and raised concerns that "seem to be important enough to warrant further investigation and corrective action if they are verified." Stoner's chief worry was the switch to ball powder, he told Payne.

But such alarms came far too late. The U.S. military already had shipped tens of millions of rounds of M16 ammunition to Vietnam. The vast majority of that ammo used ball-powder propellant.

11.

"TRAGEDY AND BETRAYAL"

Believe it or not, do you know what killed most of us?
Our own rifle.
—Marine writing to his family

Fred Monahan was startled awake by shouts in the darkness. What was that dreamy gibberish? Words? Commands? His exhausted brain delivered a foggy answer: he was hearing Vietnamese. He was in Vietnam. He was in a war. The twenty-year-old Marine lance corporal sat bolt upright. He could barely see. His glasses were smeared after an hours-long rainstorm. He was sopping wet and his body was shaking. He sat on a small mud shelf in a bunker about the size of a Volkswagen bug's back seat. He had dozed off after the grunt who was supposed to relieve him never showed up. It was May 3, 1967, but what time was it? Monahan had no idea. He heard more shouting and clambered to the bunker's opening. Automatic rifle fire erupted to his left and right. Grenades and mortars exploded nearby. In the drizzly fog, ghostly shouts came from down the hill. He knew enough Vietnamese to understand the phrase: Die, American! Die, American! He lifted his M16 toward the bunker entrance but didn't fire. He saw shadows—lots of them—moving up the steep trail below. He estimated they were about as far from him as home plate to first base on a baseball diamond. He crawled over and dropped a phosphorus grenade on one group below a cliff; he heard the moans of the dying and wounded after the explosion. A corpsman with a wounded Marine—the man's hand was blown off—came up asking whether they could get into the bunker. Monahan let the men in and asked the corpsman to load up M16 magazines. An enemy soldier threw a grenade, which exploded in a puddle in front of the bunker, spraying Monahan with singeing, muddy water. If he hadn't been wearing his glasses, he would have been blinded. The enemy troops shouted taunts at him in Vietnamese. He hurled American taunts back. They crept closer, but in the darkness he wasn't sure where they were. They opened fire with AK-47s, sending green tracers flying by his head. One tracer knocked a soggy cigarette out of Monahan's mouth. To draw fire away from the bunker, Monahan took off his helmet and set it on a branch a few feet away, creating a silhouette that enemy riflemen mistook for a Marine. Raising his rifle, he aimed, pulled, and held the trigger, blasting out a full magazine on automatic. Red tracers flew at the green tracers. He took out the empty magazine, loaded another, and sprayed again. He popped in a third magazine, but after three rounds something horrific happened: his M16 stopped firing.

Monahan crouched to try to clear the rifle's chamber, but he couldn't get the spent shell out. "I thought, what in the world is going on here? I couldn't get the thing to extract," he recalled. "I thought somehow I got the only rifle in Vietnam that jammed up."

He ducked in the bunker and grabbed the wounded Marine's rifle. It fired a few times, but then it jammed too. He cleared both guns, but after a few rounds they both jammed again. He took turns firing the guns in short bursts, and clearing them when they froze up. He wondered whether they were overheating. Maybe it was the rain and mud. The North Vietnamese snuck closer, steadily firing their AK-47s. Grabbing one of his rifles, Monahan dove into a nearby trench, where he found two dead Marines. Out of the gloom, a North Vietnamese soldier lunged at him. Using his M16 as a club, Monahan beat the man with the rifle butt. When he had him on the ground, Monahan instinctively switched to drive the barrel end of the rifle into the man's face, though he didn't have a bayonet. The barrel pushed into the man's eye socket and into his brain. The man went limp. Monahan had just killed the only way he could with a rifle that wouldn't shoot. He scampered back to his bunker and found he was alone. The corpsman and the wounded Marine had fled up the hill. Monahan's only protection was the two jammed rifles, one Claymore antipersonnel mine, a knife, a Catholic pendant that his girlfriend gave him, and a pocket Bible that he carried in part to honor his mother, a woman with Quaker roots who cried when she learned he was going to war. He had the Bible open that morning to Psalm 91: "Thou shalt not be afraid for the terror by night; nor for the arrow that flieth by day." He shouted more taunts. "This is it, so I'm going down swinging," he recalled thinking. "I'm going to die anyway, the sooner the better." He shouted to Marines up the hill, asking someone to throw him an M14. Most of his company recently had been issued the new "black rifles," but he knew the engineers in his company still had M14s and he trusted they would work. A Marine rushed down the hill, firing his M14 at the enemy, but just before he reached Monahan's bunker, he was killed. Monahan pulled the Marine's limp body to the entrance to use as "a bullet catcher. I hope he would have done the same with me," he recalled. Grabbing the man's M14, he fired the remaining bullets. The gun worked perfectly and he killed the enemy soldier who had just taken his comrade's life. Out of ammunition for the M14, Monahan again figured he was about to be killed. But daylight arrived, burning away the fog and bringing U.S. aircraft—jets, helicopters, and fixed-wing gunships—into the sky. Menaced by bombs, rockets, and bullets, the North Vietnamese retreated into the forest.

Monahan crawled out of his hole to behold the aftermath of one of the fiercest fights of the war. "There were dead bodies all over the place," he recalled. Echo Company, Second Battalion, Third Marines, had about two hundred men when they bedded down that night in an abandoned North Vietnamese camp on a low hill in the remote northwestern tip of South Vietnam.

By morning, thirty-one of the Marines were dead and many others wounded. More than a hundred men in the unit were awarded the Purple Heart. Some won citations for valor, including Monahan, who was awarded the prestigious Navy Cross. As he walked the demolished camp, Monahan learned from other Marines that his problems with jammed rifles had been a nightmare for many of those fighting that night. Black rifles all over Echo Company's perimeter had stopped working. Monahan and others found dead Marines lying in foxholes next to cleaning rods and jammed rifles. They found one dead Marine with a jammed rifle who had killed at least six North Vietnamese with his knife before being overpowered.

The morning after the fight, survivors gathered around their commanding officer, who asked the exhausted men whether any of their rifles had malfunctioned. Monahan estimated that 40 percent of the men raised their hands. All guns have some percentage of malfunction in combat, but that level of jamming was atrocious. The few men in the unit carrying M14s did not experience malfunctions on that magnitude; in fact, the M14 was the only rifle Monahan fired that awful night that worked.

Everyone suspected the M16's ammunition. The officer ordered the men to bring up their remaining M16 rounds and dump them into the muddy grass. In a scene that reminded Monahan of "some kind of African war dance," the angry Marines spilled out the shiny brand-new bullets, then stomped them into the earth with their heavy boots. Monahan and his fellow Marines hated the M16 after that horrible night. "I was pretty well disgusted," he said. "I knew when something was worthless." Asked more than five decades later to sum up his company's experience with the gun in Vietnam, Monahan said with his voice quaking, "Tragedy and betrayal."

Marines' guns jammed throughout the battle zone of what would become known as "the Hill Fights"—twelve days of combat near the Marine base at Khe Sanh in late April and early May 1967. U.S. fighters reported problems with M16s in other parts of Vietnam as well. About five months earlier, U.S. Army officers at LZ X-Ray had praised the M16's performance, and top military officials had used that praise to push for a massive requisition of the weapon. Now the Hill Fights undermined the Pentagon's narrative that the new rifle was going to help the United States win the war.

As the conflict intensified, the U.S. military worked frantically to supply fighters with M16s. By August 1966, all army combat units under Westmoreland's command had been supplied with the rifles. The Marines planned to distribute M16s to all of their Vietnam combat units by spring of the following year. Colt thrived thanks to its exclusive rights to produce the M16, and its manufacturing operation in Connecticut went into high gear. By December 1966, Colt was producing twenty-five thousand rifles a month for the army—but that wasn't enough to meet demand.

The Pentagon had spent almost a year trying to increase M16 production, and had begun moves to buy manufacturing rights from Colt so it could contract for more rifles from other manufacturers. "We now have a very substantial requirement for the M16s," McNamara told a House committee.

Public concern over whether U.S. fighting men would have enough M16s drew the attention of Congress. Democratic representative L. Mendel Rivers of South Carolina, the House Armed Services Committee chairman, set up a special subcommittee on May 3, 1967, to investigate M16 production. That was the very day Monahan fought for his life in Vietnam.

The three-member committee included Democratic representative Speedy Long of Louisiana and Republican representative William Bray of Indiana. It was chaired by Democratic representative Richard Ichord Jr. of Missouri. All three men represented rural districts and were conservative Vietnam War hawks. Long was a vocal segregationist. Bray had won the army's Silver Star in World War II in the Pacific. Ichord, who served in the navy during World War II, also chaired the House Internal Security Committee, then investigating Yippies, Black Panthers, and other leftist organizations who opposed U.S. involvement in Vietnam. He gained national notoriety as a square foil at hearings attended by theatrical self-proclaimed revolutionaries such as Jerry Rubin and Abbie Hoffman. Ichord loathed such protesters who often used toy M16s as props in their protests and public stunts. Abbie Hoffman recounted in *Yippie Manifesto* (1969) that he came to a committee meeting with a "bandolero of real bullets and carrying a toy M16 rifle on my shoulder. The rifle was a model of the rifles the Viet Cong steal and then use to kill American soldiers in Vietnam."

Ichord was convinced that North Vietnam, with the help of the American Communist Party, was behind much of the mayhem and protests hitting cities and colleges. He had first traveled to Vietnam with other congressmen in 1965, as the war was heating up. "I must say that before I went to South Vietnam I had some doubts about the wisdom of our presence in that country," he said in a speech he gave in Missouri after that trip. "Now I have none." He described those opposing the war as "long-haired, unwashed, and unshaven beatniks."

Rivers tasked the subcommittee with investigating "the development, production, distribution and sale of M16 rifles." On May 12, 1967, the three congressmen flew down to Fort Benning. On a tour of the base, the congressmen saw M16s and M14s fired on the range, and shot the guns themselves. They interviewed thirty-five to forty soldiers who had used M16s in Vietnam.

The following Monday, the subcommittee gathered in Room 2216 of Washington's Rayburn House Office Building, across Independence Avenue from the Capitol, to hold its first hearing. Dick Ichord, a sullen-looking forty-year-old with oiled hair combed back and puffed up so that he resembled a thin, wan version of Johnny Cash, banged the gavel at 10:15 a.m. The first witness was Robert A. Brooks, assistant secretary of the army for installations and logistics. The M16 "has been by far the most popular individual weapon to be introduced in the recent history of the Army," Brooks said. "To my knowledge, U.S. Army combat commanders in Vietnam are unanimous in their opinion that it is an excellent weapon for the combat conditions there." The congressmen were deferential to Pentagon officials at the hearing, and Ichord reported that soldiers at Fort Benning praised the gun.

But Ichord was troubled by the story of the M16's development and distribution to U.S. forces, calling it "soaked in a muddle of confusion." He then added, "And as you well know we have had confusing reports coming out of Vietnam about the performance of the M16 rifles." It was the first of several remarks, seeded amid the hearings' lengthy discussions about contracts and production schedules, that focused on the real problem: rifles malfunctioning while U.S. troops were in combat. Ichord's comments referred to a news report—which he later named explicitly in the hearing—by the journalist Bill Wordham on NBC's influential evening news program *The Huntley-Brinkley Report*. Wordham reported on May 9 that Marines in the Hill Fights and another military operation found their M16s jammed. "One sergeant, almost in tears with rage and sorrow, said that two of his men were killed because their guns would not fire," Wordham said on the program.

The subcommittee's counsel, Earl Morgan, said at the hearing that soldiers interviewed at Fort Benning cited "failure to extract" a shell after firing as the biggest problem causing jams. Military officials brushed off concerns. The next morning, Major General William John Van Ryzin of the U.S. Marines told the subcommittee, "Occasionally you may have a broken part, or a new weapon that is tight that may not function perfectly. That happens with any weapon."

When Ichord brought up the NBC report, Van Ryzin replied: "The only adverse report we have is by means of the television." He was lying.

In fact, Pentagon officials long knew that the gun was malfunctioning at an unacceptable rate in Vietnam. For at least sixteen months before the Hill Fights, the Pentagon was aware that the gun had a serious jamming problem but it didn't warn troops or limit use of the rifle, Pentagon documents at the National Archives and other repositories show. Top generals, secret multibranch committees, and leading Defense Department bureaucrats knew the jams were not solely caused by poor rifle care as they claimed publicly. Classified reports discussed numerous, interrelated problems including the switch in ammunition propellant, rusting of the rifle's chamber in jungle conditions, and disruption in the rate at which the rifle fired and reloaded. The giant bureaucracy didn't want to admit to the American public, its troops, or the enemy that anything was wrong. But confidential reports had warned that the gun, after changes made by the technical committee, had serious problems. A Colt report for the military dated November 8,

1965, found significant changes in cyclic rates of M16s fired with ball powder. In December 1965, the army's project manager for rifles wrote in a memorandum that "the functioning differences induced by one of the approved propellant types are directly related to an increased number of weapon malfunctions." An army survey of troops in Vietnam, completed in August 1966, found rusting and other problems appeared to be causing jams. By October of that year, about six months before the Hill Fights, troop complaints about the gun were so numerous that the army quietly sent teams to Vietnam to figure out what was wrong.

A "Secret Hold Close" memorandum to General Johnson in late November urged an investigation of the switch to ball powder as a major cause of M16 malfunctions. An internal Pentagon report, dated February 20, 1967, determined chrome plating of the gun's chamber—which the technical committee had decided wasn't necessary—and non–ball propellant ammunition were needed to restore the M16's reliability. The secret report was blunt: "[T]he changes identified so far are rectification of mistakes made by that same Technical Committee at the time the weapon was adopted."

Troops heading into combat were never told of these concerns. Commanders just instructed troops to keep their weapons clean and increased rifle inspections and training. The army launched an education/propaganda effort among the troops regarding gun maintenance. In December 1966, the army published a comic booklet, drawn by the famous cartoonist Will Eisner, in which a buxom woman gripping an M16 instructed soldiers on "How to Strip Your Baby." A plastic cover for the gun was referred to as the gun's "négligé [sic]." A feminized ammunition magazine shouted, "Protect me, you big strong guy!" The army also printed posters showing two Viet Cong fighters in the jungle, one holding an M16. "I got it from a guy who didn't keep it clean," the fighter said.

Marine Al White was first given an M16 during a stopover in Okinawa on his way to Vietnam. The M16's lightness unnerved him and training was minimal. "We didn't know shit about it," he said. At five feet, six inches tall and weighing 130 pounds, the young White was an "ammo humper" for a bazooka team. He carried rockets, his loaded pack, full canteens, as well as his recently issued M16 rifle and ammunition cartridges.

White, who grew up in the corn belt of central Illinois, signed up for the Marines after seeing the corps band perform on a high school field trip. He thought it would be cool to play his saxophone for the band and a recruiter assured him that was a definite possibility. During basic training he got a brief tryout, but soon it was clear the recruiter had conned him. White was headed to Vietnam. In Okinawa, White lost his virginity to a bar prostitute after his squad leader insisted he do so. At night, "[a]ll I did was screw and drink," he said. After Okinawa, White's unit was sent to live on ships of the U.S. Seventh Fleet off the Vietnamese coast as part of a quick-strike unit providing support to troops stationed in the northern part of South Vietnam. On the ship, they trained with their M16s by shooting into the water. They would stand in a queue to shoot, then fire rounds and pass it to the next guy. "We'd just take one or two shots," he said. "We didn't shoot it long enough to jam."

In late April 1967, White's unit was sent to aid a Marine base near the village of Khe Sanh. The terrain around the base was tough: steep hills covered with thick tree canopy and bamboo groves—a perfect place for the enemy to build deep bunkers and defensive works that could not be detected by aircraft. Knolls and valleys in between were dark and crowded with vegetation, excellent for ambushes. North of the base were three looming hills occupied by thousands of North Vietnamese regulars. The Marines named the hills 861, 881 South, and 881 North, denoting their elevation by meters above sea level. White remembered turning nineteen when he arrived at Khe Sanh. Stepping out of a helicopter, he stood in awe as jets and artillery pounded a hill in front of him. "They were bombing the fucking shit out of it," White recalled. "I thought, fuck, what a birthday present."

In his first firefight, White's M16 jammed. "I threw the son of a bitch away," he recalled. A comrade next to him was killed, so White took his rifle: "He wasn't going to need it anymore." On May 3, the night Monahan fended off attackers with jammed M16s, White lay in elephant grass nearby, trying to fire his rifle, which jammed repeatedly. "I was so fucking mad I couldn't see straight," White recalled. "Here the United States of America is giving us this plastic junk."

At one point, White was put on corpse detail, looking for dead Marines or what was left of them and putting the remains in body bags. He found dead Marines with their rifles dismantled next to them or the cleaning rods by their side. "Back to the Revolutionary War," he said.

Dick Backus, another grunt who fought that night, saw five of the men in his ten-member squad killed in the battle.

"Our government sent young men to war with a rifle that didn't shoot," he said.

In a battle nearby around the same time, Lance Corporal William J. Roldan crouched near an enemy bunker to try to unjam his M16. Before he could fix the gun, a sniper killed him. Vernon Wike, a corpsman, ran to aid Roldan. The incident was memorialized in a now famous sequence of black-and-white photographs taken by Catherine Leroy, a French freelance photographer who accompanied the men. The photos show the frantic Wike trying to aid the fallen Roldan, then realizing in anguish that his comrade was dead. The photos were published on May 19, 1967, in a large spread in *Life*. The article made no mention of jammed rifles.

Back on the ships after the Hill Fights, many Marines panicked about having to go back into combat with M16s. "I never want to see one again as long as I live. I hated it," Monahan said. At one point, he dismantled his rifle and threw a piece of it into the South China Sea to avoid having to fight with the weapon. Al White recalled after the battle handing in the rifle on the ship, and the officer in charge giving him a hard time because the serial number didn't match the one he was assigned. "He really started eating my ass," White recalled. "I said, 'It's up on that hill. If you want it so bad, go up and get it.'" Word came down to the grunts to stop talking about any M16 problems. One

Marine captain at the Hill Fights issued a statement praising the gun, declaring, "Not one malfunction occurred in the entire company during this fight." Marine Corps Commandant General Wallace Greene held a press conference at the Pentagon to, in his words, "correct the faulty impression that some people seem to have that the Marine Corps is dissatisfied with this weapon."

On May 10, during the Hill Fights, the army announced it officially had adopted the M16 as a standard rifle worldwide in addition to the M14. Behind the scenes, many military officials were panicked that the M16's problems were coming to light. Hallock retired, believing he would be made a scapegoat for the gun's problems. General Johnson, the army chief of staff, approved renewed testing of the gun and its ammunition.

While Marines could be stopped from talking to reporters, they couldn't be stopped from writing to their families. Letters poured back to the United States with requests for different weapons, cleaning oil, and lubricant. Marines wrote to parents, siblings, girlfriends, and friends about harrowing experiences when their M16s jammed. News of the problems soon made their way to Congress. On May 22, 1967, Democratic representative James J. Howard from New Jersey stood up on the House floor.

"Mr. Speaker, the Members of the House as well as millions of Americans have been greatly disturbed over recent reports that the M16 rifle presently being used in Vietnam is unreliable," Howard said. He added that he had written to McNamara and the Ichord committee that morning for explanations.

Howard quoted from a letter written by an unnamed Marine to his family living in Howard's district. Large portions of the letter, without naming the Marine, had been published two days earlier in the *Asbury Park Evening Press*, a New Jersey newspaper. From the context of the letter, it was clear the Marine had participated in the Hill Fights.

"Practically every one of our dead was found with his rifle torn down next to him where he was trying to fix it," the Marine wrote, adding, "There was a newspaper woman with us photographing all this and the Pentagon found out about it and won't let her publish the pictures. They say they don't want to get the American people upset. Isn't that a laugh?" Howard then read the most damning sentences of the Marine's letter: "Believe it or not, do you know what killed most of us? Our own rifle."

12.

"BORDERS ON CRIMINAL NEGLIGENCE"

Mistakes were made and errors in judgment committed under
the pressures involved in accelerated introduction
of this new weapon system.
—Pentagon official

Terrifying stories from soldiers and Marines flooded in from families to congressional staff and made their way to Ichord's subcommittee. Families feared that the military would retaliate against their loved ones, so they often did not reveal names. Some letters gave details about specific engagements, and named men who died because their guns stopped working. In one letter, a young Marine only identified as Bert recounted to his parents the harrowing story of the death of his eighteeen-year-old friend and comrade, Lance Corporal David C. Borey of Pittsfield, Massachusetts, in a seven-hour firefight not far from Da Nang on May 13, 1967:

> More than half the company was pinned down and couldn't get back to safety for all those seven hours. In our company we had eight killed and 20 wounded. Dave Borey was one of the ones killed. This is how it happened—like you said Dad—we are all complaining about the M16 when it works you can't beat it—but it jams so goddamn easy. The only cover we had was a 5" dike

to hide behind. There was a steady flow of lead going back and forth and rifles were jamming left and right. And when they jam the only thing you can do is poke a cleaning rod down the bore and punch out the empty shell. Borey had the only cleaning rod in our group and he was running up and down the lines punching out the bores. I knew he was going to get it and I think he did too. A man needed the cleaning rod so Dave jumped up and started running towards him. As soon as he got up he was hit in the foot. He was about 10 feet in front of me and he called to me and said, "Hey Bert, I'm hit." He couldn't stay there because bullets were hitting the dirt all around him. He had to get back to the dike. I told him to get up and run and I'd shoot grazing fire into the hill line where the VC were. I got out 3 magazines and fired 60 rounds to cover him—but as he was running a goddamn VC hit him in the back. As soon as he fell down I threw down my rifle and ran out to him, picked him up, and carried him to the dike. But he was already dead when I put him down.

A grunt from Montana wrote to his parents about a battle in which 50 out of 125 men had rifle jams. A man from Southern California sent a letter from a Marine who complained that in one clash, "Mine jammed on me five times and I popped only 280 rounds! The round will fire, but it won't eject; it just stays in the chamber, so you have to get a ramrod and poke it out. Just like Daniel Boone and those guys." The Marine said the gun was directly responsible for comrades getting killed.

On June 1, 1967, the three congressmen—Ichord, Bray, and Long—flew to Vietnam to get a firsthand look at how the gun was doing. They questioned as many fighting men as possible. While most of the soldiers reported few problems with the gun, the team interviewed at least five hundred Marines, and about half of them said the gun had serious problems.

When the congressmen returned to Washington, they received tips that many of the soldiers in Vietnam had not been truthful. One soldier wrote to his sister, "Everyone that was selected to go to be interviewed was either a squad leader or a team leader or someone who had been asked, 'Has your weapon ever malfunctioned on you?' If the man said, 'Yes,' he didn't go. If he said, 'No,' he went. They made sure that the men that the investigators interviewed from our company were picked people that they could bust if they said the wrong thing . . . [Y]ou can guess what the investigators found out from these people—Nothing!" Another woman wrote that she and her brother, a Marine captain, saw General Greene say on television that Marines liked their M16s. "My brother groaned," she wrote. "[A]nd when I said, 'What is wrong?' he said, 'There will be no more complaints because they have issued an order that if you do, you will be severely reprimanded, or perhaps even threatened with court-martial.'"

If the military hoped to quash the story about M16 malfunctions, Ichord's committee made sure that didn't happen. Throughout the summer, committee hearings were dominated by questions about how the gun was made; who profited; what changes the army made to Stoner's original invention; how troops were trained on the new guns; and how the rifles worked in battle. Top Pentagon officials, Colt representatives, Bob Macdonald, and even Eugene Stoner testified.

The possibility of a cover-up angered Ichord, and his questioning of military officials shifted sharply after the Vietnam trip, from deference to a prosecutorial tone. This anti-hippie, pro-war, Middle America politician had lost trust in the military: they were lying about the gun and he knew it. "It stands as a shocking example of muzzling by our military leaders on a subject that can mean life or death to our combat soldiers," he said at one hearing. "This committee is interested in only one thing, and that is arriving at the truth, and correcting the difficulties affecting the lives of our fighting men in Vietnam."

When the subcommittee convened on June 21, 1967, the first person to testify was Eugene Stoner. Since leaving ArmaLite, Stoner had worked as a consultant for various military contractors. He invented the Stoner 63 rifle—briefly a competitor to his AR-15/M16—for Cadillac Gage in suburban Detroit. He also consulted for TRW's weapons division in Port Clinton, Ohio, set on Lake Erie. He bought a large home by the lake on Catawba Island, just outside of the town. Reports of guns jamming in Vietnam troubled Stoner deeply, his daughter Sue remembered. He was angry about changes the military had made to the gun. The shy man was not eager to testify before Congress, but he wanted to set the record straight.

Reporters packed a Washington hearing room as Stoner came in to testify. Ichord sensed Stoner was uncomfortable being in the spotlight.

"Won't you come forward, Mr. Stoner, and have a seat there, and we will proceed informally," he said.

Stoner sat at the witness table.

"I think this morning, Mr. Stoner, to kick the matter off we would like for you to just informally give us your version of the development of the M16 and what part you played in it," Ichord said. "You may proceed as you wish."

"You want the historical end of it?" Stoner asked.

What followed was a highly technical history of the AR-15 from the man who created it. Asked about the gun's modifications, Stoner distanced himself.

"I want to reiterate that I have not been associated with Colt for the last 2 or 3 years," he said. Stoner focused most of his testimony on the army's decision to use ball powder in the gun's ammunition. He designed the gun for commercially available IMR-type powder. When he was told, after the fact, that the army had made the switch he warned army officials "it would be very, very risky." Stoner had said that the ammunition would cause more fouling when fired, and as deposits built up in the chamber, it could cause shells to get stuck. One official had asked him to sanction the propellant switch, he told the committee. But the official told him the technical committee had already approved the change. "I said, 'So why are you asking me now?' and he said, 'I would have felt better if you had approved of the package.' And I said, 'Well, we both now don't feel so good.'"

The core issue, in Stoner's estimation, was the increased rate of fire. The ball powder sped up the firing of the gun and upset Stoner's system.

The gun operated because of the precise amount of energy derived from recirculating gas expelled when bullets were fired. Any change "can cause, you name it, problems all the way up and down the line," Stoner said.

Stoner was most comfortable when talking about technical issues, but the committee also wanted to discuss the gun's function: killing. Ichord said that a soldier told him that he fired his M16 at a Viet Cong and struck near the man's eye, and "his whole head was reduced to pulp."

Stoner offered a scientific explanation.

"A little bullet, being it has a low mass, it senses an instability situation faster and reacts much faster," he said. "So, therefore, this is what makes a little bullet pay off so much in wound ballistics." Larger bullets tended to bore a straight hole through the human body, he said. "The small bullet will go unstable faster, and therefore create a larger wound cavity than you would normally expect."

Stoner didn't want to anger anyone in the military and threaten future contracts or design work. Ichord asked Stoner whether the changes the army had made had ruined the gun. Stoner was evasive.

> ICHORD: Now, the thing that concerns me is that the recent experience in Vietnam just doesn't stack up with the reported tests, the test down at Fort Benning and the earlier tests and use in South Vietnam. But with all the changes, we might not be dealing with the same weapon which you tested at Fort Benning. Is that a correct statement?
>
> STONER: Well, it is quite possible, if you say there has been this many changes made . . .
>
> ICHORD: We understand that. Well, the thing is more complicated and involved than we at first thought, and this is a very sensitive matter. The thing that concerns me is that so many men over there are losing confidence in the weapon, and I am sure as a weapon designer and one who has had great experience in this field, you realize the seriousness of a man losing confi-

dence in his weapon, being jittery that it might malfunction on
him at any time when he has to use it . . .

STONER: This I think is the worse [*sic*] thing that can happen, is
that if these things get out in the open.

ICHORD: They are already out in the open, that is the problem . . .

STONER: My interest in this thing, of course, is as a designer of,
I would say the original AR-15, is to try to make sure the troops
get the best they can possibly get. I have no ax to grind with anybody in the military, or Colt, or anyone else . . . I certainly don't
want to get in between on this thing.

Stoner answered many questions, but he was eager to get away from
the press attention without saying the wrong thing. He would say years
later that with "the magnitude of the problems that were going on I
was completely disgusted and amazed and everything else." Robert G.
Bihun, a mechanical engineer at TRW who worked closely with Stoner,
said the inventor was furious about the attacks on his gun, because the
mistakes were all caused by the military.

"He told me one time that all that bullshit about the AR-15 jamming
wasn't because of the rifle but because of the goddamned U.S. government changing the ballistics, the propellant," Bihun said. "He always
believed in the AR-15–M16, because he knew it was the propellant."

After Stoner's testimony, Ichord asked him to advise the subcommittee on technical issues. As the military, Colt, and others responded
to the inquiry, they found the congressional questioning more pointed.
Stoner's own view toward his invention was characteristically detached.
Days before the Ichord committee's report was made public, reporters started putting Stoner on the spot. One asked him about inventors'
moral responsibility for their creations. Stoner replied that "inventing
guns is no more immoral than inventing automobiles or mouse traps or
working in a missile factory." The reporter wrote that Stoner felt "that it
is not the grocer's responsibility when a housewife dumps rat poison in
her husband's orange juice, nor Jack Daniels' [*sic*] fault for the nation's
drunks."

Ichord grilled Colt engineers and military officials at the hearings. One key Colt witness was Kanemitsu "Koni" Ito, the company's top rifle engineer who led teams investigating M16 problems in Vietnam. "I was shocked," he said. "I had never seen equipment with such poor maintenance." Ito, a decorated army veteran, had helped Stoner during the AR-15 Alaska tests in 1958. As soon as he retired from the army in 1963, he joined Colt to work on mass-producing Stoner's gun. Ichord was incredulous at Ito's explanation that maintenance was the primary cause of jams.

"You are not saying the improper maintenance was the sole cause of all of the malfunctions in Vietnam, are you?" he asked.

Ito hedged, saying it could be environment, the ammunition, or the soldiers that were at fault—or perhaps a combination of all three: "Well, you can never say it was the sole cause, because you have the elements also against you. You may have the powder against you. And you also have the man."

Howard Yount, who eventually rose to the rank of colonel, also testified. He had overseen the M16 technical coordinating committee and was project manager for the gun's military adoption from March 1963 to June 1967. He testified that he had no evidence that the switch to ball powder had any negative effects, though he acknowledged it increased the cyclic rate.

Yount told the committee that he spoke with Stoner about the change in propellant, but said the two didn't discuss the M16. A stunned Representative Long asked, "You didn't discuss it with him, with regard to the M16?" When Yount said he probably did but didn't recall the conversation, a flabbergasted Ichord jumped in.

"Is there knowledge of anyone in your command, or anyone in the Army talking to Mr. Stoner about the conversion to ball propellant before the conversion was made?"

"Not to my knowledge; no, sir," Yount replied.

Yount was caught in an awkward, career-threatening situation. Ichord pressed Yount and other officials to acknowledge that the switch was to blame.

"I cannot buy some of these reports that I have seen that it is entirely the fault of the men out there in the field not cleaning their weapons," Ichord said. "You can't be wet nursing a weapon."

When Ichord later asked about what testing was used to determine the efficacy of the switch to ball powder, Yount admitted, without naming names, that the decision wasn't made on the basis of any tests, but instead on "direction."

Ichord: "Where did that direction come from?"

Yount: "Well, as many decisions which were made on this rifle, this decision emanated from the Department of the Army staff, sir. It was further coordinated with the Department of Defense, and Secretary McNamara personally approved it."

Around the time of the hearings, the army reassigned Yount to a post in Korea.

Ichord's committee tried to determine who ordered the fateful switch. Army brass contended that the switch was a reasonable decision, but admitted they had not done much testing. "We conducted tests, not as extensive perhaps as we might have liked, but the tests we conducted at the time gave us no indication that our supposition, that it was a low-risk matter, was anything to worry about," testified Major General Roland "Andy" Anderson, director of army procurement.

The evasive responses infuriated Ichord.

"We are asking the Army to give us the facts on this matter, the full facts, so that we can make a report," Ichord said. "And I doubt very much that if the committee had not received a tip in Vietnam to look into this ammunition that we would have ever explored it and have developed the whole record. I think the record without doubt sustains the fact that the crux of the problem—you had other problems, surely—started with this conversion to ball propellant."

A tense Anderson replied, "Mr. Chairman, I don't know quite how else to respond. There is nothing that I know of that we have withheld from the committee. There is nothing on this subject that I know of that throws any additional light on the controversial switch, so to speak, to ball powder."

The army asserted that any problems with the M16 were minor, and it was well on the way to fixing them. In a statement released to the subcommittee, the army stated ball powder was a less expensive propellant, but "the Army has not in any case ever compromised the required standards of technical performance in order to take advantage of the lower cost."

The army's public relations effort on behalf of its modified M16 was overwhelmed by letters reaching Congress from soldiers and Marines. The letter that received the most publicity was written by Lieutenant Michael Chervenak. The Marine lieutenant wrote, "My conscience will not let me rest any longer." He wrote that on July 21 his company was in a battle in which at least forty of their M16s jammed. He sent the letter to the Ichord committee, New York senator Robert F. Kennedy, his local Pennsylvania newspaper, and *The Washington Post*. "I believe that the cold, hard facts about the M16 are clouded over by a fabrication of the truth for political and financial considerations," he wrote. "I have seen too many Marines hiding behind a paddy dike trying to clear their rifles to accept these explanations any longer."

Ichord released his committee's final report on the M16 malfunctions, with thirty-one findings and recommendations, to the public on October 19, 1967. It blasted the Pentagon for mishandling adoption of the M16 and called for significant changes so that "future weapons not suffer the same fate."

"The manner in which the Army rifle program has been managed is unbelievable," the report stated. "The existing command structure was either inadequate or inoperative. The division of responsibility makes it almost impossible to pinpoint responsibility when mistakes are made. There is substantial evidence of lack of activity on the part of responsible officials of highest authority even when the problems of the M16 and its ammunition came to their attention."

The report was scattershot, focusing on some problems, such as the impact of ball powder, but paying little attention to others, such as corroded receivers. Though the document was rushed and unsystematic, the overall message it conveyed was clear: the Pentagon, under pressure

to meet war demands, and corporations, seeking fat government contracts, sent men to war with a defective rifle and little training or cleaning equipment.

Some of the report's key conclusions were:

- The army's switch to ball propellant for M16 ammunition caused
  malfunctions and the decision "was not justified or supported by
  test data."
- The army's decision to allow Colt to use IMR propellant instead of
  ball powder in its tests at the factory was a huge mistake. The army
  issued troops as many as 330,000 rifles that had high chances of
  jamming if they fired ball-powder propellant ammunition.
- Changes made by the army to Stoner's gun were costly, unnecessary, or harmful to the gun's performance. The army's delay in
  dealing with the malfunctions, a problem it created, "borders on
  criminal negligence."

To deal with the M16's problems in the middle of a war, the committee urged cleaning equipment be supplied to all troops in Vietnam
and called for extensive training to take place. It urged the ball-powder
propellant being used in ammunition be replaced with ammunition
using a fully tested, safer propellant.

But the names of those responsible for the M16 malfunctions were
absent from the report. The only military official the committee called
out was retired Army Major General Nelson Lynde Jr., a Colt consultant and former Ordnance Corps commander. Ichord's committee
found that Lynde's assertion that he had nothing to do with M16 production was proven false by the company's own records. While Lynde's
consulting work for Colt may have been legal, "the subcommittee does
seriously question the wisdom of such action in view of the suspicion
aroused by this type of association," the report stated. Any public casti-
gation of military officials stopped there.

The report did not call for a criminal investigation into what happened or a full accounting of who was responsible. Stoner said years

later that the report avoided calls for punishing those responsible as part of a deal between Ichord and the Pentagon.

"The committee decided that they identified who the real culprits were, but they decided in the interest of the morale of the army that they'd better not do anything about it," Stoner recalled. "And Ichord told me, he says, 'They know who they are and they will fix the problem a lot faster than we [*sic*] putting them in jail and having someone else new come in and fix the problem.'"

Earl Morgan, the committee's counsel, was asked by the journalist James Fallows more than a decade after the investigation whether he thought collusion among the military, Colt, and other companies contributed to the M16's problems. He suspected so, but the committee couldn't prove it, he said.

Ichord's reluctance to call out names and punish military officials was influenced by deep concern about the U.S. war effort, at that moment foundering with mounting losses. The United States had about 450,000 troops in Vietnam, and Americans were coming home in body bags every day. The Johnson administration and the military faced increasing resistance from the public, not just over conduct of the war but over why America was fighting the war at all. Two days after the report was released, close to a hundred thousand people gathered at the Lincoln Memorial to protest. About thirty-five thousand people then marched on the Pentagon. Ichord, who held such protesters in contempt, was loath to aid the peace movement with more bad news about the military. But that's exactly what he had done. The report, with its damning conclusions, received widespread coverage on television, radio, and in newspapers. A reporter called Stoner at his Ohio home to comment. Stoner said that he had warned the Pentagon not to switch the propellant. "In drawing up the specifications, the Army settled on a powder which is not really compatible with the weapon," he said. *The Kansas City Times* ran a political cartoon showing a sergeant handing a soldier an M16 and a slingshot. "Here's Your M16, and This Is Your Backup Weapon When It Jams," the sergeant said. One of the most damning assessments came in a *Washington Post* editorial: "If the

New Left were to set out to compose an insider's indictment of the 'military-industrial complex,' it could hardly match the report which a congressional committee has submitted on the M16 rifle." Edward Ezell, then a university instructor researching the history of U.S. military small arms, delivered a stark assessment in an essay for a North Carolina newspaper: "The American soldier needs and expects reliable weapons. The M16 is not such a rifle."

In November, Westmoreland returned from Vietnam to speak at the National Press Club in Washington. He told the audience the M16 was "the best infantry firearm our troops have ever taken into battle, but it does require care. There have been a few complaints which are well known to you. There are a few so-called bugs in the weapon which don't render it ineffective, but which if these guns are corrected, and they are being corrected, it will entail less maintenance."

This tone of unwavering support for the gun had been set by Robert McNamara. On October 18, just a day before the report was released to the public, McNamara sent a memo to his leadership team in which he delivered an upbeat assessment. "[T]he M16 rifle is clearly the best available rifle for the Southeast Asia environment," he wrote. By November, McNamara announced he was leaving his post as defense secretary to head the World Bank.

Would fewer Americans have died if the M16 ammunition had not been switched? Undoubtedly, but no one ever investigated how many soldiers needlessly died. Would an unaltered M16 have performed in Vietnam better than the M14? No one ever examined that issue.

One powerful figure within the army wanted answers. General Johnson, army chief of staff, ordered a special panel to investigate what went wrong and who was to blame. Johnson, then approaching retirement, wanted someone to pay for the screwups that had cost soldiers' lives. But some of his staff worried about public perception. A memorandum marked "For Official Use Only, Sensitive," recommended top brass avoid commenting on the report or say as little as possible. Another confidential memo about the switch in propellant stated, "Hindsight indicates that it was a serious mistake," but added, "This office does not have any information concerning the rationale causing the mistake." Johnson scrawled in the memorandum's margins: "This must be checked out and an audit trail established to pin down the specific individuals responsible for making shipments and conducting acceptance tests."

When the Ichord report came out, both of the companies involved issued statements denying any mistakes. Olin Mathieson, the maker of ball powder, defended its product. Colt launched a monthslong lobbying effort arguing Colt was not responsible for any problems caused by the army's changes; the M16 was an excellent rifle; and Colt should remain the military's sole source for the weapon. A top Colt executive and Ito visited the Pentagon to urge the army not to contract with any other companies to make M16s. The men stated that any problems in Vietnam were the result of improper maintenance. The pitch didn't work. Army leadership, long irritated with Colt, had already put out other bid requests to make M16s.

Colt president George Strichman sent a company report to General Johnson that stated, "The sub-committee also concluded that no blame could be attributed to the design of the rifle."

This statement angered Johnson. "Your paraphrasing of the Ichord Committee conclusions, without comment, leads the reader to conclude that Colt is totally exonerated of responsibility for any problems encountered on the M16 rifle," the general wrote. "I cannot subscribe to such a position. It is evident that either Colt underestimated the cleaning requirements for the rifle under field conditions or was overly enthusiastic."

Colt turned to Matthew Ridgway, the former army chief of staff who had served on Colt's board since 1955, to smooth things over. Ridgway wrote to Westmoreland, stating the M16 was a great weapon, but "[c]ontinued deceptive and actually false statements emanate from high sources in Washington and elsewhere, and receive widespread acceptance throughout press and other media." He demanded that Westmoreland, his onetime subordinate, give him data on the rifle's problems. He made no mention of his Colt connection, but everyone knew his ties. An anxious Westmoreland had his staff pass the letter on to General Johnson. The general's response to Ridgway was frosty, pointing out, "The M16 rifle system is particularly sensitive to changes in operating energy levels."

ABC Television broadcast an episode of its news program *ABC Scope* titled "The M16: What Went Wrong?" A reporter in Vietnam asked a U.S. soldier about the gun's problems and what he could do if he didn't have a cleaning rod. "Pray," the soldier replied. At the end of the program, Stoner appeared on camera briefly, describing the rifle and making technical observations, but making no comment about the controversy. Army officials declined to speak on camera.

A worried President Johnson asked Frank Mayborn, a pro-war Texas newspaper publisher and longtime friend, to join a tour of Vietnam. The trip was ostensibly to investigate troop morale, but Johnson asked Mayborn to secretly question troops about the M16. Around the same time, an army survey team was sent over to also question troops about the rifle. But both groups arrived as Vietnam was engulfed in one of the largest military operations of the conflict: the Tet Offensive. Starting on January 30, 1968, North Vietnamese and Viet Cong fighters launched attacks all over South Vietnam, even hitting the U.S. embassy in Saigon. The scope and ferocity of the attacks stunned American military leaders and the public. However horrible Tet was for the U.S. war effort, the mayhem proved beneficial for the M16, cutting short the Mayborn and army survey team tours.

Television news broadcasts were dominated by images of GIs holding M16s over their heads along muddy walls and shooting off whole magazines on automatic, a practice known among the troops as "spray and pray." The M16's problems took a back seat to the war.

The closest thing to a public apology from the army about the M16 malfunctions came in February 1968, in the midst of Tet. "Mistakes were made and errors in judgment committed under the pressures involved in accelerated introduction of this new weapon system," John S. Foster, the Pentagon's director of Defense Research and Engineering, acknowledged in a letter to the House Armed Services Committee.

In another letter, the army tepidly apologized for troops being told to lie to Ichord's committee. An army lobbyist wrote to Ichord "that in some instances those to be interviewed were told 'Don't go up there and tell them the weapon is not any good or tell them it's all good.' While this remark was probably intended to suggest that soldiers should give a balanced report considering all aspects of the rifle's performance, it should not have been made."

General Johnson—with only a few months left before his retirement—still pressed to find what went wrong and who was responsible for the gun malfunctions. But his investigators made little headway. On June 1, 1968, Johnson's review panel issued a confidential report. "The M16 rifle program was atypical of Army management programs and was further complicated by intense emotionalism throughout the Government," it concluded. "This rifle entered the inventory as an 'off-the-shelf' procurement and did not go through the normal research and development process." While the United States ramped up the war in Vietnam, "[c]hanges were made in the M16A1 and its ammunition by trial and error." When McNamara announced he would be sending tens of thousands of M16s to Vietnam, the army made no plans to ramp up training or cleaning equipment, the panel found. One of the more damning conclusions, buried in an appendix, blasted how the army accepted the switch to ball powder without making sure such a move was safe.

The panel's report named no names and dismissed the possibility of intentional negligence. It delivered no heads to General Johnson. But it didn't matter anymore. Johnson—the only top military official who wanted to find answers and punish those responsible for the M16 debacle—was headed out the door. Many in the army had expected him to be appointed chairman of the Joint Chiefs of Staff, but instead the general was forced into retirement, according to a biographer. Johnson left his post in early July 1968 and his replacement as army chief of staff was none other than William Westmoreland, shipped home from Vietnam to ride a desk until his retirement in 1972. With General Johnson's departure from the Pentagon and Westmoreland's arrival, impetus for further M16 investigations fizzled. The last thing Westmoreland wanted to do was draw attention to a failed rifle adoption that he had set in motion for a failed war that he had overseen.

The public also moved on, consumed by the chaos of a failing war, the assassinations of the Reverend Martin Luther King Jr. and Senator Robert F. Kennedy, riots, peace protests, bombings on campuses, and, on top of it all, a presidential election. President Johnson declined to run again. Many advocates of the military's adoption of the M16, with the exception of Westmoreland, were out of government, or on their way out. As McNamara became president of the World Bank, Curtis LeMay, retired from the air force in 1965, ran as a vice presidential candidate with the segregationist George Wallace. Midlevel bureaucrats at the Pentagon who had pushed the rifle were exiled. Godel was in prison; Hallock had "retired."

Although the war that Americans associated with the M16 was going horribly and would end in defeat for the United States, the M16 remained the military's rifle of choice. In the early 1960s, the army had initially procured a few thousand of Stoner's guns to test and examine. In fiscal year 1968, it bought more than 517,000. Colt's profits soared.

The M16 would play a key role in shifting U.S. strategy, as it tried to extricate its troops from direct combat and bolster local allies to take their place. The Pentagon supplied tens of thousands of M16s to South Vietnamese, Laotian, and Cambodian soldiers in a failed attempt to prop up those regimes. When South Vietnam collapsed in 1975, American television viewers saw images of piles of M16s cast off by fleeing government forces. Stoner's guns were in the hands of the conquering Communists.

By that time, the rifle was an improved version of the weapon the Pentagon had disastrously altered. The military had quietly fixed many of the problems it had created. The ammunition now was reliable. The gun had chrome plating in its chamber and bore. It had a new buffer to control the cyclic rate. Troops were cleaning the weapon often and receiving more training. The new version of Stoner's rifle, named the M16A1, worked better than its predecessor—but the cost to make those improvements had been bloody, full of mistakes and cover-ups.

Ichord had promised the American public that those responsible for causing the M16's malfunctions during the height of the Vietnam War would be brought to account. But Ichord's investigation had been hampered by obfuscation, misdirection, and finger-pointing by military officials. Those who lost loved ones or comrades because of the mistakes were left with only partial answers about what happened and why.

Marine Frank Bliss was handed an M16 soon after arriving in Vietnam. It jammed frequently. Decades later, he remained aggrieved that no one ever was held responsible.

"How many Marines and soldiers died at the cost of our using that rifle?" he asked. "We felt like guinea pigs."

PART II

13.

THE SPORTER

The Sporter looks like, feels like,
and performs like its military cousin.
—From an early Colt brochure for the AR-15

In February 1836, the inventor Sam Colt received a patent on a breech-loading revolver that would make him famous and rich. He was a tireless self-promoter with the single goal of selling as many guns as he could. While he awaited approval from the patent office in Washington, Colt lobbied his largest potential customer: the U.S. military. He urged officials in the army's Ordnance Department and the navy to test his new gun that could fire multiple times without reloading—an astonishing accomplishment for the time. At first, the tradition-bound military bureaucrats balked at his innovation. The Connecticut Yankee pivoted, marketing his guns to white Southerners, telling them that the inspiration for his multishot weapon had come when he was near the scene of a slave revolt and "was startled to think against what fearful odds the white planter must ever contend, thus surrounded by a swarming population of slaves."

By the 1850s, the federal government finally started buying his revolver in large quantities, and Colt used the imprimatur of that government connection to market his six-shooter to pioneers and prospectors joining America's western expansion. "These arms have no equals in quality and finish; are adopted by the Army and Navy of the United States," read one advertisement from 1861. Colt used battle scenes of Texas Rangers gunning down Comanches to promote his brand. Ahead of the Civil War, he sold guns to both the federal government and secessionist states. By the time Colt died at age forty-seven in 1862, he had produced more than four hundred thousand guns and amassed a $15 million fortune, a massive sum at the time.

The company he founded embraced his business approach after his death, and by the late 1800s, Colt six-shooters became an iconic symbol of the West, like cowboy hats or cowboy boots. As the Hartford-based Colt developed new firearms in the twentieth century, it followed the tried-and-true strategy: land large military contracts—then use those contracts as a marketing tool, a sort of unofficial stamp of approval, to market to anyone and everyone else who might buy the product. The Hartford factory kept busy primarily fulfilling military contracts, but it used any downtime to produce civilian guns with similar or exactly the same parts as the military guns. Few if any changes were required in production or worker training to make military or civilian weapons. When it worked well, it was a virtuous circle of sales and production. It was capitalism distilled and it made Colt one of the most well-known firearms manufacturers in the world.

In the 1960s, the company applied this legacy strategy to its recently acquired AR-15. Colt was making headway with McNamara's Pentagon. In 1963, the military placed an order for eighty-five thousand AR-15s, renamed M16s. That same year, Colt executives developed plans to market a version of the gun to civilians, calling it the Sporter, though the company originally considered calling it the Comanche. The gun, retailing for $189.50, was almost identical to its military counterpart, except it was semiautomatic and it was sold with a five-round magazine, fifteen rounds fewer than the standard magazine for an M16. No one thought a civilian would need any greater magazine capacity. Colt marketers hoped the Sporter could find a modest customer base among gun owners who needed a light, rapid-fire gun for backwoods or varmint hunting.

Colt reached out to influential gun writers such as R. A. Steindler, the managing editor of *Guns* magazine, to show off the Sporter and try to land some positive reviews. A Colt PR man called Steindler to find out whether he wanted to test "a civilian version of the AR-15 that would fire semi-auto." He jumped at the chance and raved about the gun in a glowing article published in the December 1964 issue of his magazine. He marveled at the gun's light recoil and military look. "The Sporter resembles the military rifle in all details, except for the full automatic firing feature," he wrote.

Colt used the rifle's military connections as a key component in its advertising. In an early brochure, the company described the rifle as "Colt's answer to the demand for a semi-automatic version of the AR-15 automatic rifle purchased by The United States Armed Forces." It boasted, "Painstaking engineering redesign efforts have resulted in a Government-approved conversion of the Colt AR-15 automatic rifle without sacrificing any performance or weight characteristics." The brochure highlighted Stoner's unique design that made it easy to keep the rifle on target while firing quickly: "Rapid semi-automatic fire is more controllable than with rifles of commercial design." In a magazine ad, Colt extolled the Sporter's similarities with the M16: "The Sporter looks like, feels like, and performs like its military cousin."

This time, the old Colt strategy wouldn't work—it would take decades for the gun to catch on and by then Colt would no longer be the primary maker of the civilian version of the rifle. Colt's early efforts to sell Stoner's rifle to civilians were a flop. The company marketed the gun as "a superb hunting partner," but sportsmen wanted polished wood stocks and crafted metal parts, not stamped aluminum and plastic. Hunters prided themselves on long-distance accuracy, on being able to fell game with a single accurate shot. What self-respecting hunter needed a rapid-fire rifle? They also saw little use for the .223 caliber bullet, just slightly larger than a .22 used by boys to shoot squirrels and rabbits, and not big enough to bring down large animals like deer. Colt produced only about 2,400 of the weapons in 1964, its first full year of production, and never made more than 5,000 a year until 1973, according to amateur historians analyzing serial number data. In contrast, Americans owned more than 90 million firearms by 1968, 35 million of which were rifles, according to the federal government.

Colt's decision to sell a civilian version of a military rifle caused no political uproar at the time—it went unnoticed. Gun control was a hot issue in the 1960s as violence flared and assassinations—including those of John F. Kennedy, his brother Robert, and Martin Luther King Jr.—rocked the nation. After his predecessor's death, President Lyndon Johnson pushed for major federal gun-control legislation, but lawmakers focused on mail-order guns like the one Lee Harvey Oswald had used to kill President Kennedy, as well as handguns used by criminals in robberies.

After years of lobbying, Johnson at last secured passage of the Gun Control Act of 1968, the most comprehensive piece of federal gun legislation since 1934, though it was much less expansive than what the White House had initially supported. "Today we begin to disarm the criminal and the careless and the insane," Johnson said at the White House signing in October 1968. "All of our people who are deeply concerned in this country about law and order should hail this day."

The NRA's opposition succeeded in trimming certain provisions from the bill—including a registry for gun owners. But the final bill passed with bipartisan support, and was largely regarded as a crime-fighting measure that was appropriate for a turbulent time. The NRA was primarily a sportsmen's association and though it did oppose the final bill, the group did not have the political force it would come to have later on. The year before the act was passed, California had enacted a law sponsored by Republican assemblyman Don Mulford that prohibited the carrying of loaded firearms without a permit. The act, supported and signed into law by Republican governor Ronald Reagan, was in direct response to Black Panther Party members carrying loaded firearms in public.

In the end, the 1968 federal law prohibited mail-order rifles like the one used to kill JFK and established a federal licensing system for gun manufacturers, dealers, and importers. The law made it illegal to sell guns across state boundaries unless through a licensed dealer. It also prohibited felons, fugitives, drug addicts, illegal aliens, and people dishonorably discharged from the armed forces from owning firearms at all.

The Sporter was not mentioned in the act—it was considered an obscure novelty, and rifles were not of particular concern to gun-control advocates at the time. A more robust gun-control act had been passed back in 1934. President Franklin Roosevelt signed the National Firearms Act, which imposed a $200 tax on machine guns and required them to be registered with the federal government. The law curtailed civilian ownership of weapons widely associated with gangster melees and bank robberies from the just-ended Prohibition era, but semiautomatics weren't covered.

If the AR-15 did not figure in the gun-control debate at the time, the black rifle was fused in the American consciousness with the war, its attendant horrors and ultimate failure. Americans for years watched news reports of exhausted soldiers trudging through rice paddies with the gun or spraying the weapon into underbrush at elusive foes. Photos in newspapers and magazines showed the gun next to the wounded and the dead.

Documentaries such as the Academy Award–winning *The Anderson Platoon* showed worried soldiers firing their M16s in the confusion of battle, as comrades died nearby. What became known as the My Lai massacre, the slaughter by U.S. soldiers of hundreds of unarmed Vietnamese civilians in March 1968, became public in 1969. Americans learned how soldiers had used M16s to gun down fleeing women, children, and elderly men. Attempts by hawks to cast the M16 as a tool for brave men fighting for democracy were met with derision. The 1968 movie *The Green Berets*, starring and codirected by John Wayne, presented M16s in a positive light. The movie featured a beefy older Wayne as an army colonel in Vietnam. It was filmed at Fort Benning and used extras and equipment (including M16s) borrowed from the army base with approval from President Johnson. Wayne, the first person to fire an AR-15 who wasn't an ArmaLite employee, gripped an M16 through much of the film and fired it during the final battle scene. The film was full of classic Wayne bravado. When a reporter in the movie complained about due process after soldiers beat a Communist spy, Wayne barked, "Out here due process is a bullet!" Such machismo played well in *The Sands of Iwo Jima* in 1949, but at the height of U.S. involvement in Vietnam, *The Green Berets* was panned by critics. Antiwar protesters picketed the film. Politicians later blasted Wayne and the military when it came out that the army provided M16s and other equipment at no cost.

Antiwar activists condemned the U.S. military for using the gun. The philosophers Bertrand Russell and Jean-Paul Sartre organized self-appointed tribunals to review alleged war crimes by the U.S. military in Vietnam. The tribunals declared that the M16's relatively small, high-velocity ammunition ripped through a body and exploded on impact just as dum-dum bullets did. The Hague Convention of 1899 had banned dum-dum bullets for use in warfare. Though the scientific evidence for the tribunal's claims was challenged by the United States, Swedish politicians and antiwar activists around the world argued that the very act of using an M16 constituted a war crime.

After the war, American books and movies presented the gun in a negative light, linking it with the horrors of war and defeat. In 1977, Michael Herr, who had been a reporter for *Esquire* in Vietnam, published his memoir *Dispatches*. The M16 figured in the book as a quintessentially American and violent tool, misused by troops trapped in a war they didn't want in a country they didn't understand. Herr watched a soldier fire his M16 into dead Viet Cong, ostensibly to make sure they were dead, but Herr presented it as emblematic of the war's overkill and casual violence. "Then I heard an M16 on full automatic starting to go through clips, a second to fire, three to plug in a fresh clip, and I saw a man out there, doing it," he wrote. "Every round was like a concentration of high-velocity wind, making the bodies wince and shiver."

In Michael Cimino's film *The Deer Hunter* (1978), Robert De Niro's character uses the rifle to spray a writhing Vietnamese soldier whom he already has set on fire with a flamethrower. In Francis Ford Coppola's *Apocalypse Now* (1979), written in part by Herr, the gun played a prominent role. American soldiers used M16s in their attack on a Vietnamese village. Men heading upriver carried the rifles as they sought to find the mad Colonel Kurtz, portrayed by Marlon Brando. When they encountered Kurtz's renegade army deep in the jungle, many of his lieutenants also held M16s next to bloodied corpses and severed heads at an abandoned temple.

Popular films linked Vietnam vets, mental illness, and M16s. One example was *First Blood*, Sylvester Stallone's 1982 story of a Vietnam vet and drifter named John Rambo who runs afoul of the law. The movie showed Stallone scrambling through the woods, gripping Stoner's rifle by its handle, as winded guardsmen struggled to keep up. The Rambo character, an ex–Green Beret who had been awarded the congressional Medal of Honor, was haunted by Vietnam flashbacks. Toward the end of the movie, Rambo's former colonel urged the tortured veteran to end his private war. "Nothing is over!" a sobbing Rambo shouted. "Nothing! You just don't turn it off!"

The gun's reputation with the public had little impact on its inventor. After the painful congressional hearings, Stoner had dropped out of the spotlight and was forgotten by the public—though his stature among weapons designers rose to an exalted state. He wore the mantle awkwardly. "He hated the attention and would complain about having to put on a suit and go talk to people," said Herb Roder, a machinist who worked with Stoner in Port Clinton at TRW. Stoner was much more comfortable in the workshop. He told everyone to call him Gene, and preferred talking with shop workers about technical problems.

"At lunchtime, I would be standing at the machine and he would come out of his office, and I'd offer him half of my sandwich," recalled Roder. "He'd sit down with me and he'd eat his half of the sandwich and we would just talk about anything."

In 1971, Stoner and Robert Bihun, an engineer from TRW, started a new weapons company, ARES Inc. Most people assumed it was named in honor of the Greek god of war. Stoner's daughter Susan remembered that it was an acronym for "Advanced Research Engineering Systems." Bihun said it stood for "Another Robert and Eugene Stoner enterprise."

Bihun, who was university trained, was amazed by how Stoner's mind worked. "I'd say, 'Look, Gene, here's what the situation is, here's what we need,'" Bihun recalled. "And he would sit there and scribble on the back of an envelope, and he would come up with a device that would solve the problem."

ARES started in Stoner's garage at his home near Port Clinton and grew to have 250 full- and part-time employees in Port Clinton offices as it won U.S. and foreign contracts. The booms of cannons resounded throughout the day from the testing grounds in Port Clinton. ARES work included a yearslong project with the shah of Iran's military to develop antiaircraft cannons. Stoner traveled to Iran often, meeting with the shah and generals. It all fell apart when Islamic revolutionaries overthrew the shah in 1979. Stoner and Bihun sold ARES to Chamberlain Manufacturing Corporation in 1987, making both men wealthy. Stoner also continued to make money from payments for Colt sales to the military, though he had nothing more to do with the gun's manufacture.

While the Sporter barely dented the larger civilian gun market, it was embraced early on by radical and extremist groups on both the far right and far left. Some argued that by using the AR-15, the oppressed could turn the tool of their oppressors against them. Others saw it simply as a weapon of war, and they considered themselves at war with society.

One of the first cases, perhaps the first case, of government agents seizing an AR-15 from an American citizen occurred in October 1964. Treasury Department agents and Los Angeles police raided the home of Robert Reign Romero, who they believed to be a member of a shadowy anti-Communist group called the Minutemen. The FBI considered it to be "a group of vigilante superpatriots" that believed citizens needed to train for guerrilla war because Communists had taken over the government, the media, and Hollywood. Romero, a movie usher in his early twenties, was charged with illegal possession of weapons and explosives. Officers seized dynamite, grenades, and thousands of rounds of ammunition from Romero's Van Nuys home, as well as numerous weapons, including seven machine guns, a Thompson submachine gun, an M1 carbine, and something agents had not encountered before: a brand-new Colt AR-15. California's attorney general linked Romero to the Minutemen in a report that he issued on extremists. Romero was fined and put on probation, and his guns were seized. Decades later, Romero denied he was in the Minutemen and said he bought the AR-15 as part of a plan to open a gun store. Romero remembered being unimpressed by the weird-looking gun and favored his traditional .22 caliber rifle. "I didn't get really into it," he said.

In the tumultuous 1960s and 1970s in the United States and around the world, self-styled revolutionary groups and militant political movements embraced firearms as symbols of empowerment for those battling oppression. No gun had more revolutionary cachet than the AK-47. It was the "people's gun," a symbol of liberation for guerrilla movements from the Philippines to Palestine, from South Africa to Nicaragua. Chinese propaganda posters featured heroic Chinese Communist soldiers gripping AKs. When the African nation of Mozambique gained independence from Portugal in 1975, the government put the AK-47 in its national emblem and on its flag. Fidel Castro gave AK-47s to Latin American leaders as gifts, a not-too-subtle call to join the revolution.

For some, the AR-15 was a potent symbol of rebellion against the powers that be. Black Panther publications carried numerous sketches of the gun. A cartoon in a December 1969 edition of *The Black Panther* newspaper showed a Black man holding the rifle and walking past several dead pigs in police uniforms. The gun was "seen in our communities carried by the gestapo pig forces. The AR-15 caliber .223 is the semi-automatic civilian model called 'sporting' model of the M16 used in Vietnam. The M16 fires either semi-auto or full auto. After the lives of many brothers were lost in Vietnam because the weapon was new and untested, it has now been de-bugged and is fairly reliable," an article in 1970 said.

Others used AR-15s in violent acts. In 1973, American Indian Movement (AIM) activists staged a seventy-one-day armed takeover of Wounded Knee, a village on South Dakota's Pine Ridge Reservation. The group did not have Stoner's gun, but the federal agents who surrounded the village had M16s—and afterward, some AIM members determined they needed similar firearms. AR-15 sales skyrocketed in the area in anticipation of a mini civil war, according to a local gun dealer. On June 26, 1975, a shootout took place in which two FBI agents, Jack R. Coler, twenty-eight, and Ronald A. Williams, twenty-seven, were killed by someone armed with an AR-15. The agents, who had handguns, fired only five rounds. Federal forensic experts determined that numerous rounds had been fired at the FBI agents, including 114 .223 caliber rounds fired from a single AR-15. Federal investigators determined the man who fired the AR-15 was Leonard Peltier, an AIM activist staying on the reservation. A federal jury found Peltier guilty of two counts of first-degree murder. During the trial, prosecutors played up the military origins of the rifle and how its ability to fire rapidly had overwhelmed the FBI agents. Peltier and his supporters have argued for decades that he did not commit the crimes, but appeals courts have upheld the conviction.

In a letter responding to a request for an interview, Peltier, in a federal prison in Florida, asked, "Why would you be writing too [sic] me asking for info about the AR15 Rifle?" He wrote that when he served in the Marines, he was trained on the M14, but did not acknowledge ever owning or using an AR-15. The Pine Ridge Reservation murders appear to be the first time a civilian version of Stoner's gun was used to kill Americans.

Around this time, the gun became a favorite of the Irish Republican Army as it battled British forces in Northern Ireland. In June 1974, four men with ties to Northern Ireland were convicted in a federal court in Baltimore of conspiring to buy AR-15s at local gun shops. They had planned to smuggle them to Irish Republican Army fighters in Northern Ireland, but British forces intercepted several shipments.

By the late 1970s, a white nationalist subculture in the United States embraced the AR-15 as a weapon it could use for what it saw as an inevitable race war. In 1978, William Luther Pierce, who founded a white nationalist organization, wrote a dystopian fantasy novel under the pseudonym Andrew Macdonald. Set in the early 1990s, *The Turner Diaries* had on its red cover a sketch of a white man and a white woman holding guns. The first edition showed the woman gripping one of Stoner's guns. A later edition showed the man firing the rifle. The novel's lead character was Earl Turner, part of a white underground resistance group. Turner used an M16 in the novel to shoot three Black people and a white sympathizer. A 1980 report by the Anti-Defamation League of B'nai B'rith found that white nationalists had set up guerrilla training centers across seven states. The groups were training with AR-15s, according to the report.

Paralleling these ominous developments was another disturbing trend: mass shootings carried out by lone gunmen. This modern American phenomenon erupted on the national scene in 1966, when a disturbed ex-Marine opened fire from the observation deck of the 307-foot-tall University of Texas tower in Austin, killing fourteen people and wounding dozens more. He used multiple weapons in his attack—not an AR-15. But the attack had profound cultural significance for the United States, inaugurating the bizarre social phenomenon of disturbed young men using guns to attack crowds of people they didn't know. The Texas shooting began a dark epoch and it was not long before mass shooters were drawn to the AR-15.

The first mass shooting of U.S. civilians with an AR-15 took place in the early morning hours of Saturday, July 23, 1977, when DeWitt Henry, a twenty-six-year-old unemployed truck driver, killed six people outside a nightclub in Klamath Falls, Oregon. Henry, whose wife had served him with divorce papers, had a history of drug and alcohol abuse and had recently attempted suicide. He drove his pickup to the club, which he had been kicked out of earlier, and began shooting at people in the parking lot. "It was somebody just sitting on a pickup truck waiting for anybody en masse he could find to pull the trigger on," said a witness. One of those killed was a woman who was eight months pregnant. Her unborn child died as well. Henry was taken into custody and he remains in prison. News stories noted that Henry had used an AR-15.

In June 1980, a forty-five-year-old former high school teacher about to go on trial for committing incest burst into a crowded Baptist church in Daingerfield, a small town in East Texas. Wearing a helmet, flak jacket, and military fatigues, Alvin Lee King carried an AR-15 and several other weapons. King opened fire with one of the other guns, then shouted to the 350 people in attendance, "This is war," and started firing again. Church members wrestled with him. King fled to a nearby fire station where he shot himself in the head with a .22 caliber pistol, but didn't die. He killed five people, including a seven-year-old girl. King hanged himself in jail.

Two years later, in Luzerne County in Pennsylvania's coal country, George Banks killed thirteen people in two homes—three girlfriends who were living with him, an ex-girlfriend, that woman's mother, seven children (five of them his own), and a bystander. He did it all with a borrowed AR-15. It remains the worst civilian mass shooting in Pennsylvania history. Banks was a misogynist gripped by unchecked anger and paranoid delusions. At the time of the shooting, the forty-year-old Black guard was working on a fantasy novel about a race war set in the state prison where he worked. At a party hours before he started shooting, Banks had admired a woman's T-shirt that read "Kill Them All and Let God Sort It Out." Banks and the woman traded shirts, angering one of his girlfriends and setting off an argument. Banks wore the shirt and military fatigues as he launched his killing spree. Banks was convicted of multiple counts of first-degree murder and sentenced to death. Later, a judge ruled Banks to be incompetent to be executed and he was sentenced to life in prison. Banks had stood on a bed to shoot down and kill a three-year-old whom a woman tried to shield, recalled Robert Gillespie, the county prosecutor who handled the case. "I felt the weapon should be banned for civilians," Gillespie said. "The devastation that was done by that gun was shocking to me." Gillespie made the lethality of the AR-15 a major part of Banks's prosecution.

Early in 1984, Tyrone Mitchell, a onetime member of Jim Jones's cult, opened fire with an AR-15 from his second-story apartment across the street from an elementary school playground in a low-income neighborhood of Los Angeles. Though most mass shooters had been white men, Mitchell was, like Banks, an exception. He was African American and his victims were as well. About a hundred children were coming out of the school to head home for the weekend when Mitchell started shooting. Children and teachers ran for cover. Mitchell emptied a thirty-round magazine in three minutes, killing ten-year-old Shala Eubanks, who bled to death in front of other children. Mitchell shot a passerby who also died. Mitchell killed himself as police closed in.

In 1987, an unemployed chemist and Vietnam veteran in Worcester, Massachusetts, saw Secretary of State George Shultz on television and announced in front of his worried mother, "Shultz, you're dead," before driving away with an AR-15, shotguns, and ammunition. The man had earlier threatened to kill President Reagan and had been hearing voices. His mother called local police, who in turn contacted State Department security. The man shouted to reporters as he was taken into custody that he was just a tourist and had planned to go hunting. "Ordinarily an AR-15 semiautomatic rifle and a sawed-off 12-gauge shotgun would not be the type of weapons a person would use for hunting purposes," a police spokesman said.

None of these incidents led to politicians' increased scrutiny of the gun as a particular concern. In fact, the only legislation dealing with firearms that Congress passed during this era was a measure to loosen gun restrictions. Ronald Reagan signed into law the 1986 Firearm Owners' Protection Act. It gave gun owners traveling through states with different gun laws more protections, allowed mail-order sales of ammunition, and prohibited a national gun registry. Helping to get the bill through the Democratic-led Congress, one provision banned the commercial sale and manufacture of new machine guns. It was the most consequential gun law since the one President Johnson had signed in 1968, and it reversed some of that law's restrictions. Yet both laws had something in common: neither mentioned the AR-15.

Stoner's patent for the weapon had expired in 1977 with little notice. The patent's end had no financial impact on Stoner or Colt, since they both continued to reap income from military contracts.

By this time, a few other companies began to build their own versions of the rifle for civilians. In the 1980s, these small gunmakers found a niche market: the growing number of gun owners who felt the world was unraveling and that they needed a military-style firearm. In 1985, the writer J. David McFarland argued in the *AR-15, M16 Assault Rifle Handbook* that the gun was increasingly popular with civilians because it was so close to the M16. The owner of such a rifle would be ready for war, McFarland wrote: "Many of the people purchasing the AR-15 today are survivalists who feel that if and when the ultimate chaos hits (whether from nuclear war, natural disaster, economic collapse or whatever), the old .30–30 that they carry into the woods every fall just won't cut the mustard in a prolonged firefight." The gun wasn't considered much use for home defense, but could be used in combat if society collapsed.

The rifle became more common at gun stores and at the range. Ads for versions of the AR-15 appeared more often in gun magazines. Marketers in the 1980s frequently used the phrase "assault rifle" to advertise AR-15s—and saw nothing wrong with the term. They sought to evoke the gun's military origins. The term had become accepted in military circles as a broad descriptor for a class of select-fire military rifles.

"The idea of calling semi-automatic versions of military small arms 'assault weapons' did not originate with either anti-gun activists, media or politicians," according to Joe Tartaro, a leading gun rights advocate who was president of the Second Amendment Foundation. "The term 'assault weapon' was first corrupted by importers, manufacturers, wholesalers and dealers in the American firearms industry to stimulate sales of selected 'exotica'-firearms which did not have a traditional appearance."

Like Colt had done before them, these small companies promoted the military connections of the gun and used the term "assault rifle" as a selling point. In an era where survivalists became a growing niche among gun buyers and Ronald Reagan focused on restoring public pride in the U.S. military, promoting these military-style firearms made great sense.

"Back then you'd open up the safe and [say] 'Oh, *this* is an assault rifle,'" said Randy Luth, the founder of DPMS Panther Arms, an early AR-15 maker. "That was more prevalent back in the eighties and early nineties . . . before all the negative press."

14.

BIG GUNS COME IN

Once you start shooting, the endorphins kick in, it's like a drug
and it's hard to stop. The guns take over and you lose control.
—Kirkton Moore

Kirkton Moore stood at the glass counter, his eyes scanning the rows of guns on the wall: Uzis, AK-47s, shotguns, and his favorite, the AR-15. The twenty-four-year-old wore a burgundy golf cap, a red and black button-down, a gold chain, khakis, and white Converse sneakers with red laces. It was the uniform for the Harvard Park Brims, one of many gangs battling in the streets of South Central Los Angeles in 1985.

A skinny woman stood next to Moore, fidgeting. She was the aunt of one of his girlfriends and he'd given her a crack rock to go gun shopping with him. Moore had a criminal record: arrests for robbery and drug sales. He needed someone else to put their name down on the purchase. A black AR-15 caught Moore's eye. He'd seen the gun in movies such as Stallone's *First Blood*.

"This is what I want," Moore thought. "We're fighting a war."

A salesman took the AR-15 down from the wall and put it on the counter next to a box of ammunition. The woman filled out the paperwork. Moore took out his money roll and peeled off nine $100 bills—the going rate for such a weapon. The salesman didn't ask questions. He handed Moore the AR-15 with no box or wrapping. In the parking lot, Moore gave the woman another crack rock.

The Harvard Park Brims took their name from the fedoras they liked to wear, and Moore would wear his with sixty-two red-tipped matches stuck in the hatband; the number represented the street they were from, and the color of the matches was a tribute to the Bloods, their much larger allies in the city's gang wars. The Brims' neighborhood was surrounded on all sides by the rival Crips, who wore blue. The Brims' survival strategy was simple: "We got to be twice as hard as these dudes."

Kirkton Phenor Moore was born in 1961. Moore and his three siblings were raised by a single mother, a social worker. He joined the neighborhood gang when he was in sixth grade and it became like his family, he said. They nicknamed him "Kirk Dog." The Brims hung out, stole from stores, smoked weed, got into fistfights and occasional knife fights with the other gangs. Shootings were rare when Moore was young. For a while, the gang only had two guns, both stolen: a .22 caliber pistol and a single-shot .410 shotgun. They'd take them to parties, but they were for show.

Crack cocaine changed everything, flooding L.A.'s poor neighborhoods with money—and guns—as gangs fought for territory, product, and customers. "The money was coming in so fast and we were spending it so fast," Moore recalled. "Gold chains, clothes, cars." Moore bought himself expensive classic cars. He had three or four girlfriends at any one time.

With their newfound wealth, the gangs also entered into an expensive arms race.

"When crack cocaine came into L.A., that's when the big guns came," Moore recalled.

Drive-by shootings became common. Their enemies, the Crips, armed themselves with semiautomatic versions of AK-47s, Uzis, and even M1 carbines. The Brims needed more firepower.

Moore, who had risen in the gang's ranks, went to Western Surplus, the store that sold gang attire and guns. Moore believed the AR-15 could be an equalizer. "In our minds, we're nothing but soldiers fighting a war," he said. "It is a war and because they got heavy artillery, you got to get heavy artillery."

An endless cycle of revenge killings swept South Central. One day in the late 1980s, the Brims were drinking and remembering some of their dead gang members.

"When you get drunk and tipsy, you get emotional and then you're like 'Let's go get these dudes,'" Moore said.

Moore and three other gang members drove to a rival gang's street in what they called an "undercover bucket," a cheap, inconspicuous car registered to someone else that they used for shootings and running drugs. Moore got out, popped the trunk, and grabbed his AR-15. Two of the other Brims had semiautomatic pistols. Moore walked up the middle of the street and opened fire with his AR-15 at the rival gang members selling drugs on the sidewalk.

"They scattered; they duck; they fall," he remembered.

Shooting the gun gave Moore a feeling of euphoria.

"Once you start shooting, the endorphins kick in, it's like a drug and it's hard to stop," he said. "The guns take over and you lose control."

The attack on the rival drug dealers lasted just minutes. The other gang fled, firing a few shots in retreat.

"How long's that fight going to last?" he said. "You've got the biggest gun, the most bullets."

Back in the car driving home, one of the younger kids told him that all the Brims needed guns like the AR-15.

The kid's view made sense to Moore. He saw himself as a soldier. He used military tactics, taping together thirty-round magazines just like grunts had done in Vietnam. He felt no moral pang about shooting rival gang members—they were the enemy.

"People get Purple Hearts for killing other people," Moore said. "Now you want me to feel sympathy when someone's trying to kill me and I kill him?"

The violence escalated and spilled out of South Central. In January 1988, a twenty-seven-year-old woman shopping in L.A.'s fancy Westwood neighborhood was killed by a stray bullet. Los Angeles police chief Daryl Gates responded by launching a massive effort to smash the gangs. Gates became a cop in Los Angeles in 1949 and later helped create the first SWAT team in the country. He became chief in 1978.

In response to complaints from civil rights groups, Gates blamed Black people for the injuries they sustained from police choke holds, claiming that their "arteries do not open up as fast as they do in normal people." Rank-and-file cops felt Gates had their back. He pushed for years for officers to be issued better weapons than .38 caliber revolvers. Such outdated firearms were no match against criminals with semiautomatic handguns, he argued. In 1986, Gates issued 9 mm semiautomatic handguns to his officers. "But by then, the arms race had escalated another notch," he later wrote.

Semiautomatic versions of AKs and Uzis flooded South Central. Investigators at the scenes of drive-by shootings started picking up thirty, sixty, even seventy spent casings. The high-velocity bullets sailed through walls and cars, hitting bystanders.

Then came September 3, 1988. It was Labor Day weekend and Moore, twenty-seven, was home after drinking with friends when he got a call from a girlfriend. She told him that Crips had attacked her and her family at a picnic. She wanted revenge.

Earlier that night, officers Daniel Pratt and Veronica Delao had been sent to an undercover stakeout in South Central. The thirty-year-old Pratt had joined the LAPD in 1982 after serving in the Marines. He started patrolling in a relatively peaceful area, but he craved action and transferred to the Seventy-Seventh Street Division in South Central. Though he had three young children at home, Pratt didn't shy from dangerous assignments. On the evening of September 3, Pratt and Delao, wearing plain clothes, drove a Chevy Camaro they used for undercover work. It was blue to make it easier for them to blend in while driving through Crips territory. Delao drove to a liquor store in South Central that had been robbed three times that day. The officers parked the car next to the store and waited.

Moore and his girlfriend, in a yellow 1976 Pontiac, a Brims undercover bucket, drove to the same neighborhood—but for a different purpose. Moore was cradling his AR-15. As they rolled by a group of Crips, Moore pointed the rifle out the window and fired multiple rounds. He hit two gang members in the legs. He also hit a young woman who was doing her laundry at her home nearby. Moore and his girlfriend sped away.

Pratt and Delao heard the gunfire. Their police radio gave bare details: a drive-by, three people down. A car with its headlights off zoomed by and the police officers gave chase, assuming it was the shooter's vehicle. Delao gunned the motor, but the car without headlights darted into an alley and then into a doughnut shop parking lot. Delao stopped the car, grabbed the radio, and described the suspect's vehicle, a yellow Pontiac. Pratt drew his handgun. The man in the Pontiac's passenger seat turned around, pointing what looked like a black rifle at them through the back window, but didn't fire. The Pontiac peeled out onto the street, the Camaro close behind. The Pontiac veered into a gas station and Pratt and Delao pulled in behind it. Pratt jumped out of the car and called for backup. The Pontiac made a U-turn around the gas pumps, then headed straight for the officers. Pratt jumped back into the Camaro and lowered himself down, gripping his gun. Who fired the first shot is a matter of dispute, but what happened next is not. As the Pontiac drove by, Moore opened fire with his AR for the second time that night, the fusillade striking the radiator and the blue metal hood of the Camaro. Pratt planted one foot on the pavement, leaned back in the seat, keeping as much of his body behind the engine block as possible. He fired with his handgun in the space between the open door and the windshield. One bullet hit the Pontiac's tire. Pratt fired fifteen times, until his gun's magazine was empty. But Moore had more firepower: his AR-15 had a thirty-round magazine. One bullet tore into Pratt's face, right above the lip. He lurched back in the seat. His empty gun clattered on the pavement. Delao rushed to his side. He was dying.

Pratt, who had been trained on the M16 in the Marine Corps, had been killed by a civilian version of Stoner's gun, just a few miles from where Stoner first invented it. Pratt's widow, Andria, was pregnant with the couple's fourth child when she got the news.

The day after the shooting, Gates pounded the table as he spoke at a press conference. "You have an officer," Gates said, "a young man like this, who is a member of the family, who also has a family, who has a child he will never see . . . four young kids growing up without a father, because you've got no-good miserable sons of bitches out there . . . this society continues to allow to roam the streets."

Pratt's death by an AR-15 was too much for the chief. "I decided it was time to try to halt this nonsense," Gates later wrote.

Gates began a campaign to ban AR-15s and other semiautomatic weapons from civilian use. Gates had never backed gun-control efforts in the past, but the chaos in Los Angeles drew him to the conclusion that AR-15s, Uzis, AK-47s, and similar weapons didn't belong in what he called "a complex urban society." Gates's strident position on assault weapons cost him friends. One suggested that if Gates needed help in dealing with the criminal element, he should ask the ACLU from now on.

Gates joined other big-city police chiefs. Joseph McNamara, the police chief of San Jose, California, warned that semiautomatic weapons like AR-15s should be banned or "the U.S. is going to look like Beirut, with police officers walking around with these weapons slung over their shoulders—police are going to demand equal firepower." Rank-and-file officers feared for their lives, recalled Robert Scully, a Detroit cop who was head of the National Association of Police Organizations, a large association of police unions. "For police officers in Detroit and other cities the weapon of choice was the .38 police special—six rounds and you've got to reload," Scully recalled. "We were terribly outgunned on the street with the AR-15s and the AK-47s."

The day after Pratt's murder, Moore—who had gotten away—watched the news about the killing and claimed that it was then he realized he had shot a cop, not a Crip. Because of the blue car and officers wearing plain clothes, Moore said he thought he'd been firing at rival gangsters. Moore and his girlfriend went to Las Vegas to hide out. He left behind everything, including the AR-15 used in the shooting. Police recovered it from the trunk of one of his cars.

About two thousand people attended Pratt's funeral at a cemetery in Covina, California. Police helicopters passed overhead and Chief Gates handed a flag to Pratt's widow.

The LAPD considered Moore the prime suspect. On Sunday, October 23, about two months after the killing, the television program

America's Most Wanted reenacted Pratt's killing for American television viewers and publicized a $40,000 reward.

Moore, knowing he was trapped, turned himself in. He was convicted of first-degree murder and sentenced to life in prison without the possibility of parole.

In November, Gates and McNamara, along with other law enforcement leaders in California, began working with the state attorney general, a Democrat, to draft legislation banning what they called "assault-type" weapons. In Sacramento, California's capital, the Democratic lawmakers David Roberti and Mike Roos, both from the Los Angeles area, vowed to sponsor the legislation in the coming session. Roberti and Roos knew it would be a tough fight against the NRA. But they had new allies: police chiefs and rank-and-file cops. Many Americans at the time—and almost every officeholder—viewed police officers as heroes in the fight against violent crime that was skyrocketing in American cities in the late 1980s. The backing of the police might just be enough to offset opposition from gun owners.

15.

BUSH BAN

I'm getting pretty sick and tired of presenting flags to widows
and little kids and trying to explain away why it is we have an
arms race in the United States.

—Los Angeles police chief Daryl Gates

When George Herbert Walker Bush ran for president in 1988, his campaign won the backing of the National Rifle Association. Bush wanted the support of the group, with its almost three million members and large reservoir of campaign funds, to help him win over the blue-collar voters who had carried Ronald Reagan to victory for two terms. Unlike his predecessor, who had a folksy, cowboy image, Bush was a New England patrician, viewed by many Americans as elitist and aloof. He was prone to malaprops, and known for his cautious approach to thorny issues. On gun policy, he took cues from police chiefs. As a young Texas congressman, he backed the 1968 Gun Control Act. Others from the Texas delegation voted against it, but Bush explained to constituents that the bill had an "emphasis on helping local law enforcement." During the 1988 campaign, Bush accused Democratic candidate Michael Dukakis of being a gun-control advocate. The NRA spent millions to defeat Dukakis and printed ads like "DUKAKIS WANTS TO BAN GUNS IN AMERICA." Guns ended up playing only a minor role in the presidential campaign, which was dominated by Bush's attacks on Dukakis for being soft on crime.

But three days before Bush was sworn in as president, guns—specifically military-style semiautomatic rifles—became a pressing issue in America. On January 17, 1989, a man armed with an AK-47 opened fire on a crowded elementary school playground in Stockton, California. Patrick Purdy fired his rifle 105 times from the edge of the schoolyard, killing five children and wounding thirty-one others, before he killed himself. The twenty-four-year-old targeted Cleveland Elementary School because it was in a neighborhood of Southeast Asian immigrants. Two weeks before the attack, the white out-of-work welder cursed Vietnamese immigrants while drinking at a Stockton bar. "You're going to read about me in the papers," he told other patrons.

It was the worst shooting at an elementary school in the country's history. Hilary Rogers, a Stockton school trustee, was stunned. "Do we need a plan where kids are told to hit the deck like air raid drills we used to have when I was a kid?" she asked.

At first, the response from the Republican White House was muted. Reagan didn't say anything publicly about the school attack. When Bush gave his inaugural address on January 20, he gave no indication of how he would respond to the massacre.

Americans clamored for the new president to take action. They saw photos of crying parents and frightened teachers. They heard accounts of children running from gunfire. They saw images of the AK-47 that Purdy had used and were surprised to learn that anyone could buy such military-style, semiautomatic rifles at gun stores. At that time, most rifle owners in America were hunters. Most used wood-stocked bolt or lever-action guns. If they had a semiautomatic rifle, it didn't look anything like an AK-47. Purdy's gun resembled something that fighters would carry in the Middle East. Even the man who sold Purdy the gun for $349.95 at a gun store in Oregon said he rarely stocked AKs and had only ordered one because a few customers had been talking about them.

The Stockton schoolyard massacre prompted a moment of deep reflection among liberals, conservatives, police chiefs, and even gun industry executives about whether these types of guns—including

AR-15s—belonged in civilian hands. It shifted America's political discourse away from handguns to military-style semiautomatic rifles, a shift that would have long-lasting consequences.

Before Stockton, the leading gun-control group Handgun Control Inc. struggled to get lawmakers to introduce legislation to ban military-style semiautomatic rifles, recalled Bernie Horn, a Handgun Control Inc. attorney. "The Stockton schoolyard massacre was like 9/11 for the gun debate," Horn remembered. "It changed everything. Where before I was calling up legislators saying, 'Would you introduce a bill?' Now they were calling me and saying, 'I want to ban assault weapons.'"

Federal and state lawmakers proposed bills targeting the AK-47s and guns like them. Ohio Democratic senator Howard Metzenbaum introduced a bill to regulate them in the same way that the United States regulated machine guns: banning new manufacture and forcing current owners to register their weapons with the federal government. "We know of only one instance in which [an AK-47] was used for hunting," Metzenbaum said, "when a psychopath in California went hunting for school children." In California, Democrats introduced a similar ban with the support of police leaders such as Chief Daryl Gates and even the state's Republican governor, George Deukmejian.

These lawmakers immediately seized a rhetorical advantage by calling the guns they were seeking to ban "assault rifles." Though the phrase had been used by gunmakers for marketing in the 1980s and some of the nation's leading gun writers had adopted it as well, gun-control activists found they could use it to advance their cause. When Art Agnos, a California state assemblyman, proposed legislation to restrict the sale of such guns in 1985, he described them as "assault rifles." Agnos filed the bill after an out-of-work security guard used a semiautomatic version of an Israeli gun in his massacre of twenty-one people at a McDonald's in Southern California. Agnos was focused on the Uzi, but he also included the AR-15 because it was the semiautomatic version of the gun he'd used while in the military. Agnos said he used "assault rifle" to describe the AR-15 because of its military pedigree and because it was the phrase the gun industry used.

"It didn't hurt that it had an ominous interpretation," he added. "Assault is a serious word."

Agnos never got his bill passed. But the phrase "assault rifle" caught on among gun-control advocates. Josh Sugarmann, founder of the Violence Policy Center in Washington, popularized the term as he lobbied lawmakers for stricter gun laws. Sugarmann had worked as the spokesman for the National Coalition to Ban Handguns, but he realized by the 1980s that a federal ban on handguns was unlikely. He decided to focus on guns such as AK-47s, Uzis, and AR-15s, which he labeled "assault weapons." Sugarmann issued a report in late 1988 called *Assault Weapons and Accessories in America*. He and a coauthor argued that activists could draw more attention to their cause by focusing on these guns. "The weapons' menacing looks, coupled with the public's confusion over fully automatic machine guns versus semi-automatic assault weapons—anything that looks like a machine gun is assumed to be a machine gun—can only increase the chance of public support for restrictions on these weapons," they wrote. They argued that the issue could drive a wedge between police and the gun lobby. He sent the report to lawmakers and the Washington media. It was largely ignored until Stockton.

The NRA and its chief lobbyist, Wayne LaPierre, led the opposition. Though he was an important leader in the battle against the proposed gun laws, many in the gun-rights movement found him strange. LaPierre was often seen fumbling with large sheaves of paper as he walked the halls of Congress, giving him the appearance of a harried political science professor, not a Washington power broker. He was an awkward man who didn't look people in the eye. The onetime NRA lobbyist Richard Feldman said that LaPierre was like an amoeba and lacked a spine. Strangely, he seemed uncomfortable around guns. Yet LaPierre thrived in his post. He had studied the way Washington worked and became an expert at persuading lawmakers to fall in line with the wishes of his members, many of whom were one-issue voters. That issue was gun rights.

The NRA had transformed—beginning in the 1970s—from an

association of sportsmen into a political force laser-focused on fighting gun control. The key moment came at the group's 1977 annual meeting in Cincinnati when a band of Second Amendment absolutists took the reins of the NRA in a surprise parliamentary maneuver. They were angry at NRA leaders who wanted to move the group's headquarters from Washington to Colorado to focus more on conservation and sport shooting, and less on politics. The dissidents didn't want the NRA to be a Sierra Club with guns. After what became known as "the Revolt at Cincinnati," the NRA adopted a much more strident approach to gun laws. By 1989, some of the leaders of the revolt had been pushed out for being too extreme, but the NRA maintained a hard edge.

Soon after Bush's inauguration, LaPierre and James Jay Baker, another NRA lobbyist, visited White House deputy political director David Carney and reminded him that Bush had vowed to oppose any new gun laws if elected. Carney assured them that Bush's opposition to gun control "hadn't changed."

Indeed, a month after the shooting, Bush said he would fight any gun ban. "I'm not about to suggest that a semiautomated [sic] hunting rifle be banned. Absolutely not," he said.

But even Bush's family wanted him to take action. Asked whether she thought weapons like the one used at Stockton should be outlawed, Barbara Bush told a reporter, "They should be, absolutely."

Chief Gates, Bush's close ally in the "War on Drugs," pressed for the new president to restrict civilian ownership of military-style semiautomatic rifles. He told a Senate committee that "these weapons must be abolished." Much of the focus had been on Purdy's AK-47, but Gates told the senators about how Officer Pratt had been killed with an AR-15.

"That officer would be alive today if he had not been confronted by an assault rifle," Gates said, adding that gang members loved the weapons for drive-by shootings. "They don't have to aim. They don't have to be sportsmen. They don't have to be marksmen. They just spray."

The chief issued a warning to the NRA. "Those who object to gun control had better pay attention: we in law enforcement are facing up to this every day and I'm getting pretty sick and tired of presenting flags to widows and little kids and trying to explain away why it is we have an arms race in the United States."

Bush didn't want to anger the NRA, but he was uneasy over the prospect of a public battle with police. Bush had made backing police a central part of his presidential campaign. On February 19, 1989, as he readied for a trip to Asia, the president sent a memo to his chief of staff, John Sununu.

"BEFORE WE LEAVE ON OVERSEAS TRIP PLEASE ASSIGN SOMEONE IN OUR SHOP TO FOLLOW UP ON AK 47 MATTER. I DO NOT LIKE BEING OPPOSITE THE POLICE ON THIS ONE," the memo said. "I'D LIKE TO HAVE SOME SUGGESTION READY WHEN WE GET BACK. A GOOD ITEM TO GET OUT FRONT ON PROVIDED A REASONBLWE [sic] ANSWER CAN BE FOUND."

A Gallup poll found that 72 percent of Americans surveyed favored federal legislation banning the "semi-automatic assault guns, such as the AK-47."

"The dynamics of the gun control debate may be changing," a Bush domestic policy aide warned in a memo. "The numbers of citizens and police now being gunned down continues to increase. The AK-47 incident in Stockton, California, where five children were killed in a schoolyard, produced a tremendous public outcry against this particular weapon and other so-called 'assault weapons.'"

Momentum for bans swelled. On March 13, the California State Assembly voted to ban a variety of military-style semiautomatic weapons, including Uzis, AK-47s, and AR-15s. The next day the White House announced that it would temporarily block the importation of more than a hundred thousand "semi-automatic, assault-type weapons." The AR-15 wasn't included because it was made in America. Bush told reporters that there needed to be accommodation between the interests of police and sportsmen. Imports of AK-47s and guns like them had been rising from four thousand in 1986 to forty-four thousand in 1988, according to the Bureau of Alcohol, Tobacco, and Firearms. Sununu called the temporary ban "a place to draw a line that is comfortable."

After the import ban was announced, Colt, the largest maker of AR-15s, declared that it would stop selling its rifle to civilians. "We sense a great concern on the part of the government toward the possible inappropriate misuse of semiautomatic weapons," a Colt spokesman said. "We're responding to that concern." Colt's decision reflected the charged atmosphere after Stockton. But it was largely a public relations move. Military sales were how Colt made most of its money. The company had sold 279,000 semiautomatic AR-15s in the twenty-five years since it was introduced, the gun historian Edward Ezell estimated in 1989. Over the same period, it had sold millions of M16s to the military. Colt's public position was that Bush's import ban had caused the company to feel "a social and civic responsibility to review and suspend the sale of the AR-15 Sporter." The company would wait for the outcome of the Bush administration's ninety-day review of the imported weapons ban before making a permanent decision, it said.

The NRA hated the import ban, as well as state ban proposals. In the April issue of *American Rifleman*, the NRA argued that the AR-15 and other guns labeled "assault rifles" were no different from any other semiautomatic weapon. The issue's cover had photos of semiautomatic guns: hunting rifles, handguns, AK-47s, and AR-15s, under the headline "ALL THE SAME." One of the more popular guns in the country, the Ruger 10/22, was a .22 caliber varmint-hunting rifle with a traditional look that was semiautomatic. Glock's polymer handgun, then beginning to draw gun owners away from revolvers, was also semiautomatic. In the same issue, J. Warren Cassidy, the NRA's executive vice president, recast a famous anti-Nazi poem to defend people owning guns such as the AR-15.

"In America, they came first for the machine guns, and I didn't speak up because I wasn't a machine gunner," Cassidy wrote. "Then, they came for the handguns, and I didn't speak up because I wasn't a handgunner. Then, they came for the semi-autos, and I didn't speak up because I wasn't a semi-auto owner."

The NRA's staunch position caused some of the country's leading conservatives to sour on the gun organization. Former Arizona senator

Barry Goldwater, the founder of modern American conservatism who'd appeared in NRA advertisements, broke with the group over its stance on semiautomatic weapons. "I've never used an automatic or a semiautomatic for hunting," Goldwater said. "There's no need for it. They have no place in anybody's arsenal. If any SOB can't hit a deer with one shot, then he ought to quit shooting."

Pressure built in Congress, where Democrats controlled both the Senate and the House. Metzenbaum's bill advanced, but Bush's staff was more worried about a bill proposed by Senator Dennis DeConcini, a pro-gun Democrat from Arizona. DeConcini wanted to ban more than a dozen specific weapons, including Colt's AR-15. He had been backed by the NRA in the past, but he was so taken aback by Stockton that he decided to introduce the bill. "I said, 'Dennis, you're somebody who might be able to do something because the NRA likes you and you're not considered a screaming liberal,'" DeConcini recalled. His bill was much narrower than Metzenbaum's.

Inside the White House, Bush staffers searched for middle ground. In a memo entitled "Assault Weapons," they wrote that supporting DeConcini's approach would "be viewed favorably by those who are deeply concerned about the proliferation of so-called 'assault weapons,'" but it would also be viewed as "a major reversal of position by gun owners as represented by the NRA." A more promising option was to support restrictions on sales of magazines that could hold a lot of rounds, they suggested. Limiting magazine capacity would make it more difficult for gang members or mass shooters to fire so many bullets.

Bush's staff found that unlike banning certain types of guns, the idea of limiting the size of magazines was politically palatable to conservatives and gun groups. The NRA would "reluctantly go along with a provision banning large magazines," they wrote.

One leading advocate for magazine-capacity limits was a titan in the American gun industry, William Batterman Ruger. Gruff and outspoken, Ruger was a legend among gunmakers. He had turned a boyhood love of hunting into one of the country's largest gunmakers, Sturm Ruger & Co. Ruger designed the guns he wanted to own, said Jim

Sullivan, the ArmaLite draftsman who worked on the AR-15. Sullivan went to work for Ruger in the late 1960s to help design the Mini-14, a wood-stocked semiautomatic rifle that resembled the army's ill-fated M-14. The basic model, called the Ranch Rifle, was priced under $200, and when it was first introduced it outsold Colt's AR-15.

Ruger didn't like guns like the AR-15 that were civilian versions of modern military weapons. He felt they didn't comport with the image of the American gun owner. Ruger told Sullivan that he didn't want the Mini-14 to look like an AR-15 because he didn't want neighbors to call the police when they saw someone with one of his guns. Ruger sent a letter to Congress, arguing that many common handguns and hunting rifles were also semiautomatic. "THEREFORE TO DEFINE 'SEMI-AUTOMATIC FIREARM' AS SYNONYMOUS WITH 'ASSAULT WEAPON' IS AKIN TO DEFINING ALL 'HATS' AS 'HELMETS' OR ALL 'VEHICLES' AS 'TANKS,'" Ruger said. The way to limit the carnage on the streets was to limit magazine capacity.

"By a simple, complete and unequivocal ban on large capacity magazines, all the difficulty of defining 'assault rifles' and 'semi-automatic rifles' is eliminated," Ruger wrote. "Regulating large capacity magazines seems the best way to respect the rights of everyone—the hunter, target shooter, collector and the general public—while depriving the drug lords of their firepower."

The pragmatist Bush embraced Ruger's idea as a middle ground. In May, at a memorial in Washington for police officers killed in the line of duty, Bush unveiled his crime package that he planned to present to Congress. "We're going to take back the streets," he told the audience. His plan: stiffen prison sentences for gun crimes, expand the use of the federal death penalty, build more prisons, boost law enforcement funding, and limit the capacity of magazines to fifteen rounds. "One thing that we do know about these assault weapons is that they invariably are equipped with unjustifiably large magazines," Bush said. In July, the Bush administration made the import ban permanent and expanded its list of the models that were barred. It was the most significant move by a Republican president to curtail gun sales in the country's history.

The Stockton massacre, the cop killings, and the violence hitting American cities had caused a Republican president and leaders of a Democratic-led Congress to find a compromise. "They were willing to talk about it because if it made a big difference and addressed the issue that'd be great," Sununu recalled.

But many gun owners felt betrayed. Letters flooded into the White House. "When you first came out and stated you were against any further restrictions against semi-automatic rifles, pistols and shotguns, I applauded," one man wrote. "I just do not understand how you could change your position in this short time." Gun owners across the country called on Cassidy, the NRA head, to revoke Bush's membership. In Congress, the ban on high-capacity magazines that Bush had proposed was stripped from his proposed crime package by pro-gun politicians. Metzenbaum's bill went nowhere. DeConcini's narrowly passed the Senate in 1990, but it died in the House. Those who had backed compromise faced blowback from those who saw efforts to regulate semiautomatics as an attack on the Second Amendment. In 1991, Cassidy was pushed out by hard-liners in part because of his unwillingness to sever ties with Bush.

Bush's interest in gun regulations waned over the rest of his time in office, though the import ban remained in place. He faced a host of international challenges: the collapse of the Soviet Union, the invasion of Panama, and the Persian Gulf War. Throughout his presidency, gun owners never forgave him. As Bush headed toward an election year, he tried to repair the relationship. He threatened to veto a crime bill that included new background check system and a five-day waiting period for buying handguns. The legislation had been named for James Brady, Reagan's press secretary who had been shot and disabled in the 1981 assassination attempt on the president. The bill had the backing of Reagan, who also had been wounded in that attack. But Bush's veto threat helped stall the legislation in late 1991. Sarah Brady, James Brady's wife and the leading voice for gun control, said the backlash from gun owners over Bush's import ban "ultimately ensured that President Bush never lifted a finger to help with the Brady bill."

Facing a serious challenge from the Arkansas Democratic gover-nor, Bill Clinton, and the Independent candidate, Ross Perot, a Texas billionaire, Bush needed all the support he could get. The NRA had endorsed Bush four years earlier. But it didn't make an endorsement this time. The NRA wanted Bush to pay a political price for blocking imports of AK-47s after Stockton. In doing so, the group aided in the election of a man who would spearhead the most wide-reaching gun ban in American history, a ban that would include the AR-15.

16.

THREE SENATORS

Some of the difficulty in dealing with people who were working
on this legislation is that they weren't familiar with firearms.
—Brad Buckles

Howard Metzenbaum, the seventy-six-year-old senator from Ohio with a leonine shock of white hair, read the newspaper in disgust. Another mass shooting. A man had walked into a downtown San Francisco law firm and killed eight people on July 1, 1993, with two semiautomatic weapons. Metzenbaum, livid, flung the paper across the room as staffers watched. He had been fighting for years for stricter gun laws and had gotten nowhere. In the Senate, liberal colleagues looked to Metzenbaum as the "conscience of the Senate." Conservatives found him to be an obstructionist, showing little interest in compromise. An unnamed Capitol Hill staffer once called Metzenbaum a "knee-jerk liberal, with an emphasis on 'jerk.'"

The angry Metzenbaum realized it was an opportune moment to launch a renewed attack on semiautomatic weapons, including the AR-15. Polls showed that a growing majority of Americans wanted a federal ban. Democrats controlled the White House and both chambers of Congress. Though President Bill Clinton had been noncommittal on a federal assault-weapons ban during his campaign and the early days of his presidency, he now supported one.

"We finally thought we had some momentum. We had a president that we felt was supportive. We had the support of the major police groups. We felt that with the recent incidents of gun violence all of this was a perfect storm in our favor," recalled Mike Lenett, Metzenbaum's counsel on the Senate Judiciary Committee. "We moved to strike."

Three Democratic senators—Metzenbaum, Arizona's Dennis De-Concini, and one of the newest members of the chamber, California's Dianne Feinstein—led the attack. In 1989, Metzenbaum had proposed banning the manufacture and sale of semiautomatic weapons that could hold more than ten shots. But the broad prohibition, which would have included hundreds of types of guns, received just seventeen votes on the Senate floor. Prior to the San Francisco shooting, Metzenbaum had submitted a bill for a narrower ban of thirty-five weapons. Fifty-six-year-old DeConcini, whose 1989 legislation had gotten further but ultimately failed, had also submitted new legislation that banned seventeen specific firearms. Both wanted to ban the Colt AR-15.

Feinstein, sixty, was eager to join the two senators in the gun-ban efforts. Gun control was personal. City Supervisor Feinstein was at San Francisco City Hall in 1978 when a disturbed former city supervisor shot and killed Harvey Milk, a gay activist and fellow supervisor, and George Moscone, the mayor. She rushed to Milk's side to feel for a pulse, but her finger found a bullet hole instead. The assassinations made her mayor and she pushed through a citywide ban on handguns that was later overturned in the courts. Now in the Senate, she wanted to build a national reputation on gun issues.

By the fall of 1993, the three senators joined to craft a single piece of legislation, which they titled "The Public Safety and Recreational Fire-arms Use Protection Act." Despite the prosaic title, no one in Congress had any delusions: the bill was a federal ban on a class of semiautomatic weapons, including the AR-15.

These senators were not the most powerful people in the chamber. Metzenbaum was viewed by many as a crank and a contrarian. DeConcini, though widely liked, had been politically damaged by recent allegations that he was involved in an influence-peddling scandal in his home state. Feinstein was a woman just arrived to one of the most venerable old-boys' clubs on the planet. The odd group would pull off an unexpected victory.

However, in their eagerness to pass the bill, the senators made compromises that left it flawed. Their legislative efforts revealed an ignorance about how the weapons they were trying to prohibit actually worked. The result was a ban that could never achieve what they promised the American people.

The senators were focused on a range of guns, but their legislative push brought the AR-15 to broad public attention. It became a ready reference for liberal politicians, and something of a prop—a symbolic shorthand for the sinister nature of the weapons they wanted to ban. At the same time, it grew into a defiant symbol of the Second Amendment for gun-rights activists and gun owners.

The results of the legislative fight were complex and ultimately tragic. During the ten years that the federal ban was in place, the AR-15's popularity grew, and hastily worded provisions in the legislation enabled production and sales of the gun to increase. After the ban expired in 2004, sales of the rifle exploded. So did another American phenomenon—mass shootings.

In 1993, major news events propelled the senators' efforts to portray the AR-15 as a danger to society. Earlier that year, heavily armed federal agents laid siege to a doomsday cult's compound in Waco, Texas. The cult's leader, David Koresh, convinced his followers that he was the Messiah. This messiah liked guns. He collected an arsenal, including hundreds of parts to build AR-15s, in preparation for Armageddon. On February 28, 1993, seventy-six armed federal agents descended on the Branch Davidian compound, and a ninety-minute gun battle erupted. Four government agents and six Branch Davidians were killed. After a fifty-one-day standoff, Attorney General Janet Reno ordered federal agents to move in. Armored vehicles punched holes in walls and pumped tear gas inside. A fire that began during the attack consumed the compound. Koresh and seventy-five cult members, including twenty-five children, died. The government said that Branch Davidians set the fire.

In the wreckage, investigators found AR-15s that were modified to fire like fully automatic machine guns.

"The tragic situation in Waco, Texas, where four ATF agents were murdered and several others were injured, was only one of many recent examples in which criminals have used assault weapons to overpower law enforcement," DeConcini said.

The senators knew they wanted to ban the type of rifle that the cultists had used in Waco, but struggled to define the weapons as they crafted their legislation. Describing different classes of firearms in law was complex for people who knew guns; it proved extremely difficult for people who didn't.

Early state bans had been problematic. After California lawmakers banned a list of guns by their commercial product names in 1989, gunmakers simply had changed the names of their guns.

When George Bush wanted to ban AK-47 imports, the arduous task of defining terms fell to a group at the Bureau of Alcohol, Tobacco, and Firearms. The leading attorney in the group was Brad Buckles, a career bureaucrat who wore wire-rim glasses and a trim mustache. Buckles realized that American laws had never defined the military-style, semiautomatic rifles that Bush wanted to keep out of the United States. The lawyer found a phrase in the 1968 Gun Control Act that allowed foreign guns to be imported into the United States only if they were "particularly suitable for or readily adaptable to sporting purposes." The clause had been used in the past to block cheap imported handguns known as "Saturday Night Specials."

Buckles and his team used the phrase as the foundation for a test to determine whether a gun was a "semiautomatic assault rifle" that should not be allowed into the country. The criteria for the test was not an exact science. It focused on what the group called the "military appearance" of a firearm.

"Honestly, it had to come down to how they were dressed," Buckles recalled.

Buckles and the group drew up a list of military features that had no hunting or target-shooting purposes. The features included an attachment for a bayonet, a flash suppressor to conceal gunfire at night, and a pistol grip. The ATF used these features as a key test to determine whether a semiautomatic rifle could be imported. Any firearm found to be "a semiautomatic version of a machinegun" with a "military appearance" using certain ammunition wouldn't be allowed into the United States.

Buckles knew that the features test was not about how a gun fired; it was about how it looked. The features "did not directly add to the lethality of the weapon, but in combination they posed a greater public safety threat," Buckles said. "They appealed to criminals, to people who wanted to engage in mass killings."

This test was created to block imported weapons like the one that had been used in the Stockton massacre. It was not written to be a federal law or to outlaw the AR-15 rifle, which was made in America.

In 1993, the senators' staffers searched for workable legal language that would single out the weapons they wanted to ban. They turned to gun-control groups. Bernie Horn, the Handgun Control Inc. attorney, gave them a draft ban that was in part based on the test that Buckles and his team had created. The draft was one that he'd given to other lawmakers. "It was pretty much already on my computer," Horn remembered. Horn worked with the Senate staffers to draw up a more complex features test, using Buckles's import test as a starting point. If a semiautomatic rifle sold in the United States had a detachable magazine, it could not have more than one of the following military-style features: a pistol grip, a bayonet attachment, a flash suppressor, a grenade launcher, or an adjustable stock. If it didn't have a detachable magazine, the gun could have as many military features as a gun owner wanted. They also added language to ban any copies of the models that were prohibited by name.

Buckles thought using such a test for a nationwide ban didn't make sense. The language worked to ban imports, but wouldn't work well as part of a national gun law. He and his colleagues tried to warn the senators' staffers about the limitations. They visited Senate aides, lugging guns pulled from the agency's vault to Capitol Hill. They showed them that banning the features would do nothing to reduce how rapidly the guns fired. The guns would still be semiautomatic. They would fire the same bullets at the same speed—as fast as you could pull the trigger.

Lenett, the Metzenbaum counsel who worked on the ban, attended some of these meetings, and was shocked by guns like the AK-47 and the AR-15 when he saw them up close. "They really did strike me as military weapons," said Lenett, a Georgetown law school graduate who had grown up near New York City. "I'm not a big gun nut. I didn't have real experience with guns. I was taken aback." Lenett was unpersuaded by Buckles's warnings. "He's really not with us, he's a gun guy," Lenett recalled. "We took whatever he said with a grain of salt." Lenett felt that there was a strong case to be made that the military features were all designed for one purpose: to aid the shooter in his quest to kill people quickly. "Every one of those features made those guns more dangerous," he recalled thinking.

Other aides believed the military features needed to be banned because they attracted criminals, extremists, and violent loners. "These guns were made to appeal to a certain population for certain reasons—folks who imagined themselves Ramboing," said Adam Eisgrau, Feinstein's counsel on the Judiciary Committee.

Buckles was disheartened and frustrated. Whenever he heard politicians talking about the "dangerous" features on a rifle, he found himself covering his ears.

"Some of the difficulty in dealing with people who were working on this legislation is that they weren't familiar with firearms, they didn't know firearms, they had never fired a firearm," Buckles recalled.

The senators wanted to attach their legislation to Bill Clinton's massive anti-crime bill, a key White House effort that focused on funding for police and stiffer sentences for criminals. But even though Clinton and Delaware senator Joe Biden, the sponsor of the crime bill, had voiced support for the ban, they worried it would jeopardize their entire legislative package if it was attached. Feinstein pressed Biden, the chair of the powerful Senate Judiciary Committee, to do so. Feinstein recalled that he told her: "I was wasting my time to try."

The senators met to figure out how they could win enough votes for passage. They sat down with a few staffers in Metzenbaum's "hideaway office" located in the basement of the Capitol building. The spacious office was a special privilege given to long-serving senators like Metzenbaum, conveniently located near the Senate floor but removed from the public or the press. The wealthy senator from Ohio had filled his offices with modern art.

The three discussed a central issue: should such a ban be permanent? DeConcini argued for a ban that could be renewed by Congress after three years. Other senators would be more likely to back the ban if they could assess how it was working, he argued. Metzenbaum and Feinstein wanted the ban to be permanent.

Metzenbaum grumbled and said he could stomach a fifteen-year ban. Feinstein whispered with Eisgrau, her aide. She offered ten. Metzenbaum reluctantly agreed.

When Feinstein showed the legislation to Bob Walker, the top lobbyist for Handgun Control Inc., he was disappointed. He was disturbed to see that they had included a ten-year sunset clause before Senate debates had even begun. It would have been smarter to use a sunset clause as a bargaining chip if necessary, he thought.

But Walker let it go. He was busy working to pass another major gun law in the fall of 1993, the Brady Bill, which mandated background checks for gun buyers. The bill, signed into law at the end of November, required licensed dealers to run the names of their customers through a federal system to make sure they did not have a criminal record or mental health adjudication that disqualified them from owning a gun.

As the senators' legislation took shape, gunmakers lobbied to keep their companies' guns from being the ones that were on the ban list. Colt, which had resumed selling AR-15s, pressed to exempt its Sporter model from the ban. The company had filed for bankruptcy in 1992 after enduring a labor strike and the loss of a contract to produce M16s for the military. Colt needed to sell civilian firearms to stay in business. In the three years leading up to 1993, the company had sold an average of thirty-five thousand civilian AR-15s a year, accounting for about $35 million of Colt's $100 million in annual sales.

Colt's home-state senator, Democrat Joe Lieberman, urged Feinstein in private meetings to remove the Sporter from a list of guns specifically named. He passed on a letter from Colt, which argued that the ATF, not the Senate, should decide whether that particular AR-15 model met the definition of an assault weapon. Feinstein agreed. When the *Hartford Courant* learned of Lieberman's lobbying, he defended his actions. "This is a proud, old Connecticut company," he said. "It's fighting for its life now."

When the legislation was presented to the Senate, the Sporter was not named on the ban list, but the "Colt AR-15" was, underscoring the confusion and perhaps lack of understanding about firearms that reigned among many senators and their staffers. The Sporter and the AR-15 were essentially the same gun.

The senators pushing the ban were willing to horse-trade to secure votes. To win over older gun owners, they named more than 670 firearms—most of them hunting rifles—that would explicitly not be banned. The long list of protected guns included Ruger's Mini-14, a smaller version of the military's ill-fated M14. It was semiautomatic and used the same ammunition as the AR-15 and could be fitted with a high-capacity magazine.

"With so much in common, why is the AR-15 illegal and the Mini-14 legal?" *The Wall Street Journal* asked in an editorial. Its answer: "Looks."

The Mini-14 had been used in horrific crimes. In 1989, a Montreal man armed with a Mini-14 killed fourteen women at an engineering school, yelling, "I hate feminists." But the gun was popular with hunters and putting it on the list would cause too large an uproar, ban backers worried. An internal Justice Department memo noted: "It was agreed that certain weapons probably had too large a constituency to ever be worth the risk of including, including the Mini 14." The AR-15 did not have as large a constituency. Out of the 4.1 million guns built for sale in the United States in 1992, just thirty-three thousand were AR-15s.

On the evening of November 9, 1993, Feinstein walked to the well of the Senate floor and offered the trio's work as an amendment to the crime bill.

"There's no reason for weapons of war . . . to be used freely on the streets of America where they are the weapons of choice for every assassin, terrorist, gang member, drug syndicate, drive-by shooter, mafioso or grievance killer," she said. "Most troubling of these categories is the grievance killer, someone who takes out their wrath on anyone who happens to be around."

Feinstein, Metzenbaum, and DeConcini hammered home their argument on the Senate floor: criminals bent on slaughter of innocents or killing cops wanted these weapons, not everyday Americans. The ATF bolstered their claims by reporting that 8 percent of guns they traced in criminal investigation in 1993 were the types of weapons covered by the ban even though they made up just 1 percent of all guns in the United States. The senators argued that mass shootings such as the ones at the San Francisco law office and Stockton, California, playground were terrifying the public and had to be stopped. They glossed over the data that critics of their effort often stressed: handguns were used in the vast majority of murders in America. On the Senate floor, Metzenbaum declared that Americans were mowed down every day of the week with the guns they wanted to ban. Feinstein was more circumspect: "True, they're not responsible for a large number of homicides, but what they do offer is the possibility of the deranged killer, the grievance killer, to take out a whole room of people without having to reload," she told her fellow senators.

Larry Craig, the senator representing Idaho, offered a rebuttal. The NRA board member presented a Second Amendment absolutist argument: it didn't matter what a gun was used for, the Constitution protected a citizen's right to own it. "The Founding Fathers didn't specify what type of gun a citizen could have," he said, adding, "The Constitution does not speak to sporting purposes, does not speak to hunting."

The Idaho senator then said: "The gentlelady from California needs to become a little more familiar with firearms and their deadly characteristics, I say that—"

Feinstein cut him off.

"I am quite familiar with firearms," she said. "I became mayor as a product of assassination."

The ban survived a Republican motion to kill it by a 51–49 vote. Forty-six Democrats and five Republicans voted with Feinstein. Ten Democrats and thirty-nine Republicans voted against her. The result showed to the Senate, the House of Representatives, and the White House that the ban had a real chance. It was attached to the Senate crime bill later that year.

The legislation banned the manufacture and sale of nineteen semi-automatic weapons by name, including the Colt AR-15. It banned any semiautomatic weapons that failed the features test. It prohibited the manufacture and sale of magazines that held more than ten rounds. And it allowed people who already owned such guns to keep them.

The senators had shocked Washington by passing the ban. The NRA had been caught off guard. Everyone expected a fierce fight in the House, where many Republicans and Democrats representing rural districts were loyal allies of the gun group.

17.

THE END OF COMPROMISE

The AR-15 was an affirmation of our right to own firearms.
—David McCann

The highest-ranking Democrat in the House of Representatives visited the Oval Office in the spring of 1994 to deliver a warning to President Bill Clinton. Speaker Tom Foley, a tall, well-dressed sixty-five-year-old once described as having the face of a St. Bernard, told Clinton to abandon his support for the federal assault-weapons ban that had passed the Senate before it came up for a vote in Foley's chamber. "Don't push the assault-weapon ban," Foley said according to Clinton's top legislative affairs aide, Patrick Griffin, who was at the meeting.

Foley believed the ban proposal was dangerous. Despite his love of fine suits and hobnobbing with the Washington elite, Foley represented a conservative rural district on the eastern edge of Washington State. The men and women who had kept him in office since 1965 were rugged westerners who cherished their firearms. Foley had voted pro–gun rights on every major piece of legislation going back to his vote against the Gun Control Act of 1968. The National Rifle Association had backed Foley in every election, even distributing bumper stickers that read "Another Sportsman for Foley." Foley was one of dozens of rural Democrats in the western, midwestern, and southern United States who resisted gun-control measures to satisfy their gun-owning constituents.

The Speaker's argument to Clinton was not about the policy of banning weapons such as the AR-15; it was about political wins and losses. The Democratic Party couldn't afford to support banning rifles of any kind. "There were dozens of Democrats who felt that the assault weapons ban was another legislative 'third rail,' which would kill them if they touched it," Foley later recalled. Democrats would get pummeled by gun owners and lose seats in the fall elections if they were forced to vote for a ban, he said.

Sitting in a chair near the fireplace next to Vice President Al Gore, Clinton rejected Foley's plea, arguing that gun owners could be persuaded to back a ban on military-style semiautomatics. Clinton believed he could make the case to hunters that he wasn't going after their guns, he said. "He was a bubba," recalled Bruce Reed, Clinton's top domestic policy aide. "He knew what they were concerned about and he could explain to them why it would be okay." Clinton was concerned about political wins too, but mostly about his rather than his party's. The president was beset by personal and political problems. He faced an investigation into a real estate deal in Arkansas. New allegations of sexual impropriety arose, this time from a former Arkansas state employee named Paula Jones. The administration had made little progress on a major campaign promise: overhauling the American healthcare system. The inveterate campaigner decided that going after AR-15s and AK-47s was a campaign he could win. He told Foley he would strongly push for a ban. Foley grimaced, and he and the two men flanking him, Majority Leader Dick Gephardt and Majority Whip David Bonior, shook their heads. Three times, they begged Clinton not to do it. "Foley was unflinching as was Clinton," Griffin said.

Foley ended the awkward meeting with a threat. "If you support this, we will not support the bill in any shape or form," Foley said, according to Griffin. Clinton would have to get the ban through the House without the backing of his own party's leadership. The job of whipping the bill—counting the votes, twisting arms, making deals—would be left up to Clinton's White House team. "I'm terrified," Griffin, Clinton's head of legislative affairs, remembered thinking.

196 · AMERICAN GUN

One reason that he was so terrified was the NRA, the chief opponent of the ban. The gun group, now under the control of Second Amendment absolutists, launched a full-scale effort to kill the ban. The NRA wielded extraordinary influence in rural districts where the group's support was crucial for reelection. The NRA's chief lobbyist, Tanya Metaksa, who told those she met that she spelled her name "A-K, as in AK-47, S-A, as in semiautomatic," coordinated the effort. She was a tough—some said abrasive—fifty-six-year-old who had embraced the gun-rights cause as a young woman. Metaksa had participated in the pivotal takeover by hard-liners at the 1977 convention that transformed the NRA into an uncompromising champion of gun rights.

Metaksa's strategy to defeat the ban was simple: terrify House members with the prospect of angry gun owners turning against them. "You've got to understand banning a piece of metal because of what it looks like is not a negotiable stand," Metaksa later said.

Metaksa believed she could count on Speaker Foley. The NRA had backed Foley for decades. In 1978, the group gave him an eight-inch-high statue of a minuteman, which the NRA called its "Defender of Individual Rights Award."

Foley and Jack Brooks, the powerful pro-gun Texas Democrat, hatched a plan to kill the ban. In April 1994, Brooks pushed through passage of a version of the crime bill through the House. His version included funding for new cops and prisons, but didn't have the assault-weapons ban. Instead, Brooks and Foley arranged for a standalone vote on the ban, separate from the rest of the crime legislation. It was political theater. The two veteran politicians were convinced the ban would fail in such a vote.

The White House panicked and launched a public relations campaign featuring the AR-15 and similar firearms to win over the American public and pressure wavering Democrats. Clinton was tired of getting beat up by Congress, his aides recalled him saying. The ban would give him a chance to stand up and fight on principle, something voters wanted to see Clinton do more, aides wrote in a memo. "This sets up a fight between the cops and the NRA—with the President squarely on the side of the cops," the memo said.

Clinton was convinced that pushing the ban would bolster support among liberals for his crime package, which some criticized as draconian, the memo said.

Staffers set up press events with Clinton, police officers, and shooting survivors. On April 25, the White House used the AR-15 as a central prop at a Rose Garden press conference. Dayton, Ohio, police Lieutenant Randy Bean, wearing his dress blues, stood beside the president and spoke about how a man armed with an AR-15 opened fire at him and Officer Steve Whelan during a traffic stop in 1991. Bean dove for cover, but the shooter killed his partner. "This is the type of weapon that was used to kill Officer Steve Whelan," Bean said as he handed a black AR-15 to Clinton for the cameras to capture.

"It's not just Lieutenant Bean," Clinton said. "Every major law enforcement organization in this country has said we should ban semiautomatic assault weapons."

An ATF fact sheet on the AR-15 sent to newspaper editorial boards linked the Colt AR-15 to 1,802 serious crimes, including 212 narcotics investigations and 106 murders, between 1990 and 1993. The AR-15 was by far the most widely available gun named in the ban, with about four hundred thousand manufactured, according to the ATF.

National newspapers backed the White House position. "One of the great advantages we had on the gun issue was that the media was with us from the beginning," recalled Bruce Reed. But by the end of April, the White House realized it would need at least some Republican support. Wheelchair-bound Jim Brady enlisted his former boss Ronald Reagan and former president Gerald Ford to support the ban. The two former Republican presidents along with Jimmy Carter issued a letter, calling the ban "a matter of vital importance to public safety." They urged Congress to "listen to the American public and to the law enforcement community and support a ban on the further manufacture of these weapons."

Early in the morning of May 5, the day of the House floor vote, Bob

Walker, the top lobbyist for Handgun Control Inc., estimated the ban was still six or seven votes shy of passage. "I was convinced that we were going to lose," he recalled. He got a call from a key swing vote, Dick Swett, a Democrat who represented the pro-gun state of New Hampshire. Swett was willing to vote for the ban, but he wanted a personal call from Ronald Reagan to give him cover with voters. Walker got Reagan to call Swett and a half dozen other congressmen.

The last-minute efforts worked. The ban narrowly passed, 216 to 214, with 177 Democrats and 38 Republicans in favor and 137 Republicans and 77 Democrats against. Inside the White House, some of Clinton's aides danced.

Gun owners across America were enraged. Letters flooded Congress and magazines such as *Gun World*, including one from a Georgia high school senior, who wrote to say that he was against "the Clintons telling me what guns I don't need."

As Foley predicted, anger spread to his eastern Washington district even though he'd remained neutral on the ban—and hadn't cast a vote, as was his practice as House Speaker. Dave McCann, a forty-one-year-old medical device salesman in Foley's district, was furious. An NRA member who had served in the Marines, McCann purchased a Colt AR-15 in the early 1990s. It was something to shoot at the range. "The people up here knew that a .223 was not appropriate for large-game hunting, it was more of a toy," McCann recalled. But now the Democrats were trying to ban ownership of a civilian version of the weapon he once carried to defend the country, he thought. The shootings in big cities such as Los Angeles and Miami had nothing to do with his quiet life and his constitutional rights. "Don't make us responsible for the trouble that's being caused in other parts of the country," he recalled thinking.

McCann started to see the AR-15 as a symbol of defiance against federal overreach.

"The AR-15 was an affirmation of our right to own firearms," he said.

This growing anger meant trouble for rural Democrats like Foley.

Before he was elected in 1964, a Republican had held Washington's Fifth Congressional District for eleven terms. Foley built a reputation in the House as a politician who valued compromise. Soon after becoming Speaker, he brokered the 1990 budget deal with President George H. W. Bush that included tax hikes. In Foley's mind, compromising on issues was not selling out, it was how government got things done.

"There are people who think I should be more partisan, should be more aggressive, should be more combative. More hard-edged," Foley told *The New York Times*. "I don't tend to agree with it."

But one issue that he rarely compromised on was guns. He consistently had voted against gun-control measures. He made sure press photographers were present at his duck hunts.

During the summer of 1994, Foley still hoped that the ban would be dropped altogether. The Senate had passed the crime package, with an assault-weapon ban attached, and the House had passed the crime package and the ban, but as separate pieces of legislation. The initiatives needed to be reconciled. Leaders from the two chambers met to iron out details of a compromise bill they could both back and send to the White House. Though Clinton had some reservations that including the ban could hurt his reelection Metzenbaum, DeConcini, and Feinstein, backed by the powerful Biden, persuaded him to keep it in the package. That combined package would now come up for a final vote in Congress.

When Foley heard the news, he buried his head in his hands. "Oh no," he sighed.

"He was realizing the catastrophe," said Bonior, the majority whip. "The electoral catastrophe."

Foley avoided taking a public stand on the ban as long as he could. But he dropped his neutral stance that summer after a disgruntled ex-airman armed with a version of an AK-47 killed four people and wounded more than twenty others at a base in his district. Foley told reporters he would have voted for a ban to break a tie. Metaksa and others in the NRA took the statement as a betrayal.

To secure passage of the final crime bill, White House staffers satisfied a slew of quid pro quo requests from legislators, ranging from smoothing the way for new casinos to rides on Air Force One. "We were promising everything under the moon," Griffin recalled.

Responding to pressure from the White House, Metaksa sent letters to wavering lawmakers such as Democratic Georgia representative Buddy Darden, reminding them: "Our members intend to play a very active role in upcoming elections."

After a procedural snafu, a desperate White House was willing to do anything to pass the crime bill, even if it meant considering watering down the assault-weapons ban. Sitting in a conference room, Biden told Metzenbaum staffers, "Look, we've got to get this crime bill passed, the administration is riding on this bill," recalled Lenett, Metzenbaum's counsel. "Why can't you guys compromise more on this?"

Lenett told Biden the proposal to weaken the ban would make the legislation meaningless.

Biden looked up at the people in the room, paused, and then said, "Well then, fuck 'em."

And with that declaration, the ban stayed in.

On Sunday, August 21, 1994, the crime bill, including funds for more cops, more prisons, harsh sentences for violent crimes and drug offenses, and, after much sound and fury, the assault-weapons ban, passed the House 235–195. Forty-six Republicans voted for the bill. After all of his efforts to avoid taking a position, even Foley voted yes. Clinton trumpeted the result when he signed the bill on September 13, 1994. "We will finally ban these assault weapons from our streets that have no purpose other than to kill," the president promised.

The prohibitions adopted into law almost exactly matched those introduced in the Senate in 1993. Nineteen semiautomatic weapons, including Colt's AR-15 and any copycat versions, were no longer allowed to be made or sold in America. Neither were magazines that could hold more than ten rounds.

NRA leaders, seething from their defeat, launched a scorched-earth campaign during the fall elections. Metaksa sent a special election mailer to NRA members titled "It's Payback Time!" Donors poured

$6.8 million into the NRA's political action committee that election cycle. The gun group "had never spent the kind of money we spent in 1994," Metaksa recalled. The NRA focused on twenty-four races that fall, including rural, pro-gun Democrats who had broken with the gun group to back the ban. Targets included small-time players like Buddy Darden in Georgia all the way up to their longtime ally Speaker Foley.

The NRA ran television ads featuring the actor Charlton Heston accusing Foley of betraying gun owners. "The Speaker has stopped listening," Heston said. The NRA endorsed Foley's Republican challenger and poured $80,000 into the race. Metaksa flew to Spokane to mobilize voters like McCann. They were eager to make Foley pay. The Speaker was working with Clinton and talking about how the "AR-15 is an evil weapon," McCann recalled. "People in this part of the state didn't buy that at all."

Foley lost by just under four thousand votes. The last time a House Speaker had been defeated in an election was 1862. Foley's ouster was the crowning achievement of the NRA's campaign of retribution in the 1994 midterms. That fall, the sweeping victories helped put the GOP in control of the House for the first time in four decades (and made Representative Newt Gingrich the new Speaker). That win was, in part, proof of the growing power of the AR-15 as a political symbol for gun owners. It was a stunning defeat for Democrats; the party lost fifty-four seats that election cycle. Though Republican campaigns also stressed Clinton's tax increases, the attempt to permit gay people to serve openly in the military, and failed healthcare reform, Clinton blamed the gun group in large part for his party's failures. "The NRA was an unforgiving master: one strike and you're out," Clinton wrote in his memoir. Critics of that narrative, chief among them gun-control proponents, say Clinton's analysis was a convenient way for him to blame the wipeout on something other than his tempestuous relationship with the American public. But at the time, even they were forced to admit that gun owners had come out in force and punished politicians who crossed them.

"They were able to turn out a very single-minded, single-issue constituency, something that we have not been able to do," said Cheryl

Brolin of Handgun Control Inc. "The widespread public support for gun control that shows up in the opinion polls is not showing up at the ballot box."

Foley saw in his political demise a new, uglier politics emerge over guns. Gun-rights advocates, he wrote in his memoir, "had an aspect of an increasingly hard-edged policy . . . you were either with them on everything, or against them . . . there was no middle ground."

18.

BAD BOYS

They weren't members of our club.
—Gun industry executive on companies making civilian AR-15s

The highlight of Dick Dyke's youth came when he learned an entire tap-dance routine from the legendary Gene Kelly at a dance convention at Radio City Music Hall. Dyke had grown up in a house with no indoor plumbing in the mill town of Wilton, Maine. He saw music, theater, and dancing as his escape. He was accepted to an acting and dance school in New York City. But his parents, a wool factory worker and a policeman, refused to pay. So Dyke went to Husson University in Bangor, to study business.

After college, Dyke embarked on a successful career in salvaging failing businesses, from lumber companies to accounting firms. In 1976, he purchased a bankrupt gun company called Bushmaster Firearms for $241,000. By the 1990s, Dyke had turned that company into a viable enterprise by selling a semiautomatic version of Stoner's gun and gun parts to American consumers at a time when few other gunmakers besides Colt did so. The gun was cheap and easy to make. Stoner's patent had expired, and because Stoner had designed the gun for easy mass production, Dyke could get machine shops to churn out parts at a low cost. All his employees had to do was assemble the guns and ship them out. From 1976 to 1994, the company grew from a basement in

Portland, Maine, to a warehouse staffed by about a dozen employees in an industrial park in nearby Windham. The gun appealed to a small segment of gun buyers that included survivalists, veterans of recent wars, and collectors. The federal assault-weapons ban threatened to destroy the little business. With the stroke of President Clinton's pen, it seemed that Bushmaster could no longer sell its main product, the XM-15 rifle.

"We thought, 'Oh my God we're going to be out of business,'" recalled Izzy Anzaldua, who designed guns and worked in sales for Bushmaster. "We're done, I'm going to work at 7-Eleven the rest of my life."

But before giving up, the people working for Dyke—or Mr. Dyke, as employees called him—decided to see whether they could figure out how to modify their rifles and keep selling. They hoped that with a few alterations to the appearance of their gun, they could keep their company alive. Bushmaster executives studied the wording of the federal ban to see how they could get around it. It looked easy. "When these idiots wrote [the legislation], they wrote it cosmetically," Anzaldua said.

Anzaldua and others took an XM-15 to the machine shop.

"We took a band saw and cut the freaking bayonet lug off," he recalled. The banned bayonet lug was just a small squarish chunk of metal underneath the front sight of the rifle. Next they unscrewed the flash suppressor, a little metal piece at the end of the barrel that hid the flash of a gunshot.

Anzaldua and others fashioned a gun that looked very much like the version of the AR-15 that Bushmaster was selling before the ban. And it shot just the same. Bushmaster workers crated it up and sent it to the ATF, seeking approval to sell their new version. "I didn't know what the hell they were going to do," he said.

ATF officials gave the Maine company the green light. Within months of the much-heralded federal assault-weapons ban going into effect, Bushmaster was back in business, and it was selling more guns than ever. Some gun-control advocates later blamed the ATF for being too lenient. But top officials at the agency such as Brad Buckles, who later became ATF director, said that the way the senators had written the ban gave the agency no choice but to rely on the legislation's military features checklist.

Other small companies making versions of Stoner's rifle followed suit. DPMS Panther Arms, headquartered in an old dental office in a small town in Minnesota, made its first $1 million in 1994. Mark Westrom, an army veteran working out of an old horsemeat-processing plant in Coal Valley, Illinois, revived the old ArmaLite brand to sell his version of the gun. His little company flourished. Olympic Arms, in Olympia, Washington, had been selling AR-15s and parts since 1975, but now it saw sales orders pour in. Bushmaster's executives became millionaires. The ban was supposed to stop all manufacture and sales of AR-15s in the United States. Instead, it created a sustained and unprecedented demand for civilian versions of Stoner's rifle, which had never really caught on with the gun-buying public before. "If you want to sell something to an American, you tell him he can't have it," Westrom said.

The prospect of the 1994 assault-weapons ban sparked an AR-15 frenzy. More than 62,000 AR-15s were built for sale in the United States in 1993, nearly double the previous year. In 1994, that number climbed to 103,000.

"The crime bill was introduced and it just spun the market right through the roof," recalled Mark Eliason, head of sales at Bushmaster. "We couldn't build enough of them."

Sales skyrocketed; so did profits.

"A rifle that cost $740 the day before the enactment of the bill now turned into a $1,500 gun," Anzaldua said.

Claude Warren, a Bushmaster vice president, made almost $1.8 million in 1994. The average salary for a professional baseball player that year was about $1.2 million.

Some gunmakers took advantage of a provision in the ban that allowed owners of the AR-15s already in circulation to keep their guns, sell them, and leave them to their progeny. Mark Westrom interpreted it to mean that any rifle manufactured before the ban went into effect could legally be sold afterward. He read the law's provisions like a puzzle: How could he meet the letter of the law and still produce and sell AR-15s?

"Every clause they had, I would come up with a workaround or a counter," he said.

As the ban bore down, Westrom "made" as many guns as he could. He bought "a whole shitpot of receivers," he said, referring to the central part of the rifle that housed the firing mechanism. The receiver was the only part of the gun that carried a serial number from the manufacturer. Westrom took ten receivers at a time, added the remaining parts, and videotaped employees shooting the guns. The videos were his legal proof that the guns had been "manufactured" before the ban went into effect. Then he disassembled them, and reassembled the next ten using receivers with different serial numbers. By the time the ban went into effect on September 13, 1994, Westrom and his seven-man crew had "manufactured" nearly three thousand AR-15s in this manner. He stored the videotapes in a vault at the police department across the street should the federal government ask questions.

Four hundred miles northwest of Westrom's operation was DPMS Panther Arms. As the ban moved toward passage, Randy Luth, the company's forty-year-old chief executive, sold more AR-15 receivers than ever before. "Send us another thousand, send us another thousand!" Luth remembered hollering into the phone to his manufacturer. In the spring of 1993, Luth had sold AR-15 receivers for $69.95 apiece. By September 1994, when Clinton signed the ban, Luth was selling those same receivers for $375 each. They cost him just $22 each to make. "We were millionaires in 1994," Luth recalled. "We had a million dollars in the checking account."

AR-15 companies like Luth's were outcasts of the gun industry in the 1980s and early 1990s. "I was the black sheep of the family and then I get into black rifles and I'm the black sheep [with] the black rifle," Luth said. Raised by a janitor and a part-time waitress in Minneapolis, Luth was a young troublemaker, often getting into fights. He went to work in the pressroom at the Minneapolis *Star Tribune* after high school, and later at a machine shop that had military contracts to build parts for the M16 in the early 1980s. Luth was curious and restless, with a natural penchant for building things. The young employee created a new product for his shop to make: a grenade launcher that could be adapted to many different military rifles. With the help of a Florida drug runner–turned–arms dealer, Luth tried to broker a deal to sell his creation to the Contras, the CIA-backed paramilitary group fighting against the Sandinista government in Nicaragua. He flew to Honduras with the arms dealer, who helped set up meetings. "We were shooting live ammo from three hundred yards, blowing stuff up. It was great," Luth remembered. But the sale fell through when Luth's boss refused to pay the arms dealer a 10 percent commission. The arms dealer threatened to kill Luth and his boss, Luth recalled.

In 1986, Luth, married with a young daughter, set out on his own as a consultant to help machine shops land military contracts. He called his firm Defense Procurement Manufacturing Services, or DPMS for short. He discovered a lucrative sideline: buying M16 parts from military contractors and selling them to gun-show dealers or companies making AR-15s.

When Luth bought an AR-15 rifle for the first time in 1986, the gun seemed "kind of chintzy, flimsy, and cheap," he said. But Luth saw early on that the black rifles appealed to what he called an "edgy group"— and there was money to be made. These were "gun owners that wanted something cool and different looking," he said. In 1992, he began selling his own AR-15s. He quickly outgrew the old dentist's office. By 1993, he'd built a large warehouse in rural Becker, Minnesota.

Luth knew he needed a new name for his business—something cool. Colt had the horse; ArmaLite had the roaring lion. Bushmaster had the coiled red pit viper. "I came up with the black panther," Luth recalled. He designed a logo with a snarling black panther and called the company DPMS Panther Arms. The logo looked like the insignia for a heavy metal band or a motorcycle gang.

While companies such as Luth's courted the edgy crowd, traditional gun owners viewed the companies with disdain. He received strong re-actions to the guns when he displayed them at NRA conventions. "We'd have NRA members walk by and give us the finger," he said. "They were just dyed-in-the-wool NRA bolt-action members, that's all they cared about. They didn't want to see AR-15s."

Anzaldua encountered other critics at conventions—Vietnam vets. "I carried one of them in Vietnam and that thing's a chunk of shit," was one comment Anzaldua remembered hearing.

Officials organizing the annual gun industry gathering—the Shooting, Hunting, Outdoor Trade Show, or SHOT Show—tried to make it as uncomfortable as possible for AR-15 makers to market their products.

"They weren't members of our club," said a former executive from the gun industry trade group who didn't want his name used. "The AR platform was not initially viewed as a sporting firearm. Our world was the sporting firearm."

Booths at the SHOT Show were full of polished hunting rifles, shot-guns, bird calls, hunting blinds, and blaze orange clothing. The show frowned on anything that was marketed or sold with military imagery. SHOT Show officials gave Luth such a hard time that he called them the "SHOT Show Gestapo." They made him remove anything from his displays that seemed to them too militaristic. Luth and the other AR-15 companies were given booths in out-of-the-way sections on the sprawl-ing convention floor. The SHOT Show "despised AR-15 companies," said Luth.

Tensions between AR-15 makers and old-line companies came to a head in the late 1990s. AR-15 makers called a meeting with National Shooting Sports Foundation officials and demanded better treatment. Later, officials set up a special "tactical" section at the show. It started small, with just a handful of booths.

The AR-15 makers embraced the bad-boy image. They realized that with a certain segment of gun buyers, the military connection was a selling point. Traditional gun owners thought the guns looked scary, but these new customers loved the martial look. "The rifle looks scary and that's what got it [banned], but that's also what's making it popular," Eliason remembered.

Luth realized that the gun had a unique appeal. "You can take someone who's an introvert or quiet, they can buy this cool-looking weapon that makes them feel stronger, cooler, neater, edgy," he said.

Some AR-15 makers took the bad-boy image to extremes, mocking the federal ban in the names of the rifles they sold. When a *Los Angeles Times* reporter visited Olympic Arms in 1997, the controller, Bruce Bell, showed off the small company's post-ban AR-15, the PCR, or "politically correct rifle." Bell picked up another model, called the MFR, officially standing for "multi-function rifle," but unofficially it stood for "mother-fucking rifle," he explained.

The AR-15 makers promoted shooting competitions for the weapon and sponsored big-name target shooters, a stamp of approval in the gun world similar to a basketball star endorsing a pair of sneakers. They modified the gun for larger calibers more suitable for killing big game to appeal to hunters. Though hunters still didn't buy many AR-15s, the companies' effort lured popular outdoor magazines to write about their guns—free publicity.

They broadened the appeal further by advertising one of the AR-15's unique characteristics that came directly from Stoner's original design—its interchangeable parts. They sold handguards, barrels, buttstocks, triggers, pistol grips, and many other parts, in different styles, materials, and colors. The ability to swap out parts created a whole new market for rifle add-ons.

"I would compare it to custom cars and trucks, you can put mag wheels on it, you put hood ornaments on it—it's the only rifle that was easily accessorize-able," Luth said. "Why do ladies buy earrings? Why do they buy fancy purses? Why do they buy necklaces and bracelets? To accessorize." The AR-15 is the "easiest thing to accessorize in the male world other than cars and motorcycles."

For decades, Colt had been the only gun company selling the AR-15 to American consumers. Following bankruptcy and reorganization, Colt remained the clear market leader, building more than fifty thousand AR-15s, almost half of the AR-15s made in 1994. But the company faced a new crop of competitors. Despite its famous name and larger operations, Colt was at a distinct disadvantage. Unlike smaller companies, it couldn't cheaply outsource parts. It was a union shop and made all the parts for its guns at its Hartford plant. In 1994, a financier bought Colt and moved them out of their historic brick headquarters and into a less costly warren of metal warehouses on the edge of town. Though Colt still had military contracts for the M4, a smaller version of the M16, the company focused more on the civilian market in an attempt to boost profits. Following Bushmaster's lead, Colt engineers also developed an AR-15 they could sell under the ban called the Match Target. "The law itself was not designed properly to prevent assault weapons from being sold," Colt chief executive Ron Whitaker said.

While AR-15 sales soared in America despite a supposed ban, another country across the world outlawed every AR-15 old or new. In contrast to the American approach, Australian politicians moved with lightning speed to ban ownership of all semiautomatic rifles, with few exceptions, after that country's worst mass shooting. On April 28, 1996, a gunman armed with a Colt AR-15 rifle and other weapons went on a shooting rampage in the Tasmanian tourist town of Port Arthur. Martin Bryant, a twenty-eight-year-old handyman with profound psychological problems, killed thirty-five people and wounded twenty-three others.

Prime Minister John Howard, in office for not even two months, faced a national crisis. The center-right politician, known for his "awesome ordinariness" as one commentator put it, felt that the country wanted him to act. In his first press conference after the shooting, he announced he was prepared to ban all semiautomatic weapons. He marshaled support from political and police leaders. He encountered resistance from farmers, sport-shooting groups, and rural lawmakers, but he refused to make concessions. Australia's constitution had no protection for gun owners.

Twelve days after the massacre, Howard announced that he had reached an agreement with the leaders of all the country's states and territories. Unlike the U.S. law, Howard's ban didn't define the weapons by military features or product names. It banned the entire class of semiautomatic rifles, including AR-15s, with limited exceptions. It did not grandfather in existing weapons; it prohibited all of them, old or new. It did not contain a sunset clause; it banned them once and for all. The government launched a buyback program for all such guns in civilian hands.

"This represents an enormous shift in the culture of this country towards the possession, the use and the ownership of guns," Howard said in announcing the ban on May 10, 1996. "It means that this country, through its governments, has decided not to go down the American path."

Back in the United States, violent crime was dropping overall, but mass shootings continued to make news. In February 1997, two heavily armed bank robbers fired 1,100 rounds in a daytime gun battle with police on the streets of North Hollywood in Los Angeles. They carried an AR-15 and three AK-47s, all illegally converted to fire automatic. The robbers' bullets flew into businesses and cars. The men fired at a hovering police helicopter. Los Angeles police, armed with pistols and shotguns, commandeered five AR-15 rifles from a nearby gun store to try to match the bank robbers' firepower. Miraculously, no one other than the two bank robbers was killed, but several officers and bystanders were wounded.

"Even before last week's gun battle, the 1994 federal assault-weapons ban was widely seen as a failure, both by gun control advocates and opponents," the reporter David Bloom told viewers on an *NBC Nightly News* report. "Walk into any gun dealer in America . . . and you can still buy semiautomatics with the same firepower, almost identical characteristics to those banned two and a half years ago."

The large magazines that had been banned were easy to find too. *Shotgun News* carried hundreds of pages of black-and-white ads for guns and accessories. Issues from the late 1990s were loaded with ads for high-capacity magazines or clips, as some in the industry called them then. Twenty-round, thirty-round, and forty-round mags for the AR-15 sold for as low as $8.90, $9.90, and $12.90. Drum magazines that held a hundred rounds were sold by a company called C-MAG for $695 each: "AR-15/M16 Pre-Ban 100 round military drum magazine with loader and carrying case," the ad said. Under the law, any magazine over ten rounds being sold was supposed to have been made before the 1994 ban went into effect. But no one had any way of knowing, and no one, including federal and state officials, was checking.

Gun-control advocates such as Josh Sugarmann of the Violence Policy Center blamed the industry for "thumbing their nose at the American public, at the assault weapons law, at those who face these weapons." The NRA blamed the lawmakers who came up with the ban. "It's ridiculous," said Wayne LaPierre. "I mean, how guns look have nothing to do with what a gun's about, which is the way it shoots."

In August 1997, sixty-two-year-old Carl Drega, enraged over disputes with local officials in rural New Hampshire, shot and killed two state troopers, a newspaper editor, and a judge with his Colt AR-15. Drega's rifle had been manufactured before the 1994 ban. At a press conference following the shooting, the local police chief said Drega's use of an AR-15 made police, armed with handguns, feel like they had brought "a tennis racquet to a machine gun fight."

In 1999, the problem of mass shootings again took over the front pages. On April 20 of that year, eighteen-year-old Eric Harris and seventeen-year-old Dylan Klebold shot their way into Columbine High School near Littleton, Colorado. They murdered twelve fellow students and one teacher, as many of the victims pleaded for their lives. The two outcasts wounded another twenty-four people and unsuccessfully tried to set off bombs in the cafeteria. They roamed the campus for forty-seven minutes before they shot themselves, ending what was then the deadliest school shooting in American history. Harris and Klebold didn't use an AR-15 in their attack. One of the weapons that the killers used, a TEC DC-9, had been banned by name in 1994. But the gun they used had been built before the ban, and the teens had little trouble buying it from a friend. A few months later, *60 Minutes* reporter Leslie

Stahl played a clip of President Clinton saying, "We will finally ban these assault weapons from our streets that have no purpose other than to kill." The reporter dismissed the statement as a good applause line as she stood at a Miami gun show. "There are literally hundreds and hundreds of the AR-15—like this—the TEC-9 and all the others on the banned list. And this is just one show in one city," she said. In the report, Senator Feinstein spoke about the ban's shortcomings.

"If I could have gotten fifty-one votes in the Senate of the United States for an outright ban, picking up every one of them, 'Mr. and Mrs. America, turn them all in,' I would have done it," Feinstein said. "I could not do that. The votes weren't here."

AR-15 makers paid no attention to the media hand-wringing in 1999—they were too busy building and selling guns. Sales had dipped in the mid-1990s as the immediate buying frenzy caused by the ban receded. But a new panic hit the country that sent them soaring again. Americans grew concerned that a computer glitch in the storage of calendar data, labeled Y2K, would cause computers across the world to malfunction, ruining businesses and governments, throwing banks into chaos, causing widespread power outages, and upending civilization. Doomsday preppers set up bunkers in remote locations, stocked up on food supplies, and bought weapons in anticipation of mayhem. Gunmakers capitalized.

"During the panics, there's a lot of money to be made," said Westrom, the head of ArmaLite.

Bushmaster even made a special rifle for the computer-glitch crisis, inscribed with "Y2K Limited Edition" on the receiver. The gun sold out quickly, recalled John DeSantis, the company's chief executive.

"People were just concerned there was going to be mass rioting in the streets," DeSantis said. "A lot of the crazies bought semiautomatic rifles and yeah, we exploited that situation."

The little band of AR-15 companies built 70,000 rifles for sale in 1998, and 113,000 in 1999. More AR-15s were manufactured that year than in any other since Colt launched the Sporter in 1964. The federal assault-weapons ban had not only failed to stop sales of guns that were prohibited—it had sparked more interest in them from gun buyers.

By the late 1990s, Bushmaster had become a market leader for AR-15s. DeSantis, whom Dick Dyke hired to run Bushmaster in 1998, drove much of the company's success. A trained engineer, DeSantis had worked for more established weapons firms and he brought that expertise to the little company.

One of the first things he did to modernize Bushmaster was to ask Dyke to buy him a computer. DeSantis began to chart sales of the AR-15s down to the day. He noticed that spikes were correlated to events in the news such as the Y2K scare, a terrorist attack, or a mass shooting.

"Hunting rifles, you have a season; shotguns, you have a season; AR15s, there's no season," DeSantis recalled. "You could put on the news in the morning and you could see that because of a certain event that business was crazy." DeSantis reset Bushmaster's business model—so supply would meet erratic demand.

When DeSantis came to Bushmaster in 1998, the company brought in about $7 million in sales revenue, he recalled. That figure wasn't remarkable, but the margins were shocking. The sale price of their AR-15 far exceeded cost. In business, this measure of financial health is called gross margin: sales revenue less the cost of making the product expressed as a percentage. Gross margin isn't the same as profit because there are other business expenses, but at Bushmaster it was the primary number that executives kept their eyes on. When DeSantis showed up, the company's gross margin was 40 percent, far higher than other businesses', he said. The large margins were possible because AR-15 parts were relatively simple and cheap to make. They didn't require the expensive machinery or skilled labor needed to build other types of guns such as crafted wood-stocked hunting rifles, he said. Bushmaster could outsource parts production to any machine shop.

"We shifted all the burden to the suppliers," DeSantis recalled. "The suppliers had to hire all the machinists and buy all the machine tools and all that stuff. All we did was assemble. It was a nice model."

The "nice model" worked well for the boom-and-bust nature of

AR-15 sales. If business slowed, Bushmaster didn't have to lay off workers or have machinery sit idle. If sales ramped up, Bushmaster just ordered more parts. DeSantis figured out ways to increase margins even more. He hired a new purchasing manager who pressured suppliers to lower prices. He "browbeat everybody, reduced prices on everything coming in, so [the margins] got bigger and bigger," DeSantis said. Soon, Bushmaster was selling a single AR-15 for $750 to $900 that cost between $250 and $300 to build. The distributors who bought Bushmaster guns marked them up again before putting them on the shelves.

By the time the decade came to a close, the company that Dyke had purchased from bankruptcy for $241,000 was raking in millions. In 1999, Bushmaster built more than 64,000 rifles to be sold in America, far surpassing Colt, which that year made fewer than 30,000. Bushmaster's ability to crank up production when the market was hot crushed the lumbering Colt with its aging factory and union obligations. Other AR-15 companies also thrived. That year, ArmaLite made 8,000 rifles; Olympic made 7,400 and DPMS made 6,900.

Flush with cash, Dyke bought himself a white Rolls-Royce, DeSantis recalled. Dyke's money also went to his many other businesses, as well as philanthropy and politics. He had founded the Richard E. Dyke Center for Family Business at his alma mater, donating $265,000 for the building, the single largest donation in Husson University's history. In 1999, Dyke was appointed to be the chief fundraiser in Maine for the presidential campaign of GOP frontrunner George W. Bush. Dick Dyke had arrived.

But shootings involving Bushmaster's guns put the owner on the defensive. Martin Whitfield, a Los Angeles police officer who struggled to walk after the North Hollywood shootout, filed a lawsuit against Bushmaster. When the Associated Press learned in July 1999 that Dyke had a position with the Bush campaign, a Bush spokesman said Bush had no idea that Dyke was a gun manufacturer. Dyke resigned from the fundraising post, saying, "I just don't want to be any baggage."

The backlash showed that Dyke, despite his financial success, expensive suits, and high-end cars, remained an outcast. He was still one of the guys making those dangerous black rifles.

That stigma would soon dissipate, with the election of the man Dyke had supported for president. When George W. Bush was elected in 2000, AR-15 makers expected their future would be bright under the new Republican administration presidency. They had no idea.

19.

A PRECISE REQUEST

My name is Eugene M. Stoner.
—Letter from the inventor to Marine general

Eugene Stoner was wealthy by the early 1980s, in large part because of royalties for M16 sales to the U.S. military. Stoner and his second wife, Barbara, tired of Ohio winters, purchased a large property on the Florida coast in Palm City, north of Miami. They built a hangar for Stoner's Bölkow helicopter; his childhood love of flying was now a hobby that he pursued with the finest German-made machines. Stoner had a novel idea for their new house. He hoped to build it with the material that made his famous AR-15 possible: aluminum. He sketched out the idea for a home sitting atop a tall pedestal made entirely of anodized aluminum so it could withstand the corrosion caused by the salty, humid climate. The pedestal would protect the home from flooding and let them live above the mosquitoes, he told his family. He imagined it like a water tower with an elevator. When he explained the idea to his daughter Susan, she laughed.

Stoner's metal home was never built. But his imaginative plans showed that as he entered his sixties, he was still a compulsive inventor fascinated by lightweight metals. He spent late nights scribbling designs, much as he had in the family's garage in Los Angeles decades earlier. But now he no longer struggled in obscurity. Within the firearms industry, he was a demigod. His M16 was the official rifle used by the American military. For each one sold by Colt, he had received a royalty—1 percent of the sale price of every gun or $1 per gun, whichever was greater, according to his family. He also received royalties on parts that Colt sold to repair the guns. Although his patent on the gas system that made him famous had expired, he continued to receive royalties for years after because of the way the agreements were structured.

His daughter Susan said her father never talked about how much money he earned. Nor did her mother, Jean, who received half the total from their divorce. By the early 1990s, Colt had sold at least 6 million M16s to the military and other armed forces around the world. The company also had sold about three hundred thousand semiautomatic AR-15s on the commercial market. Stoner made money from ARES, outside consulting, and other patents. The money allowed him to fly around in his own helicopter as well as a private jet, a Dassault Falcon 20.

Stoner's second marriage was a happy one. In 1965, one year before Jean Stoner married Stoner's former patent attorney, Tom Mahoney, Stoner married Barbara Hitt, a schoolteacher. Stoner and Barbara met on a blind date in Detroit while Stoner was consulting at Cadillac Gage. Barbara was surprised by how shy and quiet the inventor was. On their date, he pulled a slide rule from his pocket and asked her whether she knew how it worked. She was surprised when he called for a second date. The second date went better, the two ending up alone on a dance floor.

The courtship was quick, and the marriage lasted for the rest of Stoner's life. He and Barb traveled around the world together; she even accompanied him to Iran. Barb learned to fly a helicopter. Stoner told her that she should know how to fly one if anything happened to him. Barb took care of Stoner, overseeing the running of their home so he could work on his inventions. None of his inventions became as well-known or as profitable as the lightweight rifle he built at ArmaLite.

He was proud that American fighting men still used his gun on missions around the world. They used it in the Panama invasion in 1989, the Persian Gulf War in 1990, and the Battle of Mogadishu in 1993. The problems that had plagued the gun in Vietnam were re-solved with ammunition changes, repeated testing, and tweaks to the M16 itself. Scott Neil first used Stoner's gun in combat in Panama as a twenty-one-year-old squad leader for the Seventh Infantry Division. He carried the updated M16A2. He was struck by the ease of shooting and found that the rifle's ergonomics were superior to a gun like the AK-47.

"The magazine drops out quickly," he said. "The AK and some oth-ers, you kind of have to sweep the magazine out and retain it. With the M16, you can quickly dump it and put in another."

In Panama, Neil and his unit fought through the jungle to Panama City. The rifles rarely jammed, but they did have minor issues. To fight in the dark, the men attached cumbersome flashlights to their guns with hose clamps. Another problem was that newer soldiers wasted am-munition in the panic of battle. As squad leader, Neil yelled, "Control your fire!" at eighteen-year-olds firing on full automatic. "It only takes three minutes and they've shot every bullet and yet most engagements take an hour," Neil recalled.

To reduce ammunition being wasted, the army developed a new ver-sion of the gun. Ever since the pray-and-spray days of Vietnam, military officials had fretted about this problem. So they removed the full-auto option from the rifle, giving soldiers guns that could fire either as semi-autos or in three-round bursts.

"You feel like you're being told you're too stupid," Neil said. "But that's exactly why they did it: because you're too stupid."

Some soldiers didn't like the restriction and at least one former Ma-rine hated it. Stoner visited the Marine Corps headquarters in Arling-ton, Virginia, just before the three-round burst limiter was adopted to protest the change. The M16 was a great rifle because it could lay down lots of fire, he argued. Stoner pleaded with General Paul X. Kelley, then the corps' commandant, but to no avail. Stoner viewed it as yet one more example of how the military bungled his creation. It was a re-minder of how the rifle he had invented was no longer his.

Stoner showed little interest in commercial versions of his weapon being sold by Colt, Bushmaster, DPMS Panther, and others. But the commercial AR-15 makers revered Stoner as a firearms genius. They viewed him the way that computer fans viewed Steve Jobs—a man ahead of his time. Unlike Jobs, Stoner was no showman; he cringed at the adulation. Bushmaster's Izzy Anzaldua recalled how he once took a break from manning his company's booth at a conference. He was eating at a table when Stoner quietly sat near him.

"I said 'Oh my God, you're Eugene Stoner,'" Anzaldua remembered. "He looks at me and says, 'Can you pass the salt and pepper?'"

Stoner's daughter said that walking around the SHOT Show in Las Vegas with her father was "like walking with Elvis Presley." But Stoner wasn't into it, she said: "It made him uncomfortable, he did not like the spotlight at all."

Gun historians came to view Stoner with awe. Some published large technical tomes exploring his rifle innovations in detail. In 1988, Edward Ezell, now working for the Smithsonian Institution, interviewed Stoner at ARES in Port Clinton, Ohio. The following year, Ezell traveled to Moscow and interviewed Stoner's Cold War rival, Mikhail Kalashnikov, the inventor of the AK-47. The two men's weapons had changed forever how wars were fought, and millions of fighters across the world used their rifles.

In 1990, Ezell arranged for Stoner and Kalashnikov to meet for the first time. A Smithsonian staffer made a video recording of the two men shooting their rifles at the Marine base at Quantico, Virginia, south of Washington. Stoner, then sixty-seven, calm and portly, and Kalashnikov, seventy, intense and wiry, each fired versions of their inventions. Kalashnikov grew frustrated because he could not insert the magazine into the Chinese version of an AK. After the others tried to fix it, Stoner took the rifle and inspected it. "It's hitting the bolt," he said. He effortlessly inserted the magazine as Kalashnikov looked on.

At dinner during the Smithsonian visit, the men sparred, albeit with good humor. The story has been told in various ways by those in attendance, but in all versions Kalashnikov bragged to Stoner of the medals that he received from the U.S.S.R. for inventing the AK-47. Then he asked Stoner why he hadn't received any medals. Either Stoner or someone else informed Kalashnikov that Stoner didn't receive medals, instead he had earned millions in royalties. Kalashnikov hadn't received royalties, though the Soviet Union had paid him 150,000 rubles for winning the State Stalin Prize in 1949 for his invention.

In his later years, Stoner developed a close friendship with C. Reed Knight Jr., a young man who admired Stoner and hoped to one day have a similar career. Knight grew up in Florida and his family had wanted him to become a citrus grower. But Knight was interested in guns.

Knight's father dismissed his ambition as "rainbow dreams." Undeterred, Knight opened a retail firearms store, and began selling guns and equipment to police departments. He started working with the military, sourcing specialized weapons from around the world, he said. Knight first reached out to Stoner in the late 1970s when he was repairing some Stoner-63 guns for the military and he couldn't find the right parts. He found Stoner in the phone book and called him up out of the blue. Stoner told Knight he could have as many parts as he wanted if he came to see him at ARES in Ohio. Knight piled his family into their van on the pretense of going on a vacation—from the sunny coast of Florida to the shores of Lake Erie. Stoner gave Knight a tour and the two took an instant liking to each other. Stoner ended up giving Knight parts and tooling equipment.

The two men talked for hours about their shared passion, firearm design. Stoner became a mentor for Knight and in 1989, Knight asked Stoner to consult as a weapons designer at his growing defense firm, Knight's Armament Company in Vero Beach, Florida. The two developed new guns, but their success was uneven. In one of their first efforts, Stoner and Knight designed a polymer pistol for Colt called the All American 2000. The company, then struggling financially, hoped the new pistol would help it compete with Glock, which dominated the handgun market. When Stoner and Knight met with Colt's president about the gun, Stoner remarked, "I don't know why Reed and I are sitting here and talking to you because you still owe me money from the M16," Knight recalled. Three months later Stoner got his check and

Colt put the new handgun into production. The handgun caused a stir because it had Stoner's name on it, but it flopped after a safety recall. The pair later designed a semiautomatic precision rifle called the SR-25, and Stoner's name again generated buzz. *Gun World* magazine put the new rifle on its cover, calling it "Stoner's 21st Century Rifle," and gushed that the "Stoner name has joined those of other great designers like Browning or Kalashnikov." The military adopted the SR-25 as a sniper rifle in the late 1990s.

The most successful invention to come out of Knight's armament was not a gun. And though it would have profound ramifications for Stoner's gun, Knight was the one who thought it up. Knight devised a solution to the problem that soldiers had in Panama: they had nowhere to put flashlights on Stoner's rifle. Knight designed a mount for a flashlight that could be attached to the front of the gun.

"I am going to give your gun twenty more years of life," Knight recalled telling Stoner. Stoner replied, "That's ridiculous, no gun has ever lasted that long." Knight proved him wrong. He expanded his mount and developed it into a long piece of corrugated black aluminum that a soldier could use to clip on a flashlight, a forward grip, and other accessories. Knight designed the piece so that it doubled as a front handguard. Knight would go on to sell nearly 2 million to the military. It changed how the gun looked and what extra devices could be attached. On the consumer market, it boosted the market for AR-15 accessories.

Knight expanded his technical reference collection of firearms housed at his company into one of the largest in the world. It included thousands of items, from the world's first machine gun, the Puckle gun, to a Soviet tank. He made honoring Stoner a central part of his private museum. He hired staff to trace and purchase prototypes of the weapons Stoner invented.

During this time, Susan and her husband, Art Kleinpell, moved to Florida to live near her dad. Stoner and his son-in-law took helicopter flying lessons together, and once flew close to the presidents' noses on Mount Rushmore. They designed a lightweight speedboat together. Stoner was always inventing in his head. "You could see him thinking about things—he had a fascinating mind," Art Kleinpell remembered. "He would sit back in his horrible little chair, a little desk chair, and I could see him kind of fitting various elements together."

As politics around the AR-15 grew heated in the 1990s, Stoner stayed out of the fray. Family members didn't recall him offering his opinion about the federal assault-weapons ban.

"I know there were some shootings . . . and I know he was not happy about those," Susan recalled. "But whether to *ban* them? I don't know." Stoner was a lifelong Republican and "a Second Amendment guy," his daughter said.

When Susan told her dad that some people wanted stricter gun laws, she recalled him replying, "Who is killing that person, the gun or the person? People are pulling the trigger. It's the people doing it."

Stoner had little interest in the social and political implications of the weapon that he devoted so much time to inventing and perfecting. Stoner held politicians in low esteem and often commented that they were all lawyers passing laws to benefit themselves. Politics, often fraught with emotion and drama, made him uncomfortable. Whether discussing his guns for military or commercial use, Stoner remained clinical and avoided as much as possible the inventions' purpose: shooting people. He analyzed metals, mechanisms, and tolerances as he envisioned new rifles and cannons. But his daughter said he was detached from the consequences of his creations.

He applied that same detachment to his own mortality. In 1993, at age seventy-one, Stoner was diagnosed with brain cancer. Doctors told him that he didn't have long to live. The consensus among family, friends, and coworkers was that it came from the dangerous chemicals he used for years in his many workshops. It started out as skin cancer on his thumb caused by solvents. Benzene was probably the culprit, his daughter Susan recalled doctors telling Stoner and his family. Stoner's cancer spread from a tiny, undetected spot on his thumb through his nervous system to his brain, and then into his spinal cord. "He never really complained and he was in severe pain," Susan said. Stoner kept working, designing weapons and sketching out new designs on his home drafting table. He tried various treatments and consulted with multiple doctors, but he also prepared for his death in a meticulous manner.

On October 30, 1995, two years after his battle with brain cancer began and just before his seventy-third birthday, Stoner wrote a letter to General Charles Krulak, commandant of the Marine Corps, detailing plans for his own funeral. When he died, he wanted to be remembered for what he considered his greatest invention, the M16.

"My name is Eugene M. Stoner and I served in the Marine Corps during the Second World War," he wrote. "I am also the designer of the M16 Rifle."

He told the general that he wanted to be buried at the Marine Corps' National Cemetery in Quantico, Virginia. He requested that the general make an exception to the traditional fusillade salute by the honor guard. The honor guard normally fired twenty-one shots with their M16s in semiautomatic mode. Instead, Stoner wanted full and prolonged automatic fire. His rifle "was the first enabling infantry-man [sic] to fire effectively in long bursts, and consequently—forever changed the way American Infantry will fight their battles," he wrote.

Stoner gave detailed instructions on the types of his rifles the honor guard should use and how they should fire them. When the guard fired "full automatic" bursts, "each burst could be considered a salvo. I would like three salvos, thus maintaining the Roman Legion's tradition of striking their shields three times to honor fallen comrades."

Stoner took a dig at the military's decision to change his gun, limiting it to three-round bursts. "That is why my request is so specific requesting long bursts."

Stoner saw his life's work as "designing and developing small arms for the U.S. Government," he told the general. He didn't want to be buried in California, where he grew up and where he worked for ArmaLite. He didn't want to be buried in Ohio, where he started ARES. He didn't want to be buried in Florida, where he had spent happy years and worked with Reed Knight. He wanted to be buried among other Marines, on military sacred ground. Creating a new light rifle for U.S. fighters—not weapons for the public or other governments—was his triumph, he believed. The government had wanted a "small caliber/high velocity, lightweight, select fire rifle which engaged targets with salvos of rounds from one trigger pull," Stoner wrote. "That is what I achieved for our servicemen."

Stoner wrote that he appreciated the general taking the time to consider the special request from a former corporal. He signed off his letter with the Marine Corps motto: *semper fidelis*—always faithful.

While the letter was polite, it also carried a rebuke for the military. Bureaucrats had meddled with his gun since the beginning. "The three-shot burst limiters were just kind of a metaphor for taking a perfect weapon and figuring out how to screw it up," said Art Kleinpell, his son-in-law.

The final two years of Stoner's life were painful as the cancer spread, disfiguring his face and draining his strength. Longtime friend and co-founder of ARES Robert Bihun drove to Stoner's Florida home to sit with the inventor.

"He tried to communicate to me but he wasn't lucid," Bihun recalled. "I knew he was terminal. It was traumatic for me to see him slurring his words. I could cry right now because I loved that man so much." On the evening of April 24, 1997, Stoner died at his home. He was seventy-four. Stoner was in his workshop working on new inventions shortly before his death. One of his last projects was a prototype for a lightweight airplane wing.

The New York Times ran a short obituary three days later on page 41 under the headline "Eugene Stoner, 74, Designer of M16 Rifle and Other Arms." The United Kingdom's *Independent* wrote that Stoner was the "last of the independent small arms designers in the tradition of John Browning and John Garand." All of the obituaries recounted Stoner's struggles with the Pentagon bureaucracy, and his Smithsonian-sponsored meeting with Kalashnikov. Not one of them mentioned the civilian version of his invention.

When Stoner's family arrived at Quantico for the funeral, the sky was dark with thunder rumbling, his daughter Susan recalled.

Friends, colleagues, and military officials gathered with the family for the graveside service. Susan didn't recognize some who came. Several men in dark suits and sunglasses attended the service, but didn't say anything. She never figured out who they were. The corps honored Stoner's final request, with three pairs of Marines firing salvos with M16s set to full automatic near Stoner's flag-draped coffin. As the bursts resounded in the air, a ray of sunlight briefly pierced the gray sky and shone down on the gathered crowd, Susan remembered. Decades later, Robert Bihun spoke excitedly when recounting the honor guard firing Stoner's rifles skyward. "I heard it," he said. "I was there."

20.

AR-15 TAKES OFF

You could sell anything if it looked a little bit military.

—John DeSantis

On a bright September morning, the towers came down in monstrous gray plumes. The Pentagon erupted in flames. A jet crashed in a Pennsylvania field. America found itself at war, not against a nation but against a terrorist network from the other side of the world. Fanatics were out to kill not just American soldiers or government officials but any Americans at all, and anywhere they found them. Nowhere seemed safe. Media reports of soldiers mobilizing for war and National Guard troops deploying to public spaces brought Stoner's military rifle into the public consciousness as it hadn't been since Vietnam. Troops carrying M16s were in airports, train stations, bus stations, sporting events, and subways. Gawkers crowded around soldiers with the rifles at Manhattan intersections. A New York Army National Guard colonel told the Associated Press that he knew some people seeing troops with M16s might find them unsettling. "We are hoping, though, that most people find our presence reassuring," he said.

Now the rifle was a weapon for good guys to defeat bad guys. "Those are not toys," a mother told her son at Newark Airport. "They are keeping us safe so we can go see Grandma."

Television news broadcasts showed soldiers and Marines reporting to deployment, hugging their families goodbye, then lining up with rucksacks and M16s. Tattoo artists sold patriotic designs displaying M16s.

Weeks after 9/11, army special forces, Marines, and CIA officers armed with versions of Stoner's rifle moved into Afghanistan to hunt for Osama bin Laden. Green Berets flew secretly into the country weeks after the attacks. They carried M4s, which were smaller, more maneuverable versions of the M16. Army Sergeant First Class Scott Neil's M4 was painted a mixture of browns and tans to blend into the arid Afghan terrain. He and a small group of Green Berets, dressed like Afghan warriors, some riding on horseback deep into Taliban territory, would later be memorialized in news reports, books, and the movie *12 Strong*. The thirty-three-year-old Neil and his comrades were on a covert mission in a hostile country, armed with M4s and little else. Neil slept with the gun close beside him. He slung it over his shoulder as he rode during the day. Cut off from supplies, the men jammed their packs with twelve to fourteen magazines. The M4 worked so well he didn't even need to regularly clean it. He just dusted it off.

One night, Neil's company raided a mountain compound where Taliban and al Qaeda terrorists were hiding. A firefight erupted and Neil was pinned down. He maneuvered from building to building, firing his M4. "In three minutes, we ended up killing twenty-two guys in a small compound," Neil recalled.

Stoner's guns, including civilian versions of the M4, were banned on paper by the government because they were considered a danger to society. Now Americans saw its warriors both home and abroad using those same guns to protect them. The reputation of the rifle was resurrected. Gone were the horrors of Vietnam and emotionally tortured Rambos. The cultists, radicals, white supremacists, and violent psychos who had embraced the gun were forgotten—for the time being. The endless debates in Congress over the weapon seemed to be from another era. For many Americans, the rifle was once again a weapon for their defenders.

"These guys were our new heroes and guess what they carried?"

recalled Doug Painter, a gun industry leader. "This really became the great unexpected ad campaign for the [AR] rifle."

Sales of AR-15s rose. A man in Oklahoma spent $800 on an AR-15 and more on three handguns after September 11. "I'm definitely not a militia-type person," he said. "I don't hunt. I don't like killing things. It's just strictly out of concern for my family." An eighteen-year-old in Nevada went to a gun show hoping to trade in his AR-15 for a better version in case of more terrorist attacks, he told a reporter. "After Sept. 11, it was easier to convince my mom to let me buy one," he said. AR-15 makers embraced the newfound patriotic reputation of the gun in their marketing. For the cover of its 2002 catalog, Bushmaster used a photo of an AR-15 over a camouflage backdrop with the words "Bushmaster . . . First Choice for Defense." The company told customers that the "unbelievable acts of hate and cowardice" were being answered by "deeds of great heroism, courage and selflessness—by Americans both at home and abroad. Bushmaster has never been more proud of our country and the products we manufacture to help in her defense."

"You could sell anything if it looked a little bit military," recalled John DeSantis, Bushmaster's chief executive.

From 2001 to 2003, AR-15 production in America rose 97 percent. At DPMS Panther, Luth decorated his weapons with insignias of military units to boost sales with soldiers and veterans. "We went after that demographic because it was a no-brainer," Luth recalled. The marketing widened the appeal, as did the wars. "The army was actually educating future customers as to the success and fun of an AR-15," he said.

Patriotic fervor crushed the gun-control debate after 9/11. As leading gun-control groups prepared for a political battle in 2004 to win renewal of the federal assault-weapons ban, the movement was in disarray. The coalition that had come together in 1994 was gone.

Suburban moms were now more concerned about terrorism than guns, internal polls by the Brady Campaign to Prevent Gun Violence showed. Women in the 1990s had flooded lawmakers with calls and letters in support of the federal assault-weapons ban, but now gun-control advocates weren't sure they would.

Just a year before 9/11, hundreds of thousands of people had gathered at the National Mall in the first Million Mom March, a group of mothers who wanted stricter gun laws. Protesters carried posters showing semiautomatic rifles, including Stoner's AR-15. They held banners declaring, "Halt the Assault, Save our Children." But the rally did not have a clear political agenda and support faltered. By 2001, a Washington gathering by the Million Mom March brought a crowd of about two hundred people.

Law enforcement leaders, who in 1994 played an essential role in passing the ban, had lost their enthusiasm for the effort. Police officers knew from experience that the ban wasn't working. Unions now used their political capital to arm officers with AR-15s to match the firepower of the bad guys. William Johnson, the executive director of the National Association of Police Organizations, said that his group was no longer persuaded by the arguments for the ban. "It was hard for them to point to this as a success that had been essential for the safety of our nation," Johnson recalled.

Gun-control advocates' worries grew. "If you don't have cops up there saying, 'We don't want these things on our streets mowing people down,' you're done," said Brian Malte, a Brady staffer.

Gun-control activists fought with one another over whether to prioritize pushing for renewal of the federal assault-weapons ban. The disagreements came to a head at a rowdy summit at Brady headquarters in Washington in early 2004. At the organization's invitation, gun-control activists flew in from around the country. About forty people crowded into a conference room. The purpose was to enlist activists to pressure their representatives to support the ban. A top Brady official made the case that the ban had reduced the availability of high-capacity magazines as well as the number of shootings with the prohibited weapons. But most weren't buying what he was selling. "It didn't fly at all," Malte recalled. "There was a lot of yelling, a lot of screaming." The activists were angry because they didn't want to use what little time and money they had on something that didn't work and stood little chance of being renewed, Malte recalled. They were in favor of a stronger prohibition, but that wasn't on the table. Renewing the ban was better than nothing, Malte told them. "Better than nothing isn't really a good call to arms," he said. Everyone left bitter and divided.

As the gun-control movement splintered, the NRA grew stronger. Gun owners rushed to join the group after the 1999 Columbine High School massacre, fearful of new laws that never materialized. The group claimed about 4 million members in 2003. The NRA's magazine, *American Rifleman*, was number two in America for generating ad revenue in 2001, trailing only *Maxim*, the men's magazine that featured pictures of barely clad women. At the NRA's 2000 convention, held in Charlotte in the midst of the presidential campaign, the group's new president, the actor Charlton Heston, raised an antique rifle over his head and issued a threat to people advocating stricter gun laws. "From my cold, dead hands."

Wayne LaPierre had aligned the NRA with the Republican Party since the 1994 assault-weapons ban. This natural coalition, an outgrowth of Ronald Reagan's western brand of libertarian-tinged conservatism, had strengthened over the years. In 1992, the NRA's political action committee spent 36 percent of its campaign contributions on Democrats. By 2002, the PAC was spending just 12 percent on Democrats. The group's firm hold on the GOP became a pivotal factor as the ban came up for reauthorization; Republicans controlled the House, the Senate, and the White House. Although President Bush had said he would sign a reauthorization of the ban if Congress sent it to his desk, the NRA was confident that would never happen.

"Do we agree with the administration's position on this? No, we don't, but the real fight is going to be not at that level, but in Congress," said Chris W. Cox, the NRA's chief lobbyist.

Dianne Feinstein, the remaining member of the Senate troika responsible for writing the 1994 ban, introduced a two-page bill to renew it on February 24, 2004. It called for the law's ten-year sunset clause to be repealed without making any changes. Speaking on the Senate floor, Feinstein said making the ban permanent was vitally important.

"We were told it could not be done—but we did it," she said. "I was even told by colleagues on my own side of the aisle that I was wasting my time—that the gun lobby was just too strong. I hear many of the same arguments today. But we succeeded in 1994, and we will succeed this year."

Toward the end of her remarks she acknowledged that the ban may not have been the resounding success she had long asserted.

"And no matter whether the ban has been entirely effective or not, what is the argument for letting these banned guns back on the streets?" she asked.

Feinstein's rhetoric no longer resonated. Just 50 percent of Americans favored a ban in 2004, down from 59 percent in 2000, according to Gallup. Production of AR-15s had actually increased during the ban years. In the three decades before it went into effect, gunmakers produced four hundred thousand AR-15s. From 1994 through 2004, they built 879,000. Key researchers found what many had suspected: the ban didn't have much effect on gun violence. Two well-known criminologists, Christopher S. Koper and Jeffrey A. Roth, produced studies for the Justice Department and the Urban Institute on the ban's impact that were accepted as the most authoritative research on the subject. Koper, Roth, and their fellow researchers found that during the period before the ban and in its early stages, prices sharply rose for the semiautomatic weapons, including AR-15s. Many academics and politicians had assumed that guns grandfathered under the law would become prohibitively expensive for criminals because of their scarcity. But these researchers found that scarcity was fleeting. Gunmakers flooded the market with ban-modified guns and prices plummeted. By 1996, AR-15 prices had fallen by a third. The ban's impact on reducing injuries or deaths caused by gun violence was mixed, they concluded, since the vast majority of such incidents involved handguns. "[T]he ban's effects on gun violence are likely to be small at best and perhaps too small for reliable measurement," they wrote.

The researchers argued that "reducing criminal use" of the banned "assault weapons" and large-capacity magazines "could have non-trivial effects on gunshot victimizations." Most shooters tended to be poor shots, so those who fired more bullets hurt more people. These weapons accounted for a greater share of the guns used in murders of police and mass public shootings, "though such incidents are very rare."

Koper, Roth, and their colleagues warned that if the ban was lifted, more AR-15s would be built. "It is likely that gun and magazine manufacturers will reintroduce [assault weapons] models and [large-capacity magazines], perhaps in substantial numbers," the authors wrote. "It is also possible, and perhaps probable, that new [assault weapons] and [large-capacity magazines] will eventually be used to commit mass murder."

The ban extension did pass the Senate in the spring of 2004, 52 to 47. Massachusetts senator John Kerry, then running for president, left the campaign trail to cast his vote for the ban renewal. Feinstein declared that the assault-weapons ban would be a major issue in the campaign.

"You can be sure it's going to be in the presidential campaign as a bona fide issue," she said.

But it wasn't. Kerry didn't say much about the ban or gun legislation on the stump, fearful of alienating gun-owning voters. Throughout the campaign, Kerry prefaced any discussion of gun legislation by saying he was a longtime hunter and gun owner who supported the Second Amendment. Speaking to *Outdoor Life* magazine late in the campaign, he said, "My favorite gun is the M16 that saved my life and that of my crew in Vietnam."

The Democratic Party's official platform endorsed the right to own firearms. The party platform replaced the term "gun control" with "gun safety."

Four years earlier, Clinton's vice president, Al Gore, lost the presidential election, arguing on the campaign trail that the federal assault-weapons ban was a success. The NRA played a key role in the GOP victory, even helping swing Gore's home state of Tennessee for the GOP. Donna Brazile, Gore's campaign manager, called the Clinton administration's gun-control measures "a big factor" in the vice president's defeat. By 2004, most Democrats were avoiding discussing the ban, except Feinstein.

Feinstein pleaded for President Bush to push GOP legislators to back the extension. "Please, if you care, if you're listening, do something," she said on the program *Nightline*.

House Republicans dismissed the eleventh-hour efforts and let the ban die without a vote. House Majority Leader Tom DeLay of Texas called the ban "useless."

"It's a feel-good piece of legislation," he said. "And all it does is punish those people that are—that live by the law. And it does nothing to keep assault weapons out of the hands of criminals."

A hunting columnist for *The Grand Rapids Press* wrote that the ban's demise was "much ado about nothing." It was "a classic case of closing the corral after the cows have already split," he wrote.

The failure to renew the assault-weapons ban had little impact on the presidential election. Bush won handily.

Eric Gorovitz, who was policy director for the Million Mom March, was one gun-control activist who was glad to see the ban die. As a student at Johns Hopkins University in Baltimore, he had become convinced that gun violence was a public health crisis facing the nation. When he moved to California, he became involved in gun-control efforts there, including playing a role in that state's legislation that shut down the manufacture of "Saturday Night Specials," cheap handguns that were often used in violent crimes. Later, he worked for California's assault-weapons ban, which became a model for the federal effort. At first, he supported the federal ban. "I thought it would do something," he said. "When I got involved later I realized we never got a real ban."

Shortly after the ban expired, Gorovitz wrote an op-ed for *The Atlanta Journal-Constitution* declaring the ban "was doomed to ineffectiveness from the start because it did not properly define the guns Congress intended to eliminate." He called for a more comprehensive national gun policy, superseding state laws, to try to come to grips with what he saw as a proliferation of dangerous firearms in the country.

When Senator Feinstein's staffers saw Gorovitz's op-ed, they told him he wasn't welcome in their office anymore.

"She just wanted the credit," he said years later. "She didn't want to solve the problem."

Gun industry lobbyists pressed their advantage after the ban died. They got Congress to pass legislation they had promoted for years to limit lawsuits against gun companies. The bill declared gunmakers had no liability for the criminal use of their firearms. It passed in the Senate with fifty Republicans and fourteen Democrats, and one independent voting for it, and two Republicans and twenty-nine Democrats voting against it. Gunmakers had faced waves of lawsuits in the late 1990s and the early 2000s over shootings. In 2004, Bushmaster paid $550,000 as part of a $2.5 million settlement with families of people killed in a series of 2002 sniper attacks that terrorized the nation's capital. The store where the gunmen got the rifle paid the rest. John Allen Muhammad, a destitute, twice-divorced Gulf War veteran in his early forties, and Lee Boyd Malvo, a seventeen-year-old immigrant from Jamaica, had used a Bushmaster XM-15 to kill ten people and wound three others in a series of random attacks. The pair had also killed seven others in other parts of the country. AR-15 makers feared that such settlements with family members of people killed in shootings would put them out of business. With the Protection of Lawful Commerce in Arms Act, signed into law by President Bush in 2005, gunmakers no longer had to worry that they would be sued when their guns were used to kill Americans.

21.

HERE COME THE HEDGE FUNDS

I call them "assault" rifles, which may upset some people.
— Jim Zumbo

The new chief executive of Smith & Wesson, America's largest handgun maker, was not a "gun guy" by his own admission. Mike Golden, a short, stocky middle-aged man with a round face, bald head, and thick mustache, had never fired a gun before he took over the company. In one meeting with stock analysts, he couldn't remember the name of the revolver's cylinder, calling it a "spinny thing" after an awkward pause. Other executives in the room cringed. But Smith & Wesson's board of directors didn't hire Golden in 2004 for his firearms knowledge. They hired him to save the 152-year-old company from financial ruin.

The company had thrived for generations in the "gun valley" of the Connecticut River. Its headquarters in Springfield, Massachusetts, looked like a blocky government complex. It was just miles from the historic Springfield Armory. Now the armory was a museum, and Smith & Wesson was about to go out of business. The company's famous blue-steel revolvers were no longer essential tools for police. American gun owners had launched a boycott of Smith & Wesson after the company had cut a deal with the Clinton administration, agreeing to gun safety measures that gun-rights activists hated. Smith & Wesson was trading just above penny stocks.

Smith & Wesson's dismal economic outlook reflected broader financial troubles in the gun industry. Big cities were filing lawsuits against gun companies. Crime was falling, slowing demand for handguns. Hunting was on the decline. To make up for lost revenue, gun companies offered new product lines that had nothing to do with firearms. Ruger tried making golf club heads. Colt started making luggage. Smith & Wesson made bicycles. Smith & Wesson's London-based parent company owners, Tomkins PLC, decided to cut its losses. In 2001, it sold the gunmaker to a little-known trigger-lock company, Saf-T-Hammer Corp., for just $15 million. Fourteen years earlier, Tompkins had purchased Smith & Wesson for $112.5 million.

Smith & Wesson was an exciting change for Golden, who had climbed the corporate ladder at two well-known consumer giants, Black & Decker and Kohler Co. "It's a little more action than when I was working at Kohler when we were selling toilets," he joked on an earnings call. One of the first things that Golden did when he arrived was to buy himself golden cuff links that were miniature Smith & Wesson .44 caliber Magnum revolvers. That gun, one of the company's most well-known, had been used by Clint Eastwood's character, Harry Callahan, in the 1971 film *Dirty Harry*. That movie had come out during the company's heyday, an era that Golden hoped to re-create. He told his incredulous staff that he wanted the stock price to rise to $20 a share. He spent most of his days in his corner office, looking over financial reports. Golden pressed his team for new guns to sell. He looked to Tom Taylor, his vice president of marketing who had previously worked at Coca-Cola, to analyze industry trends. At Coke, Taylor could analyze how many cans of soda had been sold in any given period, down to the day and even the temperature. But he found a paucity of data on gun sales, so he sent his team out to gun stores to gather some. "It's getting in the car, getting on a plane, going to dealers, and saying, 'What's selling in your store?'" Taylor recalled.

His team quickly discovered that the hottest item was the AR-15, a type of gun Smith & Wesson didn't make.

"You're just sort of watching the market," Taylor remembered. "You're watching Bushmaster explode, you're watching DPMS explode."

Taylor's staff figured that the market for rifles like the AR-15 was worth about $132 million in 2005 and it was growing faster than any other class of rifle or shotgun. Sales of Stoner's rifle had risen to make up 13 percent of the nearly $1 billion market for long guns in America.

Taylor and his colleagues went to Golden, and the men gathered in an executive boardroom near Golden's office. Although the room was far from the factory floor, it was in the same massive building. It reverberated and shuddered from the forges pounding out revolver frames, Taylor recalled. When businessmen came for meetings, they often asked about the pounding. Executives would reply, "That's the heartbeat of Smith & Wesson." But by 2005, that heartbeat could not keep the company alive.

Taylor used PowerPoint slides to show Golden that the future of the company no longer lay with revolvers. The company was selling a new semiautomatic pistol and needed to expand into the AR-15 marketplace too.

"This market is exploding," Taylor said.

Except for a few half-hearted attempts at long guns, Smith & Wesson had been a handgun company for its entire 153-year history. Golden okayed the move.

"Knowing we weren't participating in the fastest-growing segment of the market—he quickly came on board," Taylor remembered.

In January 2006, Smith & Wesson announced its new gun, the M&P 15 Rifle. The lightweight gun was "based upon combat-proven design," the company said. It retailed for $1,200.

That a publicly traded American company was launching its own version of the AR-15 showed how much America had changed in the years after 9/11. The wars in Iraq and Afghanistan, the sunset of the federal assault-weapons ban, and the passage of legislation to protect gunmakers from litigation all combined to create a perfect environment for mainstream gunmakers to make, market, and sell large quantities of AR-15s.

Sales executives realized that the gun's appeal was widening beyond military veterans. Bill Silver, head of commercial sales at Sig Sauer, recalled that the tough-looking military-style weapon had what he called the "wannabe factor." "People want to be a special forces guy," he explained. Silver encouraged executives at Sig Sauer, a Swiss company known for high-end pistols, to build their own version of Stoner's rifle. "I'll sell as many as you can build," Silver told them.

These new customers driving AR-15 sales were ridiculed within the gun industry in the early 2000s, remembered Ryan Busse, a sales executive at the gunmaker Kimber America.

"The industry had these really pejorative sorts of names for this new consumer that popped up," he said. "They called them tactards as in 'tactical retards'; everybody called them couch commandos."

Busse said that fellow sales execs had rolled their eyes at the AR-15 devotees when they approached their booths at gun shows to talk about how great Stoner's rifle was. "Nobody in the industry really wanted anything to do with them or be seen with these people," he said. "Then, the market shifted." Kimber, which specialized in handguns and hunting rifles, never got into the AR-15 business. But almost everyone else did.

When forty thousand people from the gun industry, law enforcement, and the military descended on Las Vegas for the SHOT Show in February 2006, Stoner's gun was everywhere. The show "seemed to be all about the AR. There were ARs of all sizes, calibers, and even colors," wrote David Griffith, the editor of a law enforcement periodical called *Police* magazine. Griffith came across AR-style rifles that shot huge .50 caliber rounds and one that shot tiny BBs. "There were ARs with lights, lasers, grenade launchers," he wrote. SHOT Show attendees crowded around booths of companies offering new AR-15s. "You had to fight your way through the crowds at the [Sig Sauer] booth to even handle these things," one gun blogger wrote. The selling point for the Sig 556 was that it looked exactly like an AR-15, but reincorporated the piston and operating rod that Stoner had removed.

As mainstream gun companies entered the AR market, some of the original "bad boy" AR-15 makers contemplated cashing in and selling their brands. In Maine, Dick Dyke, Bushmaster's owner, told chief executive John DeSantis that he wanted to sell. The company was booming and Dyke believed he could command a high price. Dyke was paying himself about $1 million a year, according to DeSantis. DeSantis urged him not to sell; profits hadn't reached their peak. Dyke dismissed the advice and hired a broker to reach out to potential buyers.

Potential buyers showed immediate interest. In December 2005, five separate groups flew in private jets to Portland and then drove in limousines up to Bushmaster's headquarters—a few metal buildings that resembled the offices of a midsize lumberyard. DeSantis gave each group of visitors a PowerPoint presentation with charts and graphs showing profits and the company's growth. In 2004, Bushmaster brought in $46.6 million, with more than $7 million in earnings. By 2005, revenue reached $60.8 million, with $11.2 million in earnings. The visitors were surprised when they toured Bushmaster operations. The area where workers assembled more than five thousand guns a month was just eighteen thousand square feet, about one-third the size of a football field.

One group caught DeSantis's attention. They were Wall Street money men like the rest, but they actually knew something about guns. They worked for a private equity firm called Cerberus. They told DeSantis that their boss, Stephen Feinberg, liked guns and was interested in buying a gun company. DeSantis had never heard of the man.

Most Americans had never heard of Feinberg or his Manhattan-based private equity firm, even though the businesses it controlled had more than $30 billion combined in annual sales. "What's Bigger Than Cisco, Coke, or McDonald's?" *BusinessWeek* asked in a headline. Cerberus oversaw businesses that had little to do with each other, including National and Alamo car-rental companies, Formica Corp., and 226 Burger King restaurants. The forty-five-year-old Feinberg kept a low profile. He refused interviews, and the firm's bare website didn't list the companies it ran.

Feinberg was the son of steel salesmen and grew up in a small town north of New York City. His intelligence got him into Princeton. After college, he worked on Wall Street as a trader before cofounding Cerberus at the age of thirty-two. He and a partner named the hedge fund after the snarling three-headed dog that guarded Hades in Greek mythology. They chose the image to show how vigilant the firm would be with investors' money. Feinberg's playbook was simple and successful: buy undervalued companies, usually with money he borrowed, slash costs by firing employees and other means, and sell the companies for a large profit.

Feinberg's fortune grew; he reportedly earned about $50 million in 2004 alone. But he didn't spend his wealth on the traditional indulgences of the rich and powerful.

"While other hedge-fund managers are collecting fine French wines and flying around in private planes, he drives a Ford truck and drinks Budweiser," a friend told *BusinessWeek*.

Feinberg liked to hunt. He hired a renowned sniper to teach him how to hit targets over great distances. The former Marine Steve Reichert was known for shooting an enemy combatant in Iraq from more than a mile away, one of the longest recorded kills in American military history. Reichert taught Feinberg how to read the wind and adjust his aim. Feinberg studied trajectories as he did company financials. On a trip to Colorado, he reportedly climbed an eleven-thousand-foot mountain and killed a giant bull elk with one shot.

When Dick Dyke unsealed bids for Bushmaster, Cerberus had made the highest offer: $76 million—315 times what Dyke had paid for the company in 1976. Almost all of the $76 million would go to Dick Dyke and his son, Jeff, who together owned about 98 percent of the company. Dyke was thrilled but Bushmaster's employees were worried about a private equity takeover. DeSantis, who remained on as chief executive, wondered why Feinberg, a Wall Street giant, wanted to buy Bushmaster. Feinberg's Cerberus controlled sprawling international operations. Why did he want little Bushmaster?

"He never got involved with a company that was worth less than a billion dollars," DeSantis said. "Seventy-five million or whatever— that's small potatoes for him."

But the Bushmaster purchase was just the first step in Cerberus's grand plan to shake up and ultimately dominate the gun industry. Feinberg's point man on the project was George Kollitides II, a Columbia MBA who had first learned about the importance of margins by calculating the cost of gas for his childhood lawn-mowing business. After the United States invaded Afghanistan, Kollitides came up with the idea to invest in private companies aiding the war effort, including those manufacturing firearms, according to his deposition in later court proceedings. But the military market for guns was smaller than he expected and he worried about its volatility. No war meant fewer sales. Instead, Kollitides grew intrigued by the U.S. civilian gun market. "There was a gigantic thriving commercial market and there may be an opportunity there," he recalled. He was amazed by the fact that one-third of Americans owned guns—a huge built-in customer base was waiting to be sold more product.

But the gun industry at the time was a fractured ecosystem of small companies. Most gunmakers were privately owned and the two publicly traded companies, Smith & Wesson and Ruger, were worth a combined $330 million at the end of 2005, a small sum by Cerberus's standards. Kollitides decided to apply a standard private equity practice: buy up and consolidate. If the plan worked, the company could sell gun owners every kind of firearm they wanted, including ARs, and bring down the cost of production through scale. "There is cost-cutting opportunities which generate your return," he said. He set out to build a billion-dollar gun company.

Kollitides understood the AR-15 to be central to this mission. The market for the gun had been growing about 8 percent every year from 1998 to 2005. "I would challenge you to find a consumer product that grows at eight percent consistently for seven years," he recalled. "As an investor, this would excite me."

Kollitides seized upon an emerging realization in the gun industry: the AR-15 had become its financial savior. Almost two hundred thousand AR-15s were built for sale in America in 2006, a new record. Smith & Wesson's stock rose above ten dollars.

America's leading gun companies embraced Stoner's rifle, but some of the gun world's most well-known personalities still found the military-style weapon off-putting. One such celebrity was Jim Zumbo, a Stetson-wearing outdoorsman from Wyoming and a well-known writer for *Outdoor Life* magazine, a popular journal for hunters and fishermen. Zumbo hosted a television show on the Outdoor Channel, and many gun owners considered Zumbo to be *the* authority on hunting. "He's like our Michael Jordan," said Linda Powell, who worked in public relations for Remington Arms and often hunted with Zumbo. Readers and viewers paid close attention to the guns Zumbo used. "It's kind of like with sports figures, you look at the tennis shoes they wear, what kind of gear or equipment they're using and you aspire to use the same thing your hero uses," Powell said. Powell's company, Remington, known for its hunting rifles and shotguns, sponsored Zumbo's television show.

"Jim carrying our gun on his hunt and Jim wearing our hat—that sells a lot of guns," she said.

That all changed in February 2007, when the sixty-six-year-old Zumbo was out on a coyote hunt in Elk Mountain, Wyoming. On the first day, the hunting party shot coyotes and then returned to the lodge. As they stowed their guns, Zumbo saw someone with an AR-15. "What the hell is that doing here?" he asked. The guide who owned the gun said the rifle was becoming more common on coyote and prairie dog hunts. Zumbo was aghast, telling the young man that it didn't look like a hunting rifle. With that conversation rattling in his head and a scotch in hand, Zumbo fired up his laptop to update his *Hunting with Zumbo* blog on the *Outdoor Life* website. His editors had been telling him to post items that sparked conversation. He typed out a post and hit send. The blog post was titled "Assault Rifles for Hunters?"

> The guides on our hunt tell me that the use of AR and AK rifles have a rapidly growing following among hunters, especially prairie dog hunters. I had no clue. Only once in my life have I ever seen anyone using one of these firearms . . .
>
> I call them "assault" rifles, which may upset some people.

Excuse me, maybe I'm a traditionalist, but I see no place for these weapons among our hunting fraternity. I'll go so far as to call them "terrorist" rifles . . . Sorry, folks, in my humble opinion, these things have no place in hunting. We don't need to be lumped into the group of people who terrorize the world with them, which is an obvious concern. I've always been comfortable with the statement that hunters don't use assault rifles.

Zumbo finished up the hunt, bagging a couple of coyotes. The first indication that anything was wrong came when Linda Powell called him as he drove home. Complaints were pouring in about the blog post, she told him. Next, Zumbo got a message to call Ted Nugent, the Detroit rock musician and celebrity NRA spokesman. "Zumbo, you fucked up," the rocker told him. Zumbo logged online and saw hundreds of comments. "You are a fucking POS, fuck you Zumbo, go suckle on Hillary Clinton's bosoms a little more, you uninformed fucktard, good day, sir," one reader commented. Hundreds of readers canceled their subscriptions to *Outdoor Life*. "If these are 'terrorist rifles,' then are you calling me, a law abiding, Constitution defending, family man a terrorist?" another reader wrote.

Zumbo appended a hasty apology to his blog, saying the post was the "biggest blunder in my 42 years." Remington dropped their sponsorship, and the Outdoor Channel suspended his show.

"In what might be considered the fastest career collapse in history, Jim Zumbo—for decades one of the nation's most visible outdoor writers and broadcasters—has lost everything in a matter of only a few days," one outdoors columnist wrote.

Zumbo's downfall showed that the AR-15 had become a key cultural icon for gun owners.

"The industry, all the organizations, had no clue that the AR-15 owners were that strong," recalled Randy Luth.

Though Remington didn't make AR-15s, Linda Powell said she was later informed that the orders to drop Zumbo had come from Cerberus, the private equity firm that was in the process of buying the company. With Bushmaster, Cerberus was already the largest AR-15 maker in the country. Cerberus couldn't tolerate being associated with writers who attacked the AR-15. "It was strictly business for them," she said. AR-15s were too important to the bottom line. Zumbo was expendable.

Cerberus closed the deal for Remington, paying $118 million and assuming the company's $252 million debt. Remington was the next big step in Cerberus's quest for gun-industry domination. Feinberg even made moves to acquire Colt. One day at the Manhattan headquarters, Feinberg pulled DeSantis into a conference room. If Cerberus bought Colt, it would have an entrée into the lucrative world of military contracts, DeSantis recalled Feinberg telling him.

"Do you want to make money?" DeSantis asked Feinberg.

"Of course I do," he answered.

"Then don't buy Colt," DeSantis said.

But Feinberg insisted, so DeSantis traveled to Hartford to meet with Colt executives. "Feinberg wanted that company so bad he could taste it," he recalled. Colt's asking price was over $200 million. DeSantis advised Feinberg against it. Cerberus put in a bid, but well below the asking price. The deal never happened.

Cerberus's efforts to build a firearms conglomerate were not the subject of mainstream media coverage. But in the world of firearms, everyone was talking about the empire he was building. "Holy mackerel, this ain't good for me," Randy Luth, the owner of the second-largest AR-15 maker, DPMS, recalled thinking. Luth decided to sell his company to Cerberus.

Rumors circulated in internet chat rooms that the billionaire George Soros—the investor and supporter of liberal causes despised by conservatives—was behind the deals with the goal of shutting down production. Eventually, the NRA would issue a statement, seeking to dispel the rumors.

By controlling DPMS and Bushmaster, Stephen Feinberg's gun firm became by far the largest manufacturer of AR-15s in America. The two companies combined to produce 118,000 ARs in 2007, nearly half the number made in the United States that year. The compounded annual growth rate for the long-gun market—hunting rifles, shotguns, etc.—was 5 percent from 2004 to 2007. The rate for the AR-15 market was 36 percent. The men running the new gun conglomerate were sure they could sell even more. They launched a camouflage AR-15 model under the Remington brand, hoping to draw hunters to the semiautomatic rifle. They increased credit lines for wholesalers, the middlemen who bought the guns from manufacturers and then sold them to gun shops. Under Dyke, Bushmaster could send $250,000 worth of AR-15s to its largest wholesaler, but nothing more until the wholesaler paid up. Feinberg's group raised the limit to $750,000, allowing Bushmaster to produce and sell its guns at an even faster pace. "As soon as that opened up, we just went crazy," DeSantis recalled. Bushmaster and DPMS leaned on suppliers to reduce costs with their massive buying power, further increasing profit margins.

The 2008 presidential election also supercharged the AR-15 market. The leading candidates for the Democratic nomination—New York senator Hillary Clinton and Illinois senator Barack Obama—avoided talking about guns, even after a college student killed thirty-two people at Virginia Tech. He was armed with two semiautomatic handguns. One candidate, Delaware senator Joe Biden, then trailing in the polls, called for a reinstatement of the federal assault-weapons ban. As the field narrowed, Clinton and Obama accused each other of wanting to restrict gun ownership. When news leaked that Obama said at a fundraiser that it was not surprising that small-town voters "cling to guns," Clinton attacked. She talked about how her grandfather had taught her to shoot a gun. "It's part of culture. It's part of a way of life," Clinton said. Obama responded that Clinton was "talking like she's Annie Oakley."

During the only Democratic primary debate in which guns were discussed at length, Clinton pledged to reinstate the ban that her husband had signed into law fourteen years earlier. Obama took no position on the ban during the debate, though on his website he had promised to reinstate it.

In the midst of the 2008 presidential race, the U.S. Supreme Court ruled for the first time that the Second Amendment protected an individual's right to keep and bear arms. The 5–4 ruling in *District of Columbia v. Heller* embraced an interpretation of the Second Amendment that the NRA and its allies had been arguing for years. For the majority, the conservative Justice Antonin Scalia wrote that the first clause of the Second Amendment—"A well regulated Militia, being necessary to the security of a free State"—did not limit the second clause—"the right of the people to keep and bear Arms, shall not be infringed." The Second Amendment guaranteed the "individual right to possess and carry weapons in case of confrontation," Scalia wrote. Scalia left open the possibility of regulating or limiting what he called "dangerous and unusual weapons," but he didn't specify which ones. Pro-gun lawyers prepared challenges to state assault-weapons bans, believing that the decision in *Heller* meant such bans were unconstitutional. Gun-control advocates readied their defenses, arguing such bans were the limitations that Scalia had in mind.

Obama, by then the presumptive Democratic nominee, delivered a cautious response to the decision, saying he supported an individual right to own guns, and some gun-control measures. His remarks were part of a strategy to appeal to working-class voters in key swing states such as Pennsylvania and Ohio. The Democrat learned from watching what happened to his predecessors in 2000 and 2004 that talking gun control didn't help Democrats win national elections.

But Obama's moderate stance made no difference to the NRA. The group announced it would spend a record $40 million to defeat him and back Arizona senator John McCain, the Republican nominee. The gun group warned its members that if Obama were to be elected, sweeping gun-control measures would follow: "Never in NRA's history have we faced a presidential candidate—and hundreds of candidates running for other offices—with such a deep-rooted hatred of firearm freedoms." The NRA launched a website, GunBanObama.com, and claimed he would be "the most anti-gun president in American history."

The NRA's campaign fueled AR-15 sales. Gun shops taped up NRA posters declaring, "On the Second Amendment, Don't Believe

Obama!" Dealers at gun shows displayed photos of Obama and advised shoppers to "Get 'em before he does." On Wall Street, investors were thrilled with the fear that was fueling sales. One analyst queried Smith & Wesson's Golden on an earnings call about the "atmospherics on the pre-election buildup" and the growth potential for gun sales.

"Some of the growth in tactical rifles is pre-election buying," Golden said. "You talk to some guys that have been in the industry for a while and they think it's only going to continue to increase as we get closer to November, depending on how things are looking."

By the end of October, things looked good for Obama—and the gun industry. For the three months that ended on October 31, 2008, sales of Smith & Wesson's version of the AR-15 rose 308 percent when compared to the same three months the prior year.

"M&P 15 sales were helped by a consumer promotion as well as what appears to have been speculation on the outcome of the presidential election," the company told investors.

On November 4, 2008, Barack Obama became the first Black U.S. president. As he spoke to a large crowd in Chicago's Grant Park that night, he cast his victory as a triumph of hope over the politics of fear. But with his election, panicked gun owners rushed to buy AR-15s. In Florida, a salesman at Shoot Straight Tampa spent hours "fitting assault rifles to the palms of gun-hungry customers," the *St. Petersburg Times* reported. Jim's Pawn Shop in Fayetteville, North Carolina, was selling fifteen to twenty AR-15s every day: "It's been an absolute madhouse," a manager said. In Texas, a Fort Worth gun shop called Cheaper than Dirt! sold $101,000 in firearms and accessories the day after the election, an all-time high. One customer said he was motivated to buy an AR-15 after receiving postcards from the NRA. The FBI conducted more background checks for firearms purchases that November than in any other month since the modern background-check system was instituted in 1998. AR-15 makers called it "the Barack boom."

All that year, Bushmaster's fleet of GMC trucks were in constant motion, picking up parts from machine shops and delivering them to the Maine industrial park. Warehouse workers put in six days a week,

HERE COME THE HEDGE FUNDS · 249

from seven in the morning to eight at night, assembling rifles by hand. By the end of 2008, Bushmaster had built a record 85,700 ARs, a 44 percent increase from the year before.

"In those days you could sell anything you could make," recalled John DeSantis. DPMS, the private equity group's other AR manufacturer, made 94,500 ARs that year, a 60 percent jump. At least twenty-six different gun companies made 444,000 AR-15-style rifles for sale in the United States in 2008, representing nearly 10 percent of all guns made in the U.S. that year.

The sales bonanza persuaded even the most conservative gunmakers to join in. Ruger, whose founder had resisted making ARs for decades until he died in 2002, launched its first AR-15 model in 2009. Colt decided in 2011 to reenter the commercial AR-15 market. The decision was made by the chief executive, Gerry Dinkel, who was brought in to save the company. The company's controlling shareholder wanted Dinkel to bring in more sales from foreign militaries. But Dinkel felt that the only way to make up for declining U.S. military sales was to add the commercial AR-15 sales to the international business. "It almost didn't matter how many rifles were being sold out there, the fact that people could now buy a Colt rifle, as opposed to somebody else's rifle, would guarantee a strong market share for us," Dinkel remembered.

At a London pub in late 2010, Dinkel made his pitch to a major Colt shareholder. He said that sales of ARs on the commercial market could add up to $100 million in annual revenue. Sales of Colt's new AR-15 were robust and helped to keep the company afloat. "Everybody was happy," said Dinkel.

Executives at Feinberg's gun firm moved to grab an even larger share of the expanding AR-15 market. They changed the company's name from American Heritage Arms to Freedom Group. They pushed their AR-15s into big-box stores such as Walmart, slashing the prices of their low-end rifles to get them on the shelves of America's largest retailer. They wanted to sell as many as possible. "With Cerberus and them, it's all about the numbers and volume," remembered Luth, who was still in charge at DPMS.

Money poured into Freedom Group and other gun companies, while every other business sector struggled as the global financial crisis plunged the United States into a recession. America's Big Three automakers were on the brink of insolvency. The value of Cerberus's substantial stakes in Chrysler and General Motors' financing arm, GMAC, plummeted. Feinberg's investors withdrew more than $4.77 billion in response to the losses.

Feinberg's private equity firm now looked to the gun company as a source of funds. Freedom Group filed to go public in October 2009, hoping to raise $200 million. The company boasted to potential investors that it was the largest producer of AR rifles in America, controlling 49 percent of a fast-growing market. Net sales of the gun increased by $50 million in the first six months of 2009 when compared with the same period of the previous year. Freedom Group's prospectus predicted that sales of Stoner's rifle would grow even more by courting a new generation of AR-15 owners.

While growing up in California's Coachella Valley, Eugene Stoner liked making things explode. He built a primitive cannon and a rocket that accidentally smashed into the side of his parents' house. *(Photograph courtesy of Susan Kleinpell)*

Stoner served as a Marine during World War II. "Imagine being twenty years old, obsessed with guns, cannons, and then being able to work with the big stuff during a war," his daughter Susan said. *(Photograph courtesy of Susan Kleinpell)*

Stoner married his high school sweetheart, Jean. When he came back from the war he presented her with a gift: gun parts that he assembled into a working rifle. *(Photograph courtesy of Susan Kleinpell)*

The Stoner family: Jean and Gene with their children, Michael, Patty, and Susie (on her mother's lap). *(Photograph courtesy of Susan Kleinpell)*

Eugene Stoner, wearing his trademark bow tie, holds his creation the AR-10. The AR-15 was a scaled-down version of this gun. *(Photograph courtesy of Susan Kleinpell)*

ArmaLite's fifteenth creation was the AR-15. Here, Stoner poses with an AR-15 at ArmaLite's Costa Mesa offices. *(Photograph courtesy of Susan Kleinpell)*

President John F. Kennedy's administration embraced the AR-15 as new technology to help combat Communist aggression. Here, Kennedy holds the gun in the Oval Office on April 19, 1963. An aide holds a crossbow. *(JFK Library / Getty Images)*

Marine Lance Corporal Fred Monahan was awarded the Navy Cross for his bravery during intense fighting near Khe Sanh, South Vietnam, in May 1967. During the battle, Monahan's M16 jammed as he used it to fend off attackers. "I never want to see one again as long as I live," Monahan said of the M16, the military's designation for the AR-15. "I hated it." Here, he is at a training area on Okinawa in early April 1967, shortly after being issued the weapon. *(Photograph courtesy of Fred Monahan)*

A Marine holds his M16 as he takes cover behind a burned-out vehicle in Hue, Vietnam, during the Tet Offensive. *(Bettmann Archive / Getty Images)*

During a chance visit to ArmaLite's offices, the actor John Wayne became the first person not working for the company to fire an AR-15. He later purchased versions of the gun and bragged about his role in its history. The rifle was featured in Wayne's 1968 hawkish film *The Green Berets. (Sunset Boulevard / Getty Images)*

The Democratic senator Dianne Feinstein of California was a key advocate in Congress of the 1994 assault-weapons ban. After the ban sunsetted in 2004, she continually pushed to reinstate it without success. Here, Senator Feinstein holds a news conference in January 2013, shortly after the Sandy Hook Elementary School massacre. *(Photograph by Alex Wong / Getty Images)*

Randy Luth was one of the first gunmakers to sell AR-15s to civilians. In the 1980s and 1990s, his company, DPMS Panther Arms, was shunned by mainstream firearms firms and by traditional hunters. *(Photograph by Patrick Fallon)*

Francine and David Wheeler with their sons, Nate (left) and Ben. Ben was one of the twenty children who were shot and killed at Sandy Hook Elementary School on December 14, 2012. He was six years old. *(Photograph courtesy of the Wheeler family)*

The veteran Chris Waltz was appalled when Democratic politicians called for restricting the sale of AR-15s after Sandy Hook. Waltz launched AR-15 Gun Owners of America as a protest page on Facebook. Soon the effort morphed into a thriving business selling AR-15 accessories and, eventually, AR-15s. *(Photograph by Dustin Chambers)*

Stephen Paddock used numerous AR-15s to shoot from his
Las Vegas hotel room down at the Route 91 Harvest country music festival
on the night of October 1, 2017. It was the worst mass shooting in modern
American history. *(Photograph by David Becker / Getty Images)*

Nadine Lusmoeller was wearing these cowboy boots when she was
shot during the Las Vegas attack. Six months after the shooting,
she sought closure by burning the boots, which were stained with
blood. She spread the ashes at the site of the massacre. *(Photograph by
Nadine Lusmoeller)*

On Valentine's Day, 2018, Nikolas Cruz used an AR-15 to kill seventeen people at Marjory Stoneman Douglas High School in Parkland, Florida. Here, students are led out of the school in single file with their hands on one another's shoulders. A police officer armed with an AR-15-style rifle stands watch. *(Photograph by Joe Raedle / Getty Images)*

Protesters and police clash on January 6, 2021, as a man waves a Confederate battle flag bearing the image of an AR-15 and the words "Come and Take It." *(Photograph by Joseph Prezioso / AFP)*

While the AR-15 became a symbol for gun-rights advocates, it also became a symbol for gun-control activists. The sign here was from a May 2022 rally at the U.S. Capitol following the shooting in Uvalde, Texas. *(Tom Williams / CQ-Roll Call, Inc. / Getty Images)*

On July 4, 2022, a twenty-one-year-old man opened fire with an AR-15 on a parade in the Chicago suburb of Highland Park, Illinois. Here, law enforcement officers armed with AR-15-style rifles escort a family away from the scene. *(Photograph by Mark Borenstein / Getty Images)*

Valerie Kallis-Weber was shot twice by AR-15-wielding attackers on December 2, 2015, at a holiday gathering for government workers in California's San Bernardino County. She endured scores of surgeries and thousands of hours of therapy. "This is one of the star fighters," said one of her doctors. *(Photograph courtesy of Valerie Kallis-Weber)*

22.

THE MAN CARD

MINE IS SO DEFINITELY BIGGER THAN YOURS.
—Proposed Bushmaster advertisement

A great way to reach young men in the 2000s was to place an ad in *Maxim* magazine. With scantily clad models and regular features on sex, it was the ultimate bro bible. Every month, it delivered on the promise in its tagline, "Sex Sports Beer Gadgets Clothes Fitness." It attracted a huge following among men ages eighteen to thirty-four, a demographic coveted by advertisers. By 2005, *Maxim*'s monthly circulation topped 2.5 million. Glossy spreads for Patrón tequila, Nautica cologne, and Cadillac filled the magazine's pages. But Freedom Group's marketing team believed that *Maxim* was the perfect venue to launch a bold new ad campaign for Bushmaster's AR-15 model. They turned to one of their ad agencies, Brothers & Company, a Tulsa firm that specialized in outdoor recreation and sports marketing, to create an ad that would grab the attention of the magazine's readers.

"The mostly educated, higher-than-average-income Maxim reader isn't cracking open their new issue hoping the latest AR ad can be found there," Brothers & Company wrote in an internal memo for Freedom Group in September 2009. "We not only must cut through the clutter of advertising, we have to make our product the sexiest thing in the magazine." The agency proposed five ads that would "speak to the primal core of the Maxim reader, both with refreshingly brutal honesty and humor." The memo warned that while they "will certainly make you squirm, if you want to sell Bushmaster guns in *Maxim*, these are the ads for the mission."

They weren't subtle. The first proposed ad was a large photo of Bushmaster's AR-15 rifle, the XM-15, pointed out at the reader. Below the gun, in giant black letters, the ad copy declared: MINE IS SO DEFINITELY BIGGER THAN YOURS. At the bottom of the full-page ad it read: "If it's good enough for the military, it's good enough for you. Bushmaster. The world's finest commercial AR-platform rifle."

Other proposed ads carried equally brash messaging: HELPING MEN GROW A PAIR SINCE 1978, YOUR iPHONE JUST LOST ALL NOVELTY, IT IS NEVER TOO LATE TO BE A MAN, and CONSIDER YOUR MAN CARD REISSUED.

The men at Freedom Group declared the Man Card ad the winner. It appeared in the November 2009 issue of *Maxim* opposite a photo of the female stars of the television show *Battlestar Galactica*, wearing bikini bottoms and skimpy halter tops. Only the small print at the bottom of the full-page ad was slightly changed from the draft to say, "If it's good enough for the professional, it's good enough for you."

The men at Freedom Group were so excited about the Man Card promotion that they dedicated seven pages to it in their internal marketing plan for 2010. The presentation explained the concept behind the ad: "Every man carries an 'implied' man card, representative of his status as a man, and the privileges accompanying said status. In this ad, we imply that by buying a Bushmaster, your man card is reissued." It then described a new online phase of the Man Card campaign that would appear on Bushmaster's website that spring. Visitors to the site would have the chance to revoke their buddies' Man Cards for being a "crier" or a "cupcake." They could provide a description of the offense, such as "Jeff stayed at home to watch 'Mama Mia' with his girlfriend instead of going out to poker night with the boys," according to the presentation. Bushmaster would send an email to the accused, who would have to take a quiz to retain their Man Card. Visitors could also take a test to get their own Man Card by answering questions such as, "Which of these best expresses your inner light?" The possible answers were a kitten, a candle, or an AR-15. A kitten and a candle were the wrong answers.

Freedom Group launched a large promotional campaign for the website with ads in gun magazines, social media promotion, and a big push at the NRA annual show in Charlotte, North Carolina. "In a world of rapidly depleting testosterone, The Bushmaster Man Card declares and confirms that you are a Man's Man, the last of a dying breed, with all the rights and privileges duly afforded," the site copy read.

Freedom Group's ad campaign arrived in an era when American men were feeling particularly insecure. The Great Recession had destroyed 8 million jobs, three-quarters of which had been held by men. For the first time in U.S. history, more women were working than men. Women were outpacing men in education too, earning three college degrees for every two that men earned. The American male physique was deteriorating. In 2010, the average weight of an American male was 196 pounds, up from 166 pounds fifty years before. At work, men sat at desks staring at computer screens. At night, they stared at video games or television shows. Hunting continued to wane. Just 5 percent of Americans older than sixteen went hunting in 2006, according to the U.S. Fish and Wildlife Service. The flaccid existence of most men was mocked in popular culture. Television shows such as the animated *Family Guy* and the sitcom *King of Queens* presented fat, oblivious morons as typical American males.

Bushmaster's remedy: get an AR-15.

Yet the tough-guy image Bushmaster promoted was a paradox. The gun looked martial and intimidating, but Eugene Stoner had designed it to be easy to aim and shoot for just about anyone. Recoil was minimal, making quick follow-up shots a breeze. Shooters felt like expert marksmen at the shooting range with little practice. In many ways, the AR-15 was the ideal firearm for the modern American man: it looked macho, but he didn't have to put much effort into shooting it. Deer-hunting rifles and shotguns delivered a tremendous kick to the shoulder. Handguns required steady arms. The AR-15 was well suited for shooters of small stature, a key sales pitch made by Stoner and Colt representatives during their trips to Asia.

American civilians generally weren't using the gun for hunting. Most AR-15 owners used their rifles for shooting paper targets at the range, according to the first comprehensive survey of AR owners in 2010 by the National Shooting Sports Foundation. When asked where they had shot their AR-15 in the last twelve months, 44 percent of those queried said a public shooting range, while another 44 percent said a private shooting range. Just 19 percent said they used the gun for hunting on private land. The top reasons for owning an AR-15 in order were: target shooting, home defense, collecting, varmint hunting, competition shooting, big-game hunting, and, lastly, professional use. The typical AR owner was male (99 percent) and married (73 percent) with no military or law enforcement background (56 percent). Many paid keen attention to political discussion of gun rights. Eight in ten had purchased their most recent AR since 2008, the year that Obama was elected. AR-15 owners were richer and younger than typical gun owners. The key demographic most likely to spend more than $600 on accessories and parts were men under thirty-five who owned three or more AR-15s and made more than $110,000 a year, according to the survey. That was precisely the *Maxim* demographic.

The Man Card campaign was a sharp departure in tone from previous marketing at Bushmaster. A typical Bushmaster ad in *Shotgun News* from earlier years would feature photos of rifles and parts with detailed descriptions of their specifications. In one from 1998, Bushmaster highlighted that its rifles had "Heavy Profile Premium Match Grade Barrels," and "manganese phosphate finish for rust and corrosion protection." This ad approach, devoid of sex appeal, appealed to aging gun hobbyists who already owned a lot of guns. The percentage of American households that owned guns had dropped to 31 percent in 2010 from 50 percent in 1977. By 2004, 20 percent of America's gun owners owned 65 percent of the nation's 283 million guns, researchers from the Harvard School of Public Health found in a comprehensive survey of American gun ownership. Gunmakers worried that these older buyers were tapped out on purchases and weren't passing down the hunting tradition to their children and grandchildren. The firearms industry needed to find a way to reach younger customers.

Some gun marketers saw video games as a potential way to market their products. Gun companies and game designers made agreements to place name-brand AR-15s and other weapons in games that were popular with boys and young men. Gunmakers didn't need to seek these deals out at first; designers who wanted their games to look realistic came to them. Money rarely changed hands. But with the appearance of AR-15s in these games, the gun's makers suddenly accessed millions of potential new customers. Bill Silver, head of commercial sales at the gunmaker Sig Sauer, called putting the gun in these games "seed planting."

At Freedom Group, a marketing team prepared a memo called "Gaming Strategy" that they marked "confidential" and "for internal use only." It promoted the view that video games were an excellent way to expose a new generation to guns and turn teens and young men playing the games into gun buyers. "With increasing urbanization and access to shooting/hunting areas in decline, a primary means for young potential shooters to come into contact with firearms and ammunition is through virtual gaming scenarios," the memo stated. "Gaming allows millennials without access to shooting facilities or mentors to be exposed to shooting."

The marketing team believed that "being included in these games will be beneficial to [Freedom Group] and help create brand preference among the next generation who experiences these games, allowing [Freedom Group] to win our fair-share of these young customers."

The memo outlined how its guns should appear on-screen. Acceptable games included hunting, military, and nonmilitary scenarios where the shooter was acting legally and ethically. But games where civilian bad guys could be targets should not carry the company's name. "Previous experience tells us people will seek out the brand of the guns," the marketing team wrote. "A lack of direct branding helps to shield us from the implications of a direct endorsement while still receiving benefit from inclusion in the game."

Freedom Group's executives were amazed by how well the video-game marketing worked. "It really is irony that video games that just a decade ago were considered the number one threat to gaining new shooters is perhaps now the number one draw," one Freedom Group vice president wrote in an internal email.

"It's just another way to get their name out there," recalled Pete Blumel, a producer at the video-game designer Infinity Ward, which created the popular game franchise *Call of Duty*. One of Blumel's responsibilities at Infinity Ward was to select the weapons for the games. Once they decided on the guns, Blumel would have the actual firearms photographed from every angle so the guns would appear as realistic as possible. He had his staff meticulously record audio of real guns being fired. Stoner's rifle was included in games because it was "the American gun," Blumel said.

When *Call of Duty: Modern Warfare 2* was released in November 2009, it smashed video-game sales records. The game included a controversial level called "No Russian" that featured a mass shooting. In the level, the player had the option to kill unarmed civilians in an airport with an M4 or another weapon. Players could chase fleeing people, shooting them down and even firing at the wounded as they tried to crawl away, moaning and crying. Religious leaders condemned the brutality, but the game was well received by critics and fans.

Some gunmakers found video-game promotion distasteful and wouldn't participate. Randy Luth at DPMS Panther turned down requests to have his gun appear in games.

"I didn't want to be part of using our brand name to teach kids how to kill humans," he said.

Though he drew the line at video games, Luth found other ways to reach the demographic. He struck a deal with SoftAir USA to make BB guns that looked like his AR-15s, bearing his company's panther logo. He thought it was a safe and respectful way to introduce kids to firearms—and promote his brand.

"I felt that just like Camel cigarettes, if you introduce the kids to the brand at a young age, they're gonna remember that brand," he said. "And it worked because every day a kid's turning eighteen or twenty-one." Under federal law, Americans had to be eighteen to buy rifles or shotguns and twenty-one to buy handguns.

Gunmakers also used shooting competitions, called "3-Gun," that were gaining in popularity to market AR-15s to a younger audience. Competitors raced along a special course, firing at targets with three different guns—often a pistol, a shotgun, and an AR-15. *Junior Shooters*, a magazine devoted to youth shooting competitions and hunting, put out a special issue in 2011 on 3-Gun competitions. In those pages, young competitors raved about the AR-15.

"With such little recoil, it is easy to settle back onto a target for a second shot," wrote one sixteen-year-old competitor.

Junior Shooters featured ads from many of the major AR-15 makers. Ruger advertised a .22 caliber rifle that looked like an AR-15 model as "The Coolest .22 LR Ever." The colors of the ad were reminiscent of an ad for minty chewing gum. The magazine's editor praised Ruger's gun as "Cool, fun, and great for practice at little cost!"

As gunmakers sought out younger customers, industry lobbyists tried to soften the AR-15's image in Washington. The National Shooting Sports Foundation hired a public relations firm to come up with a new term to recast Stoner's gun and get away from the phrase "assault rifle." "We wanted a term that was more accurate in terms of its civilian perception," said Doug Painter, the group's president. The group settled on the term "modern sporting rifle" and pressed gunmakers to stop using "tactical rifle" or "assault rifle" when describing the AR-15. Industry representatives also pushed journalists to adopt the term. But few gun owners, politicians, or journalists did. Most just called them ARs.

The AR-15 marketing, from glossy magazine ads to video games, drew lots of new customers, and as targeted, many were young men. The vast majority intended to be responsible gun owners, but the gun's new image also attracted isolated and disturbed men. One of them was a twenty-four-year-old graduate student in Denver named James Eagan Holmes. Holmes had graduated with a bachelor's degree in neuroscience with highest honors from the University of California, Riverside, in 2010. He enrolled at the University of Colorado Anschutz Medical Campus the next year as a doctoral candidate.

Holmes struggled with social anxiety and obsessive-compulsive behavior that had plagued him for much of his life. He developed insomnia. He saw shadows committing violent acts on his apartment walls as he lay in bed. He stopped communicating with his few friends. He became obsessed with the size of his penis, convinced it was abnormally small.

Holmes had long fantasized about killing. Now the perverse notion consumed him. He called it "the mission." He searched the internet to learn about the best guns for killing lots of people. In late May, he bought his first one, a Glock pistol. Several days later, he bought a tactical shotgun. On June 7, 2012, Holmes failed his oral exams in the doctoral program. That same day he went to a chain sporting-goods store in a Denver suburb to buy a third gun. He paid $968.38 with his MasterCard for a Smith & Wesson M&P 15, three magazines, a sling, and ammunition. Five days later, Holmes purchased a hundred-round drum magazine online and a green laser sight for the rifle. He bought 3,370 rounds of .223 ammunition. He practiced shooting the rifle at an open-air range near the mountains. Holmes set up profiles on dating sites, including Match.com and AdultFriendFinder.com, asking potential partners, "Will you visit me in prison?"

23.

"I'M A KILLER, I GUESS"

He wanted to look like a badass.

—Craig Appel

Marcus Weaver was a Batman fan. The broad-shouldered, six-foot-four Weaver was drawn to the superhero because of what the fictional character represented: a man combating pervasive evil in a dark world. Weaver had gotten into trouble when he was younger, including drugs and stealing. Now working for a social service nonprofit in Denver, Weaver wanted to get his life back on track and help the world just like the caped crusader. "Batman is my dude," he said. Weaver admired the stoic interpretation of the character by the director Christopher Nolan in the movies *Batman Begins* (2005) and *The Dark Knight* (2008). In 2012, Nolan had finished his trilogy with a final installment, *The Dark Knight Rises*. Weaver couldn't wait to see it.

Weaver invited Rebecca Wingo, a thirty-two-year-old single mother of two, to go with him. Wingo, a cheerful waitress with long brown hair, had served in the air force and was attending community college. Weaver bought tickets to the late-night premiere at a movie theater in Aurora, a large suburb of Denver. The tickets were for Theater 9, one of the multiplex's largest theaters. The couple met up in the lobby, then found their seats. As they sat down, Wingo joked, "Are you getting sick of me yet?" The two laughed and he told her of course not. The lights dimmed. The movie started and the crowd of about four hundred people applauded.

Twenty minutes into the movie, Weaver saw smoke and heard strange noises.

"Something's whizzing at the lower level and it's hard to see what's going on," Weaver recalled.

From the second row, Jennifer Seeger saw a figure in a costume coming through an exit door near the screen, just feet from where she sat. He wore body armor and a gas mask. He held a shotgun and had a rifle slung over his chest.

He looked like a SWAT officer or a soldier, she thought. He said nothing.

The figure threw canisters that made hissing sounds and spewed caustic smoke. Everyone started coughing and covering their eyes.

Then he started shooting. He raised the rifle and fired into the crowd.

Seeger dove under her seat as he pointed in her direction. "All the bullet casings kept falling on my forehead. They were like singeing my forehead. And there was just gunpowder in the air. And all I hear was screaming and just bloody murder." The image that stuck in her mind was the man pointing the rifle at her.

Christopher Ramos, a twenty-year-old sitting farther back, believed he was going to die after the man sitting next to him was hit. "I hear . . . a splash noise," he recalled. "And he just jerks."

Ramos saw the shooter down below. "He was just quiet and he was literally just shooting everyone like it was, like, hunting season or something," he said. "People were standing around, he wasn't aiming for a specific person. He was aiming for as many people as he could."

Seated at the back of the theater, Weaver heard loud booms, then the rapid shots.

"It was like a thunderstorm . . . and everyone just started screaming," he recalled. "Remembering the sound of an AR-15 in that small theater—that's the thing that has given me nightmares, the beginning and that feeling of utter helplessness."

Weaver dove behind the seats and peeked through a crack.

"It looked like the devil," Weaver recalled. "And it just doesn't stop. Bam, bam, bam, bam."

The shooter paused, and Weaver sprang up and told Rebecca to run for the exits. People were piling over each other to escape. The shooting resumed. Weaver fell over into the row of seats behind him. He got up and ran to the lobby. He saw a police officer rushing to the theater. He called out to say that he couldn't find his friend Rebecca.

As he was talking, a girl came up to Weaver and said, "Your arm is bleeding."

Weaver looked over at his right shoulder. He couldn't move his arm.

"It's drenched in blood," he recalled. "I had been shot and I didn't even know it."

He scanned the panicked crowd. Where was Rebecca?

The first 911 call came in at 12:38 a.m. In the background, the dispatcher heard shooting and screaming. A minute later, someone called from the theater. The dispatcher heard more shots as a person shouted into the phone, "Help us please" and "Please help."

Gerry Jonsgaard, an Aurora police sergeant, rushed to the theater thinking he was responding to a gang shooting. He saw crowds pouring out of the theater, many with bullet wounds. He ran into Theater 9. Bodies were everywhere and blood covered the floors and seats. The veteran officer was overwhelmed. He opened an exit door to clear the room of smoke. He stood at the doorway for a moment, trying to collect himself.

"We see trauma. We see heartache, death, destruction on a daily basis. I mean, that's what we do," he later said. "But the volume of this night was just beyond your senses."

Jonsgaard saw the body of a little girl lying at the doorway. Though he knew he was violating crime-scene protocol, he ordered men to take her lifeless body outside to emergency workers.

"No child is going to stay in that scene," he said. "It was horrific enough without having my officers step over the body of a little girl right at the rear door."

The girl was six-year-old Veronica Moser-Sullivan.

Aurora officer James Waselkow, who had served in the army in Afghanistan, was startled to see a military rifle on the ground outside the exit door. What was that kind of weapon doing at a movie theater? The gun lay near a bloody pink flip-flop. Officers Jason Sweeney and Jason Oviatt, positioned outside in the parking lot, noticed a figure in body armor and wearing a gas mask standing near a car.

"When I first saw him, I thought he was a cop," Oviatt said.

But something was off. The man seemed confused. The two officers realized that his gas mask and body armor were not standard issue for the city's SWAT team. The officers called out to the man. They approached the man and handcuffed him.

Sweeney and Oviatt arrested James Holmes, but they didn't believe at first that he was the sole shooter. It didn't seem possible that one person could cause so much horror in so short a time.

Hospitals were deluged. At the University of Colorado Medical Center, many of the wounded arrived in police cars, not ambulances. Doctors triaged patients, putting those with less serious injuries in the hallways; the hospital had run out of beds.

Tom Sullivan woke up in the early hours of that Friday morning to get ready for his predawn shift as a distribution clerk at a Denver post office. He went to bed at about 7:00 p.m. every night, then woke about 2:30 a.m., made himself some coffee, and packed his lunch before heading to work. He often turned on the television to watch sports-game recaps. That morning he turned on the television and instead of sports, newscasters were talking about a mass shooting in Aurora.

"I was thinking Alex might have gone to the movie theater last night but that's not the one he normally goes to. I'd better call him," he recalled.

Alex was his son. July 20 was his birthday, and he now was twenty-seven. It was a tradition for Alex to go to the movies for his birthday.

Tom Sullivan's call to his son's cell went to voice mail. He wished Alex a happy birthday and asked him to call him, so his mother—who was still sleeping—wouldn't worry when she woke up and saw the news. A short while later, he called again. He left another message: "This looks like it's really serious stuff. Please call me."

On his way to work, Sullivan drove by the Century 16 Theater, which was lit up by lights from police cars and ambulances. Throughout the morning he called his son's cell phone every half hour. At about 6:30 a.m., his wife called. Sullivan assumed she had seen the news and he tried to calm her.

"I said, 'Don't worry, he's probably just sleeping, but there has been this shooting,'" he said. His wife cut him off. "She just started screaming, saying Alex has been shot."

Sullivan rushed to a nearby high school where families of people hurt or killed at the theater were told to gather. His wife and daughter met him there. They were shuttled into a room with eleven other families. Sullivan couldn't stand waiting there. He and a police officer drove to three hospitals. His son wasn't in any of them. The family later learned that Alex, with his wife out of town, had gone to the Century 16 Theater for his birthday with coworkers. Before going, he posted on his Facebook page: "#TheDarkKnightRises OMG COUNTING down till it start cant wait going to be the best birthday ever." Alex was killed and many of his coworkers were injured.

In one hospital, Marcus Weaver lay on a bed as doctors tried to figure out what to do with the bullet fragments in his shoulder. A television in the room blared nonstop coverage of the shooting. Weaver called Wingo's friends and family—anyone he could think of—to find out whether there was any news about her. The next morning, Wingo's father confirmed in a Facebook post what Weaver had dreaded: Rebecca Wingo had been killed.

"I lost my daughter yesterday to a mad man, my grief right now is inconsolable," Steve Hernandez wrote.

All this carnage was the result of James Holmes firing weapons for a mere eighty-two seconds. He first fired a shotgun, then threw the spent gun to the ground and picked up his M&P 15 rifle. He fired more than sixty rounds from a hundred-round drum attached to the weapon before it jammed. In less time than it takes to watch three television commercials, the gunman killed twelve people and wounded scores more. Some people were not shot but were injured trying to flee in a panic.

James Holmes's mind had been unraveling in the months before the shooting. The pale Holmes wrote down his delusions and bizarre plotting in a spiral computation notebook. On one page he labeled the book "Insights into the Mind of Madness." A few pages later he called it "Self Diagnosis of Broken Mind." In one section, he wrote the word "Why?" repeatedly. Other pages were filled with conspiratorial ramblings and strange equations. Holmes believed that people could gain points from the universe if they killed others. Holmes came to believe that the only way to save himself from his monstrous depression and avoid suicide was mass murder. He considered bombing, biological warfare, and serial murder, but settled on a mass shooting.

"Maximum casualties, easily performed w/ firearms although primitive in nature. No fear of consequences, being caught 99% certain," he scribbled in his notebook.

He decided to attack a movie theater—with large crowds and little security. He estimated police would respond within three minutes. He made a to-do list: "Research firearm laws and mental illness. Buy handgun. Committed.-Shotgun,—AR-15, 2nd handgun, Wildcard: explosives."

He wrote on July 13, "Embraced the hatred, a dark k/night rises." Days before July 20, Holmes put black contacts in his eyes, dyed his hair red, donned body armor, and took selfies in his apartment. He posed with his AR-15. Holmes changed his appearance and took the photos because he wanted "to differentiate myself from who I normally was," he said later.

"This is what a killer looks like," he said. "That I'm familiar in the ways of weaponry and body armor, that I'm a killer, I guess."

Holmes was drawn to the AR-15 in part because it looked scary, said Craig Appel, an Aurora homicide detective who interviewed Holmes.

"That warrior mentality, that was his big issue," Appel recalled. "He wanted to look like a badass."

In the theater that night, Holmes—wearing body armor, helmet, and gas mask—could barely see where he was shooting, he said later. He just fired where he saw movement, or people cowering behind seats. When the AR-15 jammed, he pulled out the drum magazine and tried to insert another magazine. But the gun still didn't work. He staggered up an aisle for more light to see, but he couldn't get the gun to fire. The jamming of his chief weapon deflated the killer. "I wanted to fix the AR-15 . . . Once I couldn't fix it, I kind of left," he said later. Holmes fired his handgun a few times, but then he stumbled outside, dropping his AR-15 on the ground.

Holmes knew little about firearms and his ignorance saved many lives that night. When he practiced at the rifle range, he thought he was mastering the weapon, but in fact he was fouling his gun each time he fired. He never cleaned his firearms because he didn't know that he needed to do so. He never learned how to clear a jam—standard procedure for any serious firearm owner. He bought a hundred-round drum magazine, an unreliable device.

"The fact that this guy is self-taught shows how easy it is to shoot these things," said Rich Orman, one of the prosecutors in the Holmes murder trial. "He would have found a way to kill everyone in that theater by other means if he had to, but the AR-15 makes it so much easier."

By his own estimation, Holmes was a bad shot. But he figured it didn't matter since he would be attacking an enclosed theater with hundreds of unarmed victims.

"It's a great gun for killing lots of people really quickly," Orman said. "That's why these guys use it. That's why the Army uses it."

The Aurora shooting reignited the national gun debate when neither political party wanted to talk about the divisive issue. Democrat Barack Obama was seeking reelection against the Republican Party's presumptive nominee, Mitt Romney. The Obama campaign needed to win key midwestern states where hunting was popular. Romney needed to win over suburban voters, especially women, and hard-line, pro–Second Amendment stances didn't play well.

Speaking to the National Urban League, Obama suggested he would back some restrictions on gun ownership, but he offered no specifics. He said gun owners had rights under the Constitution, but they must agree "that AK-47s belong in the hands of soldiers, not in the hands of children." Romney argued passing new gun-control laws wasn't the answer, but also said Holmes shouldn't have been allowed to own a gun.

"We can sometimes hope that just changing the law will make all bad things go away," he said. "It won't. Changing the heart of the American people may well be what's essential, to improve the lots of the American people."

Political observers on both sides of the issue called the two candidates out for the wishy-washy stances.

"How long will elected officials, from the White House on down, be allowed to evade hard questions about why tragedies like Aurora occur and what might be done to prevent them?" asked an editor at the Toledo newspaper *The Blade*.

Dianne Feinstein went on Fox News offering the same solution she had made in the early 1990s: an assault-weapons ban.

"I have no problem with people being licensed and buying a firearm," she said. "But these are weapons that you are only going to be using to kill people in close combat. That's the purpose of that weapon."

The NRA was quiet after the shooting. Just hours after Holmes's attack, the NRA's "American Rifleman" Twitter account posted, "Good morning, shooters. Happy Friday! Weekend plans?" The organization deleted the tweet in response to criticism. The organization said the person managing the account wasn't aware of the Aurora shooting, despite wall-to-wall news coverage.

After the Aurora massacre, no major federal legislation was proposed and many Americans moved on. But a few disturbed men, far from forgetting, obsessed over this massacre and others. In internet chat rooms, they traded details about the shootings, including the weapons the killers used. They wrote about the killers and massacres as if they were talking about their favorite sports stars and games. One was Adam Lanza, a thin, pale twenty-year-old who lived with his mother in Connecticut. He spent hours hunched at his computer inside a darkened room. He had covered the windows with black plastic trash bags to keep the light out. He compiled lists of killers. He made edits to their Wikipedia pages, updating details about the guns they used. He registered as "Smiggles" on an online forum devoted to the Columbine High School killers. After the Aurora massacre, he exchanged emails with an online acquaintance about Holmes's popularity with fans, whom he called "Holmies." Lanza wrote that he didn't understand why the Holmies thought the Aurora shooter was "just a poor misunderstood puppy who needs help." He dismissed the massacre as unoriginal. "I don't really understand why Aurora shooting was considered such a big deal all-around, as if such a thing had never happened before."

On his computer, Lanza had a detailed spreadsheet of more than four hundred mass murders from all around the world, going back to the 1800s. The first column on the spreadsheet listed the number of people killed, followed by the number wounded, the name of the killer, and then the weapon that was used. In other columns he tracked locations; dates; how the massacre ended; whether the attacker was dead, in prison, or freed; the attacker's age and sex; and whether the guns had been purchased legally. One of the last entries involved twenty-eight-year-old Michael Kenneth McLendon, who on March 10, 2009, shot his mother and several relatives with a Bushmaster XM-15 in Alabama. He also fired indiscriminately at strangers. McLendon, who had been depressed about not achieving his goal of becoming a Marine, killed ten people, then committed suicide during a police shootout.

Lanza too wanted to join the military, though he was frail and beset by mental problems. He'd been diagnosed with Asperger's syndrome and obsessive-compulsive disorder. He refused to shake people's hands or touch doorknobs. At the barber shop, he cringed at the buzzing of hair clippers. He changed his socks up to twenty times a day.

Lanza's parents divorced in the fall of 2009 and the couple agreed that Adam, then seventeen, would continue to live with his mother, Nancy Lanza. She sought to connect with her loner son by sharing her love of guns. She had grown up hunting in New Hampshire, and she told one of her neighbors that she "loved the feeling and power of a gun in her hand." She taught him to shoot a .22 caliber rifle when he was five. She went target shooting with him as a teen. As he approached his eighteenth birthday, Lanza, who weighed 112 pounds and was nearing six feet, told his parents he wanted to enlist. "What do you do?" his father told *The New Yorker.* "You tell him, 'Adam, that's unrealistic'?"

On March 29, 2010, a few weeks before her son turned eighteen, Nancy Lanza drove to Riverview Gun Sales in East Windsor, Connecticut, a gun shop about sixty-five miles northeast of their home. She bought a Bushmaster XM-15 model that had a sixteen-inch barrel, four inches shorter than a traditional AR-15. Its short, light design tracked the military's M4s, which soldiers favored for close-quarters combat.

The gun that she bought was modified by Bushmaster to comply with Connecticut's assault-weapons ban that had been passed in 1993. Connecticut lawmakers had intended to outlaw weapons like the AR-15. But their law used a features test like the moribund federal ban, and it was easy for gunmakers to remove the offending features and keep selling their rifles. Nancy Lanza dutifully filled out the State of Connecticut Department of Public Safety form as though she was buying it for herself. But the gun was likely a birthday gift for her son. He was turning eighteen; he was about to become a man.

24.

"YOU WOULDN'T UNDERSTAND"

I have no illusions about how hard the task is in front of us.
But I also have never seen the nation's conscience so shaken
by what happened at Sandy Hook.

—Joe Biden

Six-year-old Benjamin Wheeler's nickname was "Crash," which was short for "Crash, Hop-along, Hurt Himself, Jawbreaker, Shiner, Split Lip, Gash Eye, Face Plant, Nose Buster Wheeler." The energetic boy's parents, David and Francine, added to his name with each new childhood mishap. He buzzed around their home, running, jumping off furniture, tripping, and falling. Ben had brown hair that was always tousled and round cheeks that grew rounder when he smiled. He was always eager to tell his family something in his lispy voice, often interrupting his older brother, Nate, at the dinner table. Ben never slowed down when he was awake; sometimes at bedtime, he would fall asleep midsentence.

"Nothing moved fast enough for him," David said.

David and Francine were living in Queens when Ben was born on September 12, 2006. The couple had been in New York City for years, working as actors and musicians. They met in 1998 when David hired Francine's singing trio to perform at his comedy and variety show, and they married in 2001. When Nate was born three years later, the couple's late-night lifestyle shifted from clubs to cribs. Francine recorded an album of children's music called *Come Sit Beside Me*. Songs such as "Good Morning, Mr. Bagelman" and "Love Somebody, Yes I Do" were written over a diaper-changing table. They sang them to their two children to help them sleep.

By the time Ben was born, the couple was looking for a home in Newtown, Connecticut, where they had friends. The bedroom community had great schools and low taxes, and was an hour-and-a-half drive from the city. The town of 26,700, with its woods and winding roads, reminded David of where he had grown up in New Hampshire; a meeting of the country and the suburbs that he called the "woodburbs." The young family's move to Newtown in 2007, with four-year-old Nate and fifteen-month-old Ben, was noted in the weekly *The Newtown Bee*. "As fun as theater life is, it is also demanding, and when she and her husband decided to start a family, Ms. Wheeler began to think it was time to get out of show business," the newspaper reported. "We wanted a piece of lawn, somewhere quiet, somewhere with good schools," Francine told the *Bee*.

Most Newtown residents were wealthy. The Wheelers made ends meet. Francine gave piano and voice lessons and sang with a music group. David found work as an art director for an interior decor company.

Both of their children, first Nate and then Ben, attended their local public school, Sandy Hook Elementary. Francine and David were impressed by the school's principal, Dawn Hochsprung, a five-foot, two-inch dynamo whom David described as "unstoppable." She ran the school with a firm but caring hand.

Ben eagerly awaited each day of kindergarten. "He loved everything about school; he couldn't wait to go," David said. "If anything, he was overly enthusiastic, which for a teacher can be a challenge." Ben's mom taught him to play the piano. His favorite song was "The Bonnie Banks o' Loch Lomond," which he would pick out on the piano with one finger and sing loudly, "You'll take the high road and I'll take the low road!" He was a goofball and a ham. He played tricks on his older brother, hiding his favorite teddy bear or dressing it in a strange outfit. For first grade, Ben was assigned to a teacher who David and Francine thought would not be the best fit. They wanted "someone who was a little more forgiving of that boy energy," David recalled. Principal Hochsprung assigned Ben to Amanda D'Amato's class for the 2012 school year.

In the early morning darkness of Friday, December 14, 2012, David and Francine readied their two boys for school. It was parental chaos as usual. Ben woke with the sniffles. Francine asked David whether she should keep him home. He didn't have a cough or a fever. "Your day is going to be turned upside down if you keep him home, he's going to be fine," David said. Complicating the morning, Francine planned to take David's Honda Fit and drop it off to get snow tires installed. David had to take Francine's Toyota Corolla to work. Halfway into David's fifty-mile commute, Francine called his cell. The boys' backpacks were in the trunk of her car, which meant they didn't have their books, supplies, or lunch bags. Francine improvised, giving Nate and Ben their lunches in brown paper bags. Nate had to go to school early for a book club. Francine asked Ben whether he wanted to go to Starbucks after dropping Nate off and before he had to go to class. He said yes. As she rushed to load the dishwasher, Ben asked her one of those deep, non sequitur questions that children sometimes ask: "Mom, what does forgiveness mean?" It's when somebody does something wrong and you forget about it, she told him. Ben shrugged.

Francine drove through wintry woods to Sandy Hook. She dropped Nate off, then drove with Ben to Starbucks. They talked as Francine sipped coffee and Ben guzzled chocolate milk. Ben told his mom that he wanted to be a paleontologist just like Nate wanted to be. He also wanted to be a lighthouse keeper, he said. She drove Ben back to school and gave him a hug. He ran inside. Ben's teacher wasn't there that day so the class had a substitute.

Around 9:40 a.m., drivers on Riverside Road near the school stopped their cars when they spotted a group of five children running and waving their arms. They didn't have coats or backpacks. The children frantically told the drivers that a man was in their school with a gun. He was killing everyone. One of the women called the school, but no one answered. She dialed 911. Get down to the station and bring the children, an officer said.

At the station, one of the boys said that he had been sitting in his first-grade class when he heard loud noises from the hall. The door swung open and a "bad man" came in and started shooting. The gunman was wearing "army clothes" and had a "bazooka," the boy said. A girl told the officers that she didn't want to die, she wanted to live, so she ran the fastest she could out of the school.

One of the first officers dispatched to the school was William Chapman. His heart was pounding as he drove his patrol car full speed. He did breathing exercises to calm himself and unlocked the department-issued AR close to his seat. At the school, he grabbed the gun and jumped out. He released the charging handle of the rifle, putting a round into the chamber. He heard rifle fire from inside the school. He turned his selector switch from "safe" to "fire." He motioned to two fellow officers to move forward.

Inside the school lobby, the officers found shell casings and shattered glass. Acrid gunpowder hung in the air. As the others gave him cover, Chapman knelt to check the vital signs of two women lying on the floor. No pulse. Chapman and another officer made their way through the school. In classroom 9, they found teachers huddling in shock. One woman was bleeding. Across the hall, Chapman opened the door to classroom 10 and saw a Glock handgun lying on the floor. He went in, his AR-15 at his shoulder. On the floor he saw a skinny man wearing fatigues and a tactical vest. Blood pooled around the man's head. He'd shot himself. Chapman moved farther into the room and saw the bodies of children and teachers. An AR-15 lay near them.

Chapman felt his heart breaking as he walked around the room.

"No, no, no," he said.

Everyone was dead. Then he came across a girl huddled by the legs of a table. She still had a faint pulse. He slung his rifle across his back and ran to the hallway, calling for an ambulance. He picked up the girl and sprinted out of the building. He ran across the parking lot, praying that she would live and telling her that she was safe, that Jesus loved her, and that he was protecting her. "Come on sweetie, come on sweetie," he said.

Connecticut State Police Sergeant Bill Cario saw no one when he first walked into classroom 8, Ben's classroom. But as he made his way farther in, he saw two women lifeless on the floor. Beyond them, he saw an open door. He looked inside the little bathroom; he couldn't comprehend what he was seeing. After a moment, he realized it was the face of a little boy, lying on top of a pile. A pile of what? He looked down. He was looking at a pile of children.

Cario told Patrick Dragon, a fellow state trooper, that he thought one boy in the bathroom might still be breathing. Dragon found a brown-haired boy and cradled him in his arms as he ran down the hallway. Dragon told the little boy that his family loved him and that he was a hero for trying to protect his classmates. They laid him on a blanket in the back of a police SUV and Cario climbed in. The boy was unresponsive but he was breathing and Cario kept talking, trying to comfort him until the ambulance drove him away.

Cario went back to classroom 8's little bathroom to try to find more survivors. Looking at the bullet holes and blood spatter, Cario realized all of them had been shot inside that little, windowless room. He took the children's bodies out one by one and placed them in a row on the classroom floor until he ran out of room. Cario tried to tally the number of dead in the school, but he couldn't count beyond the low teens and he kept getting confused. "This will be the worst day of your life," he told paramedics as he escorted them inside.

David Wheeler was working at his office when Francine called: something had happened at Sandy Hook. A few minutes later, Francine called again: it was a shooting. He headed out the door. His phone buzzed. A text from Francine: "Meet us at the firehouse. I have Nate but I don't have Ben yet." David made it to near the school at around 10:45 a.m. Police cruisers, ambulances, television news trucks, and parents' cars crowded the road. David parked and ran over a hill to the firehouse. He found Francine and Nate.

"I remember everyone in the building trying to find a charger for their iPhones," David recalled. "I remember increasingly large numbers of people with dark-colored windbreakers with letters on the back showing up."

David paced the firehouse, calling area hospitals to give them a description of Ben.

"There were a lot of people screaming and wailing," he recalled. In the men's room, David ran into his friend Jeremy Richman, whose daughter Avielle was Ben's friend. Richman was crying. He had seen a girl who was Avielle's friend and who was in the same classroom as Ben. Richman told David the girl had brain matter in her hair and she wasn't injured. David sat down with his wife.

"We have to open our minds to the possibility that Ben may not come home," he said.

Parents spent hours crowded in a small carpeted room with tables and chairs at the back of the firehouse. They learned Principal Dawn Hochsprung was dead. Some parents grew furious and pressed state troopers for answers: Where are our kids?

Then Connecticut governor Dannel Malloy arrived and huddled with police officials. David overheard the governor getting angry. He remembered the governor saying, "We do this now. We tell them now."

Then he stood on a chair and told those gathered: "Twenty-six people are dead, twenty of them are children. If you're in this room, it's because one of those children was yours."

David remembered a loud keening from all the parents. Twenty first graders were dead: Ben, Avielle, and eighteen of their classmates. Six school faculty were dead, including Ben's substitute teacher. Police found one more body at a nearby home, the gunman's mother, Nancy Lanza. Adam Lanza had killed her before driving to the school.

Sandy Hook was the deadliest shooting ever at an American K–12 school. That afternoon, President Barack Obama spoke from the White House. He wiped away tears as he spoke:

Our hearts are broken today—for the parents and grandparents, sisters and brothers of these little children, and for the families of the adults who were lost. Our hearts are broken for the parents of the survivors as well, for as blessed as they are to have their children home tonight, they know that their children's innocence has been torn away from them too early, and there are no words that will ease their pain. As a country, we have been through this too many times . . . And we're going to have to come together and take meaningful action to prevent more tragedies like this, regardless of the politics.

Investigators pieced together ballistic evidence at the school. They found eight brass casings at the front entrance where the killer shot out a large plate glass window with the Bushmaster to get past the school's locked doors. They found one casing in the hallway and sixteen in the lobby where he shot the principal and the school psychologist. In Ben's classroom, they found eighty casings. Lanza had shot two teachers and fifteen children, most of them as they tried to hide in the classroom bathroom. In Avielle's classroom, investigators found forty-nine casings from the rifle with which Lanza killed five children and two teachers. They also found two thirty-round magazines duct-taped together. Lanza had fired a total of 154 rounds from his AR-15 in less than five minutes.

Lanza left no manifesto or suicide note. State and federal investigators could not pinpoint a precise motive. The FBI's Behavioral Analysis Unit determined that Lanza's deteriorating relationship with his mother was a significant stressor before the attack.

When police searched Lanza's house, they found the remnants of his fixations: a *New York Times* article about a 2008 shooting at Northern Illinois University, three photographs of what appeared to be dead bodies, and photocopied articles from 1891 about schoolchildren being shot. Among his clothes, they found a military-style uniform. On his computer, he had videos of suicides, and movies that showed mass shootings. They found video games, including *Call of Duty* and one called *School Shooting*, where the player controlled a gunman who shot students. They found photos of Lanza holding a handgun and a rifle to his head.

None of Lanza's writings, emails, or internet comments that have been made public state why he used the AR-15 at Sandy Hook. He left a semiautomatic shotgun along with two magazines in his car outside the school. He left other guns at home, including a .22 caliber rifle. He killed his mother with the .22. But when Lanza burst into Sandy Hook, he brought only one rifle: a Bushmaster AR-15. He carried three hundred rounds of ammunition for his rifle in ten magazines, stuffed into the pockets of his cargo pants and tactical vest.

The immediate aftermath was akin to the U.S. reaction to 9/11—bafflement, sadness, horror, anger. On the day of the shooting, journalists encountered a lone woman in the road near the school, wailing, "Why? Why?" Thousands of people—including little children with stuffed animals—came to impromptu, overflow services at churches in and around Newtown. For a nation that thought it had become jaded to mass shootings, a new nadir had been reached.

Obama had promised "meaningful action" in his remarks on the day of the massacre, but his administration initially was mum about what that action might be. A spokesman for the National Rifle Association said the group had no comment "until the facts are thoroughly known."

On the day of the shooting, Senator Dianne Feinstein said, "Weapons of war don't belong on our streets or in our theaters, shopping malls and, most of all, our schools. I hope and trust that in the next session of Congress, there will be sustained and thoughtful debate about America's gun culture and our responsibility to prevent more loss of life."

In the years since the federal assault-weapons ban had expired, Feinstein had found herself unable to gather the political support needed to renew a ban on Stoner's invention. But in the weeks that followed Sandy Hook, the idea received unexpected backing. Retired U.S. Army General Stanley McChrystal, who had led American forces in Afghanistan, said on CNN that AR-15s didn't belong on the streets of America.

"That's what I want soldiers to carry," he said. "But I don't want those weapons around our schools."

National retail chains and gunmakers that had made millions on Stoner's invention tried to distance themselves from the AR-15. Walmart stopped selling AR-15s on its website and Dick's Sporting Goods stopped selling the guns in their stores.

Stephen Feinberg decided on the Monday after the massacre to sell his firearms conglomerate, Freedom Group, which included Bushmaster, the company that made Lanza's gun. He was under pressure from major investors.

"It is apparent that the Sandy Hook tragedy was a watershed event that has raised the national debate on gun control to an unprecedented level," Feinberg's firm Cerberus stated in a press release. "This decision allows us to meet our obligations to the investors whose interests we are entrusted to protect without being drawn into the national debate that is more properly pursued by those with the formal charter and public responsibility to do so."

Men who had spent their careers building and selling AR-15s were convinced that the gun would be banned once and for all. "I couldn't see how Congress or the Senate could not pass legislation after that happened," John DeSantis, who had retired as president of Bushmaster in 2010, recalled thinking.

Five days after the shooting, Obama spoke to the nation again and announced that Vice President Joe Biden would lead a task force that would make recommendations on how to prevent mass shootings.

"This is not some Washington commission," Obama assured the nation. "This is not something where folks are going to be studying the issue for six months and publishing a report that gets read and then pushed aside. This is a team that has a very specific task, to pull together real reforms right now."

As political pressure mounted in Washington, mourning parents planned funerals. Friends and family arrived at the Wheelers' home to comfort them, but what was most striking was the silence. "A very loud house became a very quiet house very quickly," David remembered. Their pastor helped plan Ben's funeral and recommended a funeral director who had been an army mortician in Afghanistan. Funeral directors discouraged many Sandy Hook parents from seeing their children's bodies. But Francine and David insisted on going to see Ben before his body was cremated. The couple sat alone with the body.

"We had that gift and that remains the hardest memory for me," David said. He brought a goodbye letter that he wrote to Ben. They brought stuffed animals and a couple of Ben's favorite toys.

The funerals for the Sandy Hook Elementary School victims began on a gray day, December 17, when Noah Pozner and Jack Pinto, both six years old, were laid to rest. Ben's funeral was held on December 20 at Trinity Episcopal Church. It was filled to capacity. David read "The Road Not Taken" by Robert Frost. A choir sang "The Bonnie Banks o' Loch Lomond."

On that same day, Freedom Group's board of directors held an emergency meeting by telephone. George Kollitides II, who had risen to become Freedom Group's chief executive, thanked the board members for meeting on short notice and informed them about Cerberus's decision to sell the company after the shooting. Kollitides also noted that gun sales continued to be strong after the tragedy. But the aftermath of the slaughter was only a brief part of the meeting. Kollitides promptly turned to other matters, including the possible acquisition of a gun barrel manufacturer for about $6 million. Kollitides argued that buying the company was a strategic move for Freedom Group. Others in the meeting noted that the deal would increase margins even further on the company's AR-15s. The board voted to authorize the acquisition.

"It was one of our higher margin products," Kollitides later said in a deposition, adding, "It was an awful horrific huge tragedy, but its impact on the long-term capital decisions of the business were not—were not a factor. We were in the business of legally making guns to legally sell to legal gun owners. So there is no other thing to do than wake up and make guns on Monday morning."

The next day, the NRA ended its silence. For a week, NRA officials had said nothing, even deactivating the organization's Facebook page and silencing its Twitter account. From a podium at the Willard Hotel in Washington, Wayne LaPierre, wearing a dark suit, a white shirt, and a striped blue tie, condemned "all the anger directed at us." A protester interjected, yelling, "It's the NRA and the assault weapons that are killing our children." LaPierre blamed a culture of violent video games and movies. He attacked the media.

"They claim these civilian semi-automatic firearms are used by the military. They tell us that the .223 is one of the most powerful rifle calibers, when all of these claims are factually untrue. They don't know what they're talking about."

At the end of his twenty-five-minute speech, LaPierre made an extraordinary proposal: the nation needed to stop mass shootings by placing armed guards in schools.

"The only thing that stops a bad guy with a gun is a good guy with a gun," he said.

A month after the massacre, Obama and Biden met with reporters to announce the task force's recommendations. With little children brought to stand near the podium, Biden told the nation that it had a "moral obligation" to act.

"I have no illusions about what we're up against or how hard the task is in front of us," Biden said. "But I also have never seen the nation's conscience so shaken by what happened at Sandy Hook. The world has changed, and it's demanding action."

Obama signed twenty-three executive actions, including one that directed the Centers for Disease Control and Prevention to research how to reduce gun violence. The measures were minor because real action had to come from Congress. The president urged Congress to reimpose the federal assault-weapons ban, and to support background checks for all gun purchases.

"I will put everything I've got into this, and so will Joe," he said.

The declaration was a departure for the president. He had been cautious in pushing changes even after a man armed with a handgun wounded Arizona Democratic representative Gabby Giffords in a 2011 shooting that left six dead. Looking ahead to his reelection campaign, Obama feared alienating voters in swing states such as Michigan and Ohio. Obama won reelection handily in 2012, but he struggled to push legislation through a newly divided Congress during his second term.

In late January 2013, Feinstein, joined by other Democratic senators, proposed a new federal assault-weapons ban that was stricter than the one enacted in 1994. The bill proposed to ban numerous AR-15s by name, including the Bushmaster XM-15 and the Smith & Wesson M&P 15.

The NRA was sure it could kill the bill, but issued doomsday predictions as it sought money from members. "I warned you this day was coming and now it's here," LaPierre wrote in a fundraising letter. "It's not about protecting your children. It's not about stopping crime. It's about banning your guns . . . PERIOD!"

Sandy Hook provoked everyone and anyone—legal scholars, professors, gun owners, victims of gun violence, columnists, talk show hosts, celebrities—to offer their views about AR-15s and gun control. The horror writer Stephen King in an essay called for a nationwide ban on the sale of rifles such as the AR-15. He wrote, "[G]un advocates cling to their semi-automatics the way Amy Winehouse and Michael Jackson clung to the shit that was killing them."

In response to the national discussion, AR-15 sales soared to unprecedented levels. In December alone, the FBI performed about 2.24 million background checks for gun purchases, an all-time record. Smith & Wesson sold nearly $32 million worth of its AR models in the three months that ended January 31, a 59 percent increase from the same period a year earlier.

Into this charged atmosphere—with the AR-15 at its center—came the Sandy Hook parents. The grieving group joined the fray without understanding what they were about to face. All they knew was that they wanted to make the world safer for children. They hoped to salvage something lasting and important out of their monumental tragedy.

David and Francine Wheeler had never been politically active, but Ben's death changed that. They met with other Sandy Hook parents to talk about what they could do. David had fired rifles while growing up in New Hampshire, but he owned no firearms as an adult. Those meetings were "my entry into understanding the world of firearms in this country. And the more I learned, the less I could believe," he recalled.

He learned about the 2005 law that protected gunmakers from lawsuits filed by survivors and families of those killed with their weapons. As he found out more about the rifle Lanza had used to kill Ben and so many others, David was amazed that such a weapon could be sold to civilians. "I couldn't understand why a weapon that was requested by the military, designed by the military, refined by the military, how that—for the sake of profit only—could be marketed to an untrained civilian population," he recalled.

When a state task force drafting new gun legislation held a hearing in Newtown, David decided to speak. Wearing a black blazer and a dark maroon shirt, he looked up from the table where he was seated and fixed his gaze on the lawmakers on the stage.

"We lost our son Benjamin the morning of December fourteenth to an unstable suicidal individual who had access to a weapon that has no place in a home," he said. "It doesn't matter to whom these weapons were registered. It doesn't matter if they were purchased legally. What matters is that it was far too easy for another mentally unbalanced, suicidal person who had violent obsessions to have easy access to unreasonably powerful weapons."

David called for AR-15s to be registered and for at-risk individuals to be identified and evaluated by mental health professionals. Databases should be compiled and used by law enforcement to find when troubled people bought or tried to buy such firearms, he insisted. David closed his remarks by referring to the inalienable rights of life, liberty, and the pursuit of happiness referenced in the Declaration of Independence.

"I do not think the composition of that foundational phrase was an accident," he said. "I do not think the order of those important words was haphazard or casual. The liberty of any person to own a military-style assault weapon and a high-capacity magazine and keep them in their home is second to the right of my son to his life. His life."

The crowd applauded. Lawmakers stood up and clapped. The speech made national news as media outlets set it in sharp contrast to stale talking points delivered that same day in the nation's capital at a Senate Judiciary Committee hearing on guns. On his MSNBC show, the liberal commentator Lawrence O'Donnell described Wheeler's testimony as the one that "the Senate Judiciary Committee should have heard today." He then played the entire speech for his viewers.

For the Wheelers, it felt as if they were doing something to honor their dead son. But as with every public appearance in those months after Ben died, they went home afterward and collapsed into their beds, not emerging from their house for days.

The Wheelers suffered in other ways for speaking out, ways they could never have imagined before the shooting. Parents who lost children at Sandy Hook found themselves the targets of online conspiracy theorists who claimed that the massacre had been some elaborate hoax, part of a secret plot designed to take guns away from Americans. People took to social media and discussion groups to argue, without any facts, that the school massacre had been staged by what they labeled "crisis actors." They harassed the Wheelers in particular because they had done some acting before having children.

Connecticut lawmakers responded quickly to the parents' pleas. The small state that had been the birthplace of the U.S. firearms industry, where the AR-15 was first manufactured, took action to rein in ARs by the early spring of 2013. Democrats, who controlled the governor's office and the state legislature, passed a massive overhaul of the state's assault-weapons ban with the support of Republicans. Public Law 13-3 prohibited the sale of AR-15s and other semiautomatic rifles by name, including Bushmaster's XM-15. It banned semiautomatic rifles with detachable magazines and at least one of five military-style features. Anyone who owned any of these rifles was required by the law to register them. The new law banned the sale of magazines that held more than ten rounds. The law required background checks for all long-gun sales, including private transactions, and an eligibility certificate for anyone wishing to buy ammunition. It gave wider latitude to authorities to deny gun purchases on mental health grounds. New York and Maryland also placed restrictions on the sale of AR-15s.

After the win in Connecticut, the Sandy Hook parents decided to take on Washington. They talked with politicians and lobbyists, seeking guidance. They met with Matt Bennett, a former Clinton White House staffer and veteran gun-control advocate at a DC law firm. Bennett felt obligated to tell them the truth about the politics of guns in Washington. He told them that the three major gun-control acts—in 1934, 1968, and 1994—had all passed when Democrats controlled Congress and the White House. Obama was dealing with a hostile GOP-led House. He explained that the 1994 federal assault-weapons ban had many flaws. He told them how its passage had doomed Democrats in the 1994 midterms. Those losses had stung many Democrats so badly that they still avoided the subject.

"I am ashamed as an American to tell you that the odds of banning the AR-15 are very, very slim," he remembered telling them.

"You cannot tell us that we can't do this," one mother said. "You can tell us what we can do, but you can't tell us what we can't do."

Bennett instead urged the group to support a gun-control bill that had a much better chance of passing: expanding the background-check system to require checks for gun sales between private parties. Federal law required anyone buying a gun from a licensed gun dealer to undergo a background check. But sales between individuals required no such checks.

"This would have had no impact on your own tragedy, and it would have had no impact on many school shootings, but it would have a lot of impact on the tens of thousands of shootings and thousands of murders every year," Bennett told the group.

Bennett had an interest in getting the group to back this bill over a difficult push to ban AR-15s. He had worked on the background-check bill in the Clinton White House after Columbine. He had resurrected the bill during his years at Americans for Gun Safety. Bennett was a firm believer that finding a middle ground on an issue, even one as divisive as guns, was the only way to achieve real change in Washington.

Most of the parents came to Washington hoping to fight for a national ban on AR-15s. Francine Wheeler and others wanted to keep pushing for it. But most agreed with Bennett's plan. They believed him when he said it had a better chance of passing.

Bennett met with Biden, Schumer, and others. Though the White House publicly supported Feinstein's ban, Biden and Schumer focused their energy on background checks, which they also believed had the better chance of passage. Senators Joe Manchin, a West Virginia Democrat, and Pat Toomey, a Pennsylvania Republican, sponsored the bill, which became known in political shorthand as Manchin-Toomey.

When Feinstein learned that the Sandy Hook parents were backing the background-check legislation, she was angry, Bennett recalled. Feinstein had no choice but to press on with her bill. On February 27, 2013, she held a hearing in which both sides echoed their talking points from the 1990s.

Congressional debate about the AR-15 rifle had devolved into a tired Punch-and-Judy show, with one notable exception: a doctor spoke to the senators about wounds caused by AR-15s. Medical professionals had for the most part stayed on the sidelines on gun issues. But as mass shootings became more common, emergency room doctors started speaking out. The doctor who appeared before the committee that day was Dr. William Begg, the director of emergency medical services at Danbury Hospital in Connecticut. EMTs brought two Sandy Hook victims—a girl and a boy—into his emergency room.

Begg described the children's injuries. His clinical description was reminiscent of ARPA reports from Saigon to the Pentagon four decades earlier, except he was describing wounds to American children, not enemy fighters.

"Most of the victims actually didn't come in. And we have such horrific injuries to little bodies," he said. "When a child has three to eleven bullets in them and it's an assault-type bullet, it explodes inside the body that does not go through in a straight line, it goes in and then it opens up. That is not a survivable injury."

As the votes on the ban and the background-check bill neared, Obama traveled to the University of Hartford in Connecticut to speak in support of both measures. The president said he had spoken with Francine Wheeler and that she was "determined not to let what happened that day just fade away."

Afterward, the Wheelers and several other Sandy Hook families flew back on Air Force One. On the flight, Obama spoke candidly, David Wheeler remembered. "He was talking to us for a while and that's when he said, 'Look, this is not going to be easy. This may not go your way and you have to be ready for that,'" Wheeler recalled.

The Wheelers and other families spent a week walking the halls of the Hart Senate Office Building. They carried pictures of their children to each meeting.

They met with Senator Rob Portman, an Ohio Republican, who had recently broken with his party to speak out in favor of gay marriage—after one of his sons told him he was gay. The senator was moved as he listened to the parents' appeals. A boy who'd lost his brother and came with his parents asked the senator how many lives the background-check legislation might save in Ohio. The questions from the boy caused Portman to cry. He told the families that he believed the legislation would save lives, but he couldn't vote for it. He could not risk straying twice from party orthodoxy. "You did that to advocate for your son. I don't understand why you can't do this for everyone else's," replied Nicole Hockley, who had lost her son Dylan.

The Wheelers and others met with Iowa senator Chuck Grassley, a conservative with an "A" rating from the NRA. As the parents spoke, David noticed that Grassley was not looking at them, but instead was looking down at the floor. He was crying. Grassley said he had young grandchildren and he kept repeating, "I can't imagine, I can't imagine." Avielle Richman's mother, Jennifer Hensel, told the senator that she was from Iowa and urged him to support the background-check legislation. Grassley, still looking down, said the calls coming into his office from constituents were overwhelmingly against the bill. He had to listen to his constituents, he said. David Wheeler and the others pressed him: Why couldn't he use his position to help push the bill through?

"You wouldn't understand," Grassley said.

The meeting unsettled David Wheeler. "Here are these people in their oak-paneled offices, surrounded by the riches of long government service and they can't look you in the eye, and they weep and look at the floor, and tell you, 'You wouldn't understand,'" Wheeler said. "And we all sat there just shocked. How can you stand there and tell me about something you think I don't understand? Who is it in this scenario who's really not understanding?"

At the end of the week, Francine and David Wheeler flew home. They were exhausted and needed to take care of Nate. They didn't stay for the Senate vote, scheduled for April 17. The White House invited the Wheelers and other parents to stand with Obama in the Rose Garden for a press conference after the votes were tallied.

"I just couldn't do it," Francine said. "It had taken everything out of me."

On the day of the Senate vote on Manchin and Toomey's background-check bill, other Sandy Hook parents sat in the gallery. Hockley tried to count the votes on her fingers but she kept losing track. They needed sixty votes to move the amendment forward. The final tally was 54 senators in favor and 46 against. Six votes short. The vote on Feinstein's ban came next. It failed by a 40–60 vote. Afterward, Hockley and other parents stood in the Rose Garden with Obama, who said it was "a pretty shameful day for Washington."

Obama then embraced each of the parents. "When he gave me a hug, I just wanted to melt into him," Hockley recalled.

The *New York Times* editorial board declared: "Newtown, in the end, changed nothing." An academic researcher who analyzed polling in the months after the massacre found "that the Sandy Hook shooting did not significantly alter the polarized and politicized nature of the gun control debate in America."

Back in Newtown, Francine Wheeler felt betrayed by the American political system. The couple had met with so many politicians who had wanted to hear about Ben's life. But in the end, all of that effort did nothing, she said.

"We go home and then Ben is still not here," Francine said. "They get to go on and we don't."

Every bit of the Wheelers' lives was weighted with Ben's absence. What-ifs haunted them. What if they had kept Ben home that day?

What if they hadn't had him switch classes? One morning, David woke with an urge to go to Sandy Hook Elementary, to see the place where Ben was killed. The school had been closed since the shooting and the district was planning to demolish the building. David told Francine that he was going to go. She erupted. How can you go?

He needed to see Ben's classroom, he told her. He wasn't sure what he wanted to find. A connection with Ben? Something. Francine couldn't go, she said. It was just too painful. A state trooper drove David to the school in a squad car. His wife's pastor and the detectives who worked on the case joined him at the boarded-up school. Inside, everything that had been touched by the massacre was removed. In Ben's classroom, the carpet was gone. The windows were gone. Investigators had taken anything stained with blood or marked by a bullet as evidence.

"I was struck by how small the room seemed," David remembered. "I'd been there before when it was full of desks and kids and it felt bigger. Usually you walk in an empty place that you're familiar with, full of furniture and it feels enormous. But this felt small, and the bathroom felt even smaller."

After a short time, David told the detectives that he wanted to leave. It was too much. He thought he was leaving the place where his son had died. But as he walked out, he ran into State Trooper Patrick Dragon. Dragon was the one who had gone into the bathroom and picked Ben up, still breathing. The officer told David that as he carried him to the ambulance, he had whispered to the boy that his family loved him. The ambulance had taken Ben to Dr. Begg's hospital, where the boy had died despite doctors' efforts. Learning this new information was a balm for David.

"He was surrounded by people who were trying their level best to save his life," David said. "And that's a gift."

David called state trooper Scott Blair to help process what he had seen at the school. Blair had become close with the Wheelers, driving them to public events and protecting them from the media.

David remembered telling Blair after the visit: "'Scott, that weapon in that room,' and this is what I said to him, these are my words. I said, 'They were in a fucking blender.' And they were. They were. They were in a blender. And he didn't disagree with me. He didn't try to rationalize or soften or give me some factual detail that would have disproved it. He didn't at all."

25.

MOLON LABE

If everyone who owned an AR-15 was a psycho,
you'd all be dead.
—Chris Waltz

Chris Waltz was appalled. He felt Democrats were using the Sandy Hook tragedy to tell him he wasn't responsible enough to own an AR-15. He had trained on M16s in the army and carried one into combat in Panama. He had been a firearms instructor and taught his wife and four daughters how to shoot and handle AR-15s safely. He owned AR-15s and loved to shoot them. He followed safety protocols at the rifle range and kept the weapons locked securely in a gun safe at home. He had never committed a crime. What did a lunatic in Connecticut have to do with a law-abiding veteran and family man living in small-town Georgia?

"I didn't understand how you could blame a whole society for the actions of one madman, and then penalize the whole society for that, when you had people who day in and day out, millions of people, who used it responsibly," he said.

At the kitchen table, Waltz complained to his wife about the liberal politicians who were trying to pass laws to ban the AR-15 after Sandy Hook. They didn't even understand how the guns worked. His wife grew so tired of his ranting that on many nights she just left the room and went to bed—even though she agreed with him.

Waltz found himself alone and seething at the kitchen table night after night. Dressed in a T-shirt and pajama bottoms, the muscular forty-nine-year-old with close-cropped hair opened his laptop and logged onto Facebook. On discussion threads on gun-rights pages, he found lots of people agreed with him that Obama's statement about "meaningful action" on the day of the school massacre was code for wanting to crack down on AR-15 ownership. Feinstein's quick introduction of a bill to accomplish just that proved politicians were coming for their firearms. They didn't understand how many AR-15s were owned by people like him.

"If everyone who owned an AR-15 was a psycho, you'd all be dead," he said.

It was time to stand up.

Three weeks after Sandy Hook, Waltz created a Facebook page called "AR-15 Gun Owners of America." The chief motivation was anger, Waltz remembered. Night after night his wife had urged him to let it go, to come to bed. He couldn't. He needed to reach out on social media to other gun owners, to rally them. Sandy Hook and Aurora were horrible, but they weren't the chief danger to the nation. They were excuses that the liberals were using to take away guns.

The first thing that he posted that night was something he took from a blogger, a meme titled "2011 Deaths." It began with a photograph of an AR-15. Next to the photo were the words "323 by these." Below was a photo of a hammer: "496 by these." Below the hammer were photos and stats for people killed by knives, drunk driving, and medical malpractice. At the bottom of the meme was this sentence: "You are SIX HUNDRED TIMES MORE LIKELY to DIE by using your OBAMACARE, than by a semi-automatic rifle. Sooo, feel sick?"

Waltz followed up with a flurry of posts and reposts. He started reading about the Three Percenters, a militia movement founded in 2008 that believed only 3 percent of the colonists had fought to gain American independence. The loosely organized group believed an armed citizenry was needed in modern times as a bulwark against governmental tyranny. Waltz embraced those beliefs.

He took jabs at Obama and other Democrats on his page. He posted links to news stories about AR-15s from conservative news sites or commentary from gun-rights bloggers.

"If I really wanted to poke the bear, I would put something out there for the Second Amendment community to say, 'This is what Obama is doing, have you heard the latest?' and that'd just inflame everybody and you'd get all sorts of comments," he said. He started discussions about technical aspects of the AR, rifle equipment, and ammunition. Long threads among the gun's fans ensued, further fueling interest in his page.

In those initial days, Waltz once bragged to his daughters that he had reached fifty likes on some posts. They rolled their eyes and laughed. But as talk of an AR-15 ban intensified in Washington, Waltz's one-man Facebook page took off.

One early post showed a photograph of an AR-15 painted red, white, and blue. The post read in part, "To some, the AR-15 is a symbol of American freedom. To others, it's a weapon of mass destruction." The first person to comment on the post wrote, "To some, it's a symbol of freedom. To others, they're insecure, uneducated liberals."

Waltz found that a lot of people shared his anger, and they came flocking to his page to vent. He had tapped into gun-rights activism that was centered on Stoner's rifle.

Within a month of the page's launch, the AR-15 Gun Owners of America had 100,000 followers. Weeks later, it rose to 200,000, then 300,000. Waltz paid Facebook for some advertising and more followers poured in.

"We became big really quick, only numbers-wise, but we weren't anything really," he recalled. "It was me, sitting at the table, but people didn't know that."

His Facebook followers asked Waltz whether they could buy decals, T-shirts, and badges with the group's logo. But Waltz didn't have a logo, or even a group. He hired an online design service and chose a patriotic red, white, and blue badge logo. It had the silhouette of an AR-15 in between a red *A* and blue *R*, and red stripes reminiscent of the American flag behind the number 15. The creator, Waltz later learned, was "a little old lady in a print shop in Indonesia." The defense contractor paid $3,000 to print up shirts and badges. He stored the merchandise in his daughter's former bedroom. It quickly sold out. He ordered more and added other badges, one showing a skull with military-style lettering to appeal to veterans.

"It kind of exploded," he recalled. Asked how much time he spent on his new effort in 2013, Waltz said, "Every waking moment when I wasn't working."

For many gun owners, the initial outpouring of shock and grief after Sandy Hook evaporated, replaced by their long-standing suspicion of the government's motives. Distrust of politicians and the media was heightened by perpetual mistakes and misstatements in the press about AR-15s. Media reports sometimes incorrectly identified guns used in such shootings to be ARs. Reporters and politicians made mistakes in discussing how ARs worked or what ammunition they used. They would label them machine guns, or use the term "assault rifle." Such statements were viewed by gun owners as an intentional slight, further proof of a conspiracy to take away AR-15s.

Half a century after Eugene Stoner invented the rifle, it had arrived as the fulcrum of America's great gun divide. The Sandy Hook massacre and its aftermath sparked an outpouring of support for the AR-15. It forged a political movement not based in Washington but rising from small towns like Warner Robins, Georgia. It wasn't centered on charismatic politicians but on an aluminum and plastic object weighing about seven pounds: the AR-15. The rifle was the star of the movement. It appeared on T-shirts, hats, badges, belt buckles, anything you could label.

AR-15 owners, once derided as extremists by more traditional gun owners, now became the vanguard of a resurgent gun-rights movement. A confidential poll of gun owners conducted on behalf of Remington in the wake of Sandy Hook found that AR-15 owners were the most strident in their opposition to gun-control measures. They were more likely to have a positive view of the NRA and a negative view of President

Obama. They would be more opposed to stricter gun laws than would other gun owners. Forty-four percent of handgun owners supported stricter laws after Sandy Hook, while just 31 percent of AR owners did, the survey found. The vocal and angry AR owners led the gun-rights agenda. No compromise.

On the other side, gun-control advocates couldn't turn their outrage into a sustained political movement. Support for gun control had been episodic for years, swelling after horrific shootings but then invariably lessening as supporters turned to other issues. Liberals would march and cry out for change after each mass shooting, but the gun issue would be eclipsed by some other cause, from abortion rights to education to healthcare. Gun owners, especially AR owners, were laser-focused on a single issue: gun rights. The issue was not an abstraction for them: they were fighting for the right to keep an object they had in their homes, that they could hold in their hands. A 2015 Gallup poll found that 34 percent of conservatives only voted for candidates who shared their views on guns, while just 22 percent of liberals did the same. Gun owners consistently had outsized influence in Congress for a simple reason: they cared more about the issue and showed they cared in the voting booth and in donations.

Tim Mak, the author of *Misfire*, a critical look at the inner workings of the NRA, argued that the influential group derived its power from its members, not its deep pockets. Mak pointed to the collapse of the Manchin-Toomey background-check bill after Sandy Hook as a prime example. The NRA did an about-face, suddenly opposing the bill it had helped negotiate after it faced pressure from more extreme gun-rights groups. The NRA mobilized its members to kill the proposed legislation. "Marshaled into action, thousands of ardent Second Amendment supporters flooded Capitol Hill phone lines and crowded email accounts," Mak wrote. "Terrified lawmakers, concerned about their re-election bids, fell into line."

All the activism that transformed the AR-15 into a potent symbol of gun rights also translated into a bonanza for gunmakers.

"All of a sudden, people are buying guns because they want to own the libs and because people are telling them they can't have them and because they want to give the world the middle finger," recalled Ryan Busse, a sales executive at the gunmaker Kimber. "Rationality of the market left the building and this sort of weird emotional, political drive took over."

Smith & Wesson's AR-15 sales reached levels executives never thought possible. Revenue from rifles grew 75 percent in fiscal 2013 to a company-record $179 million. The company noted in securities filings that the surge was driven by fear of "potential legislative restrictions on the sale or makeup of firearms." America's largest producer of AR-15s, Freedom Group, saw an extraordinary spike in sales in the months after Sandy Hook. The company sold $320 million in guns just in the first quarter of 2013, a 50 percent increase from the same period in 2012. Stephen Feinberg's firm had promised to sell the company after Sandy Hook. But gun sales grew, and the firm ended up not selling. By the end of 2013, Freedom Group's firearms sales totaled $1.3 billion. "The orders are coming so fast, they can't make guns fast enough," said a Republican state senator of the company's upstate New York plant.

American gunmakers made 1.9 million AR rifles for sale in the United States in the year after Sandy Hook, the most they had ever manufactured in a single year. The output represented 17 percent of the record 10.8 million guns built in America that year. Once they were all sold, it would bring the number of AR rifles in private hands in the United States to more than 7 million.

Chris Waltz always had an entrepreneurial bent. In the army, he had a travel business. He sold cruises, airplane tickets, and vacation packages to fellow soldiers. Later, he sold herbal dietary supplements. He owned "Tikis by Design," and sold tiki-style bars, huts, platforms, and tables. He imported bamboo products from China to sell to zoos, hotels, restaurants, and other businesses. But these business ventures never took off. He still had piles of bamboo and dismantled tiki huts stored in his backyard.

But his AR-15 Facebook page quickly became a successful business. He initially sold T-shirts and badges, but then began selling AR-15 accessories like scopes from an American company that manufactured them in China. Waltz cleared $100,000 in scope sales alone in the first year, he said. He sold other parts for the gun: magazines, pistol grips, sights, anything a gun owner could want for their AR-15. As long as Waltz didn't sell the receiver, he didn't need to be a licensed firearm dealer. He built up a customer base from Florida to Alaska. He filled his home with plastic racks to store gun parts, accessories, and shirts. It drove his wife crazy, so he leased space on a commercial strip in Warner Robins, Georgia, behind a hearing-aid store and a beauty salon. He hung a sign over a doorway that said, "Have you hugged your AR-15 today?" He hung a Three Percenter flag up in a hallway. Within months, he had six employees, including two of his daughters and his wife.

In 2015, Waltz got a federal firearm license so he could sell AR-15s. At first, he just sold receivers. Then he started selling fully assembled guns. Whenever politicians started talking about gun control, sales spiked.

He bought a large motorboat, then another. He helped his kids out with their finances. He shopped for a second home in Florida with his wife. Within a year, Waltz had gone from angrily typing at his kitchen table to owning a thriving AR-15 business.

The gun had become legendary. Its fans linked it to historic events long before the gun was ever invented. They emblazoned it on American revolutionary flags and Confederate battle flags. One popular slogan associated with the gun came from a famous battle in ancient Greece. Three hundred Spartans led by King Leonidas faced off against a much larger Persian army at a narrow pass called Thermopylae. The historian Plutarch described a supposed exchange between Leonidas and the Persian leader Xerxes. The Persian leader demanded that the Greeks lay down their arms. Leonidas's defiant reply: μολὼν λαβέ. The phrase transliterates as "Molon labe." The English translation: "Come and take them."

At the beginning of the Texas Revolution in 1835, Texans fought off Mexican troops trying to seize a cannon. The Texans created a flag with an image of the cannon, a star, and the phrase "Come and take it." In 2006, the blockbuster movie *300* depicted the famous Greek battle. American gun activists adopted "Molon labe" and "Come and Take It" for their cause. By the time of Sandy Hook it was linked to the AR-15. Bumper stickers, buttons, patches, T-shirts, and caps bearing "Molon labe"—sometimes in Greek lettering and often next to a silhouette of Stoner's gun—proliferated. A gun developed for the U.S. military and a phrase supposedly said by a Greek king facing certain death fused as a symbol of a new strident, libertarian gun-rights movement.

Perhaps no American embodied this new mythos more than C. J. Grisham, an outspoken five-foot-five army master sergeant stationed at Fort Hood in Texas. Three months after Sandy Hook, the thirty-eight-year-old was hiking with his fifteen-year-old son in a rural area not far from the base. Grisham had a Colt AR-15 slung across his chest. Carrying a rifle was a habit that he developed growing up on a farm. The gun also gave him comfort. After a tour in Iraq, he constantly feared that he would be ambushed, a symptom of his PTSD. The AR-15 calmed him. It was the same type of gun that had kept him safe in combat.

"It's like a security blanket," he said.

As Grisham and his son walked along a road that day, a woman became alarmed and called police. The responding officer approached father and son and, without asking, grabbed Grisham's AR-15 and pulled it toward him.

"Is there some reason why you have this?" the officer said.

"Because I can," Grisham answered.

For a split second, Grisham grabbed for the butt end of the rifle as it hung between them, pointing toward the ground. The officer slammed Grisham onto the hood of his car and handcuffed him.

Grisham was arrested for resisting arrest. He argued with the officers that under Texas law he could carry any rifle, including his AR-15. Grisham's son recorded the arrest on cell phone video, and Grisham posted it to YouTube as a clarion call to fellow gun owners.

Grisham organized a protest in the city where the arrest took place.

About four hundred people, many carrying AR-15s, showed up and marched in the streets of Temple, Texas. The police put snipers on the rooftops, took pictures of the crowd, and brought in federal law enforcement officers for support. Throughout the summer of 2013, Grisham and supporters armed with AR-15s showed up in coffee shops, restaurants, grocery stores, and department stores. Grisham's activism was fueled by the anger and humiliation he felt over the arrest. Every protest he attended, he did so with his AR-15 slung across his chest like it was the day he was arrested. The gun was loaded with a full magazine and one round in the chamber. "It was kind of my finger in the air toward the police officer who arrested me," he said.

He started an organization called Open Carry Texas and gained thousands of followers. The group became a political force in the state. Conservative politicians sought Open Carry's endorsement. His movement to normalize carrying weapons in public, especially AR-15s, made national news in August 2013 as part of an event called "Starbucks Appreciation Day." The coffee chain had won gun-rights activists' favor by resisting calls from gun-control advocates to ban firearms from its ten thousand stores.

A new gun-control group, Moms Demand Action, condemned their plans. The group had been created by an Indiana mother after Sandy Hook. Her idea was to model her group after Mothers Against Drunk Driving, and chapters sprouted up around the country. Moms Demand Action countered the pro–gun rights day with a boycott called "Skip Starbucks Saturday."

Starbucks became an unexpected battleground for America's fight over the AR-15. Police arrested Grisham's supporters numerous times for carrying firearms at the stores and charged them with disorderly conduct for displaying firearms "in a public place in a manner calculated to cause alarm" under Texas law.

Sandy Hook parents called on Starbucks to ban guns from their stores. Starbucks chief executive Howard Schultz told customers not to bring their guns to Starbucks anymore, but stopped short of a policy banning firearms. Moms Demand Action claimed victory; Grisham kept going to Starbucks with his AR-15. The two groups battled in the public square. Grisham called Moms Demand Action members "thugs with jugs." They labeled him "downright scary." America's culture war over the AR-15 was raging. It had spilled from the halls of Congress to kitchen tables, to Facebook, and into the local coffee shop.

26.

TRUMP SLUMP

Everybody built a ton of ARs, thinking that
Hillary would be elected.
—Mark Westrom

Executives at America's largest gunmakers all loved Donald Trump. They backed his unorthodox candidacy for president, raising millions of dollars to support him. Stephen Feinberg and other high-finance panjandrums hosted a fifty-thousand-dollar-per-plate fundraiser in the summer of 2016 at Manhattan's Le Cirque restaurant for super PACs tied to the Republican National Committee and Trump's campaign. Ruger chief executive Michael Fifer announced a $5 million challenge grant to the NRA's political arm.

But their operating budgets, supply orders, and capital outlays told a different story: they were all betting heavily on a Hillary Clinton victory. They were certain that the Clinton presidency would result in a renewed battle to ban AR-15s and send sales of the rifle even higher. On the campaign trail, Clinton called for a new federal assault-weapons ban and said that Australia's much stricter prohibition was worth considering. It was a sharp departure from her last run for president. The shift was driven in part by recent polls showing increased support for stricter gun laws after a series of mass shootings, including Sandy Hook.

Production went into overdrive. On a February 2016 earnings call,

Ruger's Fifer predicted "a step-up of demand if a Democrat wins the election." Gunmakers produced more than 2.2 million ARs for sale in 2016, a single-year record and a 63 percent increase over the year before.

"Everybody built a ton of ARs thinking that Hillary would be elected," recalled Mark Westrom, the former owner of ArmaLite who worked as an industry consultant.

In about a decade, the gun industry that once shunned the AR-15 now relied upon it for profits. ARs generated $780 million to $1 billion in revenue in 2013 for gunmakers, compared to no more than $93 million in 2004, according to two researchers at the Naval Postgraduate School in Monterey, California. By 2013, at least seventy-six companies were making the gun, up from only thirteen in 2004, the researchers found. By 2016, the number of AR-15s made in America more than doubled sales of Ford's F-series pickup trucks, the bestselling line of trucks in the country.

The boom had been fueled in part by Americans who worried that AR-15s would be banned. Industry executives called it "fear-based buying" and labeled these customers "anxious buyers." They represented the largest pool of potential first-time gun owners, according to an internal gun industry report.

"Most of the Anxious Buyer segment have grown up always wanting to own a firearm, and their suspicion that they will not be able to fulfill this desire encourages them to buy sooner rather than later," the report stated. "If asked, an Anxious Buyer might tell you, 'I want to buy a firearm before it's too late.'"

AR-15s were "more frequently targeted for sales restrictions" and therefore were the "best bets" for gunmakers to sell to this group, the consultants concluded.

Gunmakers anticipated that calls for a new assault-weapons ban after mass shootings and during the presidential election would drive sales.

In December 2015, a couple armed with two AR-15s—a Smith & Wesson M&P 15 and a DPMS Panther Oracle—killed fourteen people and wounded twenty-two others at a holiday gathering of county government workers in San Bernardino, California. Syed Rizwan Farook, who worked as a county health inspector, and Tashfeen Malik, his wife, fired more than a hundred rounds in under three minutes before fleeing. As the couple sped away, Malik pledged allegiance to the leader of the Islamic State terrorist group on her Facebook account. Hours later, police killed the two in a shootout. The massacre was the deadliest terrorist attack in America since 9/11 and the worst mass shooting since Sandy Hook.

In June 2016, a gunman opened fire at Pulse, a gay nightclub in Orlando, Florida. Omar Mateen, a twenty-nine-year-old security guard who also pledged allegiance to the Islamic State, killed forty-nine people and wounded fifty-three others before police killed him. It was the deadliest mass shooting in modern U.S. history at that time. Mateen used a Sig Sauer MCX semiautomatic rifle. The rifle's design closely resembled an AR-15 and used the same ammunition. But the gun's internal workings were slightly different.

Such calamities were increasing, researchers found. From 2000 through 2007, the country averaged seven active-shooter incidents a year. But from 2008 through 2015, the number rose to eighteen such incidents each year, according to FBI data. The Texas State University criminologist J. Pete Blair, who led the research, found in additional analysis that AR-15s were used in only 24 of 250 active shooter incidents between 2000 and 2017. But many people had come to associate such events with AR-15s. The reason was simple: these guns were used in some of the largest and bloodiest attacks such as Sandy Hook, Aurora, and San Bernardino.

With each new tragedy, Clinton delivered speeches calling for a new ban.

"You walk into class. You're driving your baby around in a car seat, going to church, somebody has an automatic weapon, or even worse an assault weapon that is a military instrument of war, and you're somehow supposed to be able to stop that with your own gun," Clinton said on the campaign trail. "That has never made any sense."

Clinton strategists believed for the first time since the 1990s that gun control, and specifically going after the AR-15, was a winning issue with the Democratic base. A Gallup poll found that 77 percent of Democrats surveyed backed stricter gun laws.

There was no question the NRA was going to back the Republican nominee in 2016, but Trump seemed an unlikely pick at first. Trump had written a book years earlier in which he stated that he supported the federal assault-weapons ban. During the campaign, he distanced himself from that position in a question-and-answer session with the popular gun-owners blog *Ammoland*.

"Gun-banners are unfortunately preoccupied with the AR-15, magazine capacity, grips, and other aesthetics, precisely because of its popularity," he told the blog.

The NRA endorsed Trump in May 2016, and the group went on to spend $30 million on ads attacking Clinton and backing Trump. The GOP's platform, adopted that July as Trump became the party's nominee, declared: "We oppose ill-conceived laws that would restrict magazine capacity or ban the sale of the most popular and common modern rifle." It also opposed "restoration of the ill-fated Clinton gun ban."

Weeks before the election, Ryan Busse, who worked at the gunmaker Kimber, had dinner with James Debney, Smith & Wesson's chief executive. Smith & Wesson's sales were soaring. Its stock price was trading above $20 a share for the first time in its history. Debney said that he supported Trump but his company would do well no matter who was president, Busse recalled.

Busse didn't see it that way, telling Debney: "If he wins, your sales are going to fucking tank, man."

Trump won, stunning the world. His supporters, including AR-15 makers, were ecstatic. But a month later, the first signs of business trouble appeared. The FBI reported that background checks fell sharply. Two months later, Smith & Wesson warned Wall Street that demand was softening "as a result of reduced political pressures on firearm laws and regulations." Debney tried to spin it on an earnings call, saying there were still "thoughtful" buyers out there looking to buy his products.

But AR-15 makers hadn't grown because of "thoughtful" buyers;

they had grown from panic buying. Smith & Wesson's stock plunged below $10 by the end of 2017. "There is no fear-based buying right now," Debney lamented on an earnings call.

What the industry labeled the Trump Slump devastated AR-15 makers. In Georgia, Chris Waltz's sales dropped immediately for his internet business, AR-15 Gun Owners of America. "We saw it right away," he said.

Dealers tried to return AR-15s they couldn't sell to distributors and distributors tried to return them to manufacturers.

"We were maxed out on rifles, we were maxed out on handguns, and then it just never happened. Boom," recalled Michael Cargill, owner of Central Texas Gun Works, a gun store in Austin, Texas. "As soon as Trump got in, everyone got comfortable and demand just wasn't there."

Gunmakers tried to reinvent the AR-15 by introducing new calibers, colors, sizes, and models. They sought to attract new customers; for example, making pink AR-15s in hopes of attracting female gun buyers. They also sought to create new versions of the rifle to appeal to gun owners who already had a gun safe full of AR-15s but would buy a new type just to add to their collection. In the fall of 2017, Springfield Armory, a private company that had taken the historic armory's name, introduced a smaller version called an AR-15 pistol. The gun looked like a smaller copy of an AR-15.

"When it starts to slow down, people come out with new products," said Steve McKelvain, Springfield's president.

Springfield tried to appeal to more diverse customers. A video promoting its AR-15, called "the Saint," included thumping rock music and showed younger adults, men and women, white and African American, firing the gun in slow motion.

At Palmetto State Armory in South Carolina, designers tried to develop an AR-15/AK-47 hybrid. It looked like the classic Russian AK, but it fired .223 rounds like an AR-15.

"You've got to make it fresh because everyone's already got an AR," said Kris Vermillion, creative media director.

Smith & Wesson came up with more colors for its M&P 15-22

Sport, hoping to draw in women and young shooters. It already had pink, purple, camouflage, and "Harvest Moon Orange." It added "Robin's Egg Blue Platinum." The NRA promoted Smith & Wesson's little .22 caliber gun that looked like an AR-15 as a good choice for a child's first rifle.

But sales stalled. Feinberg's Freedom Group, a leading AR-15 maker that now went by the name Remington Outdoor Company, was hit the hardest. Revenue plummeted from $865 million in 2016 to $603 million in 2017. Remington struggled to pay off its massive debts as sales dropped. The company filed for Chapter 11 bankruptcy in 2018. Cerberus had built the nation's largest gun conglomerate with the AR-15 as a profit driver. With Donald Trump's election, it turned out to be a bad bet.

"The shine is coming off the nickel," said Mark Kresser, former chief executive of the gunmaker Taurus Holdings Inc.

Business empires built on the AR-15 rose and fell. Political debates about the role of AR-15s in American society flared and died down. Mass shootings erupted with sickening frequency.

Memory of the man who invented the rifle faded. His family worried about his legacy.

Whenever a mass shooting made the news, Susan Kleinpell found herself praying that the shooter had not used her father's invention. She grew concerned that her dad—whom she remembered as a quirky, soft-spoken, brilliant man—was becoming irreparably associated in the public mind with mass killers. She had never owned one of her father's weapons, but her abiding love for her dad's memory weighed on her heart.

After the Orlando shooting, she decided to say something. Even though Mateen had not used the exact type of rifle that her father invented, the shooting prompted a reporter to track down the Stoner family. Susan was on vacation and eating with her husband and friends at a restaurant in Paris when her cell phone rang with a U.S. number she didn't recognize. Worried that it was an emergency, she answered. It was a reporter from MSNBC. He wanted to know what Eugene Stoner would have thought of his gun being used in mass shootings. His question was stupid, she thought.

"Of course, he would be horrified by children being killed like Newtown," she thought to herself.

At first, Susan said she didn't want to comment. But the reporter pressed and Susan said she would think about it. She wrote out a short statement a few days later and gave it to him. It was the first time Stoner's family had spoken to the press about mass shootings.

"Our father, Eugene Stoner, designed the AR-15 and subsequent M16 as a military weapon to give our soldiers an advantage over the AK-47. He died long before any mass shootings occurred. But, we do think he would have been horrified and sickened as anyone, if not more by these events."

But Susan felt the reporter distorted the statement in his television report, jumbling facts to make her father seem, from the grave, to be calling for gun control. She had carefully crafted the statement to say only that his intent when inventing the weapon was for it to be used by the military.

The Stoner family statement, and MSNBC's interpretation of it, made headlines. But the news faded after a day. His invention was so far beyond him now, a cultural object batted around by political partisans and internet warriors. Most Americans had no idea of the origin of the name AR-15, or what Stoner's innovations had been. They didn't know the gun's Vietnam story, or how the civilian version of the gun was long rejected by most gun owners. People unfamiliar with guns confused it with the AK-47, just because it sounded similar. They associated ownership of such a rifle with being a terrorist or psychopath.

Gun owners spun tales about Stoner. To them, he was some kind of Second Amendment hero, a rugged individualist with a deep mistrust of government. Many gun owners chastised liberals for believing that *AR* stood for "assault rifle," insisting instead that it stood for "ArmaLite Rifle." Gun owners felt this knowledge was further proof that they knew what they were talking about when it came to the rifle, and gun-control advocates didn't. In fact, the *AR* stood for "ArmaLite" or "ArmaLite Research."

For both sides of the gun debate, the AR-15 had come to have no history or inventor; it was now just a cultural chew toy for angry partisans.

It had arisen from America's past as a cultural icon, pure evil for one group and sterling freedom for another. Susan realized after the cable report aired and then faded from the news cycle that no one really cared what her dad thought. All those years: tinkering in his garage, writing out schematics on napkins, working in the Hollywood offices of Arma-Lite, meeting with generals, testifying in Washington, seeing his invention adopted by the U.S. military. Of all his inventions, he was most proud of the AR-15. He made sure it was fired at his burial. But her dad's thought and effort for so many years—the crowning achievement of his life—had been reduced to a fleeting sound bite amid the sound and fury of America's endless gun debate.

27.

BURNING BOOTS

You live in that nightmare.
—Nadine

Nadine Lusmoeller bought her first pair of cowboy boots when she moved to Las Vegas in 2010. They were light brown with a simple stitched design. Nadine, reserved, with short blond hair and glasses, was born in a small town in the German countryside. But she dreamed of being an artist and going to America. As soon as she graduated from university, she traveled to the United States for the first time. She fell in love with American music, especially country and western. Back home in Germany, she found herself daydreaming about the United States. She returned as much as she could.

"Every time I came over here, it kind of felt like home," she recalled. She was drawn to the West, with its wide-open spaces and big skies. For ten years, Nadine applied for the green-card visa to work in the United States. At age thirty-two, she lucked out.

Once she was in the States, nothing could make her leave. Shortly after moving to Las Vegas, Nadine was attacked by a man with a hand-gun. He demanded her purse and when she refused he struck with his gun. She woke up in the hospital with a gash on her skull. Her family implored her to come back to Germany. She stayed. She waitressed at Applebee's and worked other minimum-wage gigs before landing an office job at Tesla, the electric-car company.

Nadine rarely went to the casinos. She only went to the Strip for one reason: country music concerts. A friend offered her a free pass to the Route 91 Harvest country music festival. When she read the list of acts, she knew she had to go because one of her favorites, Jason Aldean, was playing on Sunday, October 1, 2017.

Dressed in jeans, a black T-shirt, boots, and her tan cowboy hat, Nadine headed out that afternoon to the Las Vegas Village, a fifteen-acre outdoor venue. The festival was packed. She waded into the crowd of about twenty-two thousand people and made her way toward the stage. Just after 10:00 p.m., Aldean started singing his love song "When She Says Baby." Nadine was happy to be with so many other country music fans, listening to a song they all knew by heart.

She and everyone around her swayed to the music. But then Aldean suddenly stopped and ran offstage. Bright floodlights turned on the crowd. Nadine felt something whiz by the front of her face. What was that? Did someone throw something? Something else whizzed by and snatched the cowboy hat off her head. Something wet splashed against her body. The woman next to her fell. The whizzing seemed to come from everywhere, all at once. People fell to the ground all around her. People screamed and ran. Others crouched to hide.

Nadine didn't know what to do. A man shouted for her to hide under the stage. She climbed over a barrier and someone shoved her under the stage. Nadine fell into the dark and landed hard. Her arm crashed into something metal. She cradled the injured arm; she could feel it was broken. A bone was protruding from her skin. Around her, other concertgoers huddled. Two women wailed next to her.

She heard crashing sounds. The noises grew louder. Shafts of light appeared in the gloom as bullets pierced holes in the stage above her. She decided to run. She clambered out from beneath the stage and ran toward crowds fleeing the concert. She looked down to see where she was going and saw piles of belongings on the ground: purses, clothing, hats. She saw people lying next to them. The people weren't moving. She swallowed, closed her eyes, and ran. The jagged cracking sounds resumed. She felt a sharp pain in her left thigh—like someone had smashed her thigh with a baseball bat as hard as they could. She fell. She blacked out.

The Las Vegas massacre was the deadliest mass shooting carried out by one person in American history. In about ten minutes, the gunman killed and wounded more people than the mass shooters in Stockton, Columbine, Virginia Tech, Aurora, Sandy Hook, San Bernardino, and Orlando combined. Using AR-15s, Stephen Paddock killed 58 people and wounded 413 others with bullets or shrapnel that night. Another 456 people were injured in the stampede to escape or in other ways. The 927 casualties—injuries and deaths combined—topped the 759 casualties from the 1995 Oklahoma City bombing. More Americans were killed that night than were killed in any single battle in twenty years of war in Afghanistan.

Political leaders said it was a tragedy, with President Trump calling it "an act of pure evil." But Democratic and Republican leaders didn't offer any serious solutions or new approaches. Both sides hesitated to start up the political fight yet again; they knew it would end in a stalemate. After Sandy Hook, the nation had groped for answers. Groups as divergent as the parents of the dead children and the NRA offered a range of solutions. Newspaper columnists and cable TV commentators argued over what to do. The country's political leaders wrestled with legislative proposals. After Vegas, everyone looked away. People found ways to avoid confronting the full horror of what had happened. They were country music fans. They were adults. It happened in Vegas. "Are Americans becoming 'numb' to mass shootings?" CBS News asked. The night after the shooting the Strip was as bright as usual. Visitors crowded blackjack tables and worked the slots. Everyone tried to move on. But the unavoidable fact was that a device created to protect America was wounding it. For people who lived through these horrors, their wounds—mental and physical—remained.

The man who inflicted the horror had stood in his suite thirty-two floors up in the Mandalay Bay. Paddock had fired 1,049 bullets from twelve AR-15s. He had also fired eight shots from AR-10s, which police believe he aimed at distant fuel tanks. When police finally blew open the door, they found Paddock's body and his arsenal. Brass casings littered the carpet and tiled floor. His rifles were scattered around his suite like empty liquor bottles. Paddock used a range of rifles made by leading gunmakers such as Colt, Daniel Defense, and FN Herstal. Police believed that in most cases Paddock fired one AR-15 until the magazine was empty, then tossed the weapon aside and picked up a new rifle. The guns lay on the floor, barstools, chairs, and beds. One lay underneath the legs of Paddock's corpse, his gloved hand on its butt.

No one, even those closest to Paddock, provided a motive. Las Vegas Metropolitan Police Department investigators would probe his life, interviewing relatives, his girlfriend, his ex-wife, his doctor, and casino staff. They searched his computers, phone, and internet history. He left no manifesto or suicide note. He wasn't affiliated with a terrorist group and he had no mental health diagnosis that might explain the attack. Sheriff Joseph Lombardo, head of the Las Vegas police, would say that recent gambling losses may have been a factor. Paddock saw his real estate investment–fueled bank accounts dwindle from nearly $2.1 million to $530,000 before the attack. But the sheriff said investigators weren't able to "definitively answer the why."

Paddock's girlfriend, Marilou Danley, told authorities she thought his extensive gun buying was just a hobby. She went with him to a makeshift desert shooting range located on the edge of the town where they lived. She helped set up targets at long distances. Several weeks before the attack, Paddock urged Danley to go on a trip to the Philippines to see her family. He wired her $150,000 while she was there to buy a home. She worried he was about to break up with her.

Paddock's brother "believed Paddock may have conducted the attack because he had done everything in the world he wanted to do and was bored with everything," according to police.

In the year before the attack, Paddock searched for the best place to shoot at a large crowd. He requested a hotel room overlooking the

Lollapalooza music festival in Chicago that August, but later canceled the reservation. He stayed on the sixtieth floor of the Mandalay Bay at the beginning of September. He was "constantly looking out the windows of the room which overlooked [the concert venue]," Danley told investigators. On September 5, he searched "Route 91 harvest festival 2017 attendance" on his computer.

Eric Paddock told police that his brother "would have planned the attack to kill a large number of people because he would want to be known as having the largest casualty count."

In the year leading up to the attack, he went on an AR buying spree. He spent nearly $95,000 on more than forty different guns, as well as accessories and ammunition. Thirty-one of those weapons were based on Stoner's invention: twenty-one AR-15s and ten AR-10s. From his first AR-15 purchase on October 2, 2016, a Colt M4 model, to his last on May 5, 2017, an LWRC M6IC, Paddock bought high-end rifles. The guns in his collection cost about $1,000 to $3,000 apiece. Numerous gun salesmen who assisted Paddock told authorities that he never asked about prices. Paddock always wore white gloves, the "type that a museum curator would put on if he were handling old firearms," one salesman said.

Paddock found an easy way to make his AR-15s mimic rapid-fire machine guns. He replaced the shoulder stocks on his AR-15s with "bump stocks." On semiautomatic rifles, a person can only shoot as fast as they can pull the trigger. Bump stocks used the recoil to slide the gun back and forth, bumping the trigger rapidly against the shooter's stationary finger. The devices were cheap and easy to get, just another accessory on the massive market for AR-15 add-ons.

Paddock was able to buy thirty-one ARs in a year because no federal law limited the number of semiautomatic rifles that an American could buy. Gun dealers were required to alert the ATF if a customer bought two or more handguns within five consecutive business days. Dealers in states bordering Mexico were also required to alert the agency if someone purchased two or more semiautomatic rifles such as AR-15s within five consecutive business days. That rule, which was intended to combat gun trafficking by Mexican drug cartels, didn't trip up Paddock, since he bought his firearms in Nevada and Utah.

He was America's worst nightmare: a wealthy psychopath who could pass a background check in a land where people could buy as many AR-15s as they wanted.

Dianne Feinstein told CBS's *Face the Nation* she didn't see any way that Congress could have passed a law that would've caught someone like Paddock. A month later, she cosponsored ban legislation again. Everyone knew it wouldn't pass. Unified opposition to new gun laws by Republicans after Las Vegas was aided by the reactions from survivors and families. For many of the country music fans, the shooting did not inherently mean they should back gun-control measures. Many had been strong Second Amendment supporters beforehand; they remained so afterward.

Paddock's massacre was followed by another in a small town near San Antonio, Texas. Five weeks after Las Vegas, Devin Kelley went into church on Sunday morning with an AR-15 and wearing body armor. He killed twenty-six parishioners and wounded twenty-two others. He walked along the pews, shooting children, seniors, and a pregnant woman. Kelley fired more than 450 rounds from his Ruger-made rifle. It was the deadliest mass shooting in Texas history.

Kelley had a history of mental problems and violent behavior. Authorities believed the shooting stemmed from a dispute with his mother-in-law, who attended the church but wasn't there that day. Kelley had been kicked out of the military for assaulting his wife and her child. The domestic violence conviction should have prevented Kelley from purchasing the gun he used in the attack. But the air force failed to submit the information to the federal database used for background checks. Kelley bought his Ruger AR-556 from a gun store in San Antonio in April 2016, without any problems. At the time of the shooting, Kelley had a picture of his AR as the cover photo on his Facebook page. A week before the attack, he posted a photo of the rifle on his timeline with the caption "She's a bad bitch."

On the day of the shooting, Stephen Willeford, a fifty-five-year-old plumber, was at his home down the street from the church. After he heard gunfire, Willeford reached for his AR-15, grabbed ammunition, and sprinted barefoot out the door, loading the gun as he went. As the shooter emerged from the church, Willeford fired twice at the gunman's chest. The shooter ran for his SUV and drove off. Willeford fired again, shattering the SUV's windows. Kelley drove his SUV off the road and killed himself as police closed in.

Willeford was hailed a hero, and gun-rights supporters held up his actions as proof that widespread civilian ownership of AR-15s was a societal good. Willeford said in interviews that he would not have been able to stop the gunman without an AR-15. Gun groups exalted Willeford as the "good guy with a gun." The NRA honored Willeford at its annual convention. He told the cheering crowd, "He had an AR-15, but so did I."

Las Vegas and Sutherland Springs were two of the deadliest mass shootings in U.S. history. Both shooters had used AR-15s. Their impact on American discourse on guns was slight. The media covered the shootings, but then moved on. It turned its attention to Trump's tweets and the murky Mueller investigation.

People traumatized by the attacks—there were twenty-two thousand survivors of the Las Vegas attack alone—tried to move past the horror. In the months after the attack, Nadine focused on her physical injuries. Her arm was in a cast. The pain in her left leg was sharp and constant. She went back to work. She pushed herself to see live music again. "The one thing that he could not take away from me was my love of music," she said. She decided to honor those killed by attending fifty-eight concerts. She started about two months after the shooting, going to a country music concert at a casino. She grew anxious when she saw the crowd and found herself checking behind her and looking up at balconies above the crowd. She scanned for exits. That night she met other Route 91 survivors who were also trying to return to some kind of normal. They became friends and joined a support group.

The pain in her left leg grew worse. She had trouble standing for long periods. Doctors found there were bullet fragments in her leg, cutting into nerves and muscles. They had fractured her femur too. She endured a series of painful operations and physical therapy. Nadine covered physical scars on her leg and arm with tattoos. On her left thigh, she got a black and gray American flag pierced through with bullet holes and the word "Warrior" superimposed in script. On her wounded arm, she got angel wings and the Route 91 sign with the date of the massacre.

Nadine met a fellow Route 91 survivor, Tracy Szymanski, who noticed her tattoo at a concert. Szymanski hadn't been wounded that day. She had rushed from the shooting to the hospital where she worked as director of patient transportation. When she hurried into the emergency room, she slipped because there was so much blood on the floor. "My trauma happened in my ER," she recalled. "You can never get the smell of that much blood in one room out of your nostrils." Nadine and Szymanski became close. They went to concerts together. They opened up to each other like they hadn't been able to with others. "I cry a lot more than she does and she was the one who got shot," Szymanski said.

Nadine started volunteering at hospitals and spending time with Szymanski and other friends. She returned to work full-time. She saw a therapist and it helped her cope. Her life felt full and she thought she was busier and more social than she had been before the shooting.

At the six-month anniversary of the shooting, Nadine sought closure in a personal ritual. She went to her closet and took out the cowboy boots she had worn on the night of the concert. She hadn't touched them since then. Dark stains of blood—hers and others'—discolored the tan leather. She brought them to a friend's house, where the two took them to the backyard. Nadine soaked them in lighter fluid and lit them on fire. She brought the ashes to where she had been shot. The giant area that had held twenty-two thousand people that night was now empty. She could see the golden towers of the Mandalay Bay looming from across Las Vegas Boulevard. Nadine spread the ashes on the ground.

Burning the boots didn't bring closure. On the one-year anniversary of the massacre, Nadine attended a memorial at a small garden near downtown Las Vegas where the city had planted fifty-eight trees. People brought pictures of the dead, flowers, painted rocks, and other tributes. As Nadine stood with a small crowd, she found herself overwhelmed. She felt like she was drowning; suffocated by guilt and pain. She wished she had been killed in the attack. Szymanski tried to comfort her as she cried uncontrollably. In the days and weeks that followed, Szymanski worried that Nadine might kill herself.

Nadine fell apart. Three or four times every day, she relived the massacre. Loud sounds triggered flashbacks. Once, a woman popping balloons in her office sent Nadine into a rage. Other times she would just freeze in public, then black out. She'd awaken with strangers asking whether she was okay. She struggled at work. She stopped volunteering. She felt that her therapist wasn't helping anymore. Szymanski took her on road trips across the West, trying to give Nadine time and space to open up about what she was going through.

"I had to pull things out of her," Szymanski recalled. She couldn't fully understand Nadine's trauma. "I didn't walk over bodies," Szymanski said.

Nadine was suffering from post-traumatic stress disorder (PTSD). It was well-known as a diagnosis for soldiers returning from combat. As mass shootings became more common, psychiatrists applied the diagnosis to survivors. Studies found high rates of PTSD among mass-shooting survivors even years after the incidents.

Flashbacks hit Nadine at any time, even while she slept. Nadine's only solace was Cielo, her scruffy, little blond dog. Cielo had been trained to work with people suffering from PTSD. Whenever Nadine froze or started to shake, Cielo came and touched her with his paw or sat in her lap.

"He's telling me, 'Okay, let's take a break here for a minute and it's gonna be okay,'" Nadine said.

But every day, Nadine relived the memory of running over bodies on October 1, 2017. Because of a man she never met who armed himself with twelve AR-15s, she had joined the nation's growing ranks of mass-shooting survivors, scarred for life by the experience.

"It's like you have a nightmare and as a normal person, you wake up and just forget about it," Nadine said. "But with PTSD, it's like you live in that nightmare."

28.

LOCKDOWN NATION

We call BS.

—Emma González

On February 14, 2018, the day of a mass shooting at a high school in Parkland, Florida, fifteen-year-old Lane Murdock was in the hallway at her own high school in Ridgefield, Connecticut, a wealthy New York City suburb. She saw the alert on her phone: a gunman had killed numerous students and staff. She and her friends discussed the news casually as they walked to class. They talked about how awful it was, but it didn't *feel* awful.

"It was literally like we were talking about the weather, and it happened in a school just like the one I am in now," she recalled thinking. That night at her home, Murdock let emotions take over. Seventeen dead; another seventeen wounded. Most of them were kids just like her. She felt sick to her stomach over how callous everyone had become. Ridgefield was about a thirty-minute drive from Sandy Hook—that massacre took place when she was just ten. She had to do something, anything. Taking to Change.org and social media, she created the hashtag #NationalSchoolWalkout and called for students everywhere to leave school on April 20, 2018, the anniversary of the 1999 Columbine massacre. She thought it would be a way to channel the frustration she and her friends were feeling.

Her hashtag swept the internet. Students across America announced bluntly that they'd had enough. Murdock knew little about guns, but she soon found herself getting up to speed on the AR-15, the gun used in the Parkland massacre. She couldn't believe that a military-style rifle was still so easily available to civilians—including disturbed young men—after Sandy Hook and Aurora. The rifle became the anti-symbol of a budding student movement. As rallies erupted outside schools across the country, signs displaying an AR-15 with a line through it were common. On the day of the national walkout that Murdock had started with a simple hashtag in her bedroom, students at more than 2,500 schools left their classrooms, from Santa Monica, California, to Washington. Students staged "die-ins" at schools. Others rallied outside of the White House. They carried signs declaring "#Never-Again" and "New Gun Reform Now" with hand-drawn silhouettes of AR-15 rifles.

"We were the first generation of digital natives, this was how we organized," Murdock said. "We had no money, we had no real power. The only thing we had was our attendance. Not going to class was showing how we care about this."

Parkland proved to be a key moment for America's great gun debate, launching a political youth movement to stop a problem that adults seemed incapable of addressing. It was led largely by a group of students who survived the Parkland shooting, but also by young people like Murdock in cities and towns all over the country. These kids, aided by adults who supported gun control, formed organizations to lobby lawmakers, launch school walkouts, and organize gigantic marches in Washington, state capitals, and major cities.

Their actions frightened Republicans, at least temporarily, and forced Democratic politicians to take stronger positions on gun legislation. The expected platitudes and declarations offered by adults on either side of the gun deadlock no longer mollified America's youth. They channeled their fear and anger on social media, helping to coalesce what one Parkland student labeled the "mass-shooting generation." Even as the shooter was still stalking the hallways of Parkland's Marjory Stoneman Douglas

High School on Valentine's Day, students there were posting video clips of their friends huddled and praying near the dead and wounded. David Hogg, seventeen, posted interviews with students hiding with him in a dark closet.

"I want to show these people exactly what's going on when these children are facing bullets flying through classrooms," he said. Fellow students in the United States and across the world watched the horror in real time.

One student who emerged as an early leader was Emma González. González spoke at a gun-control rally on the Saturday after the shooting in Fort Lauderdale. In a brief speech broadcast by CNN and other stations, a teary González said, "If all our government and president can do is send thoughts and prayers, then it's time for victims to be the change that we need to see."

González attacked Washington's political classes for failing to keep kids safe.

"Politicians who sit in their gilded House and Senate seats funded by the NRA telling us nothing could ever have been done to prevent this, we call BS. They say tougher gun laws do not decrease gun violence. We call BS. They say a good guy with a gun stops a bad guy with a gun. We call BS. They say guns are just tools like knives and are as dangerous as cars. We call BS. They say no laws could have been able to prevent the hundreds of senseless tragedies that have occurred. We call BS. That us kids don't know what we're talking about, that we're too young to understand how the government works. We call BS."

The crowd roared and the speech's refrain, "We call BS," became a rallying cry for young people from California to New York.

Parkland students descended on Tallahassee, the state capital, and pressed lawmakers in the Republican-led legislature to pass strict new gun laws. The "Marjory Stoneman Douglas High School Public Safety Act" raised the minimum age to purchase a rifle from eighteen to twenty-one, required a three-day waiting period for most gun sales, and banned the sale or possession of bump stocks. The legislature gave authority to police to temporarily confiscate guns from people if they posed a danger to themselves or others with a new red-flag law. The Florida bill did not ban the sale of AR-15s as the students had hoped, but it passed through the legislature and was signed into law by Republican governor Rick Scott less than a month after the shooting.

A national movement led by young people to limit access to AR-15s gathered momentum. Days after the shooting, seventeen high school students in the DC area organized a "lie-in" near the White House. Two held a handmade sign declaring "We've had enough," showing a crossed-out AR-15.

Mina Mazeikis, seventeen, helped organize a walkout at her high school in Schaumburg, Illinois, a Chicago suburb, just days after Parkland. They chanted "kids over guns" as cars drove by, honking in support. Mazeikis was moved by seeing the Parkland students protest what every kid in America had been coping with for years—the constant fear of mass shootings.

"What really made the difference with the Parkland incident was it was all over social media," she said. "They had their phones and computers with them. It was gut-wrenching. It was almost impossible not to feel the fear. Watching it with my friends, I realized, what's the difference between me and the students at my high school in Illinois and the students at Parkland in Florida? Was it location? Was it luck?"

One month after the shooting, the liberal group that had organized massive women's marches after Trump was inaugurated called for a national walkout by students and teachers. Tens of thousands of students left classrooms to stand outside for seventeen minutes, one minute for each person killed at Parkland.

Parkland students and supporters created a new organization called March for Our Lives. It held protests in Washington and across the United States and even overseas. The marches and rallies drew about 1.2 million people, making it one of the largest days of protest in U.S. history. Celebrities, including George Clooney, Oprah Winfrey, and Steven Spielberg, gave money.

An emotional peak of the Washington rally was the speech given by González, who paused remarks for the amount of time that the shooter took to fire his gun in Marjory Stoneman Douglas. González mentioned Stoner's firearm as she talked about the lives taken in the spree.

"Six minutes and 20 seconds with an AR-15 and my friend Carmen would never complain to me about piano practice," González said. "Aaron Feis would never call Kiera Ms. Sunshine. Alex Schachter would never walk into school with his brother Ryan. Scott Beigel would never joke around with Cameron at camp." González described the other victims as well. González urged America's students, "Fight for your lives before it's someone else's job."

The youth protests were so startling to the political and social status quo that many believed a fundamental change in America's relationship with the AR-15 was about to take place. A few gun owners took to social media to post videos of themselves destroying their AR-15s or announcing they were quitting the NRA. Municipalities passed local bans on AR-15s. At a meeting with the massacre's survivors held at the White House, Trump promised: "We're going to come up with a solution." He endorsed raising the minimum age to purchase AR-15s or similar firearms to twenty-one from eighteen, tightening background checks for gun buyers, and banning bump stocks, the device used in the Las Vegas massacre.

In a meeting with members of Congress, Trump and Feinstein had a seemingly cooperative and constructive conversation about gun control. "We have to act," Trump told the group in the televised event. "We can't wait and play games and nothing gets done." Feinstein brought up the assault-weapons ban legislation and Trump promised vaguely, "I'll take a look at it." At the same meeting, he admonished lawmakers, "You're afraid of the NRA."

Companies responded to customer anger by severing ties with the NRA. Delta and United Airlines eliminated discount travel programs for NRA members. Hotels, car rental companies, insurance companies, banks, cybersecurity companies, and even a hearing-aid company severed relationships with the group.

The March for Our Lives organization released a comprehensive blueprint to reduce gun violence and mass shooting, which included a permanent federal assault-weapons ban. Groups of Parkland students traveled the country, addressing throngs of other students and supporters on a "Road to Change" tour.

The giant movement was the result of pent-up frustration over how little had been done to stop disturbed young men turning to AR-15s to lash out and kill. FBI behavioral analysts in 2018 produced an extensive study of the lives of sixty-three attackers to try to find common traits. Most were single men without a job who nursed grievances, and nearly half had expressed interest in or had attempted suicide. About one in four had been diagnosed with a mental illness, and most showed signs of mental problems. The analysts discovered that they didn't "just snap"—a common myth. Instead, these murderers planned their attacks for weeks or even months. Most told others of their plans either directly or online. Only 6 percent of the killers had been previously convicted of a violent felony, which meant they had no trouble getting guns. Three out of four either legally purchased or already had the guns they used in their attacks. Unlike most other criminals, mass shooters didn't hope to get away with it. Most wanted to die. The act was a last desperate attempt by weak, isolated men to lash out at the world, deluded they would die in a blaze of glory.

Mass shooters were getting younger and were often motivated by the desire to have their names go viral as the lines between fame and infamy blurred in the reality-television and viral-video era, according to criminologists. The more people they killed, the more widely they would be known. "Put simply, public mass shooters who want to kill large numbers of victims appear more likely to take specific steps to accomplish those goals," experts on such violence concluded in one paper. "In many cases, this weapons acquisition involves obtaining multiple firearms and at least one semi-automatic rifle or assault weapon."

The semiautomatic rifle they increasingly chose was the AR-15 as they engaged in a sick contest of one-upmanship. Four of the five deadliest mass shootings in American history had come since 2012. In three of those massacres, the attackers used AR-15s and in one, the gunman used a similar rifle that fired the same ammunition. Twelve of forty mass shooters who killed four or more people in a public place from

2012 through 2018 used AR-15s. The rifle had been used just five times by the prior 123 attackers going back to 1996, according to the Violence Project, a federally funded nonprofit that cataloged mass shootings.

"There's a utility part to this, which is, it is just a very efficient killing machine and so if you're trying to kill a lot of people, this is a good choice," said James Densley, a criminal justice professor at Metro State University in Minnesota who cofounded the Violence Project. "But then there's the sort of copycat component—which is if you want your mass shooting to conform with audience expectations of what a mass shooting looks like, you have to use the same props that the past mass shooters have used in their performances too."

Nikolas Cruz, the Parkland shooter, was a poster child for this dark phenomenon.

"I hate everyone and everything," the high school dropout said on a video on his cell phone just days before the shooting. "With the power of my AR, you will all know who I am . . . I had enough of people telling me that I'm an idiot and a dumbass."

Later that day, he made another recording, this time showing his face. His eyes were sunken.

"Hello. My name is Nik and I'm going to be the next school shooter of 2018," he said. "My goal is at least 20 people. With an AR-15 and a couple tracer rounds, I think I could get it done. Location is Stoneman Douglas in Parkland, Florida. It's going to be a big event. And when you see me on the news, you'll all know who I am." Cruz laughed and mimicked gun sounds.

Cruz had a long history of violent behavior. He killed chickens, squirrels, toads, and lizards as a boy growing up in the suburbs north of Miami. He once beat a duck to death with a tire iron. He fantasized about suicide and cut his wrists. In early 2017, he was expelled from Marjory Stoneman Douglas High School for disciplinary problems and failing grades.

Cruz had a volatile relationship with his mother, Lynda, who adopted him and his brother. One time he hit her so hard that he knocked her teeth out. He wore a Donald Trump "Make America Great Again" hat to mock his mother's liberal views. After she died of pneumonia in November 2017, he took a picture of the urn holding her ashes next to the hat.

One of Cruz's favorite songs was "Pumped Up Kicks," a 2010 hit by the band Foster the People. The song tells the story of a troubled kid planning to shoot fellow students with his father's "six-shooter." The chorus includes the lines: "All the other kids with the pumped up kicks / You better run, better run, faster than my bullet." The catchy tune became an anthem for kids who felt bullied at school and imagined taking revenge.

But Cruz wasn't interested in something as tame as a "six-shooter." He wanted an AR-15. After he turned eighteen, he purchased a Smith & Wesson M&P 15 for $560 from a local gun shop. Asked later why he bought the rifle, he said a demonic voice helped him pick out the AR while he was searching on the internet. Cruz owned other guns, but the AR-15 was the voice's favorite gun, he said. He spent much of his free time cleaning his guns or shooting in the woods. He even slept with them, his brother said.

After his mother died, a family friend called the Broward County Sheriff's Office to report that Cruz was suicidal and collecting guns. "This could be Columbine in the making," she said. Another woman called the FBI, worried about Cruz "getting into a school and just shooting the place up."

On Valentine's Day, shortly after 2:00 p.m., Cruz took an Uber to Marjory Stoneman Douglas. The skinny nineteen-year-old wore a baseball cap and a maroon shirt with the logo of the high school's junior ROTC. Just before entering the school, he searched for "Pumped Up Kicks" on YouTube on his cell phone to listen to it again.

Inside Building 12, where freshmen had their classes, Cruz set off the fire alarm. Students filed out of their classrooms. He shot at fleeing students and staff in the hallways and fired into classrooms. Windows shattered as students cowered under desks and behind filing cabinets.

Eden Hebron, a fourteen-year-old wearing a reddish-pink shirt for Valentine's, was sitting with her best friend, Alyssa Alhadeff, also fourteen, in their fourth-period English class in Room 1216. They were working on essays for a state standardized test, but the two girls were goofing off, making each other laugh. When they heard a series of bangs coming from the hallway, Alhadeff told Hebron the noises sounded like gunshots.

"Bullets, Alyssa? That's funny," Hebron said to her. "You know we're in Parkland, right?"

The noises grew louder. They dropped to the floor and crouched under a table, then Alhadeff moved to hide under the teacher's desk a few feet away. Hebron watched Alhadeff's worried face as the gunshots came closer.

"When you are hearing gunshots, like, all you can think about, you know, is I'm next," she recalled. "I was thinking, 'This is my last moment. These are literally like my last minutes of life.'"

Hebron looked over at her friend. "He shoots her," she recalled. "She kind of, you know, falls back. And she's, there's blood everywhere."

Police eventually came into the classroom and told them to run as fast as they could away from the school.

Cruz fired his AR-15 until it jammed. In six minutes, he fired 140 rounds. He dropped the gun and blended in with throngs of fleeing students but was arrested about an hour later.

AR-15s were front and center in everyone's mind. Police across the country responded to other shootings, threats of mass violence, and false alarms, arresting troubled students and seizing AR-15 rifles. In the early morning hours of April 22, 2018, a naked, deranged man with an AR-15 stormed into a Waffle House in Nashville, Tennessee, and killed four people. As the man was reloading, a customer wrestled the gun away and threw it over the counter. The man ran into the night but was captured after a manhunt. James Shaw Jr., the twenty-nine-year-old who grabbed the rifle, urged more restrictions on ARs. "A Formula One race car is for a racer," he said. "An AR-15, M16's, .223s . . . those special specific guns are meant for people that have some kind of training."

The shooter, Travis Reinking, also twenty-nine, had a history of mental illness and strange behavior. Reinking, wearing a pink dress, threatened a man in 2017 with an AR-15 in his home state of Illinois. Later that year, he tried to enter the White House grounds. Illinois authorities revoked his right to own firearms but didn't seize the weapons. Instead they handed them over to Reinking's father, telling him to lock them up. When Reinking attacked the Waffle House, he used that same AR-15. The father was later convicted in Illinois of unlawfully giving his son the weapons back, including the AR-15.

Once again, many gun-control advocates were convinced that outrage would lead to significant action on national gun control, including restrictions on the sale of AR-15s.

Lane Murdock remembered feeling the excitement of those days, of being a part of change. She believed something substantive would happen. She was wrong.

"I learned it was a pretty cutthroat business," she said of politics.

By late spring it was clear no significant gun-control legislation would be coming despite Trump's promise. NRA officials had met with Trump privately at the White House and, afterward, the president was in lockstep with the gun group. Trump and Vice President Mike Pence spoke at the NRA's annual convention in Dallas that May. Before a cheering crowd, the president said the answer to school shootings like Parkland was to arm teachers. He pledged that he would protect gun rights. "You're going to keep those rights," he said. "You're going to be so happy."

Fred Guttenberg, whose daughter, Jaime, was killed at Parkland, spoke at a small rally near the NRA convention and called for raising the age limit to buy AR-15s and other reforms. One supporter carried a sign that read "AR-15 is a WMD," meaning a weapon of mass destruction.

A larger group of men with AR-15s strapped to their bodies staged counterprotests, heckling Guttenberg as he spoke. They paraded around the park with giant "Come and Take It" flags adorned with images of AR-15s. One man wore a shirt with an image of an AR-15 that read: "No One Needs An AR-15? No One Needs A Whiny Little Pansy Either But Here You Are!"

All the while, mass shootings involving AR-15s kept erupting. On October 27, 2018, Robert Bowers, a forty-six-year-old anti-Semite, walked into Tree of Life Congregation, a Pittsburgh synagogue, during Shabbat morning services. Bowers wrote online that he was angry about a Jewish organization supporting Central American migrant caravans. "I can't sit by and watch my people get slaughtered. Screw your optics, I'm going in." He used a Colt AR-15 and three handguns, killing eleven people. "All Jews must die!" he shouted. Some of those he shot had survived the Holocaust. After police wounded Bowers in a gunfight, he surrendered.

It was the deadliest anti-Semitic attack in U.S. history. In December 2018, the Trump administration banned bump stocks, the devices used in the Las Vegas massacre. It was the only significant action taken by the Trump administration on guns after Parkland.

The post-Parkland movement had a lasting impact on Democratic Party politics. More liberal politicians called for the outright ban of AR-15s with little fear of being voted out of office. They used the AR-15 as shorthand for why gun laws needed to be tightened.

They pointed to moves by other countries to ban sales of the gun. In 2019, New Zealand banned most semiautomatic weapons after a white supremacist, anti-Islamic Australian man armed with two AR-15 rifles attacked two mosques during Friday prayers, killing fifty-one people and wounding dozens more. He livestreamed his attack on Facebook.

"Christchurch happened, and within days New Zealand acted to get weapons of war out of the consumer market," New York Democratic representative Alexandria Ocasio-Cortez tweeted. "This is what leadership looks like."

Democrats also pointed to Australia, which had not experienced a major mass shooting since its wide-reaching ban on semiautomatic rifles had gone into effect in 1996.

In the Democratic Party's crowded 2020 presidential primary, every candidate called for tightening restrictions on semiautomatic rifles like the AR-15. No candidate was more vocal than Beto O'Rourke, the Texas representative. In August 2019, a thirty-nine-year-old Texas man who'd been fired from his job went on a shooting spree, driving around Midland and Odessa, shooting at other drivers and passersby with an Anderson Manufacturing AM-15. He killed seven people and injured twenty-five before police killed him. The man had been prohibited from owning guns because a court had found him mentally unfit. He bought his AR-15 in a private sale, which didn't require a background check.

At a televised Democratic presidential primary debate in Houston weeks later, O'Rourke was asked whether he stood by his gun buyback policy, which some considered federal confiscation. O'Rourke did not equivocate.

"The high-impact, high-velocity round when it hits your body shreds everything inside of your body because it was designed to do that so that you would bleed to death on a battlefield, not be able to get up and kill one of our soldiers," he said. "When we see that being used against children, in Odessa, I met the mother of a fifteen-year-old girl who was shot by an AR-15. And that mother watched her bleed to death over the course of an hour because so many other people were shot by that AR-15 in Odessa and Midland, there weren't enough ambulances to get to them in time. Hell yes, we're going to take your AR-15, your AK-47, we're not going to allow it to be used against our fellow Americans anymore."

The audience—in Texas's largest city—cheered so loudly that O'Rourke couldn't be heard for a moment, with some standing and raising their arms in support. He went on to say gun owners and non–gun owners could find common ground, but the sound bite "Hell yes, we're going to take your AR-15" quickly spread across social media and on television. Gun-rights groups trumpeted the clip—minus the reference to the Odessa-Midland shootings—as proof the Democrats were coming for people's guns. O'Rourke's donations skyrocketed. His campaign sold T-shirts bearing the phrase "HELL YES, WE'RE GOING TO TAKE YOUR AR-15." He didn't win the Democratic presidential nomination, but that sentiment—once unutterable by Democrats hoping to win the White House—made its way into the party's 2020 platform. "Democrats will ban the manufacture and sale of assault weapons and high capacity magazines," the platform stated.

Democrats argued that the previous ban had been a success because the nation experienced a sharp increase in mass shootings after it was lifted. There had been fifty-six mass shootings in which four or more people were killed in a public place in the past ten years, compared to thirty-three during the ten years the ban was in place. The attacks were growing in both frequency and deadliness. The five deadliest mass shootings in the country's history had all taken place since the ban lapsed in 2004. Christopher Koper, the researcher who had evaluated the federal ban for the Justice Department, argued in a 2020 paper that lives likely could have been saved if it had remained in place, but not because of a ban of any specific firearm. Koper concluded that fewer people would have been killed in each mass shooting primarily because of the restrictions on large-capacity magazines. "Considering that mass shootings with high-capacity semiautomatics are considerably more lethal and injurious than other mass shootings, it is reasonable to argue that the federal ban could have prevented some of the recent increase in persons killed and injured in mass shootings had it remained in place," he wrote. Future magazine restrictions could reduce the number of deaths in mass shootings by 11 to 15 percent, though it would take a long time because of all the magazines already floating around, Koper concluded. The gun ban itself had done little to stop such attacks, he argued.

Koper's thesis was borne out in at least one prominent instance when California's prohibition on magazines holding more than ten rounds appeared to limit the carnage in a mass shooting. On the last day of Passover in April 2019, an anti-Semitic nineteen-year-old burst into a synagogue near San Diego armed with a Smith & Wesson M&P 15. Timothy Earnest fired about ten shots, killing one person and wounding three others. In the brief time when he fumbled to switch out the empty magazine for a new one, congregants rushed at him and he fled. But California's decades-old assault-weapons ban had not stopped the sales of AR-15s as gunmakers came up with legal workaround models like they had done under the federal ban. The husband-and-wife terrorists who killed fourteen people and wounded twenty-two more in San Bernardino in 2015 also used AR-15s that were purchased in California.

Unlike Earnest, they were able to obtain thirty-round magazines despite the state law.

In the five months after Parkland, twenty-four states across the country, including fourteen with Republican governors, enacted at least fifty new gun-control laws. Many passed red-flag laws allowing authorities to temporarily seize guns from dangerous individuals. Some passed bans on bump stocks. New Jersey and Vermont passed restrictions on high-capacity magazines. "This was a year of unparalleled success for the gun-control movement in the United States," the Pew Charitable Trusts' online publication declared.

But for many young people swept up in activism after Parkland, the initial enthusiasm gave way to disappointment.

Eden Hebron, who saw her friend Alyssa murdered at Marjory Stoneman Douglas, joined other students in leading rallies and calling on politicians to provide more mental health services and ban AR-15s. But she became disheartened by the partisan politics.

"Inside it felt like, 'What are we even doing this for?'" she said. "There is this division in this country. It makes me really angry. It makes me really upset. Because I know there is a solution, I think. We just haven't been able to find it yet."

Hebron spent years in therapy to process the trauma she suffered on February 14, 2018. Often, she wanted to forget it all ever happened, and part of her hated talking about it since it forced her to relive the horror. But years of suffering taught her that she had to face the ugly reality of what happened to understand it, accept it, and change the future. The country needed to do the same thing, she said.

"As much as I try to move past it, I know that you have to go to the problem to heal the problem," she said.

Murdock found the activism wore her down. People yelled at her at rallies. Some carried guns. She received nasty and threatening social media messages. When she graduated from high school, she took some time off before leaving the United States to attend college in Scotland. Living in a country where private ownership of semiautomatic rifles was uncommon was liberating—and unnerving. When she went to concerts or large gatherings, she still found herself nervous. In classrooms, she scanned for exits. Her Scottish classmates never had such concerns.

"We will always be a country that will have more guns," she said of the United States. "Fixing this problem is going to be an extremely long process. I don't think I will ever really return to the U.S. when I graduate."

29.

COME AND TAKE IT NATION

I'm going to war. I'm bringing the big cock.
—Oath Keeper about bringing his AR-15 to Washington, DC, for January 6

Demonstrators, young and old, Black and white, walked through a wealthy St. Louis neighborhood on their way to the mayor's house, drumming, singing, and chanting. The murder of George Floyd by a Minneapolis police officer had sparked a nationwide protest movement in the summer of 2020. When the demonstrators veered onto a private street of large, expensive homes, a doughy sixty-three-year-old man wearing a pink Brooks Brothers polo shirt and khakis emerged from his mansion built to look like an Italian palazzo. The man looked out over a tall hedge and cradled a Colt AR-15.

"Get the hell out of my neighborhood!" Mark McCloskey shouted.

McCloskey moved to the front steps of his mansion, where he was joined by his wife, Patricia. She waved a pistol. They didn't fire their guns. The incident, captured on video, went viral on the internet, and the couple became the target of widespread derision. Some gun owners joked about the awkward manner in which McCloskey held his rifle. Others mocked them as the ultimate example of white suburban busybodies. One meme showed the armed couple with the label "Mr. & Mrs. Boomer."

But the surreal incident underscored the fact that America had entered a tumultuous era in which the AR-15 was everywhere. The image of the AR-15 had become a political and cultural symbol infused with meaning far beyond the gun debate. People put its image on T-shirts, banners, bumper stickers, and coffee mugs. To scorn it meant you were a Democrat and a liberal who backed stricter gun-control laws. To embrace it meant you were pro-gun, conservative, likely pro-Trump. It became a tribal emblem, immediately signaling where you stood on the American political spectrum. One Republican congressional candidate, Andrew Clyde, who owned a gun store in Georgia, put the image of an AR-15 next to his name on his campaign signs. The phrase "Protect the 2nd" ran below the gun's barrel. Clyde, who had never held office before, won in a landslide.

On social media, memes proliferated, from a George Washington impersonator firing an AR-15 to a photo of the rifle with the phrase "It's because I'm black isn't it? Fight AR-15 semi-auto discrimination." One meme showed a muscular Donald Trump in desert fatigues holding Stoner's rifle and the American flag. Donald Trump Jr. joined in, posing on Twitter with an AR-15. The gun's magazine bore an image of Hillary Clinton behind bars.

Businesses appealing to conservatives embraced the gun—even as larger corporations distanced themselves from gun rights in general. One car dealership offered vouchers for an AR-15 and a Bible to car buyers. Black Rifle Coffee became the Starbucks for the right, selling coffee roasts with firearms-themed branding. The founder, Evan Hafer, a former Green Beret, named the company after his service rifle. "This is going to piss people off," he recalled thinking. "And I just kind of embraced it." In 2020, the Salt Lake City–based company brought in $163 million, nearly double its sales the previous year. In addition to its coffee, the company sold merchandise bearing its logo: a silhouette of an M4.

Prominent Republican leaders argued an AR-15 had become necessary for personal protection. Republican senator Lindsey Graham said in 2019 that homeowners could use them against looters after hurricanes. Gun-rights groups trumpeted stories of people using AR-15s to defend their homes, including a report that a pregnant mother had used an AR to confront two intruders who were pistol-whipping her husband. She shot and killed one intruder; the other fled. Even some survivors of mass shootings—including mass shootings that involved AR-15s—touted the gun as a way to keep safe. Taylor Winston, a Marine Corps veteran, became a hero during the Las Vegas attack, shuttling the wounded in a pickup truck from the festival to hospitals. When he returned to his home in San Diego, one of the first things he did was buy an AR-15. Winston was familiar with the weapon, having used an M4 in Iraq, but he had never owned a civilian version. The Las Vegas attack was a "reminder of how evil and dark mankind is," and owning an AR-15 made him feel safe, Winston said. He became a vocal gun-rights advocate. "It is a great equalizer," he said of the rifle.

By 2020, AR-15 prices ranged from thousands of dollars to just a few hundred bucks—and the guns came in myriad sizes, shapes, colors, and brands. American civilians owned about 19 million ARs, up from about 400,000 a quarter of a century earlier. By the end of 2021, that number jumped to more than 20 million.

During the protests and riots of the summer of 2020, self-appointed sentinels claiming they were working to restore order armed themselves with AR-15s. Many worried it was only a matter of time before those guns went off. In early August 2020, during Black Lives Matter protests in Portland, Oregon, people called police to report a man in tactical gear pointing a semiautomatic rifle at protesters. One person told police, "He definitely has an AR-15." In fact, the man carried a pellet gun made to look like an M4. The man called police for help when protesters confronted him. What would happen if someone came to one of these protests with a real AR-15?

On the night of August 25, 2020, seventeen-year-old Kyle Rittenhouse, armed with an M&P 15, stood outside a car dealership in Kenosha, Wisconsin. Two days earlier, Kenosha police had shot a Black man, paralyzing him and igniting protests. Rittenhouse and a friend, who was also armed, said they were there to protect the business from looters. Rittenhouse wasn't allowed to purchase such a gun because he was under eighteen, so a friend bought the rifle for him. Later when asked why he wanted an AR-15, he said, "It looked cool."

Protesters shouted at Rittenhouse about his gun. One man, Joseph Rosenbaum, thirty-six, pursued Rittenhouse across a parking lot. Cell phone videos of the incident showed Rosenbaum, who was unarmed, throwing a plastic bag at Rittenhouse. The teenager fired his rifle. Rosenbaum continued to approach Rittenhouse, who fired four more shots. The bullets shattered Rosenbaum's pelvis and punctured his lungs and liver. Rittenhouse ran away while talking into his cell phone.

"I just killed somebody," he said.

Rosenbaum was declared dead at a nearby hospital. A crowd pursued Rittenhouse and he tripped and fell. Twenty-six-year-old Anthony Huber tried to grab Rittenhouse's rifle and hit the teenager with a skateboard. Rittenhouse fired one round into Huber, who staggered back and collapsed. Huber later died. Rittenhouse shot another man armed with a pistol in the right arm.

Police charged Rittenhouse with multiple homicide and weapons counts but at a highly publicized trial in 2021, a jury acquitted him. Gun-control groups blasted the jury's verdict. Gun-rights groups praised it and exalted Rittenhouse as a hero.

While politicians and talk show hosts argued over the AR-15, extremists whose objectives were much darker than "owning the libs" embraced the gun as a tool for mass violence. Secretive groups, plotting to plunge the nation into civil war, saw the AR-15 as an essential weapon.

In Michigan, men armed with AR-15s slung across their chests marched into the statehouse in Lansing to protest pandemic restrictions ordered by Gretchen Whitmer, the Democratic governor. A smaller group also trained with the gun while preparing to carry out a plot to kidnap the governor. Authorities foiled the plan.

A white nationalist group calling itself "the Base" plotted to attack a large gun-rights rally in Richmond, Virginia, in January 2020. The men believed that by sparking mass violence, they would hasten the collapse of society and bring about a race war. They trained with AR-15s in the Georgia woods. "You realize that they're just going to call us terrorists," one of the men said shortly before FBI agents arrested them.

The rally in Richmond went on as planned under tight security. The governor banned any guns on the state capitol grounds, but they were allowed outside barricades. An estimated twenty-two thousand people attended, including people carrying AR-15s and an enormous black banner that read: COME AND TAKE IT.

The Boogaloo Bois, antigovernment extremists, showed up at Black Lives Matter marches wearing Hawaiian shirts and carrying AR-15s. The Boogaloo Bois' long-term goal was to push the country into civil war, which they referenced among themselves with the phrase "Let's boogie." In late May 2020, Steven Carrillo, an active U.S. Air Force sergeant, wrote on Facebook that the protests were a "great opportunity" to attack federal agents. Carrillo, armed with a homemade AR rifle variant, drove to Oakland, California, and opened fire from a van outside of the federal courthouse, killing one security guard and injuring another. Authorities pursued Carrillo deep into the Santa Cruz Mountains. During a shootout, he killed a deputy and injured another before being arrested.

Extremists such as Carrillo had learned to build AR-15s that couldn't be tracked by the government. Beginning in the 2010s, a cottage industry arose employing Stoner's design to build untraceable weapons, which police started calling "ghost guns." The gun's easy assembly made it simple. Under federal law, the only part of a gun that was deemed a firearm was the receiver, the metal or polymer piece that housed the firing mechanism. Manufacturers were required to stamp receivers with serial numbers. Anyone buying a serialized receiver was required to undergo a federal background check just as they would if they purchased a completed gun. Police used those serial numbers to trace weapons used in crimes. However, gun hobbyists found that if they took a receiver that wasn't quite completed—and didn't yet have a serial number—they could finish making it in their workshops with tools as simple as a drill press. This allowed them to build a complete rifle without a serial number and avoid ever undergoing a background check. Federal law allowed people to make such guns for themselves.

Small companies started selling complete kits with unfinished receivers and all the parts needed to build "ghost" AR-15s. Ghostguns .com advertised their products as "Unserialized. Unregistered." Do-it-yourself videos appeared on YouTube, teaching how to build ARs in less than an hour. Some people began fabricating unserialized receivers using 3D printers. Gun hobbyists pioneered making the homemade weapons, but criminals, gang members, extremists, and mass shooters took up the practice. A Northern California man, who was prohibited from possessing firearms because of a restraining order, killed five people in a November 2017 rampage using ARs that he made himself. By 2020, American law enforcement agencies had recovered about twenty-four thousand ghost guns in criminal investigations, many of them AR-15s. A federal counterterrorism task force warned that "criminals and violent extremists continue to seek ways to acquire firearms through the production" of ghost guns.

On January 6, 2021, President Trump addressed more than ten thousand supporters gathered for what was billed as a "Save America" rally on the National Mall not far from the White House. Trump refused to accept his defeat by Democrat Joseph Biden in November's presidential election, claiming the results were fraudulent. Electors in Congress were set to certify Biden's victory within hours.

"If you don't fight like hell, you're not going to have a country anymore," he said.

People in the throng waved MAGA flags and other pro-Trump banners. One person waved a white flag with a black silhouette of an AR-15. Another held aloft a Confederate battle flag with a large AR-15 in the center. Both banners carried the same slogan: COME AND TAKE IT.

After Trump returned to the White House, thousands marched to the Capitol. Police stationed there fired tear gas to disperse the hostile mob. A man waved the AR-15 Confederate flag amid the smoke as rioters broke through barricades and poured into Congress—an unprecedented act in American history that would leave at least five people dead and shake the foundations of the republic.

Many who came that day considered the AR-15 a tool of their political resistance. In November 2020, when Trump lost, Christopher

Quaglin, an unemployed electrician from New Jersey, wrote on his Facebook page, "I'm going to war. I'm bringing the big cock." Prosecutors interpreted that to mean his AR-15 rifle. About two weeks before January 6, Quaglin posted a photo of his AR-15 in his SUV. His caption: "so bad ass." Police arrested him for attacking officers at the Capitol.

Members of the Oath Keepers, a right-wing militia group, led the most organized effort to bring AR-15s and ammunition to Washington. "We aren't getting through this without a civil war," Stewart Rhodes, the group's leader, told members in a chat group after the election. Oath Keeper groups, self-labeled "QRFs," a military term meaning quick reaction forces, brought AR-15s and thousands of rounds of ammo and other weapons to a Comfort Inn in Arlington, Virginia, a ten-minute drive from the Capitol. As the riot got under way, Edward Vallejo, who was in charge of the hotel operation, repeatedly asked Oath Keeper leaders to give him the green light to send men with guns over to the Capitol.

"We are at WAR," Vallejo messaged.

The FBI swooped down on Vallejo and other Oath Keepers. Agents fanned out across the country to arrest hundreds of others involved in January 6 and crack down on extremists. The raids and prosecutions gutted the ranks of such groups and weakened—at least temporarily—their ability to use violence to achieve their political ends.

But as COVID lockdowns ended and Americans began to gather once again, another pervasive and stubborn danger resurfaced with a vengeance: mass shooters.

30

BEYOND THE TALKING POINTS

I don't think you get the toothpaste back in the tube.
—Democratic representative Mike Thompson on banning AR-15s

The AR-15, created by Eugene Stoner in the 1950s to aid American soldiers, had by the early 2020s become fused in the public mind with the slaughtering of American civilians. The nation relived the nightmare of mass shootings like a traumatized survivor, swinging between grief, anger, and numbness. Liberals blamed the NRA and the gun industry. Conservatives blamed the media and mental illness. The AR-15 remained at the center of the rancorous, stalled debate. President Joe Biden and other prominent Democrats called for a federal ban on AR-15s, just as they had in the 1990s. Republicans argued that more guns would solve the problem and passed new state laws to make it easier to carry them in schools, churches, restaurants—anywhere people came together.

The nation needed new answers as mass shootings resumed. In March 2021, a twenty-one-year-old used a Ruger AR-556 pistol to kill ten people in a Boulder, Colorado, grocery store. He was wounded in a shootout with police and surrendered. In April, a former FedEx Corp. employee in Indianapolis used two AR-15s to kill eight people at his old workplace before killing himself. The nineteen-year-old had a history of suicide attempts and profound depression.

The pandemic had granted a brief respite, but these springtime mass shootings brought the country back to this awful reality—and the familiar stalemate. President Biden called for a new assault-weapons ban in a speech to a joint session of Congress. He had helped pass a ban about three decades before and believed it could be done again. The National Rifle Association reacted by calling for more Americans to arm themselves. "The real 'problem' with guns is too few people carry one. Truth," the NRA tweeted days after the Indianapolis shooting.

By this time, many gun-control advocates had stopped pushing for an assault-weapons ban. The head of the House caucus on gun safety, Mike Thompson, a Democrat from California, said of Biden's speech: "He's always felt that way." But Thompson did not believe that a new ban was politically possible or practical. If the sale of new ARs was prohibited, there would still be millions of them in civilian hands.

"I don't think you get the toothpaste back in the tube," Thompson said.

Instead, Thompson favored new approaches that would make it more difficult for people with evil intent to obtain AR-15s. More focused measures besides broad bans could win bipartisan support, he believed. Both sides needed to get beyond the "bumper sticker mentality," he said.

Even some congressional aides who had helped write and pass the federal assault-weapons ban now saw it as a lost cause. Tom Diaz, a former Schumer staffer, watched mass shootings disappear in Australia after that country banned most semiautomatic weapons in 1996. He believed that American politicians had a similar opportunity in 1994 when Democrats controlled the White House and Congress and AR-15 owners were a small minority of gun owners. At the time, the majority of Americans favored a strict ban.

"That was the last great chance that America had to change the course of the commercial destiny of the firearms market," Diaz said. "At that pivotal moment in time, we blew it. Had this passed in an effective form, I think the gun industry would have turned in another direction."

The political force behind the NRA's old arguments was also crumbling. In the spring of 2021, as the gun debate flared, the group's leaders were consumed by internal scandals and power struggles. New York State's attorney general sued to dissolve the 150-year-old gun group, accusing LaPierre and others of enriching themselves at the expense of NRA members. During legal proceedings, LaPierre admitted that he'd made a mistake by not disclosing that he and his family often took free vacations in the Bahamas on a 108-foot-yacht that was owned by an NRA vendor. LaPierre also admitted he received $275,000 worth of Italian suits and other clothing that were paid for by the NRA's former ad agency. LaPierre's foes within the gun world seized upon the admissions as they mounted a campaign to oust the aging leader. More strident gun-rights groups stepped in as the NRA weakened, but these smaller groups did not have the same clout in Washington.

Beyond the Beltway, beyond the grinding drone of partisan talking points, a wide-ranging group of younger political leaders, pragmatic gun-industry executives, free-thinking scholars, and desperate law enforcement leaders began offering new, intriguing solutions. In some places, law enforcement leaders began to question long-standing tenets of gun-rights orthodoxy. Grady Judd, the conservative sheriff of Florida's Polk County, became a leading advocate for the state's red-flag law, which allowed his deputies to temporarily take away firearms from people threatening violence. Judd had long endorsed Republican candidates and had been appointed to a council on juvenile justice by President Trump.

A sheriff in a conservative part of Central Florida would have risked his political career in previous years by promoting gun-control measures. But after Parkland, Sheriff Judd vowed he would do everything he could to prevent such a horror from happening in his jurisdiction. He saw Florida's new red-flag measure as his most effective tool. Under the law, judges could order the temporary seizure of firearms even if the person hadn't been charged with a crime. The sheriff hired a lawyer dedicated solely to filing red-flag petitions with the courts. Authorities in Polk County used the state's red-flag law 874 times from 2019 to mid-2021 to temporarily remove guns from individuals, far more than police in large cities such as Chicago or New York. In one case, Sheriff Judd's office secured a red-flag order against a high schooler who threatened another student with a gun after the local police department that had arrested him declined to do so.

"I'm a conservative, I'm a Second Amendment . . . you know, red white and blue," Judd said. "But when there's someone out here running around threatening to kill people and I have a tool at my disposal and I don't use it, I have a professional and political liability for not using it."

The first red-flag law designed specifically to target mass shooters was passed in California in 2014, after a twenty-two-year-old killed six people—shooting three and stabbing three others. Police officers had visited the man's home prior to the shooting, after his parents expressed concerns over his behavior. But police felt they didn't have the authority to take away his weapons or arrest him. State representative Nancy Skinner, a Democrat from Berkeley, wrote the legislation and it was signed into law by Democratic governor Jerry Brown. But the concept of temporarily taking guns from dangerous individuals won support from some Republican politicians and gun owners. They liked that the law focused on people, not firearms. But gun owners also worried that the new laws could encroach on their civil liberties.

By 2020, nineteen states and the District of Columbia had passed such laws, with the majority of them coming after Parkland. Researchers found that the laws were effective in reducing suicide rates and showed promise in stopping mass shootings. Authorities in California seized guns fifty-eight times from individuals threatening mass shootings from 2016 through 2018, according to a study by the University of California Firearm Violence Research Center. In a case highlighted by the university's researchers, police seized an AR-15 from a twenty-one-year-old who was threatening students at his former high school.

But the application of so-called red-flag laws was uneven. In one of the most glaring lapses, the prosecutor's office in Indianapolis decided not to use the state's law against Brandon Hole before he killed eight people at the Indianapolis FedEx facility. Hole struggled with depression. His father had committed suicide. When Hole was eighteen, he bought a shotgun and told his mother, Sheila Hole, that he wanted to kill himself. She rushed to the nearest police station and pleaded for officers to do something. Police came to the house, handcuffed him, and took away the shotgun. The officers then took him to a mental health facility. But he was released within a few hours, and a few days later police promised to return his gun. The shocked mother persuaded her son to get on the phone and tell the police that he didn't want the gun anymore. Prosecutors declined to bring a red-flag case that would have prevented Hole from temporarily buying guns, since he had already given up the shotgun. His mother was appalled. That summer, Hole bought two AR-15s.

"Someone as angry as that should not be allowed to possess a gun," she said. "He should have been red-flagged."

Soon after Indianapolis, violence researchers published a report on the impact of different state gun laws on mass shootings. The findings opened up new possibilities for reform. The group included James Alan Fox, a Northeastern University professor who had studied mass shootings since the 1980s; Grant Duwe, research director at the Minnesota Department of Corrections, who wrote a book on mass murder in 2007; and Michael Rocque, chair of the Sociology Department at Bates College, who had studied mass killings for a decade.

Their research found that two policies in particular showed promise. First, laws requiring a permit to purchase or possess a gun could reduce the number of mass shootings. A handful of states such as Illinois, Connecticut, Massachusetts, and New York required residents to get a license to purchase weapons. The process took much longer to complete than a typical background check at a gun store, which usually took a few minutes. The authors determined that mass shootings had 60 percent lower odds of occurring in states that required permits to purchase guns than in those that didn't.

Speaking about the report's findings, Rocque theorized that the license requirement disrupted a mass shooter's preparation. "Maybe it's throwing up some roadblocks that make people change their mind or stop the process of planning," he said.

The second policy that showed promise was restricting large-capacity magazines. This policy didn't reduce the number of mass shootings, but it did reduce the number of people killed during such events. Such restrictions were associated with a 38 percent reduction in deaths and a 77 percent reduction in nonfatal injuries. Nine states and the District of Columbia had such laws in place. "Although reloading a magazine with a fresh clip or swapping firearms may take only a few seconds, it does present an opportunity for would-be victims to escape and for bystanders or law enforcement to intervene," the researchers wrote.

Rocque had expected that state assault-weapons bans would be associated with lower rates of mass shootings. For decades, both sides in the debate over AR-15s expended enormous amounts of political energy pushing for passage or fighting adoption of these bans. But Rocque and his colleagues found the bans had no impact. "We actually didn't see any association," he said. The state bans, which used features tests to define prohibited weapons, didn't stop the sale of AR-15s or similar guns.

"The features that define an 'assault weapon' are not necessarily relevant to the actual lethality of the firearm," they wrote. "What *does* translate into increased lethality, it seems—and the evidence shows—is magazine capacity."

The researchers rejected claims that the federal assault-weapons ban had reduced mass shootings during the ten years of its existence, saying research on the topic showed mixed results. One Stanford study found that eight mass shootings took place in the decade before the ban went into effect, and six occurred when it was in place. The study defined a mass shooting as six or more people killed. But data showed that mass shootings in which four or more people were killed actually increased under the ban—thirty-three during the ban, up from twenty-five in the ten years prior, according to the Violence Project, a nonpartisan research organization funded by the U.S. Justice Department. Researchers all agreed that the number of mass shootings soared after 2004 when the federal ban expired.

State prohibitions came under threat in June 2021, when U.S. District Court Judge Roger Benitez overturned California's ban, ruling it violated the Second Amendment. Judge Benitez, who was appointed by Republican president George W. Bush, wrote that AR-15s had become so common they shouldn't be targeted by special laws.

"This is not a case about extraordinary weapons lying at the outer limits of Second Amendment protection," Judge Benitez wrote. "The banned 'assault weapons' are not bazookas, howitzers or machine guns. Those arms are dangerous and solely useful for military purposes. Instead, the firearms deemed 'assault weapons' are fairly ordinary, popular modern rifles."

In his decision, Judge Benitez cited the 2008 *Heller* ruling that the Second Amendment protected the individual right to keep and bear arms. He wrote that *Heller* drew a line between guns commonly owned for lawful purposes and more unusual weapons used for unlawful or solely military purposes. The AR-15 fell into the first group and so it was unconstitutional to ban them, he argued. "The overwhelming majority of citizens who own and keep the popular AR-15 rifle and its many variants do so for lawful purposes, including self defense of the home," he wrote.

State assault-weapons bans had survived prior legal challenges even after *Heller*. In 2017, the United States Court of Appeals for the Fourth Circuit upheld Maryland's assault-weapons ban. "We have no power to extend Second Amendment protection to weapons of war that the *Heller* decision explicitly excluded from such coverage," Judge Robert Bruce King, who was appointed by Democratic president Bill Clinton, wrote for the majority. The judge relied on a sentence in the Supreme Court decision, saying that military weapons such as "M16 rifles and the like" may be banned. "The AR-15 shares the military features—the very qualities and characteristics—that make the M16 a devastating and lethal weapon of war," Judge King wrote.

The outlook for gun-control laws in the American judicial system shifted since Judge King wrote that opinion. Conservatives held a solid 6–3 majority on the Supreme Court after the Senate confirmed President Trump's nominee, Amy Coney Barrett, to fill the vacant seat left by the death of the liberal justice Ruth Bader Ginsburg. As conflicting decisions worked their way through the courts, gun-rights groups were confident that the high court would side with them against state laws restricting the sale of AR-15s.

Even as gun-rights advocates heralded a more gun-friendly judiciary, the parents of children killed at Sandy Hook struck an unexpected legal blow against AR-15 makers. In February 2022, Cerberus's gun conglomerate, which manufactured the Bushmaster rifle used by Adam Lanza, agreed to pay Sandy Hook families $73 million to settle a lawsuit they'd brought against Remington Arms Co. It was the largest settlement ever paid by a gunmaker over a mass shooting.

Joshua Koskoff, the attorney who represented the families in the suit, took a novel approach that many lawyers doubted would work. Koskoff came from a family of lawyers known for taking difficult cases. His grandfather had represented members of the Black Panther party. The Sandy Hook parents approached Koskoff to discuss suing Remington after many lawyers turned them down, telling the families it would be impossible to get past the federal law shielding gunmakers from liability when their weapons were used to kill.

Koskoff and his team focused on an exception to the federal gunmaker protection: companies could be held liable for deaths and injuries resulting from negligent marketing. Koskoff focused his lawsuit on Bushmaster's "Man Card" campaign and marketing slogans like "Opposition Forces Bow Down," arguing that such messages had drawn mass shooters like Lanza to the weapons.

In 2019, the Connecticut Supreme Court ruled—to the surprise of both gunmakers and gun-control groups—that Remington could be held legally responsible for its marketing practices. That ruling allowed Koskoff to move ahead with claims that Bushmaster's advertising violated a state law that prohibited "immoral and unscrupulous" marketing. The ruling in Connecticut—the cradle of American firearm manufacturing—reverberated throughout the gun industry. Remington filed for bankruptcy protection for a second time in as many years. Large gunmakers quickly toned down aggressive marketing. At SHOT Show in 2020, gunmakers still displayed AR-15s, but much of the marketing that played up the gun's military origins was gone.

The settlement gave a long-sought victory to the Wheelers and other parents who had endured what they saw as a betrayal by the nation's political leaders after the massacre. It excited plaintiffs' attorneys and terrified gun executives. They realized that the federal immunity law was not impenetrable. Judgments and large settlements over mass shootings had the potential to hit gunmakers where it hurt the most, their bottom line. Democrats and gun-control activists who had struggled to pass new gun-control measures saw an opening. Lawmakers in New York and California passed legislation making it easier to sue gunmakers, raising the possibility of more large settlements. Even though similar suits would later be tossed out by judges, a new angle of attack had emerged for gun-control advocates. At a press conference announcing the Sandy Hook settlement in February 2022, Koskoff said the days of these gunmakers avoiding responsibility were over.

"Immunity protecting the gun industry is not bulletproof," he said.

31.

"ARE ANY RESIDENTS SAFE
IN THIS COUNTRY ANYWHERE?"

*This is what God thought of when he sent Eugene Stoner to
design and manufacture the M16 and AR-15.*
—Buffalo mass shooter

By the 2020s, Americans had adapted—sort of—to the unnatural reality that it was possible for a mass shooting to erupt at any time or any place. Tens of millions of students and workers were subjected to training about how to run, hide, and fight. Armed security was posted at schools, workplaces, concerts, and malls. Police armed themselves with AR-15s and were trained about what to do when a call came in from a school, a park, a factory, a church. Yet even when police officers responded immediately, AR-15s still gave attackers the capability to kill lots of people before they arrived.

In August 2019, Connor Betts, a twenty-four-year-old man obsessed with mass shootings, opened fire with an AR-15 pistol with a hundred-round drum attached outside a Dayton, Ohio, bar. Betts pulled the trigger forty-one times in about thirty seconds before police stationed nearby killed him. An officer shot him with a department-issued AR-15. Dayton police officers were right there when Betts started firing. Yet Betts still killed nine people and wounded another fourteen.

"Thirty seconds," said Dayton police chief Richard Biehl. "At least 41 rounds fired by the assailant. Nine dead, 14 with nonfatal gunshot wounds, and another two dozen injured. We couldn't prevent those level [*sic*] of casualties and we were right there."

In response to shootings like Dayton, the NRA promoted the idea that armed civilians should be the first line of defense. They pointed to Stephen Willeford, the Texas plumber who fired his AR-15 at the Sutherland Springs mass shooter after he'd killed twenty-six people in a church. They would later point to twenty-two-year-old Elisjsha Dicken, who killed a mass shooter armed with an AR-15 in an Indiana mall in July 2022. The attacker killed three people before Dicken shot him with his handgun. But an FBI study of 160 active-shooter incidents between 2000 and 2013 found that cases of citizen intervention in mass shootings were rare. Five of them ended when armed citizens exchanged gunfire with the suspect. In 2021, armed citizens killed two of sixty-one active shooters, according to the FBI. In one of those instances, a police officer in Arvada, Colorado, mistook the hero for an attacker and killed him by mistake.

Was there a better way? People overseeing security at schools and workplaces became convinced they needed to go beyond defensive measures such as metal detectors and armed guards. John McDonald, the security chief of the Colorado school district where the Columbine High School shooting occurred, started a program to monitor students who made violent threats—even after they graduated. McDonald always took threats made by students, whether online or in person, seriously. "If you say you're going to kill me, I believe you," McDonald said. "And if you're going to believe the threat, you're going to have to actually manage the threat." McDonald insisted these students get counseling and that local law enforcement know about them. He assigned case managers who talked with students and ex-students regularly. The case managers monitored the students' social media and checked in with the students' therapists. Far from seeing the program as an abrogation of civil liberties, parents and teachers eagerly supported the program.

The Colorado program was tailored to deal with mass shooters, in part by better understanding the common traits they exhibited before committing a massacre. Mass shooters were often isolated young men who telegraphed their murderous and suicidal fantasies online on various social media platforms. Most had no criminal records that would stop them from walking into a gun store, completing a background check, and buying an AR-15 and ammunition.

"So many of the weapons used in these types of events are legally purchased, whereas everyday gun violence tends to be with firearms that are illegally held," said James Densley, a criminal justice professor at Metro State University in Minnesota who studies mass shooters. "Everyday gun violence is often gang related . . . When you're talking about mass shootings, it's completely different. This is just people who are going to the gun shop and purchasing a firearm with the intent to use it pretty soon after making that purchase. And the intent is to perpetrate a mass shooting."

Seventy percent of mass shooters over the past half century purchased their guns legally, according to Densley's tabulation of cases in which a determination could be made. Some studies put that percentage even higher. The attackers in Aurora, Las Vegas, Parkland, Pittsburgh, Dayton, Boulder, and Indianapolis all acquired their AR-15s within the law. "When individuals are telegraphing violent intent, that is not the time to be selling them a firearm," said Densley, who has coauthored a book with Jillian Peterson called *The Violence Project: How to Stop a Mass Shooting Epidemic*.

But American legal and regulatory systems weren't designed to stop would-be mass shooters from buying guns. Federal and state background checks scanned for criminal convictions, court adjudications of insanity, restraining orders, and dishonorable discharges from the military. The categories of people barred from buying guns were conceived in the 1960s before mass shootings became a widespread social problem and long before the AR-15 became so popular. Background checks don't look at social media or online chat rooms for threats. Authorities don't interview a person's friends and family—or anyone for that matter—during a background check. In other countries like Japan, a gun buyer must provide a doctor's note, signing off on an individual's mental fitness to own a firearm. No such rule existed in the United States.

At least one prominent gun-industry executive, whose company profited from the AR-15 boom, came to believe people wanting to buy Stoner's rifle should face a higher-level scrutiny than people buying shotguns or handguns.

"We've got a problem, a societal problem," said Gerry Dinkel, the former Colt chief executive. Dinkel thought the federal government should regulate AR-15s much like it does machine guns under the 1934 National Firearms Act. For decades, Americans purchasing machine guns—fully automatic weapons—have been required to undergo lengthy federal background checks that go beyond the rudimentary checks for other firearms. These checks required buyers to submit their fingerprints and register their weapons with the federal government. They can take months to complete. Beyond these long-standing checks, President Ronald Reagan signed legislation in 1986 banning the manufacture of new machine guns for commercial sale. So the number of such firearms in circulation was limited, driving up the cost of existing weapons—making them hard for the average person to afford. For years, machine guns just haven't been easy to get in America.

Dinkel believed the tight regulations on machine gun sales were the reason that there hadn't been a major mass shooting with a legally purchased machine gun in decades.

"We didn't really ban them, but we did an effective job at managing the circulation," Dinkel said. "What if you did the same thing with ARs?"

Dinkel believed that it was an example of a practical solution to the societal problem. It wouldn't involve taking people's ARs and it would put up some future boundaries.

"We've allowed the extreme sides to be the only discussion," Dinkel said. "Nobody's talking about something in the middle that's actually a step forward."

By 2023, no such legislation had been proposed. Such an idea was considered politically impossible.

Instead, the critical task of stopping the next mass shooter fell to friends, family, teachers, and coworkers; it was up to them to try to discern who should or shouldn't have an AR-15 and whether they were about to commit a mass shooting. Almost half of 147 mass shootings that were averted between 2000 and 2019 were stopped when friends, acquaintances, or fellow students alerted authorities, according to one study. But that ad hoc alert system often failed, and disturbed men seeking infamy or revenge continued to wreak havoc.

On May 14, 2022, Payton Gendron drove two hundred miles from his home in his small upstate New York town to the city of Buffalo, where he entered a grocery store and began shooting customers with an AR-15. A security guard, Aaron Salter Jr., a retired police officer, opened fire with a handgun and struck Gendron in the torso. But Gendron was wearing body armor. He returned fire with his Bushmaster XM-15, killing Salter. He shot and killed nine other people before police arrived and Gendron surrendered. Everyone whom Gendron killed was Black. Gendron, who is white, wanted to start a race war.

He had planned his attack for months. Just before the shooting, he posted a 180-page screed and a 673-page online diary. His writings offered an unprecedented and detailed look into the mind of a mass shooter and why he chose an AR-15 for his attack. Gendron, a community college engineering student who lived with his parents, described spending hours alone on his computer, reading racist propaganda and studying mass shootings, and guns.

"I've probably spent actual years of my life just being online," he wrote. "And to be honest I regret it. I didn't go to friend's houses often or go to any parties or whatever. Every day after school I would just go home and play games and watch YouTube, mostly by my self [sic]."

He devoted pages of his ramblings to racist justifications for killing people whom he had never met. He wrote at length about his hatred of Black people, Muslims, and Jewish people. He spoke in reverential tones about the white supremacist Brenton Tarrant, who shot and killed fifty-one people in two New Zealand mosques in 2019. He wanted to emulate Tarrant, who had used two AR-15s. Gendron believed that using an AR-15 would enable him to kill more people—and get more attention.

"The AR-15 and its variants are very deadly when used properly. Which is the reason why I picked one," he wrote. "Plus, the media loves to hate on the AR-15, which may increase media coverage and public outlash."

Gendron researched New York's gun laws as he made plans to purchase his weapon. Under New York's Safe Act, passed after the Sandy Hook massacre, residents were not allowed to purchase semiautomatic rifles with a detachable magazine and more than one military-style feature such as a pistol grip or bayonet mount. Magazines that could hold more than ten rounds were also prohibited. Gendron purchased a Bushmaster XM-15 that was compliant with the Safe Act and didn't have a detachable magazine. Although the eighteen-year-old had been evaluated at a mental health facility for threatening to kill himself and others just before his high school graduation, officials had not used the state's red-flag law to block him from owning firearms. Gendron owned a hunting rifle that his father gave him, and later purchased a shotgun. Just months before the attack, he purchased his AR-15, the Bushmaster.

"I had to buy a cucked version of this before illegally modifying it," he wrote, using a derogatory internet slang term—short for "cuckold"—implying the gun was weak or effeminate.

Gendron posted photographs showing how he easily modified the gun with a screwdriver and other tools so he could swap magazines quickly, mocking what he saw as a toothless state law regarding AR-15s. "The NY safe act didn't prevent me from buying an 'assault rifle' legally and acquiring high capacity magazines," he wrote. He wrote that he purchased used thirty-round magazines for $5 each from a flea market, because it was against the law to buy new ones in New York State.

Gendron also believed that the state's tough gun laws gave him the upper hand in any firefight that might break out during his attack. "I actually feel reassured that any legal CCW [a concealed-carry certification for a firearm owner] would be limited to ten rounds per mag, or anyone carrying a legal rifle or shotgun is limited in the same way," he wrote. "If the civilians I will be killing had guns that weren't limited, I would be much more afraid than I currently am."

He watched online videos about ARs and shooting them. He practiced firing his Bushmaster in the woods and grew comfortable with how easily he was able to do so, even in body armor. He panicked in March when his rifle malfunctioned, worried that he would not be able to carry out a mass shooting. If "my AR is broken than [sic] fuck. I'll have to change my plan entirely," he wrote.

He discussed every part of his rifle: the muzzle, barrel, receiver, handguards, buffer system, charging handle, bolt, trigger, even the sling to carry the rifle on his shoulder. He ranked AR manufacturers, categorizing his own gun, which he believed to be an older Bushmaster model, "in the low-tier but works most of the time." His writings were conversational, written as advice to his imagined audience of future mass shooters. In one digression, he added this note: "(I'm not a firearm expert, also legally I am required to tell you not to disobey gun laws (but in reality you can do whatever you want to))."

As he collected his arsenal, he warned himself, "Always make sure to watch out for glowies," meaning undercover federal agents who might seek to entrap him. He hated the federal government, believing it to be controlled by Jews. On March 1, 2022, he watched President Biden's State of the Union address on television. The president called once again for a new federal assault-weapons ban. Gendron mocked Biden's oft-stated remark that Americans don't need assault rifles because deer don't wear Kevlar vests. "How many times do we have to teach you this lesson old man?" he wrote. "They're not for hunting. They're to keep the freedom of civilians."

He took photos of his new AR and wrote about it with enthusiasm in his internet diary.

"It has a rifle gas tube and handguard, unthreaded muzzle, 20 in barrel, pistol grip, fixed carry handle, and fixed A2 stock," he wrote. "This is what God thought of when he sent Eugene Stoner to design and manufacture the M16 and AR-15."

At the Tops supermarket in Buffalo that Saturday afternoon, Gendron killed grandmothers, fathers, sisters, caregivers, and community volunteers, ranging in age from thirty-two to eighty-six. Andre Mackniel, fifty-three, was buying his three-year-old son a birthday cake. Ruth Whitfield, an eighty-six-year-old grandmother, was stopping for a bite to eat on her way home from visiting her husband in the nursing home. Heyward "Tenny" Patterson, a sixty-seven-year-old church deacon, regularly volunteered to drive people to the grocery store if they didn't have cars. Gendron chose the store's location because it was in a Black neighborhood.

"I think the question that we need to ask ourselves: Are any residents safe in this country anywhere?" Buffalo mayor Byron Brown said the day after the shooting. "Whether it is urban, suburban, rural, no community seemingly is safe from these mass shootings."

Ten days later, another troubled man inflicted yet another massacre, this time at an elementary school in Uvalde, Texas. Armed officers waited in hallways for more than an hour while a man armed with an AR-15 shot and killed nineteen children and two teachers, and wounded seventeen others. It was one of the worst failures by police in response to a mass shooting. Students and teachers made desperate 911 calls as they waited for officers to rescue them. "I don't want to die," a ten-year-old student told a dispatcher thirty-seven minutes into the attack. "My teacher is dead. My teacher is dead. Please send help, send help for my teacher. She is shot but still alive." An eleven-year-old smeared herself in her classmate's blood to play dead, fearing that the shooter would return to her classroom. Over an hour after the first officers arrived at the school, a team of border patrol agents breached a classroom and killed eighteen-year-old Salvador Ramos.

Before that day, Ramos had never fired a gun of any kind, according to investigators. He had searched the internet for the most basic information, such as what kind of ammunition an AR-15 fired and whether a magazine could be reused after being emptied. He looked up how to buy "juggernaut armor," which didn't exist in real life because it was armor from a video game. May 16, two days after the Buffalo shooting, was his eighteenth birthday, the first day Ramos was legally allowed to buy a semiautomatic rifle in Texas. He went online and ordered a Daniel Defense DDM4 V7, a high-end AR-15-style rifle, for $2,054.28 and had it shipped to a gun store in Uvalde. The next day, he bought a Smith & Wesson M&P 15 at the same store. He ordered 1,740 rounds of 5.56 ammunition that were delivered to his grandmother's house, where he lived. The owner of the gun store later told the FBI that Ramos seemed like a normal guy with no telltale signs of problems, but customers told investigators that he was wearing all black and "appeared odd and looked like one of those school shooters." He shared photos of his rifles on the internet and told others about his purchases. "Givin me school shooter vibes," one friend messaged him. He told his online acquaintances that he would be "all over the news" and many of them suspected the worst.

He saved news stories about the Buffalo attack and spent time with his cousin's son, who went to Robb Elementary, learning details from the child about his schedule and how lunch periods worked at the school. On the morning of May 24, 2022, Ramos texted with an online acquaintance from Germany that he'd shot his grandmother in the head and was going to "shoot up a elementary school rn." She texted back one word: "Cool."

Within weeks, survivors, doctors, and parents who lost children in Uvalde and Buffalo testified before Congress. Dr. Roy Guerrero, Uvalde's only pediatrician, described seeing "two children whose bodies had been pulverized by bullets fired at them, decapitated, whose flesh had been ripped apart." The only clue to the children's identities was their "blood-spattered cartoon clothes still clinging to them," he said. Guerrero urged Congress to act and find ways to keep guns like AR-15s out of the hands of men like Ramos. "The thing I can't figure out is whether our politicians are failing us out of stubbornness, passivity, or both," Guerrero said.

Killers were using AR-15s more often in massacres. Eight of the fifteen mass shooters who killed four or more people in a public place in 2021 and 2022 used ARs, according to the Violence Project.

The last one in 2022 took place in late November, when a disturbed man wearing body armor and shouldering an AR-15 burst into Club Q, a LGBTQ nightclub in Colorado Springs, Colorado. He killed five people and wounded nineteen before being overpowered by patrons, including an army veteran. Police had the suspect in custody within six minutes of the first emergency call. Novelist Stephen King tweeted the afternoon after the attack: "Another mass shooting. Don't know if it was an AR-15 style rifle, but am guessing it was. The psychos love them."

In the summer of 2022, President Biden again called for a new assault-weapons ban. But the president also backed a new push to raise the minimum age for buying AR-15s from eighteen to twenty-one in America, just like for handguns. There was a growing consensus in America that these guns weren't just like any other hunting rifle or shotgun and shouldn't be governed by the same rules. Nearly three-quarters of Americans—including most Republicans—supported raising the minimum age to buy them to twenty-one, according to one major poll.

In the weeks after the Uvalde massacre, Senator John Cornyn, a Republican from Texas, and Senator Chris Murphy, a Democrat from Connecticut, hammered out a modest bipartisan bill to address mass shootings and gun violence. The deal was possible because the old stubborn warriors in the battle over guns in America were losing their vise grip on the issue. Murphy, driven by the memories of the Sandy Hook massacre in his home state, pushed to become the Democratic Party's new leader on guns in place of the aged Dianne Feinstein. He was more open to new ideas such as red-flag laws, less wedded to the legislative approaches of the past like the assault-weapons ban. Cornyn, driven by the massacres in Texas, had an A+ rating from the NRA, but he believed there should be a way to prevent troubled young men from buying rapid-fire weapons. The NRA, beset by internal scandals, had little energy or focus to apply the pressure on Congress it had in the past.

The package that Congress quickly passed in the summer of 2022 provided funding for school safety and mental health programs. It included money for states to implement and enforce red-flag laws. It closed what had come to be known as the "boyfriend loophole" in a law that prevented spouses convicted of domestic abuse from owning a gun. It did not raise the age limit for purchasing AR-15s, but it expanded background checks to include juvenile records for buyers under twenty-one years old. It imposed harsher penalties for gun trafficking.

The media and politicians hailed the package as the most significant gun-control legislation to come out of Congress since 1994. The truth was the legislation was the *only* gun-control bill of any substance that Congress had passed since that time. The legislation proved significant for two reasons: conservatives and liberals worked together to address aspects of the mass-shooting crisis, and it signaled the emergence of new leaders in Congress on gun issues. But the legislation itself was modest. It gave funding to states that already had red-flag laws on the books—but it did not mandate them elsewhere. It required background checks to look at juvenile criminal records—but most mass shooters didn't have criminal records that disqualified them from buying guns. It imposed new penalties for gun trafficking—but most mass shooters bought their guns legally, not from gun traffickers. The praise for the bill showed how low Americans' expectations had fallen regarding their political leaders' ability to do anything serious about mass shootings.

Even as promising ideas—special licensing, red-flag laws, having schools and businesses monitor people who've made threats—gained traction and new leaders on gun issues started to emerge, many leaders in both parties had yet to signal a willingness to move beyond sloganeering toward comprehensive solutions. Some gun-control advocates have come to accept that Stoner's invention is here to stay. The technological genie is out of the bottle. More than 20 million AR-15s—perhaps as many as 25 million—are in civilian hands in the United States. More are sold every day. But some in the gun industry and beyond also now think Stoner's invention could be more stringently regulated to keep it away from dangerous people. The AR-15 was an engineering feat, created by the persistence of trial and error. Solving the unintended societal consequences of Eugene Stoner's creation would require the same doggedness by America's leaders.

Fewer than ten days after the president signed the Bipartisan Safer Communities Act into law, another mass shooter attacked with an AR-15. On the Fourth of July, crowds gathered for a parade in the affluent Chicago suburb of Highland Park. As the festivities began, a twenty-one-year-old man wearing a dress to disguise himself climbed up to the low roof of a restaurant with the rifle. Robert "Bobby" Crimo III had a history of violent behavior, including threatening to kill family members. Yet he still obtained a state permit to buy guns, which he used to purchase his Smith & Wesson M&P 15.

Crimo looked down on a quintessential American scene: an Independence Day parade. Families gathered on sidewalks to see a spectacle honoring the nation's founding. The fun had begun at 9:30 a.m. with a "Children's Bike and Pet Parade." Now with the official Fourth of July parade under way, many of those children stood with their parents holding red, white, and blue balloons and standing next to their small bicycles and tricycles festooned with streamers. Adults sat in red, white, and blue chairs and some wore red, white, and blue hats. Floats, marching bands, and other community groups moved down the street as people clapped and cheered. American flags were everywhere: large ones hung from lampposts; small ones were stuck in planters. Parade participants and onlookers waved Old Glory as marching band music resounded down the street. The event was more than just a Norman Rockwell ritual; it was a reclaiming of normalcy, an effort—replicated across the country that July Fourth—to reestablish community after the grueling years of COVID-19, lockdowns, political tensions, and unrest. One could only imagine that Eugene Stoner would have been gratified by the scene. Preserving this America was what he thought his work was all about. Sixty-two years earlier to the day, the Air Force General Curtis LeMay had picked up Stoner's gun to shoot watermelons. He thought the gun would be great for American fighting men.

But Crimo now used Stoner's invention to attack that America. In a few minutes, he fired more than seventy rounds down into the crowd. He shot indiscriminately. Video footage showed terrifying images of families with small children running from the gunfire. Crimo killed seven people before fleeing. Two of the dead were young parents, Kevin and Irina McCarthy. Their two-year-old son, Aiden, was found wandering and crying near their bodies. A news photo showed a police officer weeping amid the carnage.

32.

VALERIE'S ROAD HOME

I'm traveling in someone else's life.
—Valerie Kallis-Weber

Valerie Kallis-Weber and Harry Bowman stood up to stretch their legs and chitchat during a break at their work holiday party. Neither wanted to be there. Harry, forty-six, was a statistical analyst, quiet and not one for crowds. Valerie, fifty-eight, a policy specialist, had work to do. She was only seven weeks into a new job with San Bernardino County, and she was trying to finish a report. When the party invite came via email, Valerie tried to get out of it, but her boss told her it included mandatory training. She had to go.

On the morning of December 2, 2015, about eighty people who worked for the county public health department gathered for the party. A tall Christmas tree stood on one side of the conference room. Long tables were adorned with fir boughs. Sweets, baked goods, and soft drinks sat on a large table.

Party organizers had planned games, prizes, and awards. But before the fun, public health workers had to endure a training session. Many of them inspected restaurants, landfills, and pools in the county, America's largest by land mass. Stretching from the Los Angeles area to the Nevada state line, this large swath of the Inland Empire was a conglomeration of tract homes and sprawling shopping centers set amid barren mountains dotted with spindly desert trees and shrubs. Valerie had come to the area from Ohio with her high school sweetheart at age nineteen and made it her home, raising her only son as she pursued a career in public service.

That morning, Valerie wore a green Chico's pantsuit. She had earrings to match, and cream shoes with a cream Coach purse. The blond woman with dark brown eyes always liked to dress well, even for events she didn't want to attend. She got to the party at 8:00 a.m., before most of her team, and sat with Harry.

Harry's cubicle was close to hers in the office. He had two daughters, ages eleven and fifteen. He was a whiz with numbers, but he was shy, like many engineers. Valerie wasn't shy at all. Her coworkers described her as "spunky" and "a pistol." She liked to tease and joke with people, asking lots of questions. Her gregarious, conversational style was an inherited trait as the daughter of Greek immigrants. She was playful and sometimes blunt. Valerie brought energy to her work for various state and local governments. These days she found herself thinking about her approaching retirement. She caught herself fantasizing about traveling and spending time with her new granddaughter, River, then less than a year old.

Yet here she was, early on a midweek morning in a conference room decked out with a bureaucratic take on festive. Before anyone could dive into the cookies or sugary drinks, they all had to watch a mind-numbing video called *Learning with Lana*, which demonstrated proper techniques for landfill inspections. Next, they watched videos showing people who worked in the department, a blooper reel of workers being silly. Then a woman passed out wireless handheld clickers to buzz in for a trivia game about the videos they'd just sat through. When the woman handing out the clickers came by a table where several health inspectors were sitting, one of the inspectors wasn't there.

"Where's Syed?" someone asked.

His jacket lay on a chair. People at the table told the woman to leave a clicker, assuming that Syed Rizwan Farook, a quiet twenty-eight-year-old health inspector, would return soon.

During a break shortly before 11:00 a.m., everyone milled about the room. Some took pictures in front of the Christmas tree. Others went to the restroom or headed to the food table. Valerie, Harry, and others who worked in administration were laughing about the videos they'd just watched.

Valerie heard a loud noise; she thought it was a garbage truck emptying a dumpster outside the building. Boom, boom. The doors to the hallway swung open. A tall man clad all in black with a ski mask covering his face stepped inside. He raised a black rifle to his shoulder.

Bam, bam, bam, bam, bam.

"I've been hit!" Harry yelled, and fell to the floor.

Valerie thought it was some kind of training exercise.

A second figure, wearing a ski mask and carrying a rifle, came into the room. Valerie locked eyes with the second person. A woman with dark eyes. The woman's rifle flashed. A bullet hit Valerie in the shoulder and she fell. Facedown, heart pounding. Blood soaked through her pantsuit and pooled around her. Valerie played dead, hoping the shooters would move on. She looked over at Harry. He was completely still. I have to stay that still, she thought.

She lost consciousness. The black-clad attackers pushed into the crowded room, firing their rifles. One of them shot Valerie a second time. The bullet tore through her pelvis. Though she would have no recollection of doing so, Valerie crawled toward a door, leaving a thick trail of blood. Ambulance workers got her onto a stretcher and wheeled her outside. She regained consciousness and saw emergency workers cutting off her brand-new pantsuit. She wanted to protest, but she blacked out.

Valerie lived. But her body was damaged forever. The life she once imagined in retirement was replaced with a daily battle to overcome physical and psychological wounds from the attack. Two easy pulls of an AR-15's trigger changed everything.

At Loma Linda University Medical Center, just outside of San Bernardino, Dr. David Turay, the chief of trauma surgery, called in as many surgeons as he could on the day of the attack. He treated Valerie when she arrived.

"Big wounds, massive amounts of bleeding on the gurneys with blood pressures dropping rapidly," he recalled.

Turay recognized the wounds. He had dealt with scores of gunshot victims in his career. Bullets from handguns tended to carve straight, narrow channels through the body. These were caused by bullets from an AR.

"Assault rifles like the AR-15, I mean this thing leaves craters," he said.

Surgeons sliced open the left side of Valerie's chest. They saw that a bullet had severed a major vein and her left lung had collapsed. The doctors clamped the vein to stop the bleeding and inserted tubes so she could breathe. They drained her lung so she didn't drown in blood. The doctors packed gaping wounds in her perineum, thighs, butt, and vaginal area with fistfuls of gauze. A bullet had obliterated the blood vessels that crisscrossed Valerie's pelvis. Doctors used catheters to inject synthetic agents to try to stop the massive internal bleeding.

Once she stabilized, they took X-rays. The bullets had torn through her body like tornadoes. Her pelvis was shattered. Pieces of bone were out of place, like a flowerpot dropped on a sidewalk. Small bone fragments were embedded throughout her lower belly. Her intestines were shredded. Bullet fragments had embedded deep in the tissue of her pelvis and the left side of her chest.

That night Valerie lay doped up in a hospital bed. Her body was destroyed but she was alive.

The next day, Valerie's blood pressure plummeted and her left hand grew ice-cold. Her left arm was dying due to a lack of blood getting to the arm. Doctors rushed her back to the emergency room and cut open her chest yet again. They discovered that a major artery that sent blood to her arm was destroyed. Surgeons took a vein from her leg and grafted it into her arm to restore blood flow. If it didn't work, they would have to amputate.

Valerie's wounds didn't heal. The "high velocity ballistic injuries" were slow to heal and prone to infection, one of her surgeons noted in her chart a week after she'd been shot. The bullets from the AR-15 "created large cavitating wounds that were not amenable to bedside wound care," he wrote. To clean her wounds, the doctors had to meticulously remove dead or infected tissue with scalpels. Then, they washed the wounds with saline solution and repacked them with gauze. They had to perform this procedure repeatedly in the days and weeks that followed.

Doctors discovered that Valerie's shoulder injury was more severe than they first thought. The bullet had torn through the web of nerves that fanned out from her spinal cord to her shoulder, arm, and hand. The doctors decided not to amputate, but they doubted Valerie would ever be able to use her arm again.

Doctors were pessimistic that Valerie would ever fully recover. Valerie, slipping in and out of consciousness in her hospital bed as a new year approached, had no idea what lay ahead. She would have to endure scores of surgeries, thousands of hours of painful physical therapy, grim diagnoses, battles with insurance providers, blunt realities about what her damaged body could no longer do, abiding fear and anger over the violence that she witnessed and endured, guilt over surviving, contemplation of suicide, and an endless host of other profound or quotidian challenges. Such an epic shitstorm may have sunk a person with less of a stubborn streak.

Valerie Kallis was born in 1957 in Lorain, Ohio, a steel manufacturing town on Lake Erie near Cleveland. She was born the same year that Eugene Stoner developed the AR-15. Her father, James Joseph Kallis, a son of Greek immigrants, rose to become chief of the Lorain Fire Department. When James wasn't at the firehouse, he was working at his father's diner, the Nickel Plate. He married Valerie's mother, Mary, after his parents sent him back to Greece to find a wife.

Valerie was the second of three children, and the kids all grew up steeped in Greek culture. Family life revolved around the dinner table, with plates of pastitso, a layered meat dish, and dolmades, stuffed grape leaves. The Kallis home was lively and loud. The Kallis women were known for being stubborn. Mary came to America from Greece at twenty, speaking no English and not knowing anyone except her husband. She created a life for herself and her children by force of will and she conveyed that strength to her kids. Young Valerie inherited that willfulness. "You can't tell Valerie no," her mother said. "If she wants to do it she's going to do it." Growing up, Valerie and her sister frequently battled, especially over who would clean up after dinner. Their father once grew so tired of the bickering that he picked the dishes up and smashed them one by one until the girls stopped yelling.

In high school, Valerie was on the trampoline team, performing routines where she flipped and twisted through the air. She had a blue Ford Mustang convertible and drove it fast. She dated a football player, and they made plans to marry as soon as they graduated. Valerie's parents hated the idea. They wanted her to go to college, find a career, and, most importantly, marry a Greek. Valerie didn't listen. At age nineteen, she married her boyfriend at a Salvation Army chapel with only her grandmother in attendance. "I had other dreams for Valerie," her mother said years later. Her husband joined the air force and was assigned to Norton Air Force Base in San Bernardino. They drove off to California.

Young with two incomes and no children, the couple spent weekends in Las Vegas, going to concerts and gambling. But the idyll didn't last. Their fiery love was tumultuous, ranging from passion to anger. It grew worse after they had a son, David. When the boy was five, the couple divorced and Valerie moved with her son back to Ohio. The divorce was ugly, but a decade later, her ex-husband came to win her back. Valerie's family objected, but again she didn't listen. The couple moved back to Southern California. He begged her to marry him again and she agreed. It lasted six months. This time, she left him for good.

Valerie, now a single woman living alone with her son, had two handguns in her home for protection. In 2007, she was awakened by a noise in the middle of the night. When she came into the living room she saw her teenage son hogtied as one man held a gun to his head and another man stood nearby. The men were high on meth and looking for things to steal. She didn't have time to get to her guns. The robbers stole money, jewelry, electronics, and anything else they could fit into Valerie's BMW and her son's Hyundai. The police caught one of the men because of the tracking system on her son's car, but the other got away. Valerie saw a therapist at the time to cope with the trauma.

After the home invasion, Valerie went back to work at California's child support services agency. At the same time, she pursued a master's degree in business administration. She retired in 2009 and held a series of contract jobs before going back to work for San Bernardino County in October 2015. When her staff became overwhelmed by an unwieldy project, she urged them to break it down into a series of small tasks. "There is only one way to eat an elephant: a bite at a time," she told them. Valerie earned a good salary and stoked her pension. She had a spacious one-story home in a quiet neighborhood in Riverside, southwest of San Bernardino.

Her family back in Ohio was thrilled that Valerie had settled down and seemed to be thriving after the rocky marriage. They were impressed with her gumption. "What's a positive synonym for 'tough bitch'?" said her nephew Michael Janasko when describing his aunt.

The kitchen became Valerie's favorite place to be. She entertained guests with elaborate dinners, and she even tried out for a Food Network program, making avgolemono, a lemon egg soup.

Then came the shooting. Fourteen people were killed and twenty-four others, including Valerie, were wounded.

When they heard about the shooting, her mother, Mary, and Valerie's sister flew to California that night. When Mary saw her daughter unconscious and hooked up to machines, she wept and kissed her daughter's cheek, crying her name. Valerie underwent two dozen surgical procedures during her first month in the hospital. Doctors installed a colostomy bag and a catheter so she could go to the bathroom. They cut a hole in her windpipe so she could breathe. They inserted a feeding tube so she could get nutrients. They installed a filter to prevent blood clots from reaching her heart or lungs. The wounds in her pelvic area often became infected. She had a reaction to an antibiotic that made her skin look red and scaly. She had high fevers. She spent seven weeks in the intensive care unit, and another six weeks in another area of the hospital. She drifted in and out of consciousness, all the while on powerful painkillers.

Valerie "was full of piss and vinegar," according to her son. The hospital staff had to tie her wrists to the bed because she tried to escape. Once, she whispered to her visiting brother-in-law and nephew: "How much can you guys lift? Get me the hell out of here."

Fears and depression consumed her. She panicked that other shooters would scale the hospital and climb in through a window to kill her. She was convinced a third attacker was hunting survivors. In mid-January, Valerie told doctors she wanted to kill herself. They gave her medication to stabilize her mood. The trauma and stress affected everyone in Valerie's family. Mary had a stroke at Valerie's house, where the family was staying. She was taken to Valerie's hospital. "Could you put her on the same floor to make it convenient?" Valerie's weary sister asked the staff.

After ninety-three days in the hospital, doctors decided that Valerie could leave. An ambulance drove her to her Riverside home to be with her visiting family and her cats, Gizmo and Panda. Valerie couldn't walk and she couldn't move her left arm, so the ambulance workers rolled her inside in a wheelchair, then lifted her into a hospital bed.

At home, Valerie didn't have enough nurses to care for her complex medical needs. She found the state workers' compensation program slow and stingy. Despite Valerie's extensive injuries, workers' comp determined she didn't need around-the-clock care. Mary, eighty-three, had to cover when nurses weren't there. Mary would cook for Valerie. She'd make spanakopita, pastitso, and leg of lamb. When the food was ready, Mary would call out, "Come and eat dinner!"

"What the hell's wrong with you?" Valerie would shout from the bedroom. "I can't walk!"

Valerie's time in bed was supposed to heal her shattered pelvis and shredded insides. But in the coming months, pain in Valerie's pelvis grew. Whenever she tried to sit down, she felt an excruciating, stabbing sensation. Sitting for more than a few minutes in her wheelchair or on the couch became impossible. She couldn't walk and she couldn't sit. And soon lying down started to hurt too. What was going wrong?

When her orthopedic surgeon took X-rays, something truly strange appeared: bony growths in the soft tissue all around her pelvis. They looked like tree roots in some places and balls in others. The doctors could see that these strange growths were causing Valerie pain when she sat down. She begged a surgeon to take them out. He refused because he said they still were growing.

"I don't give a shit whether it's growing or not," she snapped. "Take it out of me now."

Valerie was suffering from a condition called heterotopic ossification, which causes bone to grow in soft tissue where it's not supposed to do so. Dr. Subhas Gupta had seen such growths in patients before, but on a smaller scale.

"If you punch a wall and break your knuckle, your knuckle grows back a little thicker than where you started," Dr. Gupta said. "That's why people with broken bones have small deformities at the site of injuries."

He had seen versions of this phenomenon when people broke bones in high-speed car crashes, but Valerie's injuries were of another order of magnitude.

"Never have I seen heterotopic ossification like that," he said.

A year after the shooting, her pelvis had grown to three times its size.

"When you look at her pelvis X-ray, it looks like a snowstorm, it just looks like everything is whited out," he said.

The bones pressed into her intestines, liver, spleen, and kidneys, taking about 25 percent of the space that her organs needed. Doctors concluded that it was the AR-15's high-velocity bullet that had caused the malformed growths. The .223 round hit Valerie's pelvic bone at such a high speed that it caused her body to overreact as it tried to heal itself. Her body was freaking out trying to heal itself by growing too much bone.

"If the body could be characterized with emotions, this would have been hysteria," Dr. Gupta said.

Military doctors had published case studies of soldiers who developed heterotopic ossification in their hips after being wounded by a high-velocity gunshot or shrapnel. The weapon that Stoner had invented for war caused Valerie injuries that doctors usually saw in combat. At least one other woman wounded in the San Bernardino shooting suffered from it too.

Valerie's surgeons decided not to operate. They feared that if they tried to remove the excess bone while it was still growing, they might trigger more growth.

Valerie's hand had become a shiny, shrunken, frozen claw. Her wrist and her fingers couldn't move and her arm couldn't straighten. She couldn't wash her hair. She couldn't put on shoes. She couldn't dress herself. She couldn't chop onions or tomatoes, the foundational elements of her favorite dishes. She couldn't braid her granddaughter's hair. She couldn't pick her up to kiss her.

The nerves that controlled movement in Valerie's left hand were dead, but the nerve fibers that transmitted the sensation of pain were not. She felt searing pain at the slightest touch on some parts of her arm. She used painkillers to make it through the day. In the summer of 2016, therapists attached electrodes to her hand to measure the electrical impulses being sent to her muscles. The chair of Loma Linda's neurology department told Valerie she'd never be able to use her hand again.

When she saw her primary physician, Dr. Haitham Juma, Valerie wept. She had fought through the pain of hand therapy sessions, holding out hope the hand might recover. She cried more than she had in all the months since she'd been shot. Dr. Juma, who had worked as a surgeon before suffering a career-ending injury, had seen how depressed Valerie was right after the shooting. He didn't want her to slip back. "Valerie, we will fight this," he told her.

Valerie struggled with post-traumatic stress disorder. She had flashbacks. One night, she saw a shooter coming down the hallway toward her bedroom. It turned out the shadows were her cats. Another time she panicked when she saw a man with an AR-15 outside her home. Where could she run? How could she run? She looked again. It was just a man changing windshield wipers on his car. She avoided crowds and refused to go into any place where she didn't think she could escape quickly.

She wore sunglasses and sat in the corner when she went for her hand therapy sessions.

Valerie spent years battling insurers to pay for her care. The county-run workers' comp delayed and denied medical services, from antianxiety medications to physical therapy. When Valerie's hair fell out from the stress and trauma, they refused to pay for a backup wig that could be used while the other was cleaned.

Eleven months after the shooting, Valerie sat on her back patio, looking out across the valley to desert hills. She had designed her backyard, with curving stony paths and drought-resistant trees. Valerie sat on a rocking chair with a special cushion to ease the pain from the bony growths inside her. She called it her "$300 cushion," a hard-fought victory in the battle with the workers' comp claims adjusters.

"I got shot here," she told a visitor, and pointed to the scars on her shoulder. "It's very far from here," she said, pointing to her withered hand. She ripped the Velcro straps off her arm brace. "I'll show you how much I can move," she said. She grimaced and her face flushed as she willed her fingers to close. They moved about a quarter of an inch. She stopped. "It feels like there's a brick attached to my hand," she said.

Valerie's mood shifted abruptly in the conversation.

"How do I feel?" she said. "I got a pee bag. I got a colostomy bag. I got medicine that we can't even put in one box. I have a room that's full of supplies. I can't get out of bed. My hair's falling out. I can't get in the shower. I can't get in the bathtub. I can't walk from one place to another. I can't sit."

She talked about being shot, lying facedown in her own blood next to the dying Harry Bowman.

"I wondered if it would've been better if I had died," she said.

During 2016 and 2017, the unwanted bone sprouting from Valerie's pelvis grew and the pain worsened. In the first year after the shooting, she had used a wheelchair, a walker, a cane, and then began to take a few steps at a time unassisted. But the growths impeded her progress. She couldn't use her right leg. Her surgeons decided to operate and remove the excess bone, despite the risks to Valerie.

Valerie was driven to Loma Linda hospital on the morning of March 6, 2017, for her thirty-first surgical procedure since the shooting, an operation more complicated and grueling than any to date.

Dr. Gupta and another surgeon used electric saws, hammers, and chisels.

"You can't cut it with a scalpel. You can't grab it and twist it. You've got to cut it like you would be cutting stone," Dr. Gupta said.

The surgeons chipped and sawed from 7:15 a.m. until 5:00 p.m. Late into the surgery, they removed a big chunk of bone but hit a blood vessel. The blood vessel had grown from Valerie's femoral artery into the bony formation to feed its growth. Blood sprayed everywhere.

When the surgeons finished, they weighed the bloody bone chunks: 2.3 pounds, just over half of what they would ultimately remove from her pelvis.

Unexpected bleeding and other complications required her to stay in the hospital for forty-five days from March to April 2017. She lost twenty-one pints of blood. Once, she was so delirious she believed that she was in a Mexican abortion clinic.

The hospital finally released her, and she returned to her house. Her family was back in Ohio. She felt alone and didn't trust anyone around her. She found herself getting angry a lot. She fired a string of home nurses. One slept on the job. Another left her stranded at a hair salon for hours. Another stole. The nursing agency lashed back, calling the police to have her committed. Two officers showed up at her house, but she convinced them she was fine. The next day, the agency called her doctors, pressing the issue.

"I was lost," she said. "I didn't know what to do."

Dr. Juma, her primary physician, as well as her neuropsychologist, stepped in, dismissing the nursing agency's request.

"When I see a fighter, I join them," Dr. Juma said.

Valerie realized she needed more help. She hired an attorney, Gary Kaplan, to battle for insurance coverage and medical care. When workers' comp refused to pay for therapy or drugs or medical supplies, Valerie called Kaplan. He would send strongly worded letters or shout into the phone, threatening lawsuits. Valerie began to feel like she had regained some control.

"Get up, get moving. Fix what you can fix," she told herself. "Put your big-girl pants on. Figure it out."

Valerie realized her recovery was her new full-time job. You eat an elephant one bite at a time. Part of her job was fighting with workers' comp. Part of her job was waking up early to be driven to therapy sessions. Part of her job was concentrating on moving her fingers or walking a few paces. Part of her job was steeling herself for yet another surgery. "I get up, I go to work," she said.

She was frustrated with her hand and arm not working. Doctors offered little chance of recovery. A doctor suggested she meet with a Loma Linda physical therapist and researcher known for exploring new therapies.

The therapist, flustered by her teasing and ribald humor, was in awe of her commitment to recovery. Valerie, though she feigned irritation with his incessant health tips, admired his dedication to her well-being. They spent hours in session as he pushed on different parts of Valerie's wounded body to get the blood flowing to her arm. He hoped he would regrow her nerves, he told her.

Valerie's hand therapists noticed that her withered left hand was warmer and more supple after these sessions. Soon Valerie could pinch and even grip some soft objects, like a tissue or a towel, between her thumb and fingers. By that July, she was able to pick up and release small plastic cones. In September, almost two years after being shot, Valerie was able to use her hand to steady onions and tomatoes while she chopped them with a knife. Nearly three years after the shooting, she was able to make a cupping motion with her palm, bringing her fingers together to pick up light items.

Three and a half years after the shooting, Valerie performed—without thinking about it—something stupendous. She took the wrapping off a granola bar while standing alone in her kitchen. She ate the bar using her left hand. Before the shooting, she wouldn't have even registered doing something so mundane. After the shooting, medical doctors had told her it was impossible. Valerie came into her hand therapist's office dancing and shimmying. The woman jumped for joy.

As the movement in her hand and arm improved, Valerie laughed more. She teased doctors and caregivers. She entertained at her home again. Valerie threw a "celebration of life" party with the help of a visiting nephew and her nurses. She invited doctors, nurses, and therapists. She felt a profound gratitude to all of the people, particularly Dr. Juma and her lawyer Gary Kaplan, who had stuck by her in her darkest hours. "These guys were like family now," she remembered thinking. She planned for days, marking recipes, noting what time each dish would go in the oven. She cooked Greek food and beef Wellington. She put out her best crystal.

Valerie's walking improved and she would go to bargain stores, pushing carts around the aisles herself. But she started to notice that every time she bent at the waist, she would feel pain in her midsection. It got to where she couldn't even bend over. Dr. Gupta, her surgeon, figured the pain was being caused by internal scarring from all of her many surgeries, from the frantic first moments in the emergency room after she was shot, to the hours-long operations to chip out bone growths. Dr. Gupta feared telling Valerie the bad news: she would have to have yet another major surgery. Patients enduring so many operations often just gave up, and he worried. The medical community even had a slang term for it: going dark. But when Dr. Gupta told Valerie the news, he found her ready to tackle the challenge. One bite at a time. She was "getting lighter and lighter, not darker and darker," Dr. Gupta recalled.

Valerie's fifty-sixth surgery since the shooting took place on October 4, 2019. When Dr. Gupta sliced her open, he was stunned by the extent of internal scarring. It radiated throughout her midsection like an octopus. He cut it out.

After the surgery, the incisions didn't heal. At home, she bled profusely. They rushed her back to the hospital and resealed the wounds with glue. The wounds opened up again. They wouldn't heal for months.

The setback pitched Valerie into a depression she had not experienced since the early days after the shooting. She bawled over the smallest things. If the window was open, she cried. If her cat ran outside, she cried.

Valerie had made it so far in four years, fighting to get back a fraction of her previous life. Yet these pelvic wounds just wouldn't heal. Stuck back in her bed, she felt all that progress she had fought so hard to achieve was slipping away. She asked herself a question over and over: What would she have done if God had given her a choice to live or die that day?

"Knowing what I have been through, I would have chosen death," she said.

On January 9, 2020, four years, fifty-seven surgeries, and more than thirty-five hundred therapy appointments since the shooting, Valerie brought a visitor along for a day at her full-time job.

On the drive to the hospital, Valerie teased her driver. At the hospital, she walked up a flight of stairs, holding on to the railing, taking one stair at a time. In her physical therapist's office, she lay down while he performed tests on her hand. He asked her to push two of her fingers together laterally while he held them apart. Valerie's face scrunched in pain. "Ow, ow, ow, ow," she mouthed.

After an hour, Valerie hobbled off to the next appointment: hand therapy. Rows of patients sat at desks while therapists manipulated and exercised their injured hands. As Valerie's therapist kneaded and pulled on her left hand, Valerie remarked she had recently taken a piece of paper from someone.

"Hold that," said Valerie, holding out a business card in between her thumb and the side of her forefinger. The hand therapist pulled on the other side of the business card as Valerie grimaced.

"Hold it, hold it, hold it, hold it," the therapist said.

She held on to it for a few seconds, grunting with effort, then let it go.

Valerie's left hand functioned a bit like a claw. She could move her fingers toward her palm but not much else.

At the end of the day, Valerie collapsed into bed. Her cats stalked into the bedroom. One nurse left, and another arrived for the night shift.

"It's like I'm traveling in someone else's life," she said.

The next day, she made stuffed cabbage for dinner. It tasted like her grandmother's—ground beef in tomato sauce with cabbage and spices—but it wasn't the same. Without two good hands, she couldn't wrap the meat in the cabbage leaves, like the recipe required. Instead, she minced the ingredients into little pieces. She called it "deconstructed stuffed cabbage."

A few weeks before the fifth anniversary of her being shot, Valerie packed up her bags and her two cats (with the help of her nurses) to move back to Ohio. Her house beneath the desert hills in Riverside had once been a symbol of an independent and successful woman. She had raised her son in that house. She had cooked elaborate dinners there. Now the house felt like a prison. "Someone was with me all the time. I couldn't drive. Everything had to be planned. My job was therapy and operations," she said. Valerie had stayed because the doctors and nurses at Loma Linda had been so supportive. She stayed because part of her had believed that things might return to what they once were.

Valerie accepted she would never recover her lost life. "This is as good as it's going to get," she thought. It was time to go home. She bought a condo on the edge of Lake Erie near the family she had left long ago. She lived on her pension and paid for her medical care with a one-time payment from San Bernardino County.

When she got to Ohio, Valerie wanted to be able to carry a gun with her. Having a handgun made her feel safe. But she couldn't get a permit. Pulling back the slide to load a round into the chamber with her crippled hand was impossible. The shooting didn't shake her views about gun ownership. She generally voted for conservative candidates; however, in 2016 she supported Hillary Clinton, whom she admired as a strong, practical female leader. In 2020, she voted for Trump. But the massacre and her debilitating injuries have caused her to wonder whether Stoner's gun belongs in civilian hands. She grilled one of her son's friends about why he owned an AR-15. "What the hell are you doing with that?" she recalled asking him. His reply: nothing.

"These weapons that you don't hunt with that go prrrrrr . . . I don't think those should be available to the public at all," she said.

Valerie often sat in a rocking chair, looking out over the vast lake that stretched to the horizon like an ocean. She snapped photos of the dramatic sunsets and sent them to friends in California. Even with her raucous family living nearby, Valerie felt a sense of peace. "I feel so safe here," she said. She cooked big Greek meals for her mother in her new kitchen. She rekindled friendships from high school. She even started dating. She bought herself a Tesla and began driving again. Her doctors at Loma Linda were so impressed by her progress that they asked her to give speeches to other victims of severe trauma and doctors who treat them. "This is one of the star fighters," said Dr. Juma.

But for Valerie, the fighting never ended. Ringing phones and chiming doorbells made her jump. One time in a parking lot, she whirled around and screamed at a man who was approaching from behind. The man was just complimenting her on her new car. She struggled in the kitchen. She bought a vise grip so she could open jars. When friends came over, she asked them to change pillowcases because she couldn't. Every night, she worked her way slowly up the stairs to her bedroom, step by step.

POSTSCRIPT: WHAT WOULD STONER DO?

We arrived at the largest gun show in America to find that the AR-15 had taken it over. The gun was everywhere in the acres of displays at the SHOT Show in January 2020. Booth after booth displayed variations of the gun. One day, buses drove attendees to the desert to fire all the latest firearms. The pop-pop-pop-pop sounds blended with the sounds of traffic nearby. We fired all types of guns inspired by Stoner's invention, even an AR-style shotgun designed by a Chinese company.

As we walked the Las Vegas convention floor, we recognized a giant image of Eugene Stoner's bow tie. The Iowa gunmaker Brownells was evoking the inventor to sell a new gun. Brownells called the gun WWSD2020. The name was a riff on the acronym for "What would Jesus do?" It stood for "What would Stoner do?"

"Eugene Stoner's ground-breaking rifles were considered visionary, futuristic, even radical," the display's text read. "If Eugene Stoner had access to today's most modern materials and manufacturing technology? This is the rifle he would build."

The commercial shrine included a larger-than-life photograph of Stoner's body, from the neck down. It didn't show Stoner's face. The decapitated ghost gripped an AR prototype, one of the ones built at the ArmaLite office in California in the 1950s.

Brownells's gun, retailing for a pricey $1,700, looked a lot like other ARs at the show. We wondered what Stoner would have thought of this marketing ploy, using his name, reputation, and at least part of his image to pull in gun aficionados. Public attention made him uncomfortable. If Stoner were alive today in the age of drones, lasers, sound weapons, and a U.S. Space Force, would he be making rifles at all?

But the acronym WWSD stuck in our heads and got us thinking: What *would* Stoner do about the AR-15 if he were alive today?

One evening, we drove to the Mandalay Bay, where Paddock used his numerous ARs to massacre Americans. Inside the hotel and casino, we walked past aisles of video poker machines in the large windowless room where Paddock spent his last morning alive. Gaggles of wide-eyed tourists wandered by. You could pick up snatches of regional accents: Southerners, Midwesterners, Californians, New Yorkers. America was in Vegas to have fun, to win money, to drink, to indulge.

The hotel made no reference to what happened on October 1, 2017. They changed the numbers of the hotel's floors; the thirty-second floor was gone. Outside, we looked up, trying to find the window to Paddock's suite. For weeks after the massacre, the shattered window stood out like a broken tooth. That night it was fixed, an indistinguishable black rectangle on a wall of dark glass. It was as though the massacre had never happened.

We walked across Las Vegas Boulevard to the giant lot that Paddock targeted on the day of the concert. The unmarked blocks-long area was enclosed by metal fencing covered by mesh and "No Trespassing" signs. Along the fence, we found plastic bags and empty beer bottles. It was quiet and dark. To the north, the Strip radiated its artificial light into the night sky. Even though no one else was around, we found ourselves speaking softly to each other.

Along one part of the fence, we found impromptu memorials: wilted white roses and faded pieces of paper that once bore notes of heartbreak. One tiny sign declared: HONOR 58. A homemade tribute hung on a metal chain. Someone had cut tin into the shapes of angels and dog tags and hung them there. Some were silver; others red. Each piece bore the handwritten name of a victim and the time they died. The desert wind swept down from the mountains, jostling the chains.

Susan Kleinpell wondered what her father's invention had become. One day, we took a trip with her to the Los Angeles garage where Eugene Stoner spent hours working on the ideas that would revolutionize firearms. It's a square, white building with a pitched roof and a black garage door set off from a white stucco home. The woman who came to the door had never heard of Eugene Stoner or his invention. As Sue walked back to the car, she said she didn't like talking to people about the AR-15. Americans had come to think of her dad's gun as the one used by mass shooters.

"It's becoming so regular, these shootings," she said. "Every time, I'm like 'Please, God, don't let it be an AR-15'—and it usually is."

Susan had come to believe that her father's invention shouldn't be sold to civilians. Her father's aim was to build a better, lighter, faster gun for the military. She didn't think he designed the AR-15 with the civilian market in mind, but she said she didn't really know what he thought.

"I personally don't think there needs to be an assault rifle out on the street," she said.

Stoner's close friends had conflicting views about what he would think today. Robert Bihun, who created ARES with Stoner, used to talk with him for hours about the AR-15's development and troubled adoption by the military. Stoner was very proud of the gun's ingenious design, "but he thought it was absolutely not for the public, for Christ's sake. I don't think that Gene ever wanted civilian use of this rifle," Bihun said. Other friends said that Stoner believed inventors weren't responsible for how their inventions were used.

In his Prescott, Arizona, workshop, Jim Sullivan, the last living member of the original ArmaLite team, said working on the rifle was the best time of his life. Around him, gun parts and drawings for new types of weapons lay neatly on drafting tables. In his late eighties, Sullivan still worked on projects every day. The complexity of engineering problems fascinated him. He had more than four hundred gun-related patents. He pulled out the original drawings for the AR-15 and smiled broadly as he described how he and Stoner created the gun. He picked up parts to demonstrate how the gun worked, explaining the firearm's functions like an excited professor. After hours of talking about barrels, bolts, receivers, and Stoner's gas system, he paused and looked down at the floor.

"There's something wrong," he said abruptly. "The U.S. has more gun deaths than the whole world and the school shootings and the mass shootings. What the hell's the matter with us?"

He looked down again. The smile was gone. The words came slowly.

"There's something wrong here," he said again.

He wondered why people who weren't soldiers would want an AR-15.

"What in the hell would civilians want it for anyway?" he asked. "What the hell do you do with it? If all you're doing is target shooting, well, just get a little .22."

He laughed. Then his expression went flat again.

"It doesn't make sense. Sick."

He was quiet.

"The whole world doesn't have this problem that the U.S. has."

Sullivan said mass shooters wouldn't be able to do what they do without inventions such as the AR-15.

"Every gun designer has a responsibility to . . . ," the old man said, pausing yet again before finishing his thought. "To think about what the hell they're creating."

Notes

1. THE BOY WHO LIKED EXPLOSIONS

12 *"It was kind of a hobby that got out of hand"*: Smithsonian Institution Archives, Washington, DC, Oral History Program, Video Collection, Twentieth Century Small Arms, Collection Division 1: (Eugene Morrison) Stoner, Sessions 1, 2, 3, http://siarchives.si.edu/research/videohistory_catalog9532.html.

12 *His father, thirty-year-old Lloyd Lester Stoner*: Information on Stoner's early life and family is drawn from author interviews with Susan Kleinpell.

13 *Gene was fascinated with launching*: Jean Stoner, transcript of unpublished interview by J. W. Gibbs, September 3, 2003.

13 *When the Great Depression hit*: Author interviews with Susan Kleinpell.

13 *Gene's family decided*: Jack Lewis, "Passing of an Icon: Gene Stoner Left His Mark on the Marine Corps He Loved!" *Leatherneck*, July 1997, 26.

13 *"He received average grades"*: Jean Stoner, transcript of unpublished interview by J. W. Gibbs, September 3, 2003.

15 *"a certain amount of experimenting on different types of machine guns"*: Smithsonian Institution Archives, Washington, DC, Oral History Program, Video Collection, Twentieth Century Small Arms, Collection Division 1: (Eugene Morrison) Stoner, Sessions 1, 2, 3, http://siarchives.si.edu/research/videohistory_catalog9532.html.

15 *On his own time*: Jean Stoner, transcript of unpublished interview by J. W. Gibbs, September 3, 2003.

15 *Stoner studied the inner workings*: Drawn from author interviews with Susan Kleinpell.

15 *In February 1947, he took a job*: Eugene Stoner, ArmaLite employment application, private collection of Susan Kleinpell.

15 *He worked in the machine shop*: Author interview with Susan Kleinpell.

16 *"Once I got established"*: Smithsonian Institution Archives, Washington, DC, Oral History Program, Video Collection, Twentieth Century Small Arms, Collection Division

1: (Eugene Morrison) Stoner, Sessions 1, 2, 3, http://siarchives.si.edu/research/videohistory_catalog9532.html.

16 *The Stoners—Jean, Gene, Patty, and Michael*: From author interviews with Susan Kleinpell.

2. MEN AGAINST FIRE

18 *On the early morning*: See Lieutenant Colonel J. F. Dunford Jr., "Strategic Implications of Defensive Operations at the Pusan Perimeter July–September 1950," USAWC Strategy Research Project, 1999, https://apps.dtic.mil/dtic/tr/fulltext/u2/a364614.pdf.

19 *At 7:00 a.m on that July morning*: Capt. Patrick J. Donahue, "The Danger of Poor Training Management: The U.S. Army in Korea—July 1950." Maneuver Center of Excellence Libraries, MCoE HQ Donovan Research Library, Korean War Student Paper Collection, https://mcoepublic.blob.core.usgovcloudapi.net/library/DonovanPapers/korea/STUP3/A-F/DonahuePatrickJ%20CPT.pdf.

19 *A day after the defeat*: "James S. Lay to National Security Council, with attachment," Harry S. Truman Library and Museum, https://www.trumanlibrary.gov/node/316187.

19 *"We may find—with overnight suddenness"*: *Washington Evening Star*, July 11, 1950.

20 *"All of the talk"*: William Shadel, "What Price Riflemen?," *American Rifleman*, March 1951, 31.

20 *Historians believe Chinese alchemists*: Clive Ponting, *Gunpowder* (London: Chatto and Windus, 2005), 11–19.

21 *After the slaughter of the Civil War*: McNaugher, *M16 Controversies*, 17–18.

22 *As far back as ancient China*: See Chinn, *Machine Gun*, 15–19.

22 *"It occurred to me"*: Ellis, *Social History of the Machine Gun*, 27.

22 *Gatling urged Abraham Lincoln*: Despite his protestations of loyalty to the United States, some officers suspected that Gatling, born in the South, had Confederate sympathies. Confederate inventors tried to create their own rapid-fire gun during the war as well, but with no success.

23 *"bears the same relation"*: William B. Franklin, *The Gatling Gun, for Service Ashore and Afloat* (Hartford, CT: Case, Lockwood and Brainard, 1874), 25.

23 *Hiram Maxim, born in 1840*: "Sir Hiram Maxim, Gun Inventor, Dies," *The New York Times*, November 25, 1916, 13.

23 *"Hang your chemistry and electricity!"*: Hiram Maxim, "How I Invented Maxim Gun," *The New York Times*, November 1, 1914, 62; Chinn, *Machine Gun*, 128.

23 *Maxim's eureka moment regarding guns*: Maxim, "How I Invented Maxim Gun," 62.

23 *"Cannot this great force"*: Chinn, *Machine Gun*, 128.

23 *Maxim guns were put into service*: Smith, *Machine Gun*, 152.

24 *During an incursion into Tibet*: L. Austine Waddell, *Lhasa and Its Mysteries, with a Record of the Expedition of 1903–1904* (New York: E. P. Dutton, 1906), 159.

24 *At the Battle of Omdurman*: Ellis, *Social History of the Machine Gun*, 85–86.

24 *John Moses Browning, the son*: Chinn, *Machine Gun*, 155–58.

24 *During World War I*: Armies in the war manufactured machine guns en masse. In 1915, the British alone produced about twenty-four hundred Vickers (Maxim) guns. By 1918, the last year of the war, it produced more than thirty-nine thousand. In addition to those guns, the United Kingdom made tens of thousands of other machine guns. So did Germany, Russia, France, Italy, Belgium, and the United States. See Ellis, *Social History of the Machine Gun*, 20.

24 *"negated all the old human virtues"*: Ellis, *Social History of the Machine Gun*, 17.

25 *The strategy didn't work that well*: The British and French models followed earlier light machine guns. The earliest such rifle was the Danish Madsen gun, first built in 1902. See Chinn, *Machine Gun*, 213.

25 *His answer was the .30 caliber*: "The designer intends the gun to be used more as a semi-automatic than as an automatic arm," a journalist for *American Machinist* wrote. See *Automatic Rifle (Browning), Model of 1918 Service Handbook*, Office of the Chief of Ordnance (Washington, DC: Government Printing Office, March 1921, revised).

25 *The military began issuing*: Browning sold the rights for the weapon to the U.S. Army at a significant discount. When his brother complained they could have gotten more money, Browning responded, "Yes, and if we were 15 or 20 years younger we'd be over there in the mud!" Browning died at seventy-one in 1926, while working in a shop on a new gun design. See Sharpe, *Rifle in America*, 71, among numerous sources.

25 *With an eight-round disposable clip*: Alec Wahlman, *Storming the City: U.S. Military Performance in Urban Warfare from World War II to Vietnam* (Denton: University of North Texas Press, 2015), 50.

26 *He first was exposed to guns*: Hatcher, *Book of the Garand*, 28.

26 *Garand started working in earnest*: Hatcher, *Book of the Garand*, 1.

26 *"She is a pretty good gun"*: Hoffman, *History of Innovation*, 14.

27 *None of the Allies had anything like it*: The Germans also developed a curved attachment so they could shoot out of a tank hatch or around corners without having to face the enemy.

27 *With German armies in retreat*: Hitler considered himself an expert on guns and he would expound at length on the finer details of ordnance and ammunition: calibers, lengths of gun barrels, the materials used, how far guns could shoot, and their function in battle. His officials found the micromanagement frustrating. See Albert Speer, *Inside the Third Reich* (New York: Macmillan, 1970).

27 *The muscular phrase echoed other Nazi labels*: Thanks to Alfred Kelly, professor emeritus of history at Hamilton College, for his input on the Nazi use of the term *Sturm*. The actual German word for "attack" or "assault" is *Angriff*.

27 *One of the earliest uses*: See *Tactical and Technical Trends*, no. 57 (April 1945) (Washington: Military Intelligence Division War Department, 1945).

28 *They also brought Schmeisser back*: The AK-47 and Nazi *Sturmgewehr* looked very similar. In 2017, outcries erupted when the statue of Kalashnikov unveiled in Moscow accidentally included a Sturmgewehr. See BBC, "Kalashnikov Statue Changed Because of German Weapon," September 22, 2017, https://www.bbc.com/news/world-europe-41367394.

29 *Though statistical support for his assertions*: See Robert L. Bateman, "The Long-Dead Hand of S.L.A. Marshall Misleads Historians," *Military History*, February 2007. Post on History.net.

29 *A top-secret army study found*: G. N. Donovan, "Technical Memorandum: Use of Infantry Weapons and Equipment in Korea" (Chevy Chase, MD: Operations Research Office, Johns Hopkins University, 1952), 18.

29 *In 1952, a study funded by the Defense Department*: Norman Hitchman, "Operational Requirements for an Infantry Hand Weapon" (Chevy Chase, MD: Operations Research Office, Johns Hopkins University, June 19, 1952), https://apps.dtic.mil/dtic/tr/fulltext/u2/000346.pdf. This finding reinforced earlier research during World War II of soldiers wounded while fighting on the Pacific island of Bougainville. See "Wound Ballistics Report: Bougainville Campaign, 1944," https://collections.nlm.nih.gov/catalog/nlm:nlmuid-46921110R-bk.

29 *"For the future, we should develop a lighter rifle"*: Garand spoke for a U.S. government film in 1954.

30 *By 1948, only 1.5 million*: Lieutenant Colonel J. F. Dunford Jr., "Strategic Implications of Defensive Operations at the Pusan Perimeter July–September 1950," USAWC Strategy Research Project, 1999, 5–6. Dunford quotes the historian and journalist Clay Blair's assessment that Truman and his defense secretary, Louis Johnson, "had all but wrecked the conventional military forces of the United States," https://apps.dtic .mil/dtic/tr/fulltext/u2/a364614.pdf.

30 *"[T]he Army of 1948"*: Omar N. Bradley and Clay Blair, *A General's Life* (New York: Simon and Schuster, 1983), 474.

30 *"If one of the camps does not capitulate"*: "Stenographic Record of a Speech by Comrade J. V. Stalin at a Special Session of the Politburo, March 14, 1948," March 14, 1948, History and Public Policy Program Digital Archive, ROC-MFA 105.11/61.15. Published in CWIHP Working Paper No. 12, http://digitalarchive.wilsoncenter.org /document/117823.

30 *The erudite Stevenson had little international or military experience*: Stevenson served briefly in the navy in 1918, but by the time his training was over, so was World War I. Stevenson's relationship with weapons included a tragedy. He accidentally shot and killed a neighbor girl when he was twelve while showing off a rifle he thought wasn't loaded. He was haunted by her death for the rest of his life.

30 *The GOP, which hadn't held the White House*: Leighton, *Strategy, Money, and the New Look*, 2–5; Ambrose, *Eisenhower*, 294–95.

31 *Eisenhower's approach, which his press handlers*: Carter, *U.S. Army Before Vietnam*, 20.

31 *"[W]hat was good for our country was good for General Motors and vice versa"*: E. Bruce Geelhoed, *Charles E. Wilson and Controversy at the Pentagon, 1953 to 1957* (Detroit: Wayne State University Press, 1979), 46.

32 *As army chief of staff*: Geelhoed, *Charles E. Wilson*, 118.

32 *"to fight tomorrow's wars with tomorrow's weapons and techniques"*: Ridgway with Martin, *Soldier*, 283, 299.

32 *New missiles, bombers, nuclear warheads*: Ridgway with Martin, *Soldier*, 296.

3. THE RIFLEMAN

33 *"This country was born with a rifle in its hand"*: Sharpe, *Rifle in America*, 4.

33 *The Cold War "inaugurated the Golden Age of the Western"*: Richard Slotkin, *Gunfighter Nation: The Myth of the Frontier in Twentieth-Century America* (New York: Harper-Perennial, 1992), 347, 352, 458.

35 *"The old pride in being"*: Paul Cardinal, "Marksmanship and the U.S. Army," *American Rifleman*, June 1951, 15.

35 *"[I]t is more important than ever"*: Merritt Edson, "Preparedness and YOU," editorial, *American Rifleman*, April 1951, 11.

36 *In August 1955, Edson went*: Hoffman, *Once a Legend*, 411–12.

4. HOLLYWOOD MOON SHOT

37 *During World War II*: Sheller, *Aluminum Dreams*.

37 *In* Aluminum on the March: Reynolds Metals Company, *Aluminum on the March*, 1956.

37 *Colt made the first*: Dick Williams, "The Origin of the Commander-Size 1911," *Shooting Illustrated*, May 17, 2018, https://www.shootingillustrated.com/articles/2018/5/17 /the-origin-of-the-commander-size-1911.

38 *Stoner called his first aluminum gun the M5*: Jean Stoner, handwritten notes, private collection of Susan Kleinpell.

38 *In the 1930s, a young Marine*: See *Hearing on the Johnson Semiautomatic Rifle Before the*

Senate Committee on Military Affairs, 76th Cong., 3d Sess., specifically S3983, a bill to provide for the adoption of the Johnson semiautomatic rifle as a standard arm of the military and naval forces.

38 *Stoner picked up the issue*: Johnson worked for ArmaLite as a consultant in the 1950s and promoted Stoner's weapons.

38 *"One of the things against the Garand rifle"*: Smithsonian Institution Archives, Washington, DC, Oral History Program, Video Collection, Twentieth Century Small Arms, Collection Division 1: (Eugene Morrison) Stoner, Sessions 1, 2, 3, http://siarchives.si.edu/research/videohistory_catalog9532.html.

39 *Out to dinner with his family*: Jean Stoner, handwritten notes, private collection of Susan Kleinpell.

39 *"They launder them. It'll come out"*: Author interviews with Susan Kleinpell.

39 *"Some felt he was difficult"*: Jack Lewis, "Passing of an Icon: Gene Stoner Left His Mark on the Marine Corps He Loved!" *Leatherneck*, July 1997, 29.

39 *"I was trying to come up with"*: Smithsonian Institution Archives, Washington, DC, Oral History Program, Video Collection, Twentieth Century Small Arms, Collection Division 1: (Eugene Morrison) Stoner, Sessions 1, 2, 3, http://siarchives.si.edu/research/videohistory_catalog9532.html.

40 *"It is amazing that anyone"*: Author interview with C. Reed Knight Jr.

40 *U.S. Patent 2951424*: In his gas system, two crucial parts, the bolt and the bolt carrier, did double duty. The bolt's main job was to lock behind the cartridge so that the gun could withstand the pressure of the explosion. The bolt carrier's main job was to lock and unlock the bolt and carry it back and forth inside the receiver. Stoner designed them so that the bolt also acted like a stationary piston while the bolt carrier acted like a movable cylinder, the patent said. When he channeled the gas in between them, it pushed the bolt carrier backward, which in turn unlocked and moved the bolt backward and ejected the spent casing. A spring sent them forward again, loading a fresh cartridge and locking the bolt behind it.

40 *The accompanying diagrams showed*: European gun designers had developed direct gas systems earlier, but the approach was never widely adopted. A Swedish military rifle produced in the 1940s also used a system that channeled gas back into the receiver, but the design was crude compared to Stoner's. With the Swedish Ljungman gas system, the bolt and bolt carrier did not double as a piston and cylinder, and the force of the gas was off-center from the rifle's axis, making it hard to control.

40 *With a lighter gun, "you'd need every available means"*: Smithsonian Institution Archives, Washington, DC, Oral History Program, Video Collection, Twentieth Century Small Arms, Collection Division 1: (Eugene Morrison) Stoner, Sessions 1, 2, 3, http://siarchives.si.edu/research/videohistory_catalog9532.html.

41 *Stoner worked on a prototype*: Currently the property of the technical reference collection at Knight's Armament Company.

41 *Historians of gun design*: Author interviews with Patrick Sweeney.

42 *"I had met George"*: Smithsonian Institution Archives, Washington, DC, Oral History Program, Video Collection, Twentieth Century Small Arms, Collection Division 1: (Eugene Morrison) Stoner, Sessions 1, 2, 3, http://siarchives.si.edu/research/videohistory_catalog9532.html.

42 *"When Sullivan talked with Stoner"*: Jean Stoner, handwritten notes, private collection of Susan Kleinpell.

43 *In July 1954, Stoner signed*: Agreement between George Sullivan and Eugene Stoner, July 1954; Thomas Mahoney, "Report on Investigation of Background of Inventions Made at Armalite Division and Contractual Relationship Between Stoner and Sullivan," September 9, 1958. Note: Stoner signed a second patent agreement with Sullivan upon being hired, promising to assign any new inventions to Fairchild. Stoner

persuaded Sullivan to exclude his garage guns—the M-6, the M-7, and the M-8 with its gas system—from this deal.

43 *Stoner's employment application with Fairchild*: Eugene Stoner, ArmaLite employment application, private collection of Susan Kleinpell.

44 *But ArmaLite's logo had a twist*: Some logos for ArmaLite instead showed a roaring, attacking lion in crosshairs.

44 *Less than a mile to the west*: The musical tribute to war veterans, *White Christmas*, and Alfred Hitchcock's film about a witness to murder, *Rear Window*, both Paramount creations, were the two top grossing films of 1954.

44 *"No doubt in anybody's mind"*: Eugene Stoner, deposition, December 22, 1960, private collection of Susan Kleinpell.

44 *Some in the office believed Sullivan*: From depositions and notes, private collection of Susan Kleinpell.

45 *"I think he put a drop"*: Author interview with Jim Sullivan. Jim Sullivan went on to a long career as a successful weapons inventor in his own right.

45 *Dorchester had worked with Sullivan*: From depositions and notes, private collection of Susan Kleinpell.

45 *One day, Dick Boutelle*: Author interviews with Jim Sullivan.

46 *The company's first weapon*: "Operations of Armalite for Year 1954," Fairchild Industries, Inc. Collection, 1919–1980, National Air and Space Museum Archives, Chantilly, VA.

46 *The AR-5 was the first*: Fairchild Industries, Inc. Collection, 1919–1980, National Air and Space Museum Archives, Chantilly, VA.

46 *The idea for the survival rifle*: See William Edwards, "The Story of the AR-10," *Gun Digest*, 1958, 109.

47 *Springfield Armory had designed*: Inspired by a visit to the armory in 1843, the poet Henry Wadsworth Longfellow immortalized the enormous complex in his famous antiwar poem called "The Arsenal at Springfield," which includes these stanzas:

> This is the Arsenal. From floor to ceiling,
> Like a huge organ, rise the burnished arms;
> But from their silent pipes no anthem peeling
> Startles the villages with strange alarms.
>
> Ah! what a sound will rise, how wild and dreary,
> When the death-angel touches those swift keys!
> What loud lament and dismal *Miserere*
> Will mingle with their awful symphonies!

48 *The forty-inch-long rifle*: Melvin Johnson, "Fairchild Aircraft Develops Seven-Pound Armalite AR-10-Automatic Rifle," *Army*, February 1957, 57.

48 *But it still weighed*: Stoner also incorporated a design element from the earlier rifle made by Melvin Johnson, the embittered gun designer whose rifle had been passed over in favor of the M1 Garand. In Johnson's gun, when the bolt locked into place behind a cartridge, it locked onto a steel extension of the barrel. In many other guns, the bolt locked onto the receiver or frame of the weapon, which meant that those guns needed heavy steel frames to withstand the force of the exploding gunpowder on the bolt. But if the bolt locked onto an extension of the barrel instead, the frame didn't need to be so sturdy; it could be made of a lighter material. Stoner applied that design change so they could make their AR-10 frame out of aluminum. ArmaLite would hire Melvin Johnson as a consultant in 1957 to help promote ArmaLite's guns. While Stoner liked Johnson's front-locking bolt, he did not care for him as a consul-

tant, according to Jim Sullivan, the draftsman. "It kind of embarrassed Stoner because Dorchester invited Johnson to come in and give him advice," Sullivan recalled. Johnson smoked cigars, waving them about as he spoke to Stoner and getting the smoke in his face. Stoner hated it, Sullivan recalled.

48 *"A break-through has been recorded"*: *Time*, July 29, 1957.

49 *The final versions of the AR-10*: Reference collection of Knight's Armament Company.

49 *One part of the AR-10*: Author interviews with Jim Sullivan.

49 *The agreement he'd signed*: Eugene Stoner, deposition, December 22, 1960, private collection of Susan Kleinpell.

49 *In exchange for*: Agreement between Stoner and Sullivan. August 6, 1956. Private Collection of Susan Kleinpell.

49 *On August 6, 1956*: Jean Stoner, transcript of unpublished interview by J. W. Gibbs, September 3, 2003, private collection of Susan Kleinpell.

50 *The December 3, 1956, issue*: "Armed Forces: The Aluminum Rifle," *Time*, December 3, 1956, https://content.time.com/time/subscriber/article/0,33009,808636,00.html.

50 *An excited Boutelle asked to see*: Jean Stoner, transcript of unpublished interview by J. W. Gibbs, September 3, 2003, private collection of Susan Kleinpell.

50 *When Stoner's wife saw Sullivan*: Author interviews with Susan Kleinpell.

50 *Jean's blowup appeared to have some effect*: Eugene Jaderquist, "Armalite's AR-10: Is This the Next G.I. Rifle?,"*Guns*, March 1957, 14.

51 *Tests at Springfield Armory in December 1956*: Roy E. Rayle, *Random Shots* (Bennington, VT: Merriam Press, 1996), 92.

51 *"Naturally this stopped the test"*: Rayle, *Random Shots*, 93.

5. SPRINGFIELD'S RIFLE

53 *"It gives the modern Army a better"*: E. H. Harrison, "The New Service Rifle," *American Rifleman*, June 1957, 15–21.

53 *"This is nothing more than the M1 Garand"*: Hallahan, *Misfire*, 440.

53 *"They labored mightily and brought forth a mouse"*: John S. Tompkins, "The U.S. Army's Blunderbuss Bungle That Fattened Your Taxes," *True*, April 1963, 36.

54 *The Belgian gun had never tested*: Rayle, *Random Shots*, 11.

54 *The leader of this group*: See Hallock, "M16 Rifle Case Study," 20.

55 *Ordnance staff were initially dismissive of the AK-47*: Chivers, *The Gun*, 5, 243, 256–57.

56 *In a lengthy article in the army periodical*: General Willard G. Wyman, "Army Rifle Marksmanship Today," *Infantry* 48, no. 3 (July–September 1958): 6–14.

56 *Wyman sponsored experiments in 1955*: "Report of Project 2709. Evaluation of M2 Carbine Modified to Fire High Velocity Caliber .22 Cartridge," United States Continental Army Command, November 5, 1955, box 62, papers of Alain Enthoven, Lyndon Baines Johnson Library.

57 *"Jackie Devers, in his work"*: "Report of Board to Review Rifle and Bayonet Problems," United States Continental Army Command, December 19, 1958, Annex Z, Colonel Richard R. Hallock Papers (MC 284), Columbus State University Archives, Columbus, GA.

57 *If the military could build missile systems*: Report of Board to Review Rifle and Bayonet Problems," United States Continental Army Command, December 19, 1958, Annex Z, Colonel Richard R. Hallock Papers (MC 284), Columbus State University Archives, Columbus, GA.

57 *But Taylor bowed to internal*: "Report of Board to Review Rifle and Bayonet Problems," United States Continental Army Command, December 19, 1958, Annex Z, Colonel Richard R. Hallock Papers (MC 284), Columbus State University Archives, Columbus, GA.

57 *The general and his entourage*: Smithsonian Institution Archives, Washington, DC, Oral History Program, Video Collection, Twentieth Century Small Arms, Collection Division 1: (Eugene Morrison) Stoner, Sessions 1, 2, 3, http://siarchives.si.edu/research/videohistory_catalog9532.html.

57 *Just days after*: McNaugher, *Marksmanship, McNamara, and the M16 Rifle*, 60.

58 *One was the AR-13*: "Fairchild ArmaLite Division Outline for Proposed Activity for 1957," Fairchild Industries, Inc. Collection, 1919–1980, National Air and Space Museum Archives.

58 *ArmaLite launched the collapsible semiautomatic rifle*: The AR-7 never caught on for the commercial market, but it did get a boost in sales in 1965 when it was used by Sean Connery in the James Bond film *From Russia with Love*. See *Dallas Times Herald*, "Spy Movie Stimulates Sale of the 'James Bond' Rifle," March 31, 1965, A31.

58 *George Sullivan had given Stoner a small raise*: Stoner employment records, private collection of Susan Kleinpell.

6. THE SPACE-AGE GUN IS BORN

60 *Military officials briefed Stoner*: Smithsonian Institution Archives, Washington, DC, Oral History Program, Video Collection, Twentieth Century Small Arms, Collection Division 1: (Eugene Morrison) Stoner, Sessions 1, 2, 3, http://siarchives.si.edu/research/videohistory_catalog9532.html.

60 *Stoner turned to the company's*: Recollections and quotes from Jim Sullivan drawn from author interviews with him.

62 *Early versions of the AR-15 weighed just over five pounds*: "Report of Project NR 2787, Evaluation of Small Caliber High Velocity Rifles—Armalite AR-15," U.S. Army Infantry Board, May 27, 1958, box 62, papers of Alain Enthoven, Lyndon Baines Johnson Library, Austin, TX; "Cordless Electric Hedge Trimmer," U.S. Patent US3212188A, Robert H. Riley Jr., Black & Decker Mfg Co., 1961.

63 *The vast bureaucracy of the Manhattan Project*: Author interview with Richard Rhodes.

64 *Jim Sullivan remembered one day*: Author interview with Jim Sullivan.

64 *In 1928, the U.S. military created*: "Report of Board Appointed to Recommend Specific Caliber for Future Development of the Semiautomatic Shoulder Rifle," September 21, 1928, Colonel Richard R. Hallock Papers (MC 284), Columbus State University Archives, Columbus, GA.

65 *Decades later, as Stoner worked*: "Wounding by SALVO Bullets," Armed Services Technical Information Agency, box 62, papers of Alain Enthoven, Lyndon Baines Johnson Library, Austin, TX.

65 *Today, .223 ammunition is one of the most*: The .223 round became the standard bullet for the AR-15, but another type of ammunition, the 5.56 round, was also developed for use in the AR-15s and was adopted for use by NATO forces. The 5.56 round uses the same-size shell casing but has slightly different pressure levels for the cartridge. Both bullets can be fired by AR-15 rifles.

67 *Velocity and mass determined*: Author interview with Beat Kneubuehl.

68 *Researchers like the military surgeon*: J. J. Hollerman, M. L. Fackler, D. M. Coldwell, and Y. Ben-Menachem, "Gunshot Wounds: 1. Bullets, Ballistics, and Mechanisms of Injury," *American Journal of Roentgenology* 155, no. 4 (October 1990): 685–90.

7. THE BUREAUCRACY STRIKES BACK

70 *When ArmaLite's guns arrived*: This information comes from author interviews with David Carson.

71 *"When it came to rifles"*: McNaugher, *M16 Controversies*, 10.

71 *In a letter before the tests*: "Evaluation of Small Caliber High Velocity Rifles—ArmaLite (AR-15)," United States Army Infantry Board, May 27, 1958, box 62, papers of Alain Enthoven, Lyndon Baines Johnson Library, Austin, TX.

73 *But testing results*: This episode is described in the Smithsonian interview. Smithsonian Institution Archives, Washington, DC, Oral History Program, Video Collection, Twentieth Century Small Arms, Collection Division 1: (Eugene Morrison) Stoner, Sessions 1, 2, 3, http://siarchives.si.edu/research/videohistory_catalog9532.html.

74 *The Infantry Board's confidential report*: "Evaluation of Small Caliber High Velocity Rifles—ArmaLite (AR-15)," United States Army Infantry Board, May 27, 1958, box 62, papers of Alain Enthoven, Lyndon Baines Johnson Library, Austin, TX.

75 *The mastermind of this campaign*: Stevens and Ezell, *Black Rifle*, 54.

75 *"the finest rifle in production"*: Scanlan [first name unknown], "Meet an Infantry Weapons Expert," *Army Times*, Sept. 30, 1961, pp. 59–60.

75 *That summer, Ordnance Corps officers announced*: "Supplemental Report of Project Nr. 2787, Evaluation of Small Caliber High Velocity Rifles—ArmaLite (AR-15)," United States Infantry Board, August 13, 1958, box 62, papers of Alain Enthoven, Lyndon Baines Johnson Library, Austin, TX.

76 *The rain test was*: See Hallock, "M16 Rifle Case Study."

77 *Before Stoner flew home*: Stevens and Ezell, *Black Rifle*, 76.

77 *In a dramatic moment*: "Report of Board to Review Rifle and Bayonet Problems," United States Continental Army Command, December 19, 1958, Colonel Richard R. Hallock Papers (MC 284), Columbus State University Archives, Columbus, GA.

78 *In their final secret report*: "Report of Board to Review Rifle and Bayonet Problems," United States Continental Army Command, December 19, 1958, Colonel Richard R. Hallock Papers (MC 284), Columbus State University Archives, Columbus, GA.

79 *"They'd already run their tests"*: Smithsonian Institution Archives, Washington, DC, Oral History Program, Video Collection, Twentieth Century Small Arms, Collection Division 1: (Eugene Morrison) Stoner, Sessions 1, 2, 3, http://siarchives.si.edu/research/videohistory_catalog9532.html.

79 *In the Arctic Test Board's report*: United States Continental Army Command, "Report of Project Nr 2787 (Arctic), Evaluation of Small Caliber High Velocity Rifles," April 17, 1959, record group 319, box 6, National Archives and Records Administration, College Park, MD.

79 *To make the guns*: Smithsonian Institution Archives, Washington, DC, Oral History Program, Video Collection, Twentieth Century Small Arms, Collection Division 1: (Eugene Morrison) Stoner, Sessions 1, 2, 3, http://siarchives.si.edu/research/videohistory_catalog9532.html.

79 *Even the final report*: Hallock, "M16 Rifle Case Study."

79 *With great bureaucratic flourish*: Stevens and Ezell, *Black Rifle*, 79.

80 *Several instances of scheming*: Author interviews with Susan Kleinpell.

80 *One deposition recounted an alleged*: Depositions from private collection of Susan Kleinpell.

80 *Thomas Patrick Mahoney was an engineer*: Author interviews with Susan Kleinpell.

81 *He had worked with Stoner*: Jean Stoner, transcript of unpublished interview by J. W. Gibbs, September 3, 2003; Eugene Stoner, deposition, private collection of Susan Kleinpell.

8. HUNTING BIG GAME

82 *Born on July 4, 1898*: *Current Biography*, 1951, 50; Kent A. Mitchell, "Richard S. Boutelle, Aviation Executive," *American Aviation Historical Society Journal*, Summer 1999, 82.

83 *The workforce swelled from two hundred*: *Industry and Agriculture* (Baltimore: Maryland Historical Society, War Records Division, Vol. I, 1950), 484–85.

83 *When his boss at Fairchild*: Kent A. Mitchell, "Richard S. Boutelle, Aviation Executive," *American Aviation Historical Society Journal*, Summer 1999, 84.

83 *The "Flying Boxcar," as it was called*: C-119s were used to resupply the besieged French outpost of Dien Bien Phu.

83 *Boutelle sided with Fairchild*: "Stockholders Taking Vote in Fairchild Fight," *The Washington Post*, July 7, 1949, 13; "Sherman Fairchild Wins Control of Aircraft Firm," *Chicago Tribune*, July 8, 1949, B7.

83 *By 1953, the company's sales*: J. S. Armstrong, "Net Earnings of Fairchild Set New Peak," *The Sun*, November 6, 1953, 30.

84 *As one aviation historian put it*: Mitchell, "Richard S. Boutelle, Aviation Executive," 87.

84 *Fairchild also signed an agreement*: The *F* did not stand for "Fokker"; it stood for "Friendship."

84 *In March 1953, Boutelle*: "Theft of MIG Strictly Private, Plotters Say," *Atlanta Constitution*, March 15, 1953, 20A.

84 *Boutelle's home was adorned*: Mitchell, "Richard S. Boutelle, Aviation Executive," 87–88.

84 *"We keep house in one"*: Eugene Jaderquist, "Armalite's AR-10: Is This the Next G.I. Rifle?," *Guns*, March 1957, 49.

85 *In Eisenhower's "New Look"*: Col. Mike Worden, *The Rise of the Fighter Generals: The Problem of Air Force Leadership, 1945–1982* (Maxwell Air Force Base, AL: Air University Press, 1998), 67, https://apps.dtic.mil/sti/pdfs/ADA338755.pdf.

85 *He directed five more such attacks*: For more information, see James M. Scott, *Black Snow: Curtis LeMay, the Firebombing of Tokyo, and the Road to the Atomic Bomb* (New York: Norton, 2022).

85 *The general, nicknamed by his men*: Fred Kaplan, *The Bomb: Presidents, Generals and the Secret History of Nuclear War* (New York: Simon and Schuster, 2020), 14.

85 *"I'll tell you what war"*: Richard Rhodes, *The Making of the Atomic Bomb* (New York: Simon and Schuster, 2012 edition), 586.

86 *"[T]o worry about the morality"*: Curtis E. LeMay with MacKinlay Kantor, *Mission with LeMay* (New York: Doubleday, 1965), 383.

86 *In 1954, Life wrote a glowing profile*: See Ernest Havemann, "Toughest Cop of the Western World," *Life*, June 14, 1954, 132–47.

87 *By the end of the decade*: George Rosen, "TV's Alltime Top Grossers," *Variety*, July 8, 1959, 1.

87 *LeMay recalled how he impressed*: LeMay with Kantor, *Mission with LeMay*, 489.

87 *In September 1954, Boutelle sent*: Boutelle-LeMay correspondence, Curtis E. LeMay Papers, 1918–1969, Library of Congress.

87 *Boutelle sent copies of Fairchild's*: Boutelle and Godfrey correspondence with LeMay, Curtis E. LeMay Papers, 1918–1969, Library of Congress.

87 *In 1955, LeMay wrote to Boutelle*: See Boutelle-LeMay correspondence, Curtis E. LeMay Papers, 1918–1969, Library of Congress.

88 *Boutelle also tapped Godfrey*: "Godfrey Guest at Fairchild; Has Fine Time," *The Daily Mail* (Hagerstown, MD), September 30, 1955, 1.

88 *The incessant bonding over hunting*: They hunted in what today is southern Chad. See James Shepley, "Helicopter Safari in Africa," *Life*, June 10, 1957.

88 *"In America, this system is carried"*: C. Wright Mills, *The Power Elite*, (New York: Oxford University Press, 1956), 74, 361.

89 *"I am sure if Joe Blow"*: Aircraft Production Costs and Profits. Hearings Before the Subcommittee for Special Investigations, Committee on Armed Services, House of Representa-

tives, Feb. 16 through March 22, 1956, 84th Cong., 2d Sess. (Washington, DC: U.S. Government Printing Office, 1956.

90 *As early as April 1956*: "Fairchild Engine Increases Outlays on Research Work," *The Wall Street Journal*, April 27, 1956, 6.

90 *"His explanation satisfied few"*: "Fairchild Engine Says First Quarter Net Fell Due to Research Costs," *The Wall Street Journal*, April 25, 1957, 18.

90 *Boutelle had married in 1935*: Richard Boutelle married Anna Luvera (Vera) Ward in 1935. See *Current Biography*, 1951.

90 *Sherman Fairchild stepped in*: "Boutelle Quits Posts," *The New York Times*, January 22, 1959, 48; "Carmichael Named Head of Fairchild," *The Washington Post*, December 19, 1958, D6.

90 *In November 1958, as his enterprises*: Walter Trohan, "Washington Scrapbook" column, *Chicago Tribune*, November 9, 1958, 1.

90 *Shortly before Christmas, Fairchild took*: "Boutelle Quits Posts," 48; "Carmichael Named Head of Fairchild," D6.

90 *"It wasn't Sherman's fault"*: Kent A. Mitchell, "Richard S. Boutelle, Aviation Executive," *American Aviation Historical Society Journal*, Summer 1999, 89.

90 *As early as September 1958*: *Hearings Before the Special Subcommittee on the M16 Rifle Program of the Committee on Armed Services, House of Representatives*, 90th Cong., 1st Sess. (May 15, 16, 31, June 21, July 25, 26, 27, August 8, 9, and 22, 1967), http://hdl .handle.net/2027/uiug.30112109164266. See Macdonald testimony.

91 *Macdonald drove*: Colonel Richard R. Hallock Papers (MC 284), Columbus State University Archives, Columbus, GA, series 3, box 54, https://archives.columbusstate .edu/findingaids/mc284.php.

91 *"The more I shot it, the better I liked it"*: *Hearings Before the Special Subcommittee on the M16 Rifle Program of the Committee on Armed Services, House of Representatives*, 90th Cong., 1st Sess. (May 15, 16, 31, June 21, July 25, 26, 27, August 8, 9, and 22, 1967), http://hdl.handle.net/2027/uiug.30112109164266, 4787.

91 *"The board would not give"*: *Hearings Before the Special Subcommittee on the M16 Rifle Program of the Committee on Armed Services, House of Representatives*, 90th Cong., 1st Sess. (May 15, 16, 31, June 21, July 25, 26, 27, August 8, 9, and 22, 1967), http://hdl .handle.net/2027/uiug.30112109164266, 4788.

91 *On January 7, 1959*: "How a Lone Inventor's Idea Took Fire," *Business Week*, July 6, 1968, Knight's Armament Co. private files, Fairchild clippings. See also *Hearings Before the Special Subcommittee on the M16 Rifle Program of the Committee on Armed Services, House of Representatives*, 90th Cong., 1st Sess. (May 15, 16, 31, June 21, July 25, 26, 27, August 8, 9, and 22, 1967), http://hdl.handle.net/2027/uiug.30112109164266, 4741.

91 *In March and April 1959*: Colonel Richard R. Hallock Papers (MC 284), Columbus State University Archives, Columbus, GA, series 33, file outline SAWS 2.

91 *The men held firing demonstrations*: In 2011, Morphy Auctions in Colorado auctioned a Colt AR-15 Model 1 test rifle, the sixth one ever made. It sold for $103,500. The auction house stated that various sources confirmed the rifle was the actual rifle Bob Macdonald had LeMay fire at Boutelle's farm. Macdonald also claimed to the rifle's owners that the weapon had been brought to Asia for demonstrations, to shoot coconuts, and, possibly, to shoot fleeing Communist prisoners in Vietnam. See https://www .morphyauctions.com/jamesdjulia/item/lot-1009-near-mythical-extraordinarily-rare -colt-ar-15-model-1-original-select-fire-test-rifle-known-as-the-coconut-rifle-42475.

92 *"The Asiatic people being small stature"*: Smithsonian Institution Archives, Washington, DC, Oral History Program, Video Collection, Twentieth Century Small Arms, Collection Division 1: (Eugene Morrison) Stoner, Sessions 1, 2, 3, http://siarchives.si .edu/research/videohistory_catalog9532.html.

92 *Macdonald cabled Colt to stop*: See Smithsonian Institution Archives, Washington, DC, Oral History Program, Video Collection, Twentieth Century Small Arms, Collection Division 1: (Eugene Morrison) Stoner, Sessions 1, 2, 3, http://siarchives.si.edu /research/videohistory_catalog9532.html.

92 *By the fall of 1959*: Hearings Before the Special Subcommittee on the M16 Rifle Program of the Committee on Armed Services, House of Representatives, 90th Cong., 1st Sess. (May 15, 16, 31, June 21, July 25, 26, 27, August 8, 9, and 22, 1967), http://hdl.handle .net/2027/uiug.30112109164266.

92 *A Colt brochure for the AR-15*: Colt Brochure, "Colt ARMALITE AR-15 for Today and Tomorrow," Records Relating to Comparisons Between the M14, AR15, and AK47 Rifles, record group 319, box 6, National Archives and Records Administration, College Park, MD.

93 *"It is not likely to be used"*: Associated Press, "Colt Announces New Auto-Rifle," *Bridgeport Post*, February 1, 1960, 10.

93 *In June of that year*: Ezell, "In Search for a Lightweight Rifle: The M14 and M16 Rifles," 313.

93 *"GOSH WE HOPE YOU CAN COME!"*: Boutelle-LeMay correspondence, Curtis E. LeMay Papers, 1918–1969, Library of Congress.

93 *"It was beautifully equipped from a shooting angle"*: Hearings Before the Special Subcommittee on the M-16 Rifle Program of the Committee on Armed Services, House of Representatives, 90th Cong., 1st Sess. (May 15, 16, 31, June 21, July 25, 26, 27, August 8, 9, and 22, 1967), http://hdl.handle.net/2027/uiug.30112109164266, 4800.

93 *LeMay was a party regular*: Hearings Before the Special Subcommittee on the M-16 Rifle Program of the Committee on Armed Services, House of Representatives, 90th Cong., 1st Sess. (May 15, 16, 31, June 21, July 25, 26, 27, August 8, 9, and 22, 1967), http:// hdl.handle.net/2027/uiug.30112109164266.

94 *After the party, Macdonald sent*: Colonel Richard R. Hallock Papers (MC 284), Columbus State University Archives, Columbus, GA, series 3, SAWS, box 54, folder 2: "The Role of Cooper-Macdonald in the M16, undated," https://archives.columbusstate.edu /findingaids/mc284.php.

94 *"We are working with the Army now"*: Boutelle-LeMay correspondence, Curtis E. LeMay Papers, 1918–1969, Library of Congress.

94 *Macdonald never heard about test results*: Hearings Before the Special Subcommittee on the M-16 Rifle Program of the Committee on Armed Services, House of Representatives, 90th Congress, 1st Sess. (May 15, 16, 31, June 21, July 25, 26, 27, August 8, 9, and 22, 1967), http://hdl.handle.net/2027/uiug.30112109164266.

94 *Boutelle died on January 15, 1962*: Obituary: "Richard S. Boutelle," *The Washington Post*, January 16, 1962, B4.

94 *He was buried in Arlington*: Mitchell Kent, "Richard S. Boutelle: Aviation Executive," *American Aviation Historical Society Journal*, 44 (March 1999): 90.

9. THE SPY WHO SAVED STONER'S RIFLE

95 *South Vietnamese army rangers*: Advanced Research Projects Agency, "Field Test Report, AR-15 Rifle," August 20, 1962.

96 *Godel disliked his stepfather*: Weinberger, *Imagineers of War*, 21.

97 *After school he worked for military intelligence*: Investigation of Governmental Organization for Space Activities, Hearings Before the United States Senate Committee on Aeronautical and Space Sciences, Subcommittee on Government Organization for Space Activities, 86th Congress, 1st Sess. (March 24, 26, April 14, 15, 22–24, 29, May 7, 1959).

97 *He was wounded twice in combat*: Investigation of Governmental Organization for Space

Activities, Hearings Before the United States Senate Committee on Aeronautical and Space Sciences, Subcommittee on Government Organization for Space Activities, 86th Cong., 1st Sess. (March 24, 26, April 14, 15, 22–24, 29, May 7, 1959); Jacobsen, *Pentagon's Brain*, 92; Weinberger, *Imagineers of War*, 21.

97 *In 1950, he was attached*: Investigation of Governmental Organization for Space Activities, Hearings Before the United States Senate Committee on Aeronautical and Space Sciences, Subcommittee on Government Organization for Space Activities, 86th Cong., 1st Sess. (March 24, 26, April 14, 15, 22–24, 29, May 7, 1959).

97 *That summer, Godel was part*: See Jacobsen, *Pentagon's Brain*, and Office of Joint History, Office of the Chairman of the Joint Chiefs of Staff, *The Joint Chiefs of Staff and the First Indochina War, 1945–1954* (Washington, DC: U.S. Government Printing Office, 2004). For bombing of hotel, see Ronald H. Spector, *Advice and Support: The Early Years, The U.S. Army in Vietnam* (Washington, DC: Center of Military History, United States Army, 1983), 111.

97 *Godel said decades later*: The North German Plain is the flat region in Middle Europe where NATO expected a Soviet invasion. See William Godel, interviewed by Huff, 1975, for a DARPA oral history of the agency, provided by Sharon Weinberger.

97 *Godel "earned a reputation"*: Weinberger, *Imagineers of War*, 25.

97 *He became known as an expert*: Richard Barber Associates Inc. for ARPA, "The Advanced Research Projects Agency, 1958–1974," December 1975, V-37.

97 *But he battled with other intelligence officials*: Weinberger, *Imagineers of War*, 26.

97 *He joined the Advanced Research Projects Agency*: In the 1970s, the agency renamed itself the Defense Advanced Research Projects Agency, or DARPA. It reverted to ARPA for a few years in the early 1990s, but today again is called DARPA.

98 *"Technically, it was all a stunt"*: Richard Barber Associates Inc. for ARPA, "The Advanced Research Projects Agency, 1958–1974," December 1975, III-23,III-24.

98 *Toward the end of the war*: In the 2003 documentary *The Fog of War*, which focused on McNamara's role in Vietnam, the former defense secretary talked about working for LeMay during the Japanese bombing. "LeMay said, if we'd lost the war, we'd all have been prosecuted as war criminals," McNamara said. "And I think he's right. He, and I'd say I, were behaving as war criminals." See https://www.npr.org/templates/story/story.php?storyId=106318407.

99 *He proposed that ARPA*: Godel's push for an office aligned with his view that one way to protect an operation from budget cuts in a large bureaucracy was to have property. "If you own real estate, they can't kill you," he said. See Richard Barber Associates Inc. for ARPA, "The Advanced Research Projects Agency, 1958–1974," December 1975, II-32.

99 *At a National Security Council meeting*: Richard Barber Associates Inc. for ARPA, "The Advanced Research Projects Agency, 1958–1974," December 1975, V-39.

99 *The ARPA effort in Saigon*: The RAND Corporation had a close relationship with AGILE, working to develop weapons systems and counterinsurgency strategies in Vietnam. See Mai Elliott, *RAND in Southeast Asia: A History of the Vietnam War Era* (Santa Monica, CA: RAND Corporation, 2010), document number CP-564-RC, https://www.rand.org/pubs/corporate_pubs/CP564.html.

99 *He showed up in South Vietnam*: Peter S. Diggins, "Godel Tells of Taking $18,000 to Asia and Starting Anti-Guerilla Center," *The Washington Post*, May 15, 1965. From CIA files.

99 *"Godel was very much an operator"*: William P. Bundy, Oral History Interview—JFK#2, March 6, 1972, John F. Kennedy Presidential Library, digital identifier: JFKOH-WPB-02.

100 *Godel became an important*: In court testimony later, a former Diệm official said Godel gave Diệm various gifts, including a rifle. It is not clear what rifle he gave to the president, but it likely was an AR-15.

100 *"The only way we lose is if the Americans come in here"*: See William Godel, inter-
     viewed by Huff, 1975, for a DARPA oral history of the agency, provided by Sharon
     Weinberger.

100 *"I know President Diệm"*: Miltob Berliner, "Testimony from Saigon," *Daily News*, May
     18, 1965. From CIA files. Diệm was convinced Americans would back a coup against
     him. He was right. In November 1963, South Vietnamese generals with knowledge
     and approval of the CIA overthrew Diệm, then assassinated him.

100 *AGILE, with main offices near the Saigon River*: "Advanced Research Projects Agency,
     Project AGILE Remote Area Conflict Research and Engineering, Semiannual Re-
     port," July 1–December 31, 1963, issued February 1, 1964 (Unclassified 1975),
     Remote Area Conflict Information Center, Battelle Memorial Institute, 35.

100 *Godel brought ten of the guns to Saigon in July 1961*: Richard Barber Associates Inc. for
     ARPA, "The Advanced Research Projects Agency, 1958–1974," December 1975, V-44.

100 *The staff held target tests*: See "Advanced Research Projects Agency, Project AGILE
     Remote Area Conflict Research and Engineering, Semiannual Report."

100 *"I neither know, nor give a damn, what the U.S. soldier needs"*: See William Godel, in-
     terviewed by Huff, 1975, for a DARPA oral history of the agency, provided by Sharon
     Weinberger.

100 *Godel pressed the Pentagon*: Dr. Robert Sproull, interview for the Executive Services
     Directorate, December 7, 2006, DARPA Case No. 13—1968.000043, Executive Ser-
     vices Directorate of the Office of the Secretary of Defense, https://www.esd.whs.mil
     /Portals/54/Documents/FOID/Reading%20Room/DARPA/15-F-0751_DARPA
     _Director_Robert_Sproull.pdf.

100 *But key military figures opposed the request*: Report of the M16 Rifle Review Panel,
     June 1, 1968, confidential, History of the M16 Weapon System, prepared by Office
     Director of Weapon Systems Analysis, Washington, DC, approved by General Ralph
     E. Haines Jr., vice chief of staff of the army, https://apps.dtic.mil/sti/pdfs/ADA953110
     .pdf, C-12.

100 *Frustrated U.S. officials in Vietnam sent their plea*: Confidential Field Test Report,
     AR-15 ArmaLite Rifle, Final Report, OSD/APRA Research and Development Field
     Unit—Vietnam, August 20, 1962, 3; Colonel Virgil Chilson to William Godel, De-
     cember 4, 1961, record group 319, National Archives and Records Administration,
     College Park, MD. Chilson wrote that the AR-15 was "considered functionally suit-
     able for large scale combat test" by units in ARVN.

101 *Macdonald handled the sale*: Colonel Richard R. Hallock Papers (MC 284), Co-
     lumbus State University Archives, Columbus, GA, series 3, box 46, https://archives
     .columbusstate.edu/findingaids/mc284.php.

101 *The first shipment arrived in Vietnam on January 27, 1962*: Research and Development
     Field Unit, Advanced Research Projects Agency, Report of Task No. 13A, Test of
     ArmaLite Rifle, AR-15, July 31, 1962, 3.

101 *Stoner heard that the tests were taking place*: Smithsonian Institution Archives, Wash-
     ington, DC, Oral History Program, Video Collection, Twentieth Century Small
     Arms, Collection Division 1: (Eugene Morrison) Stoner, Sessions 1, 2, 3, http://
     siarchives.si.edu/research/videohistory_catalog9532.html.

101 *On May 21, as the tests were under way*: J. P. Ruina, "Memorandum for the Chief of
     Research and Development, Department of the Army, Subject: Request for Informa-
     tion on AR-15 Rifle and M-2 Carbine," May 21, 1962, record group 319, National
     Archives and Records Administration, College Park, MD.

101 *U.S. advisors wrote to higher-ups*: Colonel Richard R. Hallock Papers (MC 284), Co-
     lumbus State University Archives, Columbus, GA, series 3, box 38, https://archives
     .columbusstate.edu/findingaids/mc284.php.

102 *Around this time, a key group*: Author interview with Alain Enthoven.

102 *Hitch, a slight man who had difficulty*: John Walsh, "Defense: McNamara's Comptroller Charles J. Hitch, Leaves Four Pioneering Years at DOD," *Science* 149, no. 3688 (September 3, 1965): 1074–76.

103 *On October 12 he sent a short memo*: Bill Mullen's Chronology of the M16, December 4, 1992, 20; Colonel Richard R. Hallock Papers (MC 284), Columbus State University Archives, Columbus, GA, series 3, box 54, https://archives.columbusstate.edu /findingaids/mc284.php; Robert S. McNamara, Memorandum for the Secretary of the Army, October 12, 1962, record group 319, National Archives and Records Administration, College Park, MD.

104 *President Kennedy reviewed the Hitch report*: Kenneth O'Donnell, special assistant to the president, Memorandum for Secretary McNamara, November 9, 1962, record group 319, National Archives and Records Administration, College Park, MD.

104 *McNamara responded to Kennedy*: Robert McNamara, Memorandum for the President, November 20, 1962, Records Relating to Comparisons between the M14, AR15, and AK47 Rifles, record group 319, box 3, National Archives and Records Administration, College Park, MD.

104 *"The army, some of them almost"*: Author interview with Alain Enthoven.

104 Newsweek *listed weapons and other devices*: "Canned Nucmom," *Newsweek*, November 5, 1962, 63.

105 *Curtis LeMay, who had been trying*: LeMay pressed hard at the Pentagon and in the Kennedy administration to get Stoner's rifles for the air force. The air force secured funding to purchase AR-15s beginning in 1961 and by FY1964 Defense appropriations, the branch sought thousands of the rifles. See *Department of Defense Appropriations for 1964. Hearings Before the Subcommittee on Appropriations, United States Senate, on H.R. 7179*, 88th Cong., 1st Sess. (April 24, 1963), 1235.

105 *LeMay "was absolutely adamant"*: Author interview with Alain Enthoven.

105 *In one account, LeMay*: Rottman, *The M16*, 10.

105 *Their efforts led to a handful of sales*: Colonel Richard R. Hallock Papers (MC 284), Columbus State University Archives, Columbus, GA, series 3, box 54, https://archives .columbusstate.edu/findingaids/mc284.php.

105 *On a visit to the Navy's SEAL Team Two*: Bill Mullen's Chronology of the M16, December 4, 1992, Colonel Richard R. Hallock Papers (MC 284), Columbus State University Archives, Columbus, GA, series 3, box 54, https://archives.columbusstate.edu /findingaids/mc284.php. See also Jakon Hays and Maureen Watts, "April 13, 1962 | JFK and SEAL Team 2 in Norfolk," *Virginian-Pilot*, April 13, 2016, https://www .pilotonline.com/history/article_7f62a61a-e36b-5ac0-bca0-5a71247a3756.html.

105 *Stoner credited McNamara and "the so-called Whiz Kid"*: Smithsonian Institution Archives, Washington, DC, "Oral History Program, Video Collection, Twentieth Century Small Arms, Collection Division 1: (Eugene Morrison) Stoner, Sessions 1, 2, 3, http://siarchives.si.edu/research/videohistory_catalog9532.html.

105 *The inventor was earning*: The company Stoner had helped start, ArmaLite, had been cut adrift by Fairchild and struggled on as a shadow of its former self. Only two original employees remained, George Sullivan, the patent attorney, and Charles Dorchester, his brother-in-law. The two peddled guns that looked similar to the AR-15, but their weapons lacked Stoner's technological advances, since those patents were owned by Colt. They had little success.

106 *In October 1962, the Army's General Paul Harkins*: Report of the Special Subcommittee on the M16 Rifle Program of the Committee of the Armed Forces, House of Representatives, Washington, DC: U.S. Government Printing Office, October 19, 1967, 5331.

106 *A later official ARPA history*: Richard Barber Associates Inc. for ARPA, "The Advanced

Research Projects Agency, 1958–1974," December 1975, p. V-44. The army officially designated the Colt version of the AR-15 as the M16 rifle on December 11, 1963.

106 *He found himself under federal investigation*: "We finally had to work out an agreement where he ceased to be an ARPA employee," Robert Sproull said in an interview. Dr. Robert Sproull, interview for the Executive Services Directorate, December 7, 2006, DARPA Case No. 13—1968.000043, Executive Services Directorate of the Office of the Secretary of Defense, https://www.esd.whs.mil/Portals/54/Documents/FOID /Reading%20Room/DARPA/15-F-0751_DARPA_Director_Robert_Sproull.pdf.

107 *He returned to Washington and lobbied*: "The Strange Case of William Godel," *Insider's Newsletter*, January 11, 1965. From Fairchild clippings, Knight's Armament Co. private collection.

107 *In December 1964, a federal grand jury*: Associated Press, "Ex-Pentagon Aides Deny Funds Theft," *The New York Times*, December 23, 1964, 25.

107 *His career long over*: See William Godel, interviewed by Huff, 1975, for a DARPA oral history of the agency, provided by Sharon Weinberger, 18.

10. "BRAVE SOLDIERS AND THE M16"

108 *The choppers came in low*: Drawn in part from Hal Moore, "After Action Report, IA DRANG Valley Operation, 1st Battalion, 7th Cavalry 14–16 November 1965," December 9, 1965.

109 *The Seventh Cavalry Regiment*: "Garryowen" is one word. It is a neighborhood in Limerick, Ireland.

109 *Before the men left Fort Benning*: Author interviews with Bob Edwards and Joe Marm.

110 *"The mission became quickly"*: Author interview with Tony Nadal.

110 *Stoner's gun was about to be put to the test*: They were not the first U.S. troops to carry the weapon into harm's way. A smaller army unit with M16s had been ambushed nearby on November 3, and special forces advisors had been carrying AR-15/M16 rifles in combat while on missions with South Vietnamese forces. Also, many U.S. troops sent to intervene in a civil war in the Dominican Republic in the summer of 1965 carried M16s. See Lawrence Yates, *Power Pack: U.S. Intervention in the Dominican Republic 1965–1966* (Fort Leavenworth, KS: Combat Studies Institute, 1988).

110 *The Americans were in such danger*: The battle of LZ X-Ray was the first time B-52 bombers were used to aid U.S. combat troops.

110 *Second Lieutenant Walter Joseph "Joe" Marm Jr.*: Author interview with Joe Marm.

111 *Both sides suffered heavy*: Hal Moore, "After Action Report, IA DRANG Valley Operation, 1st Battalion, 7th Cavalry 14–16 November 1965," December 9, 1965.

111 *Moore choked back tears*: Moore and Galloway, *We Were Soldiers Once*, 197–98.

111 *"Brave soldiers and the M16"*: William C. Westmoreland, *A Soldier Reports* (New York: Dell, 1980), 205; Edward Clinton Ezell, "The Search for a Lightweight Rifle: The M14 and M16 Rifles" (PhD thesis for Case Western Reserve University, June 1969), 350.

111 *On December 6, 1965*: Westmoreland, *A Soldier Reports*, 205; Ezell, "The Search for a Lightweight Rifle," 350.

111 *The next day, McNamara issued*: Hearings Before the Special Subcommittee on the M-16 Rifle Program of the Committee on Armed Services, House of Representatives, 90th Cong., 1st Sess. (May 15, 16, 31, June 21, July 25, 26, 27, August 8, 9, and 22, 1967), http://hdl.handle.net/2027/uiug.30112109164266, 5339.

111 *When the contract was finalized in June 1966*: Hearings Before the Special Subcommittee on the M-16 Rifle Program of the Committee on Armed Services, House of Representatives, 90th Cong., 1st Sess. (May 15, 16, 31, June 21, July 25, 26, 27, August 8, 9, and 22, 1967), http://hdl.handle.net/2027/uiug.30112109164266, 5341.

111 *They had flooded the Pentagon*: Colonel Richard R. Hallock Papers (MC 284), Columbus State University Archives, Columbus, GA, series 3, box 52, https://archives.columbusstate.edu/findingaids/mc284.php.

111 *A unit of the army's Chemical and Development Laboratories*: USACROL, "A Wound Ballistics Assessment of the M14, AR-15, and AK-47 Rifles," November 1962, U.S. Army Chemical and Development Laboratories, Edgewood Arsenal, MD, Biophysics Division of the Directorate of Medical Research, Lyndon Baines Johnson Presidential Library Archives, box 66.

112 *A top-secret inspector general's report*: See cover sheet and all of "Documents Relating to 'Small Caliber High Velocity Concept Versus a Larger Caliber Basic Infantry Weapons Systems for our Military Forces," October 1962–Summer 1963, Colonel Richard R. Hallock Papers (MC 284), Columbus State University Archives, Columbus, GA, series 3, box 52, https://archives.columbusstate.edu/findingaids/mc284.php.

112 *In one "FOR EYES ONLY"*: Memorandum for Mr. Vance, For Eyes Only, Colonel Richard R. Hallock Papers (MC 284), Columbus State University Archives, Columbus, GA, series 3, box 38, https://archives.columbusstate.edu/findingaids/mc284.php.

112 *M14 backers felt the fix was in*: Office of Deputy Chief of Staff for Military Operations, Headquarters, Department of the Army, Rifle Evaluation: A Study Made Under Monitorship, October 1962–January 1963, A Comparative Evaluation of U.S. Army Rifle 7.62mm, M14; ArmaLite Rifle caliber .223, AR-15; Soviet Assault Rifle AK-47, January 9, 1963, overseen by Colonel Arpad A. Kopcsak, Records Relating to Comparisons Between the M14, AR15, and AK47 Rifles, record group 319, box 3. See especially E8-E9, E13, E19. National Archives and Records Administration, College Park, MD.

112 *In an* American Rifleman *article*: Walter J. Howe and E. H. Harrison, "The First Colt AR-15 Rifle," *American Rifleman*, May 1962.

112 *The gun expert John Tompkins slammed*: John S. Tompkins, "The Army's Blunderbuss Bungle That Fattened Your Taxes," *True*, April 1963, 36–37.

113 *"The AR-15, used in South Vietnam"*: Frank F. Rathbun, "The Rifle in Transition," *Army*, August 1963, 19–25.

113 *At a 1963 Senate Appropriations*: See *Department of Defense Appropriations for 1964, Hearings Before the Subcommittee on Appropriations, United States Senate, on H.R. 7179*, 88th Cong., 1st Sess. (1963), 138–39. See also Ezell, "The Search for a Lightweight Rifle," 282.

113 *That abrupt announcement was the result*: The letter from Hallock to McGarr is undated, but the wording and sequence of previous correspondence indicate it was written in mid- to late 1963. Colonel Richard R. Hallock Papers (MC 284), Columbus State University Archives, Columbus, GA, series 1, box 3, https://archives.columbusstate.edu/findingaids/mc284.php.

113 *Enthoven was convinced the report*: Author interview with Alain Enthoven.

114 *Secret Service Special Agent George W. Hickey Jr.*: See https://www.nbcnews.com/news/us-news/accidental-assassin-jfk-theory-alleges-secret-service-agent-fumbled-gun-flna2D11634276; Peter Mucha, "Shooting Holes in Theory That a Secret Service Agent Killed President Kennedy," Philly.com, posted November 13, 2013, https://www.inquirer.com/philly/news/Shooting_holes_in_theory_that_a_Secret_Service_agent_killed_President_Kennedy.html.

114 *As the war Johnson inherited*: Associated Press, "GI's Renew Equipment Complaints," *Dallas Morning News*, March 7, 1965, Knight's Armament Co. private collection.

114 *American soldiers near Saigon*: Tom Tiede, "He Owes His Life to His Amazing Gun," Newspaper Enterprise Association, December 6, 1965, Knight's Armament Co. private collection.

114 *In the United States, army recruiters*: By 1965, recruiters were visiting state fairs and

other venues with the gun as a prop at their booths. See Kent Riffle, "Despite Scar, Sergeant Wants to Fight Cong Again," *Dallas Morning News*, October 17, 1965, Knight's Armament Co. private collection.

114 *A Dallas Morning News reporter*: Thomas E. Turner, "The M16 Rifle: A Crackerjack Weapon," *Dallas Morning News*, January 2, 1966, Knight's Armament Co. private collection, AR-15 clippings.

114 *"We are shipping everything we can possibly get"*: Hearings on Military Posture and H.R. 13456 . . . Before the Committee on Armed Services, House of Representatives, 89th Cong., 2d Sess. Hearings before the full committee and subcommittee (January–May 1966), 7571. Hearing on May 2, 1966.

114 *Some top Pentagon officials*: The military started requesting more M16s and Congress obliged. These gun sales saved Colt, which had suffered from years of tepid handgun sales, troubled management, changing ownership, and labor fights. Early AR-15s made by Colt had some quality problems, in part because the company had never made automatic rifles before. According to a document produced by the Cooper-Macdonald executive Bill Mullen, it got so bad that Macdonald demanded a meeting in New York with Colt officials to get them to improve quality control. Anxious to keep the contracts, Colt agreed. In October 1964, Colt was so eager for the military to buy its guns it offered to give the army its patent rights to the gun for free, if the Pentagon agreed to buy 540,000 guns from the company over a period of years. The army declined, unsure whether they would ever need that many M16s. In less than two years, it was clear that the Defense Department had passed up a good deal. See Bill Mullen's Chronology of the M15, December 4, 1992, Colonel Richard R. Hallock Papers (MC 284), Columbus State University Archives, Columbus, GA, series 3, box 54, https://archives.columbusstate.edu/findingaids/mc284.php.

114 *"Looks like our rifle situation"*: Report of the M16 Rifle Review Panel, June 1, 1968, confidential, History of the M16 Weapon System, prepared by Office Director of Weapon Systems Analysis, Washington, DC, approved by General Ralph E. Haines Jr., vice chief of staff of the army, appendix 9: "Audit Trail of Chief of Staff, Army Actions and Decisions Concerning the M16 Rifle." See entry for August 11, 1966, 9–11, record group 319, boxes 1–2, National Archives and Records Administration, College Park, MD.

115 *Colt, the sole company with rights*: After struggling financially for years, Colt finally had landed a big government contract thanks to the AR-15. A longtime Colt staffer who worked during this period, R. B. Myers, later wrote to a congressman that the company "probably would have been out of business today if the military contract had not been obtained." He credited the company's military connections, including its aggressive Washington lobbyists and Colt board member and former general Matthew Ridgway. "While presumably no law technically was violated, the ethics of the situation made me wonder about the actual integrity of the Defense Department," Myers wrote. See R. B. Myers to Representative Richard Ichord, July 9, 1968, Richard H. Ichord Papers, Center for Missouri Studies, the State Historical Society of Missouri, box 153—Letters, Clippings, Statements—M-16 Rifle—General Correspondence, 1967–1968.

115 *"They had really no production"*: Smithsonian Institution Archives, Washington, DC, Oral History Program, Video Collection, Twentieth Century Small Arms, Collection Division 1: (Eugene Morrison) Stoner, Sessions 1, 2, 3, http://siarchives.si.edu/research/videohistory_catalog9532.html.

115 *By the middle of 1965*: "Colt Industries Profit Spurted in 2nd Quarter," *The Wall Street Journal*, July 21, 1965, and Colt Industries' full-page advertisement in the July 20, 1965, edition of *The Wall Street Journal*, Knight's Armament Co. private collection, clippings about the AR-15.

115 *The company ran a large ad*: Colt advertisement, "The best equipped fighting men . . . ," *The Wall Street Journal*, April 6, 1966, Knight's Armament Co. private collection.

115 *The alterations were made*: Poole, *Adapting to Flexible Response*, 139–40; see also Yount information in Stevens and Ezell, *Black Rifle*, 1994.

115 *"Many of the M16's problems"*: J. David McFarland, ed., *AR-15, M16 Assault Rifle Handbook* (Cornville, AZ: Firepower Publications, 1985), 5.

115 *The army, for example, insisted*: Bullets fired from an M16 at that temperature lost accuracy. To solve the problem, a member of the air force suggested adding more spin to the bullets by tightening the twist inside the barrel. The change solved the cold temperature problem, but no one studied what that change would do to the gun's firing ability in moderate or warm temperatures. Poole, *Adapting to Flexible Response*, 139–40.

117 *Olin Mathieson's propellant, which had the formal name*: Robert E. Jordan III, "A Factual Appraisal of the M16 Rifle Program," December 12, 1967, record group 319, box 6, National Archives and Records Administration, College Park, MD; *Hearings Before the Special Subcommittee on the M-16 Rifle Program of the Committee on Armed Services, House of Representatives*, 90th Cong., 1st Sess. (May 15, 16, 31, June 21, July 25, 26, 27, August 8, 9, and 22, 1967), http://hdl.handle.net/2027/uiug.30112109164266, 4755–57; U.S. Army, "Statement on Propellants for 5.56mm Ammunition," July 27, 1967, Richard H. Ichord Papers, Center for Missouri Studies, the State Historical Society of Missouri, box 153—Letters, Clippings, Statements, M-16 Rifle—Special Subcommittee, 1967–1968.

117 *But the arsenal concluded*: Frankford Arsenal, "Tenth Memo Report on AR-15 Rifle/Ammunition System, Investigation of Alternate Propellants for Use in 5.56mm M193 Ball Ammunition," May 15, 1964, Colonel Richard R. Hallock Papers (MC 284), Columbus State University Archives, Columbus, GA, series 3, box 40, https://archives.columbusstate.edu/findingaids/mc284.php.

117 *Some tests showed*: Ezell, "The Search for a Lightweight Rifle," 334; Richard H. Ichord Papers, Center for Missouri Studies, the State Historical Society of Missouri, box 155—Letters, Statements, Committee Correspondence, "M-16 Rifle—Statements, Releases and Report, 1967–1972," "Statement on TCC Minutes of 24–25 March 1964, Discussion of Cyclic-Rate Requirements," August 7, 1967.

117 *Some critics of this switch*: Jordan III, A Factual Appraisal of the M16 Rifle Program.

118 *The committee classified the army version*: Poole, *Adapting to Flexible Response*, 138–39.

118 *Most troops simply called*: Poole, *Adapting to Flexible Response*, 138–39; and Rottman, *The M16*, 17.

118 *"Timing is everything and Murphy's Law prevails"*: Smithsonian Institution Archives, Washington, DC, Oral History Program, Video Collection, Twentieth Century Small Arms, Collection Division 1: (Eugene Morrison) Stoner, Sessions 1, 2, 3, http://siarchives.si.edu/research/videohistory_catalog9532.html. Murphy's Law posits that "anything that can go wrong will go wrong."

118 *Johnson was known as a commander*: See Sorley, *Honorable Warrior*.

118 *"The Army means people"*: Sorley, *Honorable Warrior*, 187.

118 *Colt had warned the army*: Office Memorandum, Office Chief of Staff Army. To: General Johnson. From: Lieutenant General Chesarek, Acting Director WSA, Subject: Propellant Selection for the M16 Rifle Testing, Oct. 12 1967. Record group 319, boxes 3 and 4, National Archives and Records Administration, College Park, MD.

119 *The historians Blake Stevens and Edward Ezell*: Stevens and Ezell. *Black Rifle*, 199; Poole, *Adapting to Flexible Response*, 139–40.

119 *One report from the Small Arms Weapons Systems*: The study compared the M16, the M14, another rifle developed by Stoner called the Stoner 63, ArmaLite's AR-18, and

the SPIW. Hallock designed a complex study that used computers to help simulate real combat situations for combat squads testing the rifles at Fort Ord, north of San Francisco. The idea was to simulate real war, with computers to trigger puffs of smoke and quick fires to re-create what it would be like in various firefight scenarios, including attacking, defending, and stumbling onto an enemy squad. The computers programmed the shots, and sensors tracked how the squads responded, even tracking whether return fire was close enough to drive enemy soldiers to duck. Author interview with Pierre Sprey.

119 *Pierre Sprey, one of McNamara's "Whiz Kids"*: Author interview with Pierre Sprey.

119 *"The army, out of pique, was ruining this great rifle"*: Author interview with Alain Enthoven.

119 *Wilbur Payne, a military operations expert*: Wilbur D. Payne, Chief, Office of Operations Research. Memorandum for: Director, Coordination and Analysis. Attn: Lieutenant Colonel Jank. Subject: Review of Some Technical Decisions in the M16 Weapon System, Nov. 26, 1965. Secret, confidential. Record group 319, National Archives and Records Administration, College Park, MD.

119 *The U.S. military already had shipped*: Robert E. Jordan III, A Factual Appraisal of the M16 Rifle Program, 19.

11. "TRAGEDY AND BETRAYAL"

120 *Fred Monahan was startled awake*: This battle scene was drawn from an author interview with Frederick Monahan.

122 *By morning, thirty-one of the Marines*: More than 150 Marines were killed in the Hill Fights operations.

124 *By August 1966, all army combat units*: Hearings Before the Special Subcommittee on the M-16 Rifle Program of the Committee on Armed Services, House of Representatives, 90th Cong., 1st Sess. (May 15, 16, 31, June 21, July 25, 26, 27, August 8, 9, and 22, 1967), http://hdl.handle.net/2027/uiug.30112109164266, 4434.

124 *"We now have a very substantial requirement for the M16s"*: Hearings Before the Special Subcommittee on the M-16 Rifle Program of the Committee on Armed Services, House of Representatives, 90th Cong., 1st Sess. (May 15, 16, 31, June 21, July 25, 26, 27, August 8, 9, and 22, 1967), http://hdl.handle.net/2027/uiug.30112109164266, 4470.

124 *Democratic representative L. Mendel Rivers*: Report on the Activities of the House Committee on Armed Services, 90th Cong., 1st and 2d Sess. (1967–1968), 11214–17.

124 *Abbie Hoffman recounted in* Yippie Manifesto: See Jerry Rubin, "Yippie Manifesto, Free Pamphlet Series #1" (Vineyard Haven, MA: Evergreen Review, 1969), https://ia902909.us.archive.org/26/items/Rubin-1969-the-yippie-manifesto.pdf/rubin-1969-the-yippie-manifesto.pdf%27.pdf.

125 *Ichord was convinced that North Vietnam*: See Ichord, *Behind Every Bush*.

125 *"I must say that before I went"*: Richard H. Ichord Papers, Center for Missouri Studies, the State Historical Society of Missouri, box 151, Information File/Frankford Arsenal Tests.

125 *Rivers tasked the subcommittee*: Hearings Before the Special Subcommittee on the M-16 Rifle Program of the Committee on Armed Services, House of Representatives, 90th Cong., 1st Sess. (May 15, 16, 31, June 21, July 25, 26, 27, August 8, 9, and 22, 1967), http://hdl.handle.net/2027/uiug.30112109164266, 4431.

125 *On May 12, 1967, the three congressmen*: Hearings Before the Special Subcommittee on the M-16 Rifle Program of the Committee on Armed Services, House of Representatives, 90th Cong., 1st Sess. (May 15, 16, 31, June 21, July 25, 26, 27, August 8, 9, and 22, 1967), http://hdl.handle.net/2027/uiug.30112109164266, 4451.

125 *Dick Ichord, a sullen-looking forty-year-old*: Hearings Before the Special Subcommittee on the M-16 Rifle Program of the Committee on Armed Services, House of Representatives, 90th Cong., 1st Sess. (May 15, 16, 31, June 21, July 25, 26, 27, August 8, 9, and 22, 1967), http://hdl.handle.net/2027/uiug.30112109164266, 4431.

125 *The first witness was Robert A. Brooks*: Hearings Before the Special Subcommittee on the M-16 Rifle Program of the Committee on Armed Services, House of Representatives, 90th Cong., 1st Sess. (May 15, 16, 31, June 21, July 25, 26, 27, August 8, 9, and 22, 1967), http://hdl.handle.net/2027/uiug.30112109164266, 4436.

125 *But Ichord was troubled by the story*: Hearings Before the Special Subcommittee on the M-16 Rifle Program of the Committee on Armed Services, House of Representatives, 90th Cong., 1st Sess. (May 15, 16, 31, June 21, July 25, 26, 27, August 8, 9, and 22, 1967), http://hdl.handle.net/2027/uiug.30112109164266, 4437, 4441–42.

126 *Ichord's comments referred to a news report*: Hearings Before the Special Subcommittee on the M-16 Rifle Program of the Committee on Armed Services, House of Representatives, 90th Cong., 1st Sess. (May 15, 16, 31, June 21, July 25, 26, 27, August 8, 9, and 22, 1967), http://hdl.handle.net/2027/uiug.30112109164266, 4488; Richard H. Ichord Papers, Center for Missouri Studies, the State Historical Society of Missouri, box 153—Letters, Clippings, Statements, M16 Rifle Subcommittee, 1967–1968. Transcript: "6:30 Huntley-Brinkley, NBC-TV, The M16" and "Joint Informational Services Office, 4th Marine Division Headquarters Nucleus and 5th Marine Division, FMF, and Marine Corps Base, Camp Pendleton, California. Transcript of Tape-Recorded Information Received by Telephone from HQMC (DIVINFO) 18 May 1967, Bill Worden [*sic*, actually Bill Wordham]—NBC News—Saigon." From Bill Worden's [Wordham] May 18 report: "This complication, it seems, has been going on for a year now but it did not come to light until a recent battle near the demilitarized zone. The rifle jammed so often in battle, that marines complained openly and repeatedly to newsmen. The official response was that the men were not keeping their rifles clean enough. But, in the midst of the controversy the rifle's manufacturer told industry and revealed that it was modifying the weapon."

126 *The subcommittee's counsel, Earl Morgan*: Hearings Before the Special Subcommittee on the M-16 Rifle Program of the Committee on Armed Services, House of Representatives, 90th Cong., 1st Sess. (May 15, 16, 31, June 21, July 25, 26, 27, August 8, 9, and 22, 1967), http://hdl.handle.net/2027/uiug.30112109164266, 4452.

126 *The next morning, Major General William John Van Ryzin*: Hearings Before the Special Subcommittee on the M-16 Rifle Program of the Committee on Armed Services, House of Representatives, 90th Cong., 1st Sess. (May 15, 16, 31, June 21, July 25, 26, 27, August 8, 9, and 22, 1967), http://hdl.handle.net/2027/uiug.30112109164266, 4501–4502.

126 *A Colt report*: HEL staff. "U.S. Army Technical Note 5–66: Small Arms Use in Viet Nam, preliminary results," August 1966, Aberdeen Proving Ground, MD: Human Engineering Laboratories, Richard H. Ichord Papers, Center for Missouri Studies, the State Historical Society of Missouri, box 153—Letters, Clippings, Statements, M-16 Rifle—Committee Investigations—Rifle Information File, 1967–1968.

127 *By October of that year*: Record group 319, boxes 3 and 4, National Archives and Records Administration, College Park, MD.

127 *A "Secret Hold Close" memorandum*: Office Memorandum, Office Chief of Staff, Army, To General Johnson from Director FPAO, Nov. 30, 1966. Record group 319, box 7, National Archives and Records Administration, College Park, MD.

127 *An internal Pentagon report*: "Memorandum for the Undersecretary of the Army; Subject: Modification to the M16," February 20, 1967. From Wilbur B. Payne, chief of operations research. Record group 319, boxes 3 and 4, National Archives and Records Administration, College Park, MD.

127 *"Protect me, you big strong guy!"*: Department of the Army, *M16A1 Rifle*.

127 *"I got it from a guy who didn't keep it clean"*: Analysis of the Findings and Recommendations of the M16 Committee. Record group 319, box 6, National Archives and Records Administration, College Park, MD.

127 *Marine Al White was first given an M16*: Quotes and recollections from author interview with Al White.

129 *Dick Backus, another grunt who fought*: Author interview with Dick Backus.

129 *In a battle nearby around the same time*: Colonel Rod Andrew Jr., *Hill Fights: The First Battle of Khe Sanh, 1967*, Marines in the Vietnam War Commemorative Series (Washington, DC: U.S. Government Printing Office, 2017), 41; Murphy, *Hill Fights*, 220–21.

129 *The photos were published*: Catherine Leroy, "Up Hill 881 with the Marines," *Life*, May 19, 1967, 40–45.

129 *One Marine captain at the Hill Fights*: Marine Lieutenant General L. F. Chapman Jr. to Representative James Howard, May 23, 1967, Richard H. Ichord Papers, Center for Missouri Studies, the State Historical Society of Missouri, box 153—Letters, Clippings, Statements, M-16 Rifle—Committee Investigations—Rifle Information File, 1967–1968. See also Maj. Gary L. Telfer, Lieutenant Colonel Lane Rogers, and V. Keith Fleming Jr., *U.S. Marines in Vietnam: Fighting the North Vietnamese, 1967* (Washington, DC: History and Museums Division, Headquarters, U.S. Marine Corps, 1984), 45.

130 *Marine Corps Commandant General Wallace Greene*: Ezell, "The Search for a Lightweight Rifle," 357; George C. Wilson, "Marine Chief Defends M-16 Rifle," *The Washington Post*, May 27, 1967, A6.

130 *On May 10, during the Hill Fights*: Richard H. Ichord Papers, Center for Missouri Studies, the State Historical Society of Missouri, box 153—Letters, Clippings, Statements, folder: M16 Rifle—Special Subcommittee, 1967–1968. Information for Members of Congress: "Army Adopts M16A1 As Additional Standard Rifle."

130 *Hallock retired, believing he would be made a scapegoat*: In May 1967, Hallock retired and took a job at the Bureau of the Budget. A document, presented by Alain Enthoven and written by Hallock, stated that in May 1967 Colonel Hallock retired from the army "at his own request, and accepted a position in the Bureau of the Budget, not connected with Defense work, to broaden his career." Hallock delayed working for Budget until October 1967 and consulted for Enthoven. Hallock never again returned to the army. After years of bureaucratic backstabbing in the Pentagon, "he had just had enough of it," said the military historian Dan Crosswell. "He knew he had made enough enemies higher up that he was going to get stabbed for this one." See Memorandum for record, Subject: Colonel Hallock's role in the M16 events and the rifle file, January 16, 1969, Colonel Richard R. Hallock Papers (MC 284), Columbus State University Archives, Columbus, GA, series 3, box 54, https://archives.columbusstate.edu/findingaids/mc284.php.

130 *Large portions of the letter*: *Congressional Record, Proceedings and Debates of the 90th Congress, First Session, Vol. 113—Part 10, May 15, 1967 to May 24, 1967*, Washington, DC: U.S. Government Printing Office, 1967. Rep. James J. Howard's remarks, 13381–82; Rep. James J. Howard to Robert S. McNamara, May 22, 1967. "I am sure you are well aware that the American people are quite concerned about the controversy surrounding the M16 and trust you will favor me with an early reply to my questions," Howard wrote to McNamara. The letter included a handwritten letter from a Marine, with the name redacted. See also a photocopy of the article "Marine Hits Faulty Rifle," *Asbury Evening Press*, Saturday, May 20, 1967, Richard H. Ichord Papers, Center for Missouri Studies, the State Historical Society of Missouri, box 153—Letters, Clippings, Statements, M-16 Rifle—Committee Investigations—Rifle Information File, 1967–1968.

12. "BORDERS ON CRIMINAL NEGLIGENCE"

132 *In one letter, a young Marine*: Memo to Earl Morgan from David R. Heinly, May 31, 1967, Richard H. Ichord Papers, Center for Missouri Studies, the State Historical Society of Missouri, box 153—M16 Rifle—Committee Investigations—Rifle Information File, 1967–1968.

133 *A grunt from Montana wrote*: Rep. James F. Battin to Rep. L. Mendel Rivers, May 22, 1967, Richard H. Ichord Papers, Center for Missouri Studies, the State Historical Society of Missouri, box 153—M16 Rifle—Committee Investigations—Rifle Information File, 1967–1968.

133 *A man from Southern California*: David Black to Richard Ichord, May 19, 1967, citing a May 10, 1967, letter, Richard H. Ichord Papers, Center for Missouri Studies, the State Historical Society of Missouri, box 152—Letters and more, Letters since July 1st, 1967–1968.

133 *On June 1, 1967, the three congressmen*: "Group Goes to Saigon in M-16 Inquiry," *The Washington Post*, June 2, 1967, A5. "Sen. Peter H. Dominick, R-Colo, said he fired the weapon in Vietnam and it jammed on him, twice. Ichord still defended the weapon."

133 *They questioned as many fighting men as possible*: "Visit by Rep. Ichord (D-Mo)," Richard H. Ichord Papers, Center for Missouri Studies, the State Historical Society of Missouri, box 153—Letters, Clippings, Statements, M16 Rifle—Committee Investigations—Rifle Information File, 1967–68.

133 *While most of the soldiers reported*: Hearings Before the Special Subcommittee on the M-16 Rifle Program of the Committee on Armed Services, House of Representatives, 90th Cong., 1st Sess. (May 15, 16, 31, June 21, July 25, 26, 27, August 8, 9, and 22, 1967), http://hdl.handle.net/2027/uiug.30112109164266, 5347–49.

133 *One soldier wrote to his sister*: Hearings Before the Special Subcommittee on the M-16 Rifle Program of the Committee on Armed Services, House of Representatives, 90th Cong., 1st Sess. (May 15, 16, 31, June 21, July 25, 26, 27, August 8, 9, and 22, 1967), http://hdl.handle.net/2027/uiug.30112109164266, 4580.

134 *Another woman wrote that she and her brother*: Hearings Before the Special Subcommittee on the M-16 Rifle Program of the Committee on Armed Services, House of Representatives, 90th Cong., 1st Sess. (May 15, 16, 31, June 21, July 25, 26, 27, August 8, 9, and 22, 1967), http://hdl.handle.net/2027/uiug.30112109164266, 4582–83.

134 *"It stands as a shocking example"*: Hearings Before the Special Subcommittee on the M16 Rifle Program of the Committee on Armed Services, House of Representatives, 90th Cong., 1st Sess. (May 15, 16, 31, June 21, July 25, 26, 27, August 8, 9, and 22, 1967), http://hdl.handle.net/2027/uiug.30112109164266, 4584.

134 *When the subcommittee convened*: Drawn from Hearings Before the Special Subcommittee on the M16 Rifle Program of the Committee on Armed Services, House of Representatives, 90th Cong., 1st Sess. (May 15, 16, 31, June 21, July 25, 26, 27, August 8, 9, and 22, 1967), http://hdl.handle.net/2027/uiug.30112109164266, 4544–45, 4547–48, 455,1 and 4559. Wilbur Payne testified that the barrel twist had no impact except at very low temperatures.

135 *"Well, we both now don't feel so good"*: Hearings Before the Special Subcommittee on the M16 Rifle Program of the Committee on Armed Services, House of Representatives, 90th Cong., 1st Sess. (May 15, 16, 31, June 21, July 25, 26, 27, August 8, 9, and 22, 1967), http://hdl.handle.net/2027/uiug.30112109164266, 4544–45, 4547–48, 4551, and 4559.

136 *"can cause, you name it, problems"*: Hearings Before the Special Subcommittee on the M16 Rifle Program of the Committee on Armed Services, House of Representatives, 90th Cong., 1st Sess. (May 15, 16, 31, June 21, July 25, 26, 27, August 8, 9, and 22, 1967), http://hdl.handle.net/2027/uiug.30112109164266, 4560.

136 *ICHORD: "Now, the thing that concerns me"*: Hearings Before the Special Subcommittee on

the M16 Rifle Program of the Committee on Armed Services, House of Representatives, 90th Cong., 1st Sess. (May 15, 16, 31, June 21, July 25, 26, 27, August 8, 9, and 22, 1967), http://hdl.handle.net/2027/uiug.30112109164266, 4550–63.

137 *"the magnitude of the problems"*: Smithsonian Institution Archives, Washington, DC, Oral History Program, Video Collection, Twentieth Century Small Arms, Collection Division 1: (Eugene Morrison) Stoner, Sessions 1, 2, 3, http://siarchives.si.edu /research/videohistory_catalog9532.html.

137 *Robert G. Bihun, a mechanical engineer*: Author interview with Robert C. Bihun.

137 *After Stoner's testimony, Ichord asked him*: Smithsonian Institution Archives, Washington, DC, Oral History Program, Video Collection, Twentieth Century Small Arms, Collection Division 1: (Eugene Morrison) Stoner, Sessions 1, 2, 3, http://siarchives.si .edu/research/videohistory_catalog9532.html.

137 *One asked him about inventors' moral responsibility*: William Serrin, "Ex-Marine's Invention Could Make GI an Arsenal," *Detroit Free Press*, October 16, 1967, 3.

138 *Ichord grilled Colt engineers*: *Hearings Before the Special Subcommittee on the M16 Rifle Program of the Committee on Armed Services, House of Representatives*, 90th Cong., 1st Sess. (May 15, 16, 31, June 21, July 25, 26, 27, August 8, 9, and 22, 1967), http://hdl .handle.net/2027/uiug.30112109164266, 4584–86, 4595.

138 *"You are not saying the improper maintenance"*: *Hearings Before the Special Subcommittee on the M16 Rifle Program of the Committee on Armed Services, House of Representatives*, 90th Cong., 1st Sess. (May 15, 16, 31, June 21, July 25, 26, 27, August 8, 9, and 22, 1967), http://hdl.handle.net/2027/uiug.30112109164266, 4592–93.

138 *Howard Yount, who eventually rose*: *Hearings Before the Special Subcommittee on the M16 Rifle Program of the Committee on Armed Services, House of Representatives,* 90th Cong., 1st Sess. (May 15, 16, 31, June 21, July 25, 26, 27, August 8, 9, and 22, 1967), http://hdl.handle.net/2027/uiug.30112109164266, 4611–15.

139 *"We conducted tests, not as extensive"*: Anderson submitted a written statement to the committee: "From the vantage point of retrospect, it has sometimes been suggested that the peculiar behavior of ball propellant in the M16 system should have been predicted. There was, in fact, no evidence in 1963 that the cyclic rate of the M16 would be greatly affected by the choice of propellant, provided that port pressures were controlled as they had been in the M14 and other 7.62-millimeter systems which accommodate both ball and extruded propellants. Furthermore, there was no evidence at that time to indicate that an increase of 10 percent to 15 percent in cyclic rate of fire would cause a serious increase in frequency of malfunctions. Had the Army anticipated these developments, it is most unlikely that the course chosen in January 1964 would have been the same." *Hearings Before the Special Subcommittee on the M16 Rifle Program of the Committee on Armed Services, House of Representatives*, 90th Cong., 1st Sess. (May 15, 16, 31, June 21, July 25, 26, 27, August 8, 9, and 22, 1967), http://hdl .handle.net/2027/uiug.30112109164266, 4998–99, 5000.

139 *"We are asking the Army"*: *Hearings Before the Special Subcommittee on the M16 Rifle Program of the Committee on Armed Services, House of Representatives*, 90th Cong., 1st Sess. (May 15, 16, 31, June 21, July 25, 26, 27, August 8, 9, and 22, 1967), http://hdl .handle.net/2027/uiug.30112109164266, 5000–5001.

140 *The army asserted that any problems with the M16*: "Statement on Propellants fr 5.56mm Ammunition," August 7, 1967, Richard H. Ichord Papers, Center for Missouri Studies, box 153—Letters, Clippings, Statements, M16 Special Subcommittee, 1967–1968.

140 *The army's public relations effort*: Representative Clarence Long, a Maryland Democrat, read a letter on the floor of the House in June from an unnamed officer fighting in Vietnam, declaring the M16 "is both worthless and dangerous as a soldier's primary

shoulder weapon." The officer claimed the Kalashnikov was vastly superior. "This might redden some important faces, but much more important to most of us is that it will save some lives," the letter read. Grunts had lost faith in "Mattie Mattel's Machine Gun," a wounded Marine wrote from his hospital bed in Da Nang, "I don't know why they ask generals what a private can answer better and much more truthful."

140 *The letter that received the most publicity*: First Lieutenant Michael P. Chervenak, executive officer, H Company, Second Battalion, Third Marines, to Rep. Richard Ichord, July 27, 1967, Richard H. Ichord Papers, Center for Missouri Studies, the State Historical Society of Missouri, box 154—Letters, Statements, Committee Correspondence, M16 Rifle—General and Constituent Correspondence, 1967–1972.

140 *Ichord released his committee's final report*: Hearings Before the Special Subcommittee on the M16 Rifle Program of the Committee on Armed Services, House of Representatives, 90th Cong., 1st Sess. (May 15, 16, 31, June 21, July 25, 26, 27, August 8, 9, and 22, 1967), http://hdl.handle.net/2027/uiug.30112109164266, 5368–72.

140 *It blasted the Pentagon*: "Report of the M16 Rifle Review Panel, June 1, 1968," confidential, History of the M16 Weapon System, prepared by Office Director of Weapon Systems Analysis, Washington, approved by General Ralph E. Haines Jr., vice chief of staff of the army, https://apps.dtic.mil/sti/pdfs/ADA953110.pdf. See also *Report of the Special Subcommittee on the M16 Rifle Program of the Committee on Armed Services, House of Representatives*, 90th Cong., 1st Sess. (October 19, 1967), http://hdl.handle.net/2027/umn.31951p00793094y, 5368–72.

140 *"The manner in which the Army rifle program"*: Report of the Special Subcommittee on the M16 Rifle Program of the Committee of the Armed Forces, House of Representatives, 90th Cong., 1st Sess. (October 19, 1967), http://hdl.handle.net/2027/umn.31951p00793094y, 5371.

141 *"borders on criminal negligence"*: Report of the Special Subcommittee on the M16 Rifle Program of the Committee of the Armed Forces, House of Representatives, 90th Cong., 1st Sess. (October 19, 1967), http://hdl.handle.net/2027/umn.31951p00793094y, 5354, 5368–72.

142 *"The committee decided that they identified"*: Smithsonian Institution Archives, Washington, DC, Oral History Program, Video Collection, Twentieth Century Small Arms, Collection Division 1: (Eugene Morrison) Stoner, Sessions 1, 2, 3, http://siarchives.si.edu/research/videohistory_catalog9532.html.

142 *Earl Morgan, the committee's counsel*: Fallows, National Defense, 90–91.

142 *A reporter called Stoner*: "Warned on Changes, Gun Designer Says," Detroit News, October 19, 1967, 18.

142 *"Here's Your M16, and This"*: "Here's Your M16, and This Is Your Backup Weapon When It Jams," Kansas City Times, November 20, 1967, Richard H. Ichord Papers, Center for Missouri Studies, the State Historical Society of Missouri, box 153—Letters, Clippings, Statements—Clippings and Releases.

142 *"If the New Left were to set out"*: Editorial, "The M16 Report," The Washington Post, October 20, 1967, A20.

143 *Edward Ezell, then a university instructor*: Edward Ezell, "The M16 Rifle: Our 'Least Reliable Weapon'?" Raleigh News & Observer, October 1, 1967, sec. 3, p. 4.

143 *In November, Westmoreland returned*: ABC Television Network, ABC Scope: The Vietnam War, Part 106, "The M16: What Went Wrong?," January 6, 1968.

143 *"[T]he M16 rifle is clearly the best available rifle"*: Robert S. McNamara, "Memorandum for the Secretary of the Army, Subject: Evaluation and Survey of the M16 Rifle," October 18, 1967, record group 319, boxes 3 and 4, National Archives and Records Administration, College Park, MD.

143 *Johnson, then approaching retirement*: Stevens and Ezell, Black Rifle, 265.

143 *A memorandum marked "For Official Use Only"*: Office Memorandum, Office Chief of Staff Army. To: General Johnson, Lieutenant General Chesarek. From: Acting Director, WSA. Subject: The M16A1 Rifle—Response to Ichord Report, October 26, 1967. Record group 319, boxes 3 and 4, National Archives and Records Administration, College Park, MD.

143 *Another confidential memo about the switch*: Office Memorandum, Office Chief of Staff Army. To: General Johnson. From: Lieutenant General Chesarek, Acting Director, WSA. Subject: Propellant Selection for the M16 Rifle Testing, October 12, 1967. Record group 319, boxes 3 and 4, National Archives and Records Administration, College Park, MD.

144 *Olin Mathieson, the maker of ball powder*: Stevens and Ezell, *Black Rifle*, 269.

144 *A top Colt executive and Ito visited the Pentagon*: M16 Rifle Panel report, appendix 9, Audit Trail of Army Actions on M16.

144 *"The sub-committee also concluded"*: Colt's Inc. Annual Report 1967, including George Strichman letter to shareholders, March 20, 1968, record group 319, box 7, National Archives and Records Administration, College Park, MD.

144 *This statement angered Johnson*: The Army General Harold K. Johnson letter to George Strichman, May 11, 1968, record group 319, box 7, National Archives and Records Administration, College Park, MD.

144 *Ridgway wrote to Westmoreland*: General M. B. Ridgway, personal, to General Westmoreland, April 10, 1968. General Harold K. Johnson, army chief of staff, to General M.B. Ridgway, U.S.A.-Ret., exact date mailed unclear but approved for mailing by Johnson on May 20, 1968, record group 319, box 7, National Archives and Records Administration, College Park, MD.

145 *ABC Television broadcast an episode*: ABC Television Network, *ABC Scope: The Vietnam War*, Part 106, "The M16: What Went Wrong?," January 6, 1968.

145 *A worried President Johnson*: Westmoreland knew Johnson was losing trust in him and was suspicious of Mayborn. Frank W. Mayborn, interview by Ted Gittinger, November 11, 1983, in Temple, Texas, for Lyndon B. Johnson Library Oral Histories [NAID 24617781]. See http://discoverlbj.org/exhibits/show/loh/oh. Westmoreland recounted meeting Mayborn in his own memoir, and it is also mentioned in Lewis Sorley's *Westmoreland: The General Who Lost Vietnam*, 134–35.

145 *Around the same time, an army survey team*: The survey team visited Vietnam from January 24 to February 5, 1968. See "Report of the M16 Rifle Review Panel, June 1, 1968," Confidential, History of the M16 Weapon System, prepared by Office Director of Weapon Systems Analysis, Washington, approved by General Ralph E. Haines Jr., vice chief of staff of the army. See Appendix 7, "Surveys in Vietnam," National Archives and Records Administration, College Park, MD.

145 *"Mistakes were made and errors in judgment"*: John S. Foster Jr., director of Defense Research and Engineering, to Rep. Mendel Rivers, February 15, 1968, Richard H. Ichord Papers, Center for Missouri Studies, the State Historical Society of Missouri, box 154—Letters, Statements, Committee Correspondence, M16 Rifle—Statements, Releases and Reports, 1967–1972. See also "The M16 Rifle: The Role of Cooper-Macdonald," 32–33, Colonel Richard R. Hallock Papers (MC 284), Columbus State University Archives, Columbus, GA, series 3, box 54, https://archives.columbusstate.edu/findingaids/mc284.php.

146 *In another letter, the army tepidly*: Major General Howard Penney to Rep. Richard H. Ichord, October 4, 1967, Richard H. Ichord Papers, Center for Missouri Studies, the State Historical Society of Missouri, box 153—Letters, Clippings, Statements, M16 Rifle—Committee Investigations—Rifle Information File, 1967–1968.

146 *On June 1, 1968, Johnson's review panel*: "Report of the M16 Rifle Review Panel, June

1, 1968," Confidential, History of the M16 Weapon System, prepared by Office Director of Weapon Systems Analysis, Washington, approved by General Ralph E. Haines Jr., vice chief of staff of the army, https://apps.dtic.mil/sti/pdfs/ADA953110.pdf, D-42, E-1, E-7, E-9, E-10, E-11. For same report, see Appendix 4, "Ammunition," 4–70, record group 319, boxes 1–2, National Archives and Records Administration, College Park, MD.

146 *Many in the army had expected*: Sorley, *Honorable Warrior*, 297.

146 *Johnson left his post in early July*: Sorley, *Honorable Warrior*, 291.

147 *Godel was in prison; Hallock had "retired"*: Hallock wouldn't talk about how he was treated by the army in later years, said his close friend and business partner Pierre Sprey. "Old-school army guys never talk about how bad they got screwed," Sprey said. "He would have called it whining." Author interview with Pierre Sprey, September 4, 2020.

147 *The Pentagon supplied tens of thousands*: Ward Just, "Rifle Output Stepped Up for Saigon Troops: 315,000 Now in Army," *The Washington Post*, March 31, 1968, A18.

147 *Stoner's guns were in the hands of the conquering Communists*: In the 1980s, most of the military automatic rifles captured from FMLN insurgents by the government were U.S.-made M16s. A researcher traced the serial numbers of about three thousand captured guns and found about a third were U.S. military weapons from Vietnam. How exactly they got into the hands of Central American rebels is unclear. See Chivers, *The Gun*, 363. In 2021, tens of thousands of M16s and M4s fell into the hands of the Taliban in Afghanistan when the U.S.-backed regime there collapsed.

148 *"How many Marines and soldiers died"*: Author interview with Robert Earl Bliss.

13. THE SPORTER

151 *In February 1836, the inventor Sam Colt*: Jim Rasenberger, *Revolver: Sam Colt and the Six-Shooter That Changed America* (New York: Scribner, 2020; Kindle edition), 109.

151 *At first, the tradition-bound military*: Richard A. Dillio, "Samuel Colt's Peacemaker: The Advertising That Scared the West," *History of Media Technology*, December 9, 2017, 23.

153 *Colt reached out to influential gun writers*: R. A. Steindler, "The .223 Becomes a Civilian: First Shooting Tests of Colt's Two New Sporting Rifles—In .223 Caliber," *Guns*, December 1964, 20–21, 64.

153 *In an early brochure, the company*: Colt 1964 catalog entry for the "Colt AR-15 Sporter Semi-Automatic Rifle."

153 *They also saw little use*: In an effort to drum up interest, Colt promoted a *Life* magazine photo shoot of 1962 Miss America Maria Fletcher, standing in a heavy coat and in high heels, firing the weapon at a firing range. See https://www.thefirearmblog.com/blog/2015/06/07/blast-from-the-past-miss-america-shooting-a-cutting-edge-rifle/.

153 *Colt produced only about 2,400*: See http://www.alternatewars.com/Politics/Firearms/Count/AR15_Production.htm.

154 *In contrast, Americans owned more*: "Firearms & Violence in American Life," a staff report submitted to the National Commission on the Causes & Prevention of Violence (Washington, DC: U.S. Government Printing Office, 1969), xi.

154 *"Today we begin to disarm"*: Lyndon B. Johnson, Remarks Upon Signing the Gun Control Act of 1968. Online at Gerhard Peters and John T. Woolley's website The American Presidency Project, https://www.presidency.ucsb.edu/node/237026.

154 *The NRA's opposition succeeded in trimming*: The National Firearms Act of 1934, which regulated and heavily taxed machine guns, was upheld by the Supreme Court in the

late 1930s. A push by Roosevelt in 1935 to register all firearms in the country failed to pass Congress. See "Firearms & Violence in American Life," 99–100.

155 *What became known as the My Lai massacre*: See Henry Kamm, "Vietnamese Say G.I.'s Slew 567 in Town: Vietnamese Assert G.I.'s Killed 567 Unarmed Civilians," *The New York Times*, November 17, 1969, 1; Douglas Robinson, "Army Clears Hutto in Deaths at Mylai: He Is 2d G.I. Found Not Guilty," *The New York Times*, January 15, 1971, 1. See also U.S. Department of the Army (1970, March 14), Report of the Department of the Army of the Preliminary Investigations into the My Lai Incident: Volume I, http://www.loc.gov/rr/frd/Military_Law/pdf/RDAR-Vol-I.pdf, 7–8.

155 *The 1968 movie* The Green Berets: The gun also appeared in other films around this time, including the 1967 movie *The President's Analyst*. James Coburn uses the rifle to shoot sinister telephone company henchmen.

156 *The philosophers Bertrand Russell and Jean-Paul Sartre*: Fredrik Logevall, "Russell Tribunal and the Swedish-American Conflict over Vietnam," *Diplomatic History* 17, no. 3 (Summer 1993): 421–45, https://www.jstor.org/stable/24912244. See also Martin L. Fackler, "Wound Ballistics Research of the Past Twenty Years: A Giant Step Backwards," Division of Military Trauma Research, Letterman Army Institute of Research, Presidio of San Francisco, CA, January 1990.

156 *"Then I heard an M16 on full automatic"*: Herr, *Dispatches*, 23.

157 *Popular films linked Vietnam vets*: During the filming of the movie in Canada's British Columbia in 1981, at least fourteen select-fire M16s and eleven Colt AR-15 semiautomatics as well as some other weapons were stolen from a locked truck near where the movie was being shot. The truck was supposed to be double-locked and guarded, but the weapons disappeared and investigators found no sign of forced entry. About fifty M16 replicas were untouched. The crime remains unsolved. See Aljean Harmetz, "News of Hollywood; M-G-M to Finish Natalie Wood Film," *The New York Times*, January 27, 1982, C20.

157 *"Nothing! You just don't turn it off!"*: Later movies, such as *Platoon* (1986) and Stanley Kubrick's *Full Metal Jacket* (1987), reinforced the notion that Vietnam had turned young American men into savages. M16s, emblems of American destructive technology, were prominent in both films. At the close of *Full Metal Jacket*, which was cowritten by Herr, Marines march through a destroyed city holding their M16s and singing the theme to *The Mickey Mouse Club*.

157 *"He hated the attention"*: Author interview with Herb Roder.

158 *Bihun said it stood*: Author interview with Robert Bihun.

158 *The FBI considered it to be*: See monograph "Minutemen: Extremist Guerrilla Warfare Group," Federal Bureau of Investigation, April 1965, 48.

158 *Romero, a movie usher*: Romero was ordered to never own a firearm again. Four years later, in June 1968, firefighters were called to apartments in Sherman Oaks to put out a fire after explosions shook the building. In the apartment where the explosions occurred, firefighters and police found guns, parts of machine guns, and dynamite. The man renting the apartment was Romero. Romero said in an interview that the material was not dynamite, but leftover gunpowder from the failed store. From Paul Coates, "Everybody Is an Enemy? Now Just a Minute, Men!" *Los Angeles Times*, June 19, 1968, 38; "Arsenal Uncovered in Fire; Man Surrenders," *Los Angeles Times*, June 15, 1968, 11. Also interview by authors with Robert Romero.

159 *California's attorney general linked Romero*: See California Attorney General Thomas C. Lynch's report, "Paramilitary Organizations in California," April 12, 1965, and "Arsenal Uncovered in Fire; Man Surrenders," *Los Angeles Times*, June 15, 1968, 11.

159 *Decades later, Romero denied*: Author interview with Robert Romero.

159 *A cartoon in a December 1969 edition*: Cartoon: "One Gun in the Hands of a Guerrilla

Is the Seed of a Revolution," *The Black Panther*, Black Community News Service, December 6, 1969, last page, unnumbered.

159 *The gun was "seen in our communities"*: "Organizing Self Defense Groups," *The Black Panther*, April 6, 1970, 15.

160 *In 1973, American Indian Movement (AIM) activists*: John Kifner, "Wounded Knee Is a Tiny Armed Camp: Wounded Knee Is a Tiny Camp Of . . ." *The New York Times*, March 3, 1973, 61; Laurie Johnston, "Indian Puts Onus for Losses on U.S.; Damage at Wounded Knee Laid to Fed," *The New York Times*, May 11, 1973, 78; Bryce Nelson, "Tension Between Indians, Whites Builds on Plains: Mood of Violence . . ." *Los Angeles Times*, October 28, 1974, A1.

160 *On June 26, 1975, a shootout*: "FBI Agents Remembered," *Congressional Record* 141, no. 105, June 26, 1995, S9028–30.

160 *The agents, who had handguns*: See FBI's RESMURS (Reservation Murders) posting on the Peltier case, https://www.fbi.gov/history/famous-cases/resmurs-case -reservation-murders#:~:text=On%20June%2026%2C%201975%2C%20FBI,south west%20corner%20of%20South%20Dakota.&text=Unknown%20to%20Agents%20 Williams%20and,was%20present%20on%20Pine%20Ridge.

160 *In a letter responding to a request*: Correspondence to authors from Peltier.

160 *Around this time, the gun*: By the late 1970 and early 1980s, "the ArmaLite" had become a cultural emblem in the United Kingdom for the violence in Northern Ireland. In the 1978 song "ArmaLite Rifle," the British punk band Gang of Four sang, "ArmaLite rifle, police and IRA / ArmaLite rifle, use it every day / Breaks down easy, fits into a pram / A child can carry it, do it no harm." In the 1981 song "Invisible Sun," Police frontman Sting sang, "I don't want to spend the rest of my life / Looking at the barrel of an ArmaLite."

161 *A 1980 report by the Anti-Defamation League*: Glenn Frankel, "Guerrilla-Style Training of KKK Alleged in 7 States," *The Washington Post*, October 24, 1980, A29.

161 *The first mass shooting of U.S. civilians with an AR-15*: Staff, "State's Worst Mass Murder in KF 25 Years Ago," *Herald and News*, July 23, 2002, https://www.heraldandnews .com/state-s-worst-mass-murder-in-kf-years-ago/article_47caaa64-e90d-5bd5-ab4e -5427e93598d2.html.

161 *"It was somebody just sitting"*: Associated Press, "Oregon Rifleman Opens Fire on Nightclub Patrons—6 Slain," *San Francisco Examiner*, July 24, 1977, 25.

161 *One of those killed*: Staff, "State's Worst Mass Murder in KF 25 Years Ago," *Herald & News*, July 23, 2002, https://www.heraldandnews.com/state-s-worst-mass-murder-in -kf-years-ago/article_47caaa64-e90d-5bd5-ab4e-5427e93598d2.html.

162 *In June 1980, a forty-five-year-old*: "Gunman Kills 5 At Texas Church and Shoots Self," *The New York Times*, June 23, 1980, A14.

162 *Two years later, in Luzerne County*: William Robbins, "Gunman Kills 13 in a Pennsylvania Rampage," *The New York Times*, September 26, 1982, A1; "Banks' T-Shirt: 'Kill Them All,'" *Philadelphia Daily News*, June 7, 1983, 8; "Children Who Survived Massacre Say They Saw Man Kill Relatives," *The New York Times*, June 8, 1983, A19. Banks was sentenced to death but a judge later determined he was incompetent and could not be executed.

162 *Banks had stood on a bed*: Author interview with Robert Gillespie.

163 *"Ordinarily an AR-15 semiautomatic"*: "Man with 3 Guns Seized; Reportedly Threatened Shultz," *Los Angeles Times*, November 4, 1987, C13; Sari Horwitz and Michael York, "Armed Mass. Man Charged in D.C. with Threatening Shultz: Suspect Faces Weapons Charge in D.C.," *The Washington Post*, November 4, 1987, B1.

164 *"Many of the people purchasing the AR-15"*: J. David McFarland, ed., *AR-15, M16 Assault Rifle Handbook* (Cornville, AZ: Firepower Publications, 1985), 6.

164 *The term had become accepted*: Harold E. Johnson, an army intelligence analyst, defined such weapons in an annual book on international small arms published by the Defense Intelligence Agency. "Assault Rifles are short, compact, selective-fire weapons that fire a cartridge intermediate in power between submachine gun and rifle cartridges," Johnson wrote. "Assault rifles have mild recoil characteristics and, because of this, are capable of delivering effective full-automatic fire at ranges of up to 300 meters."

164 *"The idea of calling semi-automatic"*: Joe Tartaro, "The Great Assault Weapons Hoax," *University of Dayton Law Review* 20, no. 2 (Winter 1995): 619–40.

165 *"Back then you'd open up"*: Author interview with Randy Luth.

14. BIG GUNS COME IN

166 *Kirkton Moore stood at the glass counter*: Events recounted and quotes from Kirkton Moore in this chapter are drawn from an extensive author interview with Moore in prison.

169 *He pushed for years*: Gates, *Chief: My Life in the LAPD*, 295.

170 *Pratt planted one foot*: Based on author interview with Bob Green.

170 *The day after the shooting, Gates pounded the table*: George Stein, "Officer Slain Responding to Drive-By Gang Shooting," *Los Angeles Times*, September 5, 1988, https://www.latimes.com/archives/la-xpm-1988–09–05-mn-991-story.html.

171 *"I decided it was time to try to halt this nonsense"*: Gates, *Chief: My Life in the LAPD*, 296.

171 *"For police officers in Detroit"*: Author interview with Robert Scully.

171 *About two thousand people attended*: Ashley Dunn, "Cop Tears: Some Are of Joy . . . and Others Are for a Fallen Brother," *Los Angeles Times*, September 10, 1988, https://www.latimes.com/archives/la-xpm-1988–09–10-me-1603-story.html.

171 *On Sunday, October 23*: "'Most Wanted' to reenact cop killing," UPI, October 22, 1988, https://www.upi.com/Archives/1988/10/22/Most-Wanted-to-reenact-cop-killing/1956593496000.

172 *He was convicted of first-degree murder*: He is serving a life sentence in the California state prison system. We visited him at California State Prison, Los Angeles County, located in the high desert in Lancaster, east of Los Angeles. Moore said that guns like the AR-15 should be banned. "When you get an AR, you get it for one reason: to kill a lot of people; that's what they're made for," he said. "I would abolish all military-grade weapons. Pay people and then make it illegal."

15. BUSH BAN

173 *"emphasis on helping local law enforcement"*: George H. W. Bush, "Congressman Bush's July 1968 newsletter," Thomas Collamore Files, Bush Vice Presidential Records, George Bush Presidential Library, College Station, TX.

173 "DUKAKIS WANTS TO BAN GUNS IN AMERICA": Advertisement, National Rifle Association, 1988, Emily Mead Files, White House Office of Policy Development, Bush Presidential Records, George Bush Presidential Library, College Station, TX.

174 *"Do we need a plan"*: Judy Keen and Paul Feist, "Step by Step with Killer; Are Our Kids Safe While at School?" *USA Today*, January 18, 1989, 1A.

175 *Before Stockton, the leading gun-control group*: Author interview with Bernie Horn.

175 *Federal and state lawmakers*: "Statement of Senator Howard, Senate Judiciary Subcommittee on the Constitution," February 10, 1989, Emily Mead Files, White House Office of Policy Development, Bush Presidential Records, George Bush Presidential Library.

175 *When Art Agnos, a California state assemblyman*: Author interview with Art Agnos.

176 *LaPierre was often seen fumbling*: Assessment drawn from an interview with Richard Feldman.

177 *Soon after Bush's inauguration*: David Hoffman, "Bush Being Pressed on Gun Issue; Debate Grows Over Assault Weapons," *The Washington Post*, February 16, 1989, https://www.washingtonpost.com/archive/politics/1989/02/16/bush-being-pressed-on -gun-issue/92b7d3dc-70a5-4d1c-b3fa-f7fd0a385d83.

177 *"They should be, absolutely"*: "First Lady Says Law Should Ban Assault Weapons," Associated Press, February 4, 1989.

177 *Chief Gates, Bush's close ally*: Bush greatly admired the Los Angeles chief. In March 1991, when the media and the public lambasted Gates about a video recording of his officers beating Rodney King, an unarmed black motorist, the president came to Gates's defense, calling him "an all-American hero."

177 *He told a Senate committee*: Senate Judiciary Subcommittee on the Constitution, "Hearing on Restricting Assault Weapons," February 10, 1989, https://www.c-span .org/video/?6184-1/restricting-assault-weapons.

178 *"BEFORE WE LEAVE ON OVERSEAS TRIP"*: George H. W. Bush, Memo from POTUS to John Sununu, RE: AK47's, February 19, 1989, Bush Presidential Records, George Bush Presidential Library, College Station, TX.

178 *"The dynamics of the gun control debate"*: Emily Mead, Memorandum for President Bush RE: "Assault Weapons" and Public Policy, March 5, 1989, Emily Mead Files, White House Office of Policy Development, Bush Presidential Records, George Bush Presidential Library, College Station, TX.

178 *On March 13, the California State Assembly*: Statement by William Bennett, Director, Office of National Drug Control Policy, Betsy Anderson Files, White House Office of Policy Development, Bush Presidential Records, George Bush Presidential Library, College Station, TX.

178 *the Bureau of Alcohol*: The Bureau of Alcohol, Tobacco, and Firearms later changed its name to the Bureau of Alcohol, Tobacco, Firearms, and Explosives. To avoid confusion, we refer to the bureau primarily by its acronym, ATF.

179 *The company had sold 279,000*: Letter from Edward Ezell to John Dingell, March 27, 1989, John Sununu Files, White House Office of Chief of Staff, Bush Presidential Records, George Bush Presidential Library, College Station, TX.

179 *Colt's public position was that*: "Colt Firearms Taking a Bum Rap," *American Rifleman*, May 1989, 8.

179 *In the April issue*: *American Rifleman*, April 1989.

179 *Former Arizona senator Barry Goldwater*: Davidson, *Under Fire*, 209.

180 *"I said, 'Dennis, you're somebody' "*: Author interview with Dennis DeConcini.

180 *In a memo entitled "Assault Weapons"*: Memo RE: "Assault Weapons," April 18, 1989, John Sununu Files, White House Office of Chief of Staff, Bush Presidential Records, George Bush Presidential Library, College Station, TX.

181 *Ruger sent a letter to Congress*: Sturm, Ruger & Company, "Facts to Remember When Considering 'Semi-Automatic' Firearms Legislation," John Sununu Files, White House Office of Chief of Staff, Bush Presidential Records, George Bush Presidential Library, College Station, TX.

181 *In May, at a memorial*: Joan Biskupic, "Critics on Both Sides Take Aim at Bush Anti-Crime Plan," Congressional Quarterly Weekly Report, May 20, 1989; Thomas Ferraro, "'We're Going to Take Back the Streets'; Bush's Anti-Crime Plan," UPI, May 15, 1989; "The Comprehensive Violent Crime Control Act of 1989" fact sheet, June 22, 1989, Nelson Lund files, White House Counsel's Office, Bush Presidential Records, George Bush Presidential Library, College Station, TX.

182　*"They were willing to talk"*: Author interview with John Sununu.

182　*"When you first came out"*: Letter from Wayne E. Cummings to POTUS, April 23, 1989, White House Office of Records Management, Bush Presidential Records, George Bush Presidential Library, College Station, TX.

182　*"ultimately ensured that President Bush"*: Sarah Brady and Merrill McLoughlin, *A Good Fight* (New York: PublicAffairs, 2002), 132.

16. THREE SENATORS

184　*"conscience of the Senate"*: Patricia Sullivan, "Ohio's Metzenbaum Was 'Conscience of Senate' for 19 Years," *Seattle Times*, March 16, 2008, https://www.seattletimes.com/seattle-news/obituaries/ohios-metzenbaum-was-conscience-of-senate-for-19-years.

185　*But the broad prohibition*: *Congressional Record*, Senate, May 22, 1990, 11643.

187　*In the wreckage*: U.S. Department of Justice, "Report to the Deputy Attorney General on the Events at Waco, Texas, February 28 to April 19, 1993," October 9, 1993, 309.

187　*"The tragic situation in Waco, Texas"*: *Congressional Record*, Senate, March 23, 1993, 6097.

187　*When George Bush wanted to ban*: Author interviews with Brad Buckles.

187　*The features included an attachment*: Bureau of Alcohol, Tobacco, and Firearms, "Report and Recommendation of the ATF Working Group on the Importability of Certain Semiautomatic Rifles," July 6, 1989.

188　*Bernie Horn, the Handgun Control Inc. attorney*: Author interviews with Bernie Horn and Mike Lenett. They devised separate definitions for prohibited pistols and shotguns.

189　*"I was wasting my time"*: Elizabeth Schwinn, "Feinstein Outguns Opposition to Win Assault-Gun Ban," *Oregonian*, May 8, 1994, via Factiva.

190　*Metzenbaum grumbled and said he could stomach*: Based on author interviews with Adam Eisgrau and Mike Lenett.

190　*In the three years leading up to 1993*: The sales figure comes from our analysis of ATF data. See Rachel Gottlieb, "Lieberman Helped Colt's Quietly Touted Anti-Crime Measures, Sought Exemption for Sporter, Senators Worked to Protect Gun," *Hartford Courant*, November 17, 1993, A1.

191　*"With so much in common"*: Editorial, "The Guns of Clinton," *The Wall Street Journal*, January 10, 1994, 6.

191　*"It was agreed that certain weapons"*: Jeff Brazil and Steve Berry, "Crackdown on Assault Weapons Has Missed Mark: California and the federal government restricted military-style guns several years ago. But they remain widely available because of loopholes, politics and industry ingenuity," *Los Angeles Times*, August 24, 1997, A-1.

192　*On the evening of November 9, 1993*: Senate session, November 9, 1993, C-SPAN, https://www.c-span.org/video/?52188–1/senate-session.

192　*Larry Craig, the senator representing Idaho*: Senate session, November 9, 1993, C-SPAN, https://www.c-span.org/video/?52188–1/senate-session.

193　*Ten Democrats and thirty-nine Republicans*: *Congressional Record* 139, part 19 (November 9, 1993), 103rd Cong., 1st Sess., https://www.congress.gov/bound-congressional-record/1993/11/09/daily-digest.

17. THE END OF COMPROMISE

194　*The highest-ranking Democrat in the House*: According to author interviews with Patrick Griffin, David Bonior, and Heather Foley, this meeting occurred in the spring prior to the May 5 vote on the ban legislation. In his memoir, President Clinton referenced a similar meeting that occurred later in the year.

194 *"Don't push the assault-weapon ban"*: Author interview with Patrick Griffin.

194 *"Another Sportsman for Foley"*: Janet Hook, "Foley Caught Between His Party and His Constituency on Gun Control," *Congressional Quarterly Weekly Report*, May 11, 1991, via Factiva.

195 *"There were dozens of Democrats"*: Biggs and Foley, *Honor in the House*, 234.

195 *Sitting in a chair near the fireplace*: Author interview with Patrick Griffin.

195 *"He was a bubba"*: Author interview with Bruce Reed.

196 *"A-K, as in AK-47, S-A, as in semiautomatic"*: Eric Alterman, "Grace Under Fire," *Rolling Stone*, June 1, 1995, https://www.rollingstone.com/music/music-news/grace-under -fire-63326.

196 *Foley and Jack Brooks*: Biggs and Foley, *Honor in the House*, 233.

196 *The ban would give him a chance*: Memorandum for Mack McClarty from Rahm Emanuel, Bruce Reed, Ron Klain, Jonathan Prince, RE: Assault Weapons Ban, April 20, 1994, Jonathan Prince, Speechwriting, Clinton Presidential Records, William J. Clinton Presidential Library, Little Rock, AR.

197 *On April 25, the White House*: "Assault Weapons Legislation," C-SPAN, April 25, 1994, https://www.c-span.org/video/?56345–1/assault-weapons-legislation.

197 *with about four hundred thousand*: Bureau of Alcohol, Tobacco, and Firearms. "Assault Weapons Profile," April 1994. Jose Cerda, Domestic Policy Council, Clinton Presidential Records, William J. Clinton Presidential Library, Little Rock, Arkansas.

197 *Early in the morning of May 5*: Author interview with Bob Walker.

198 *The ban narrowly passed*: In the waning minutes of the vote, neither side knew how it would play out. The last vote on the ban, after electronic voting had ended, came from the Democrat Douglas Applegate, a representative from northeast Ohio who had been known as an NRA supporter. He walked slowly down the aisle to pick up either a red card, which meant no, or a green card, which meant yes. To the dismay of the ban's opponents, he picked up a green card. "His Republican friends, and others opposed to the bill on the Democratic side, were shouting, 'no, no, the red card,'" Foley recalled. "He shrugged them off." Applegate's decision had little to do with his own views on guns or pressure from the White House. He nursed a recent grudge against the NRA. Applegate was retiring, but the gun group had refused to endorse his handpicked successor because Applegate voted for the Brady Bill. See Biggs and Foley, *Honor in the House*, 233.

198 *Letters flooded Congress and magazines*: Michael C. Clinard, "Term Paper Help," *Gun World*, July 1994, 82.

198 *Dave McCann, a forty-one-year-old*: Author interview with McCann.

199 *"There are people who think"*: See Michael Oreskes, "Foley's Law," *The New York Times Magazine*, November 11, 1990.

199 *When Foley heard the news*: Author interview with David Bonior.

200 *"Our members intend to play"*: Letter from Tanya Metaksa to George (Buddy) Darden, June 2, 1994, Legislative, Bills, George W. (Buddy) Darden Papers, Russell Library, University of Georgia, Athens, GA.

200 *Donors poured $6.8 million*: Federal Election Commission, "PAC Activity in 1994 Elections Remains at 1992 Levels," March 31, 1995.

201 *The NRA focused on twenty-four races*: Alan C. Miller, "Conservative Interest Groups Savor Wins: Politics: NRA targeted 24 races and has 19 trophies to show for its campaigning. Rich returns are also cited by Christian, anti-abortion activists," *Los Angeles Times*, November 10, 1994, https://www.latimes.com/archives/la-xpm-1994–11–10 -mn-61038-story.html.

201 *"The Speaker has stopped listening"*: John K. Wiley, "Speaker Takes Aim at Gun Lobby Ads Against Him," Associated Press, October 19, 1994.

201 *The NRA endorsed Foley's*: Kenton Bird, "Tom Foley's Last Campaign: Why Eastern

Washington Voters Ousted the Speaker of the House," *Pacific Northwest Quarterly* 95, no. 1 (Winter 2003/2004): 12.

201 *"The NRA was an unforgiving master"*: Bill Clinton, *My Life* (New York: Knopf, 2004, Kindle edition), 630.

201 *"They were able to turn out"*: Mark Johnson, "NRA Went for 19-FOR-24 on Tuesday," *Richmond Times-Dispatch*, November 13, 1994, A-5.

202 *Foley saw in his political demise*: Biggs and Foley, *Honor in the House*, 249.

18. BAD BOYS

203 *The highlight of Dick Dyke's youth*: See Alice H. Anderson, *Richard E. Dyke: Just a Man from Wilton, Maine* (Bridgton, ME: Little Market Niche of Publishing, 2011).

203 *By the 1990s, Dyke had turned that company*: Dyke called the company Quality Parts Co. for years after buying it, but then renamed it Bushmaster as AR-15 sales took off in the early 1990s.

204 *"We thought, 'Oh my God'"*: Author interview with Izzy Anzaldua.

205 *Mark Westrom, an army veteran*: When Westrom learned in 1994 that an old production manager from ArmaLite was still alive, he visited the man. By then, ArmaLite was long defunct. The elderly man, living in Southern California, received mail addressed to the firm. He told Westrom that he recently had received a letter warning that the ArmaLite trademark was about to expire. "My ears perked up," Westrom recalled. But the old production manager didn't own the trademark; it belonged to the president of a Filipino company that had owned ArmaLite at some point after Stoner left. Westrom tracked down the president of the Filipino company and purchased the name and lion logo for a price that he would not divulge but described as "very low." He renamed his rifle company ArmaLite and added the slogan "A History of Innovation."

205 *More than 62,000 AR-15s*: Jim Curcuruto's assessment of manufactured AR-platform rifles in the U.S. from 1990 to 2021. Curcuruto provided this estimate to the authors in April 2022. For years, Curcuruto worked for the National Shooting Sports Foundation, where he tallied the number of ARs and similar guns that were manufactured each year in the U.S. He used both publicly available manufacturing data published by the federal government as well as confidential numbers provided by gunmakers.

205 *"The crime bill was introduced"*: Author interview with Mark Eliason.

205 *Sales skyrocketed; so did profits*: See Jeffrey A. Roth, Christopher S. Koper, et al., "Recreational Firearms Use Protection Act of 1994, Final Report," Urban Institute, March 13, 1997. Production figures in this book for individual manufacturers regarding AR-15s are derived from the ATF's *Annual Firearms Manufacturers and Export Report* unless otherwise noted.

206 *"Send us another thousand"*: Author interviews with Randy Luth.

208 *The AR-15 makers embraced the bad-boy image*: Olympic was one of the earliest AR-15 makers in America after Colt. The gunsmith Bob Scheutz, whose passion was building rifle barrels, founded the company with his son, Brian. In the late 1970s, Scheutz got a call from a friend who said the army was destroying some old M16s and asked whether he wanted the parts. A semi tractor-trailer showed up at Scheutz's shop packed with five-foot-tall boxes. Scheutz started selling the parts and a few years later began to make his own AR-15 receivers. Soon the company was making whole rifles for customers. "The guys who were into military stuff loved it," recalled Brian Scheutz.

209 *When a* Los Angeles Times *reporter visited*: Jeff Brazil and Steve Berry, "Crackdown on Assault Weapons Has Missed Mark; California and the federal government restricted military-style guns several years ago. But they remain widely available be-

cause of loopholes, politics and industry ingenuity," *Los Angeles Times*, August 24, 1997, A1.

210 *"The law itself was not designed"*: Barbara Nagy, "Ban on Sporter Rifle Leads to New Design," *Hartford Courant*, February 7, 1995, F1.

211 *"This represents an enormous shift"*: John Howard, Press Conference Parliament House, Canberra, May 10, 1996, transcripts from the prime ministers of Australia, Department of the Prime Minister and Cabinet, https://pmtranscripts.pmc.gov.au/release/transcript-9996.

211 *In February 1997, two heavily armed*: For police, the North Hollywood Shootout, as it came to be known, had a profound impact on how they viewed the AR-15. For years, police chiefs and unions pushed to ban the guns from civilian ownership. Some departments had bought the rifles for their own use, but after the shootout, police departments started buying lots of AR-15s.

211 *"Even before last week's gun battle"*: "Profile: Where Are High-Powered Weapons Being Used by Criminals Coming From," *NBC Nightly News*, March 7, 1997.

211 Shotgun News *carried hundreds of pages*: *Shotgun News*, October 1, 1998, 34.

212 *It's ridiculous*: *NBC Nightly News*, "Profile: Where Are High-Powered Weapons Being Used by Criminals Coming From," March 7, 1997.

212 *"a tennis racquet to a machine gun fight"*: J. M. Hirsch, "Police Complain Gun Laws Too Lenient," Associated Press, August 22, 1997.

213 *Bushmaster even made a special rifle*: "Cashing In on the New Millennium," Violence Policy Center, 1999, https://www.vpc.org/studies/y2kone.htm.

213 *"People were just concerned"*: Author interview with John DeSantis.

215 *When the Associated Press learned*: Larry Margasak, "Assault Weapons Maker Resigns Bush Campaign Post," Associated Press, July 22, 1999.

19. A PRECISE REQUEST

218 *Stoner's second marriage was a happy one*: Author interviews with Susan Kleinpell and Sue Walker.

221 *Kalashnikov hadn't received royalties*: See Chivers, *The Gun*, 209. Stoner and Kalashnikov also met at a Houston gun and outdoor equipment show. Both men praised each other's guns to a reporter. Stephen Johnson, "The Riflemen: Meeting of Two Minds Behind AK-47, M16," *Houston Chronicle*, Jan. 18, 1993, 13.

221 *In his later years, Stoner developed*: Information in this section and quotes from C. Reed Knight Jr. stem from extensive author interviews.

223 *But his daughter said he was detached*: His Soviet counterpart, Kalashnikov, distanced himself from the consequences of his creation as well, but did bemoan its misuse in his autobiography. As C. J. Chivers notes in *The Gun*, Kalashnikov wrote in his memoir, "I made it [the Kalashnikov] to protect the Motherland. Then it was like a genie out of the bottle and began to walk on its own in directions that I did not want." See *The Gun*, 408.

225 *"He tried to communicate"*: Author interview with Robert Bihun.

20. AR-15 TAKES OFF

227 *Troops carrying M16s were in airports*: Katia Hetter and Rocco Parascandola, "Terrorist Attacks: Next Door to Disaster / Surrounding Neighborhoods Fall Quiet as Residents Try to Cope," *Newsday*, September 13, 2001, W48.

227 *A New York Army National Guard colonel*: Michael Hill, "NY National Guard Says It's Ready for Multiple Deployments," Associated Press, October 2, 2001.

227 *"Those are not toys"*: Randy Kennedy, "A Nation Challenged: The Airports; Guardsmen Take Positions at Terminals," *The New York Times*, October 6, 2001, B9.

228 *Tattoo artists sold patriotic designs*: Susan Welch, "Tattoos, Fingernails Flaunt Patriotism," *St. Louis Post-Dispatch*, September 20, 2001, 1.

228 *Green Berets flew secretly into the country*: The "America's Response" monument, unveiled in 2011 in Manhattan's Liberty Park, depicts an American Green Beret on horseback with an M4 slung over his shoulder.

228 *The reputation of the rifle was resurrected*: The gun did get some bad press with the invasion, when a lost U.S. Army maintenance company was ambushed in the Iraqi city of Nasiriyah. The incident became notorious because numerous American soldiers were killed and three U.S. women soldiers—Jessica Lynch, Shoshana Johnson, and Lori Ann Piestewa—were wounded in the fight and taken prisoner by Iraqi forces. Lynch and Johnson were later rescued, but Piestewa died of her injuries at an Iraqi hospital. An investigation of the attack found that many of the unit's rifles malfunctioned during the battle. Before the war, some in the military had begun arguing Stoner's rifle platform was outdated following the 1993 firefight in Mogadishu, Somalia, when U.S. Army Rangers—armed with M16s and M4s—fought off attackers but suffered nineteen killed and seventy-three wounded. After that battle, some soldiers complained the rifles didn't have enough stopping power.

228 *"These guys were our new heroes"*: Author interview with Doug Painter.

229 *A man in Oklahoma*: Robert Russo, "Nervous Americans Stocking Up: Some Stores Sold Out of Flashlights, Bottled Water," *Winnipeg Free Press*, October 25, 2001, a20; Al Baker, "A Nation Challenged: Personal Security; Steep Rise in Gun Sales Reflects Post-Attack Fears," *The New York Times*, December 16, 2001, A1.

229 *An eighteen-year-old in Nevada*: Elaine Goodman, "Gun Show Attendance on the Rise," *Reno Gazette-Journal*, December 23, 2001, 1.

229 *The company told customers*: Bushmaster Firearms Catalog, 2002, Volume 1.

229 *"You could sell anything if it looked a little bit military"*: Author interview with John DeSantis.

229 *"We went after that demographic"*: Author interview with Randy Luth.

230 *By 2001, a Washington gathering*: Beth Sheridan and Jennifer Lenhart. "This Time, No Million to March Over Guns," *The Washington Post*, May 14, 2001, https://www.washingtonpost.com/archive/local/2001/05/14/this-time-no-million-to-march-over-guns/ef9530e8-ea92-4afe-afa4-d14423f88be5/.

230 *William Johnson, the executive director*: Author interview with William Johnson.

230 *"If you don't have cops"*: Author interview with Brian Malte.

231 *The NRA's magazine, American Rifleman, was number two*: Frank Smyth, *The NRA: The Unauthorized History* (New York: Flatiron Books, 2021, Kindle edition), 154.

231 *"Do we agree with the administration's position"*: Eric Lichtblau, "Irking N.R.A., Bush Supports the Ban on Assault Weapons," *The New York Times*, May 8, 2003, A1.

231 *Speaking on the Senate floor: Congressional Record, Proceedings and Debates of the Congress* 150, no. 20 (February 24, 2004), 2d Sess., S1523–25.

232 *Just 50 percent of Americans favored*: Gallup, "Guns," https://news.gallup.com/poll/1645/guns.aspx.

232 *Many academics and politicians had assumed*: Christopher S. Koper and Jeffrey A. Roth, "The Impact of the 1994 Federal Assault Weapons Ban on Gun Markets: An Assessment of Short-Term Primary and Secondary Market Effects," *Journal of Quantitative Criminology* 18, no. 3 (September 2002): 239–66, https://www.jstor.org/stable/23366709, 262–63.

232 *By 1996, AR-15 prices had fallen*: Christopher S. Koper, with Daniel J. Woods and Jeffrey A. Roth, "An Updated Assessment of the Federal Assault Weapons Ban: Impacts

on Gun Markets and Gun Violence, 1994–2003," Report to the National Institute of Justice, United States Department of Justice (June 2004), 37.

232 *"[T]he ban's effects on gun violence"*: Koper and Roth, "The Impact of the 1994 Federal Assault Weapons Ban on Gun Markets," 239–66, https://www.jstor.org/stable/23366709; Koper, Roth, 3.

233 *"though such incidents are very rare"*: Koper, with Woods and Roth, "An Updated Assessment of the Federal Assault Weapons Ban," 83.

233 *The ban extension did pass*: Jesse J. Holland, "Senate Votes to Extend Assault Weapons Ban for Another Decade," Associated Press, March 1, 2004.

233 *"You can be sure it's going to be"*: Jesse J. Holland, "Gun Control Bill Wins Extension," Associated Press, March 3, 2004.

233 *Throughout the campaign, Kerry*: Sharon Theimer, "National Rifle Association Endorses Bush for President," Associated Press, October 13, 2004.

233 *"My favorite gun is the M16"*: Jodi Wilgoren, "In Magazine Interview, Kerry Says He Owns Assault Rifle," *The New York Times*, September 27, 2004, 33.

233 *Donna Brazile, Gore's campaign manager*: Collin Levey, "Gun-Shy Democrats Still Can't Shoot Straight," *Seattle Times*, March 4, 2004, B7.

234 *House Majority Leader Tom DeLay*: ABC News, *Nightline*, September 4, 2004.

234 *A hunting columnist for*: Bob Gwizdz, "Assault Weapons Ban Expires, with Little Impact on Sportsmen," *The Grand Rapids Press*, October 2, 2004, via Factiva.

234 *Eric Gorovitz, who was policy director*: Author interview with Eric Gorovitz.

234 *Shortly after the ban expired*: Eric Gorovitz, "Anti-Gun Fight Needs a U.S. Policy," *The Atlanta Journal-Constitution*, October 22, 2003, A19.

234 *"She just wanted the credit"*: Author interview with Eric Gorovitz.

235 *It passed in the Senate*: See https://www.senate.gov/legislative/LIS/roll_call_votes/vote1091/vote_109_1_00219.htm.

235 *In 2004, Bushmaster paid*: David Hench, "Arrests of Two Men in Washington-Area Sniper Case End Three-Week Manhunt," Associated Press, October 25, 2002; "Rifle Seized from Suspects' Car Was Manufactured in Maine; The Bushmaster AR-15 Is Praised by Gun Enthusiasts for Its Accuracy," *Portland Press Herald*, October 25, 2002, 1A.

21. HERE COME THE HEDGE FUNDS

236 *The new chief executive*: Adam Gorlick, "Renewed Vigor Makes Smith & Wesson's Day; CEO's Strategy Is for Gun Maker to Train Sights on More Markets," Associated Press in the *Houston Chronicle*, January 28, 2007, 7.

236 *In one meeting with stock analysts*: Author interviews with S&W executive.

237 *Hunting was on the decline*: From 1991 to 2001, the number of Americans who said they had hunted dropped from 14 million to 13 million even as the overall U.S. population grew. See 2001 National Survey of Fishing, Hunting, and Wildlife-Associated Recreation, U.S. Fish and Wildlife Service.

237 *Ruger tried making golf club heads*: Paul M. Barrett, "Uneasy Gun Makers Add Gentler Product Lines," *The Wall Street Journal*, March 25, 1999, B1.

237 *In 2001, it sold*: Trudy Tynan, "British Owner Sells Smith & Wesson to Arizona Company," Associated Press, May 14, 2001.

237 *Fourteen years earlier, Tompkins*: Richard W. Stevenson, "Smith & Wesson Is Sold to Britons," *The New York Times*, May 23, 1987, 33, 35.

237 *Smith & Wesson was an exciting*: Author interview with Tom Taylor.

238 *Taylor's staff figured that the market*: Smith & Wesson slideshow presentation for investors, Securities and Exchange Commission, January 26, 2006.

238 *In January 2006, Smith & Wesson*: "Smith & Wesson Enters Long-Gun Market with M&P15 Rifles," company press release, January 18, 2006, https://ir.smith-wesson .com/news-releases/news-release-details/smith-wesson-enters-long-gun-market-mp15 -rifles.

239 *Bill Silver, head of commerical sales*: Author interview with Bill Silver.

239 *"The industry had these really pejorative"*: Author interview with Ryan Busse.

239 *The show "seemed to be"*: David Griffith, "SHOT Show 2006: Report from the Show Floor," *Police*, March 1, 2006, https://www.policemag.com/339518/shot-show-2006 -report-from-the-show-floor.

239 *"You had to fight your way"*: *The Michael Bane Blog*, February 14, 2006, https://ir .smith-wesson.com/news-releases/news-release-details/smith-wesson-enters-long-gun -market-mp15-rifles.

240 *In Maine, Dick Dyke, Bushmaster's owner*: Information in this section stems in part from author interviews with John DeSantis.

240 *In 2004, Bushmaster brought in*: Freedom Group Inc., Form S-1, Securities and Ex- change Commission, October 29, 2009.

240 *Most Americans had never heard*: "What's Bigger Than Cisco, Coke, or McDonald's? Steve Feinberg's Cerberus, a vast hedge fund that's snapping up companies—lots of them," *BusinessWeek*, October 2, 2005, https://www.bloomberg.com/news/articles /2005-10-02/whats-bigger-than-cisco-coke-or-mcdonalds.

241 *Feinberg liked to hunt*: Stephen Witt, "Big Gun's Big Fail," *New York*, November 14, 2016, https://nymag.com/intelligencer/2016/11/a-billionaires-dreams-of-creating-a -guns-empire.html.

241 *When Dick Dyke unsealed bids*: Author interview with John DeSantis.

242 *"There was a gigantic thriving"*: George Kollitides, deposition in *Soto v. Bushmaster*, November 9, 2021, 46. Provided by Koskoff, Koskoff & Bieder.

242 *Most gunmakers were privately owned*: Sturm, Ruger market cap, https://companiesmar ketcap.com/sturm-ruger/marketcap.

242 *Kollitides decided to apply*: George Kollitides, deposition in *Soto v. Bushmaster*, Novem- ber 9, 2021, 58. Provided by Koskoff, Koskoff & Bieder.

243 *"He's like our Michael Jordan"*: Quotes attributed to Linda Powell are drawn from an author interview.

243 *"The guides on our hunt"*: K. J. Houtman, *Zumbo* (Crystal Bay, MN: Fish on Market- ing, 2016, Kindle edition).

244 *"Zumbo, you fucked up"*: Houtman, *Zumbo*.

244 *"You are a fucking POS"*: See http://razoreye.net/mirror/zumbo/zumbo_assault_rifles .html.

244 *"In what might be considered the fastest career collapse in history"*: Dennis Anderson, "Leg- end to Pariah; After speaking out against using assault-type rifles for hunting, well- known writer Jim Zumbo was fired from *Outdoor Life* and lost his TV show because of pressure from sponsors," *Minneapolis Star-Tribune*, March 4, 2007, via Factiva.

244 *Zumbo's downfall showed that the AR-15*: The term "Zumboed" is now used to describe individuals ostracized in the gun world.

244 *"The industry, all the organizations"*: Author interview with Randy Luth.

245 *Cerberus closed the deal*: See Jesse Barron, "How America's Oldest Gun Maker Went Bankrupt: A Financial Engineering Mystery," *The New York Times Magazine*, May 1, 2019, https://www.nytimes.com/interactive/2019/05/01/magazine/remington-guns -jobs-huntsville.html?mtrref=www.nytimes.com&assetType=REGIWALL. See also Thomas Ryan, "Remington Sold to Cerberus for $370 Million," SGBMedia, April 9, 2007, https://sgbonline.com/remington-sold-to-cerberus-for-370-million.

245 *DeSantis advised Feinberg against it*: Author interview with DeSantis.

245 *Luth decided to sell his company to Cerberus*: Freedom Group Inc., Form S-1, Securities and Exchange Commission, October 29, 2009.

246 *The rate for the AR-15 market*: Freedom Group Inc., Form S-1, Securities and Exchange Commission, October 29, 2009.

246 *"As soon as that opened up"*: Author interview with John DeSantis.

246 *"cling to guns"*: Mayhill Fowler, "Obama Exclusive (Audio): On V.P. and Foreign Policy, Courting the Working Class, and Hard-Pressed Pennsylvanians," Huffington Post, May 25, 2011, https://www.huffpost.com/entry/obama-exclusive-audio-on_b _96333.

246 *"It's part of culture"*: Sam Frizell, "Why Hillary Clinton Thinks Gun Control Can Win in 2016," *Time*, November 6, 2015, https://time.com/4101947/hillary-clinton -guns-democrats.

246 *"talking like she's Annie Oakley"*: "Barack Obama: Hillary Talking Like She's Annie Oakley," YouTube, April 14, 2008, https://www.youtube.com/watch?v=bzQxFtM9cfk.

246 *During the only Democratic primary debate*: "Transcript: Obama and Clinton Debate," ABC News, April 16, 2008, https://abcnews.go.com/Politics/DemocraticDebate /story?id=4670271&page=1.

246 *Obama took no position*: Robert Farley, "Obama Consistently on the Fence," Politifact, July 8, 2008, https://www.politifact.com/factchecks/2008/jul/08/john-mccain /obama-consistently-on-the-fence

247 *The gun group warned its members*: Ben Smith, "NRA: Obama Most Anti-Gun Candidate Ever, Will Ban Guns," *Politico*, August 6, 2008, https://www.politico.com /blogs/ben-smith/2008/08/nra-obama-most-anti-gun-candidate-ever-will-ban-guns -010821.

248 *"Get 'em before he does"*: Allison Ross, "Gun Sales Surge as Uncertainties Stoke Fears," *Palm Beach Post*, November 2, 2008, 1A; Ben Montgomery, "Fear of a Firearm Ban Fuels Gun Sales," *St. Petersburg Times*, November 8, 2008, https://www.tampabay .com/archive/2008/11/08/fear-of-a-firearm-ban-fuels-gun-sales.

248 *"Some of the growth"*: Mike Golden on Smith & Wesson Holding Corporation 2009 First Quarter Earnings Conference Call, September 4, 2008.

248 *"M&P 15 sales were helped"*: SEC filing, https://www.sec.gov/Archives/edgar/data /1092796/000095015308002067/p13705e10vq.htm.

248 *In Florida, a salesman at Shoot Straight*: Ben Montgomery, "Fear of a Firearm Ban Fuels Gun Sales," *St. Petersburg Times*, November 8, 2008, 1A.

248 *Jim's Pawn Shop in Fayetteville*: Jay Price, "Specter of Gun Regulation Prompts a Wave of Purchases," *News & Observer*, November 8, 2008, A1.

248 *The FBI conducted more*: See https://www.fbi.gov/file-repository/nics_firearm_checks _-_month_year.pdf/view.

249 *"In those days you could sell anything you could make"*: Author interview with John DeSantis.

249 *At least twenty-six different*: See Nick Clossman and Chris Long, "A Business Case Analysis of the M4/AR-15 Market," Naval Postgraduate School, Monterey, CA, September 2015.

249 *"It almost didn't matter"*: Author interviews with Gerry Dinkel.

249 *"With Cerberus and them"*: Author interview with Randy Luth.

250 *The value of Cerberus's substantial stakes*: Louise Story, "For Private Equity, a Very Public Disaster," *The New York Times*, August 8, 2009, https://www.nytimes.com/2009 /08/09/business/09cerb.html.

250 *Feinberg's investors withdrew more than*: Peter Lattman and Jenny Strasburg, "Clients Flee Cerberus, Fallen Fund Titan," *The Wall Street Journal*, August 29, 2009, https: //www.wsj.com/articles/SB125148681701267563.

250 *Freedom Group's prospectus predicted*: "The continued adoption of the modern sporting rifle has led to increased growth in the long gun market, especially with a younger demographic of users and those who like to customize or upgrade their firearms. We view this current increase in demand as having significant long-term benefits, including expanding the popularity of shooting sport categories, as well as providing an opportunity to cultivate new, and renew existing, long-term customer relationships across our portfolio of products and brands." Freedom Group Inc., Form S-1, Securities and Exchange Commission, October 29, 2009, 84.

22. THE MAN CARD

251 *It attracted a huge following*: "Maxim is ready to party; Report: Men's Magazine Hopes to Build First in a String of Branded Clubs by Early 2006," CNN Money, August 15, 2005, https://money.cnn.com/2005/08/15/news/midcaps/maxim/index.htm.

251 *"The mostly educated, higher-than-average-income"*: Brothers & Company memo entitled, "Maxim Speak," September 5, 2009. Provided by Koskoff, Koskoff & Bieder.

252 *The men at Freedom Group*: Freedom Group Marketing Plan, February 2010. Provided by Koskoff, Koskoff & Bieder.

253 *Freedom Group launched a large*: Email re: Bushmaster Man Card Marketing Launch Elements. Provided by Koskoff, Koskoff & Bieder.

253 *Women were outpacing men*: HannaRosin, "The End of Men,'" *Atlantic*, July/August 2010, https://www.theatlantic.com/magazine/archive/2010/07/the-end-of-men/308135.

253 *In 2010, the average weight*: U.S. Centers for Disease Control and Prevention reports, December 20, 2018, https://www.cdc.gov/nchs/data/nhsr/nhsr122–508.pdf, and October 27, 2004, https://www.cdc.gov/nchs/data/ad/ad347.pdf.

253 *Just 5 percent of Americans*: 2006 National Survey of Fishing, Hunting, and Wildlife-Associated Recreation, U.S. Fish and Wildlife Service. See https://www.census.gov/prod/2008pubs/fhw06-nat.pdf.

254 *Most AR-15 owners used*: National Shooting Sports Foundation, "Modern Sporting Rifle (MSR): Comprehensive Consumer Report 2010, Ownership Attitudes Towards Modern Sporting Rifles," 2010.

254 *The Man Card campaign was*: Author interview with John DeSantis.

254 *"Heavy Profile Premium Match Grade Barrels"*: *Shotgun News*, October 1, 1998, 145.

254 *But the percentage of American households*: Tom W. Smith and Jaesok Son, "General Social Survey Final Report: Trends in Gun Ownership in the United States, 1972–2014," NORC at the University of Chicago, March 2015.

254 *By 2004, 20 percent*: L. Hepburn, M. Miller, D. Azrael, and D. Hemenway, "The U.S. Gun Stock: Results from the 2004 National Firearms Survey," *Injury Prevention* 13, no. 1 (February 2007): 15–19, https://www.ncbi.nlm.nih.gov/pmc/articles/PMC2610545/.

255 *Bill Silver, head of commerical sales*: Author interview with Bill Silver.

255 *At Freedom Group, a marketing team*: Freedom Group, "Gaming Strategy, Internal. Draft, For Internal Use Only. Confidential." Provided by Koskoff, Koskoff & Bieder.

256 *"It really is irony"*: Email from John Trull to colleagues RE: *Rolling Stone*, May 26, 2012. Provided by Koskoff, Koskoff & Bieder.

256 *"the American gun"*: Author interview with Pete Blumel.

256 *When* Call of Duty: Modern Warfare 2 *was released*: Chris Gaylord, "Modern Warfare 2 Sales Nuke All Previous Records," *Christian Science Monitor*, November 12, 2009, https://www.csmonitor.com/Technology/Horizons/2009/1112/modern-warfare-2-sales-nuke-all-previous-records.

256 *"I didn't want to be part"*: Author interview with Randy Luth.

257 *"With such little recoil"*: *Junior Shooters*, 2-Gun & 3-Gun Competitions Special Issue, Spring 2011, 49.

257 *"Cool, fun, and great for practice at little cost!"*: *Junior Shooters*, Summer 2010, 22.

257 *The National Shooting Sports Foundation*: Author interview with Doug Painter.

258 *In late May, he bought*: Michelle Castillo, "Colo. Shooter Purchased Guns Legally from 3 Different Stores," CBS News, July 5, 2016, https://www.cbsnews.com/news /colo-shooter-purchased-guns-legally-from-3-different-stores.

258 *That same day he went*: Matthew Nussbaum, "Aurora Theater Shooting Trial, the Latest from Day 31," *Denver Post*, June 15, 2015, https://www.denverpost.com/2015/06 /15/aurora-theater-shooting-trial-the-latest-from-day-31/.

23. "I'M A KILLER, I GUESS"

259 *Marcus Weaver was a Batman fan*: Quotes and recollections from Marcus Weaver drawn from an author interview.

260 *The movie started and the crowd*: TriData Division System Planning Corporation, "Aurora Century 16 Theater Shooting, After Action Report for the City of Aurora," April 2014, 10.

260 *From the second row, Jennifer Seeger*: Suzanne Malveaux, Mike Brooks, Elizabeth Cohen, "Colorado Shooting; Woman Narrowly Escapes Shooter," transcript, *CNN Newsroom*, July 20, 2012.

260 *Christopher Ramos, a twenty-year-old*: Malveaux, Brooks, Cohen, "Colorado Shooting; Woman Narrowly Escapes Shooter"; David Fahrenthold, Sari Horwitz, and Bill Turque, "Deadly Rampage at Colorado Theater," *The Washington Post*, July 21, 2012, A1.

261 *The first 911 call*: TriData Division System Planning Corporation, "Aurora Century 16 Theater Shooting, After Action Report for the City of Aurora," April 2014, 144.

261 *Gerry Jonsgaard, an Aurora police sergeant*: Interview of Aurora police sergeant Gerry Jonsgaard, "In Their Own Words: The Aurora Theater Shooting Responding Officers," 9News–Denver, July 17, 2017, www.youtube.com/watch?v=X97sLzH4ykw.

262 *Aurora officer James Waselkow*: Interview of Aurora police officer James Waselkow, "In Their Own Words: The Aurora Theater Shooting Responding Officers," 9News–Denver, July 17, 2017, https://www.youtube.com/watch?v=lILU9zfe9BU. See also Michael Pearson, "Prosecutor Releases Images from Colorado Theater Shooting," CNN Wire, September 11, 2015.

262 *Officers Jason Sweeney and Jason Oviatt*: TriData Division System Planning Corporation, "Aurora Century 16 Theater Shooting, After Action Report for the City of Aurora," April 2014, 20–21.

262 *"When I first saw him, I thought he was a cop"*: Interview of Aurora Police Officer Jason Oviatt, "In Their Own Words: the Aurora Theater Shooting Responding Officers," 9News—Denver, July 17, 2017, https://www.youtube.com/watch?v =LVOZnlCI2xE.

262 *The two officers realized*: TriData Division System Planning Corporation, "Aurora Century 16 Theater Shooting, After Action Report for the City of Aurora," April 2014, 20–21.

262 *At the University of Colorado Medical Center*: Author interview with Dr. Barbara Blok.

262 *Tom Sullivan woke up*: Author interview with Tom Sullivan.

263 *Before going, he posted*: Lynn Bartels, "Aurora Theater Shooting: Alex Sullivan Remembered for the Many Friends He Loved," *Denver Post*, July 21, 2012.

263 *"I lost my daughter yesterday"*: Jordan Steffen and Lindsay H. Jones, "Aurora Theater

Shooting: Father of Victim Rebecca Wingo Is 'Inconsolable,'" *Denver Post*, July 21, 2012.

263 *All this carnage was the result*: TriData Division System Planning Corporation, "Aurora Century 16 Theater Shooting, After Action Report for the City of Aurora," April 2014, 48; "Aurora, Colorado Commemorates 1-Year Anniversary of Theater Shooting," WBNS-TV, Channel 10, July 20, 2013, https://www.10tv.com/article/news/aurora-colorado-commemorates-1-year-anniversary-theater-shooting/530–4abe161b-588c-4456-a2fc-5690340bb029.

264 *He considered bombing, biological warfare*: Holmes's notebook, 48.

264 *He made a to-do list*: Holmes's notebook, 53.

264 *"Embraced the hatred, a dark k/night rises"*: Holmes's notebook, 54.

264 *Days before July 20*: Reid, *A Dark Night in Aurora*, 96.

264 *"to differentiate myself from who I normally was"*: Dr. Jeffrey L. Metzger, James Eagan Holmes, Case Number: 12CR1522, Sanity Evaluation, September 3, 2013, 5.

264 *"This is what a killer looks like"*: Reid, *A Dark Night in Aurora*, 96.

264 *"That warrior mentality, that was his big issue"*: Author interview with Craig Appel, former Aurora, Colorado, homicide detective and one of the first officers to interview James Holmes after the shooting.

265 *He staggered up an aisle*: See William Reid's videotaped interview with James Holmes, August 1, 2014.

265 *"I wanted to fix the AR-15"*: William Reid's videotaped interview with James Holmes, August 1, 2014.

265 *"It's a great gun for killing lots"*: Author interview with Rich Orman, May 18, 2021; Dr. Jeffrey L. Metzger, James Eagan Holmes, Case Number: 12CR1522, Sanity Evaluation, September 3, 2013, 3–4.

265 *Speaking to the National Urban League*: Michael A. Memoli and Seema Mehta, "Obama Suggests Support for Some Gun Restrictions," *Los Angeles Times*, July 25, 2012, https://www.latimes.com/world/la-xpm-2012-jul-25-la-na-obama-romney-guns-20120726-story.html.

266 *"We can sometimes hope"*: Seema Mehta, *Los Angeles Times* wire service, "Romney Says Theater Gunman Shouldn't Have Had Any Weapons," *St. Paul Pioneer Press*, July 26, 2012, A16.

266 *"How long will elected officials"*: David Kushma, Opinion: "Mr. Obama, Mr. Romney, Break Your Silence on Guns," *The Blade* (Toledo, Ohio), July 29, 2012, https://www.toledoblade.com/DavidKushma/2012/07/29/Mr-Obama-Mr-Romney-break-your-silence-on-guns/stories/201207290032.

266 *Dianne Feinstein went on Fox News*: Chris Wallace interview with Dianne Feinstein, Ron Johnson, *Fox News Sunday*, July 22, 2012.

266 *One was Adam Lanza*: State of Connecticut Office of the Child Advocate, "Shooting at Sandy Hook Elementary School: Report of the Office of the Child Advocate," November 21, 2014, 105.

267 *On his computer, Lanza*: Lanza's school shooter spreadsheet, https://schoolshooters.info/sites/default/files/Lanza_spreadsheet.pdf.

267 *He'd been diagnosed*: Sandy Hook Elementary School Shooting Reports, Connecticut State Police, File number 00091417.

267 *He changed his socks up to twenty times a day*: Sandy Hook Elementary School Shooting Reports, Connecticut State Police, File number 00017458.

267 *She had grown up hunting*: Federal Bureau of Investigation, Sandy Hook Elementary School Shooting Part 1 of 3, 41.

267 *She taught him to shoot a .22 caliber rifle*: Sandy Hook Elementary School Shooting Reports, Connecticut State Police, File number 00196017.

268 *"What do you do?"*: Andrew Solomon, "The Reckoning: The Father of the Sandy Hook Killer Searches for Answers," *The New Yorker*, March 10, 2014, https://www.newyorker.com/magazine/2014/03/17/the-reckoning.

268 *On March 29, 2010*: Sandy Hook Elementary School Shooting Reports, Connecticut State Police, File number 00013039.

24. "YOU WOULDN'T UNDERSTAND"

269 *Six-year-old Benjamin Wheeler's nickname*: All information, recollections, and quotes from the Wheelers in this chapter are drawn from author interviews with the Wheelers in 2020 and 2021 unless otherwise noted.

270 *The young family's move*: Nancy Crevier, "Come Sit Beside Me—And Sing," *Newtown Bee*, December 28, 2007, https://www.newtownbee.com/12282007/come-sit-beside-me-and-sing/.

271 *Around 9:40 a.m., drivers on Riverside Road*: State of Connecticut Department of Emergency Services and Public Protection, "Sandy Hook Elementary School Shooting Reports," File numbers 00101180, 00003250, and 00184096.

272 *At the station, one of the boys*: State of Connecticut Department of Emergency Services and Public Protection, "Sandy Hook Elementary School Shooting Reports," File number 00198959.

272 *A girl told the officers*: State of Connecticut Department of Emergency Services and Public Protection, "Sandy Hook Elementary School Shooting Reports," File number 00177428.

272 *One of the first officers*: State of Connecticut Department of Emergency Services and Public Protection, "Sandy Hook Elementary School Shooting Reports," File number 00258158.

272 *On the floor he saw*: State of Connecticut Department of Emergency Services and Public Protection, "Sandy Hook Elementary School Shooting Reports," File number 00026724.

272 *An AR-15 lay near them*: In the report, Chapman stated the weapon had a collapsible stock.

272 *Chapman felt his heart*: State of Connecticut Department of Emergency Services and Public Protection, "Sandy Hook Elementary School Shooting Reports," File number 00258158.

272 *Then he came across a girl*: State of Connecticut Department of Emergency Services and Public Protection, "Sandy Hook Elementary School Shooting Reports," File number 00002060.

273 *Cario went back to classroom*: State of Connecticut Department of Emergency Services and Public Protection, "Sandy Hook Elementary School Shooting Reports," File numbers 00026724 and 00073537.

275 *"Our hearts are broken today"*: Obama White House archived website, "President Obama Speaks on the Shooting in Connecticut," December 14, 2012, https://obamawhitehouse.archives.gov/blog/2012/12/14/president-obama-speaks-shooting-connecticut.

275 *They found one casing*: Office of the State's Attorney, Judicial District of Danbury, Stephen J. Sedensky III, State's Attorney, "Report of the State's Attorney for the Judicial District of Danbury on the Shootings at Sandy Hook Elementary School and 36 Yogananda Street, Newtown, Connecticut on December 14, 2012." November 25, 2013, 17.

275 *Lanza had shot two teachers*: Office of the State's Attorney Judicial District of Danbury, Stephen J. Sedensky III, State's Attorney, "Appendix to Report of the State's

Attorney for the Judicial District of Danbury on the Shootings at Sandy Hook Elementary School and 36 Yogananda Street, Newtown, Connecticut on December 14, 2012," November 25, 2013, A84, https://www.reuters.com/article/us-usa-shooting -connecticut/newtown-school-gunman-fired-154-rounds-in-less-than-5-minutes -idUSBRE92R0EM20130328.

275 *The FBI's Behavioral Analysis Unit*: Federal Bureau of Investigation, "Sandy Hook Elementary School Shooting Part 03 of 03," accessed at FBI Records: The Vault.

275 *When police searched Lanza's house*: Office of the State's Attorney Judicial District of Danbury, Stephen J. Sedensky III, State's Attorney, "Report of the State's Attorney for the Judicial District of Danbury on the Shootings at Sandy Hook Elementary School and 36 Yogananda Street, Newtown, Connecticut on December 14, 2012," November 25, 2013, 26.

276 *He left a semiautomatic shotgun*: State of Connecticut Department of Emergency Services and Public Protection, "Sandy Hook Elementary School Shooting Reports," File number 00259452.

276 *He carried three hundred rounds*: Office of the State's Attorney Judicial District of Danbury, Stephen J. Sedensky III, State's Attorney, "Appendix to Report of the State's Attorney for the Judicial District of Danbury on the Shootings at Sandy Hook Elementary School and 36 Yogananda Street, Newtown, Connecticut on December 14, 2012," November 25, 2013, A137, A141.

276 *On the day of the shooting*: Tom Leonard, "The Shooter Kept Banging on the Door Yelling: 'Let Me In!' but He Didn't Get In," *Irish Daily Mail*, December 15, 2012, 4–5.

276 *Thousands of people—including little children*: Jennifer Swift, "Mourners Gather to Hold Vigils for Newtown School Shooting Victims," *New Haven Register*, December 14, 2012, https://www.nhregister.com/news/article/Mourners-gather-to-hold-vigils -for-Newtown-school-11520308.php.

276 *"until the facts are thoroughly known"*: Tom Cohen, "Wiping Away Tears, Obama Mourns Children Killed in School Shooting," CNN, December 14, 2012, https:// www.cnn.com/2012/12/14/us/obama-school-shooting.

276 *"Weapons of war don't belong"*: Dianne Feinstein, "Statement on Connecticut School Shooting," Government Press Releases by CQ Transcriptions, December 14, 2012.

276 *Retired U.S. Army General Stanley McChrystal*: From Piers Morgan, "Gun Control Debate," CNN, January 12, 2013. The authors also contacted retired U.S. General David Petraeus, who led U.S. troops in Iraq and Afghanistan. In 1991, Petraeus was an officer at Fort Campbell in Kentucky. During a live fire exercise, a soldier tripped and fired one round from his M16, hitting Petraeus. "It felt like the greatest blow imaginable hitting me in the upper right back (as it exploded out of my back)," Petraeus wrote to the authors. Asked whether it changed his view of the rifle, he wrote, "Not really, though it confirmed that a single round even in the chest does not necessarily put one down and out . . ." Petraeus considered the military's current AR, the M4, to be a good rifle. Asked about the ARs popularity among civilians, he wrote, "I think I can understand the fascination with shooting a weapon used on the battlefield." Asked about its use in high-profile mass shootings, he only wrote one word: "Troubling."

277 *Walmart stopped selling AR-15s*: Peter Dreier, "Roots of Rebellion: Massacres and Movements: Challenging the Gun Industrial Complex," *New Labor Forum* 22, no. 2 (Spring 2013): 92–95.

277 *Stephen Feinberg decided on the Monday*: Sharon Terlep and Mike Spector, "Talk of Selling Gun Maker Started Just After Shooting," *The Wall Street Journal*, December 18, 2012, https://www.wsj.com/articles/SB100014241278873249070204578187623794707396.

277 *"It is apparent that the Sandy Hook tragedy"*: Cerberus Capital Management, "State-

ment Regarding Freedom Group, Inc.," December 18, 2012, https://www.prnewswire
.com/news-releases/cerberus-capital-management-statement-regarding-freedom-group
-inc-183889361.html.

277 *"I couldn't see how Congress"*: Author interview with John DeSantis.

277 *"This is not some Washington commission"*: Office of the Press Secretary, "Remarks by
the President in a Press Conference," Whitehouse.gov, December 19, 2012, https:
//obamawhitehouse.archives.gov/the-press-office/2012/12/19/remarks-president-press
-conference.

278 *The funerals for the Sandy Hook*: Dan Barry, "With the Why Elusive, Two Boys, Two
Burials," *The New York Times*, December 18, 2012, 1.

278 *Ben's funeral was held on December 20*: See Danielle Lynch, "Mourners at Funeral for
Ben Wheeler, 6, Fill Church Past Capacity," *New Haven Register*, December 20, 2012,
https://www.nhregister.com/news/article/Mourners-at-funeral-for-Ben-Wheeler-6-fill
-11507232.php.

278 *On that same day*: George Kollitides, deposition in *Soto v. Bushmaster*, November 9,
2021, 235. Provided by Koskoff, Koskoff & Bieder.

278 *"It was one of our higher margin products"*: George Kollitides, deposition in *Soto v.
Bushmaster*, November 9, 2021, 238. Provided by Koskoff, Koskoff & Bieder.

278 *For a week, NRA officials*: David Keene and Wayne LaPierre, transcript: "Remarks
from the NRA Press Conference on Sandy Hook School Shooting," *The Washington
Post*, December 21, 2012, https://www.washingtonpost.com/politics/remarks-from
-the-nra-press-conference-on-sandy-hook-school-shooting-delivered-on-dec-21-2012
-transcript/2012/12/21/bd1841fe-4b88-11e2-a6a6-aabac85e8036_story.html.

279 *A month after the massacre*: "Remarks by the President and the Vice President on Gun
Violence," January 16, 2013, https://obamawhitehouse.archives.gov/the-press-office
/2013/01/16/remarks-president-and-vice-president-gun-violence.

280 *"I warned you this day"*: Davis Merritt, "Davis Merritt: Time for 2nd Amendment Ab-
solutism Is Gone," *Wichita Eagle*, January 22, 2013, https://www.kansas.com/opinion
/opn-columns-blogs/article1107008.html.

280 *The horror writer Stephen King*: Stephen King, *Guns* (Philtrum Press, 2013, Kindle
edition), 20, 22.

280 *In December alone, the FBI*: NSSF analysis of NICS data. Excludes permit checks and
gives the best proxy for gun sales. Note: not all these were ARs.

280 *Smith & Wesson sold nearly*: Smith & Wesson Holding Corporation, Form 10-Q, Securities and Exchange Commission, March 5, 2013, 20.

281 *the liberal commentator Lawrence O'Donnell*: Lawrence O'Donnell, "The Last Word,"
MSNBC, January 30, 2012, accessed on YouTube via Courage California, https://
www.youtube.com/watch?v=LTtH6SmruJI.

282 *Public Law 13-3 prohibited*: Veronica Rose, "Summary of Gun Provisions in 13–3,"
https://www.cga.ct.gov/2013/rpt/2013-R-0216.htm.

283 *They met with Matt Bennett*: Quotes and recollections from the Wheelers and Bennett
come from author interviews with them.

284 *Bennett met with Biden, Schumer, and others*: Charles Schumer, as a congressman, had
been instrumental in pushing for passage of the assault-weapons ban in 1994. He
became a senator in 1999.

284 *On February 27, 2013, she held a hearing*: U.S. Senate Judiciary Committee, *Hearing
on the Assault Weapons Ban of 2013*, February 27, 2013, https://www.judiciary.senate
.gov/meetings/location-change-hearing-on-the-assault-weapons-ban-of-2013.

284 *The doctor who appeared*: U.S. Senate Judiciary Committee, "Hearing on the Assault
Weapons Ban of 2013," February 27, 2013, https://www.judiciary.senate.gov/meetings
/location-change-hearing-on-the-assault-weapons-ban-of-2013.

284 *The president said he had spoken*: The White House, Office of the Press Secretary,

"Remarks by the President on Reducing Gun Violence—Hartford, CT," April 8, 2013, https://obamawhitehouse.archives.gov/the-press-office/2013/04/08/remarks -president-reducing-gun-violence-hartford-ct.

285 *They met with Senator Rob Portman*: This re-creation is drawn from multiple author interviews of people who were at the meeting.

285 *The Wheelers and others met*: This re-creation also is drawn from author interviews of people who were at the meeting.

286 *It failed by a 40–60 vote*: U.S. Senate, Roll Call Vote, 113th Cong., 1st Sess., "Question: On the Amendment (Manchin Amdt. No. 715)," April 17, 2013, https://www .senate.gov/legislative/LIS/roll_call_lists/roll_call_vote_cfm.cfm?congress=113 &session=1&vote=00097.

286 *"a pretty shameful day for Washington"*: The White House, Office of the Press Secretary, "Statement by the President," April 17, 2013, https://obamawhitehouse.archives.gov /the-press-office/2013/04/17/statement-president.

286 *The* New York Times *editorial board*: Editorial Board, "The Senate Fails Americans," *The New York Times*, April 17, 2013, A26.

286 *An academic researcher who analyzed*: Kevin H. Wozniak, "Public Opinion About Gun Control Post–Sandy Hook," *Criminal Justice Policy Review* 28, no. 3 (April 1, 2017): 255–78.

25. MOLON LABE

289 *Chris Waltz was appalled*: Information in this chapter relating to Waltz stems from author interviews with him unless otherwise indicated.

290 *The first thing that he posted*: Some of the statistics cited in the meme were roughly accurate, based on FBI uniform crime data and estimates of the extent of U.S. medical malpractice. Others were way off. The FBI reported 323 people had been killed by long guns in 2011, not just semiautomatic rifles. The number of people killed by ARs that year was far fewer than 323, but the meme implied the deaths had all been caused by ARs. Such social media propaganda wasn't about exactitude. The message of the meme was simple: AR-15s kill a lot fewer people than many other things. Authors' papers via Waltz.

292 *A confidential poll of gun owners*: Fabrizio Ward, "Gun Owners & Gun Control," Prepared for WCSR (Remington Counsel). Provided by Koskoff, Koskoff & Bieder.

293 *A 2015 Gallup poll found*: Justin McCarthy, "Quarter of U.S. Voters Say Candidate Must Share View on Guns," Gallup, October 19, 2015, https://news.gallup.com/poll /186248/quarter-voters-say-candidate-share-view-guns.aspx.

293 *Tim Mak, the author*: Tim Mak, *Misfire: Inside the Downfall of the NRA* (New York: Dutton), 2021), 77.

293 *All the activism that transformed*: In 2013, Americans bought more guns than they ever had before. There were 14.8 million background checks for gun purchases that year, an all-time record since the modern background-check system came online in the 1990s. More than 7 million of those background checks that year were for rifles, also a record.

293 *"All of a sudden"*: Author interview with Ryan Busse.

294 *Smith & Wesson's AR-15 sales*: The company's fiscal year ended in April. See SEC filing, https://www.sec.gov/Archives/edgar/data/0001092796/000119312513270582 /d522688d10k.htm.

294 *The company sold $320 million*: Emily Miller, "Bushmaster CEO Breaks Silence on Newtown School Shooting," *Washington Times*, June 14, 2013, https://www .washingtontimes.com/news/2013/jun/14/bushmaster-ceo-reflects-on-newtown.

294 *By the end of 2013*: Michael Corkery and Tiffany Hsu, "Gun Makers Are Reeling Even as Threat of Regulation Recedes," *The New York Times*, February 16, 2018.

294 *"The orders are coming so fast"*: Adam Sichko, "Remington Arms 'Can't Make Guns Fast Enough' in Upstate NY," *Albany Business Review*, December 13, 2013.

294 *American gunmakers made 1.9 million*: Curcuruto assessment.

294 *The output represented 17 percent*: "Firearms Commerce in the United States: Annual Statistical Update," Bureau of Alcohol, Tobacco, Firearms and Explosives, 2016, https://www.atf.gov/file/108316/download.

295 *"Come and take them"*: The Greek historian Herodotus wrote extensively about the battle and the Persian invasion, but he made no mention of this exchange.

296 *Perhaps no American embodied*: Author interviews with C. J. Grisham.

296 *Three months after Sandy Hook*: "Did This Texas Cop Infringe on a Father's Second Amendment Rights?" *Amarillo Globe-News*, October 16, 2013, https://www.amarillo.com/story/news/state/2013/10/16/did-texas-cop-infringe-fathers-second-amendment-rights/13297465007.

296 *Grisham organized a protest*: John H. Richardson, "The American Revolution of C.J. Grisham," *Esquire*, November 1, 2015, https://classic.esquire.com/article/2015/11/1/the-american-revolution-of-c-j-grisham.

297 *His movement to normalize*: Casey Mutchler, "Coffee Cup in Hand, Gun in Holster; Firearms Advocates Show Appreciation to Starbucks," *Washington Times*, August 9, 2013, https://www.washingtontimes.com/news/2013/aug/8/coffee-cup-in-hand-gun-in-holster.

297 *The coffee chain had won*: "Starbucks' CEO on Guns," *The Wall Street Journal*, September 18, 2013, https://www.wsj.com/articles/BL-233B-121.

297 *A new gun-control group*: Michael Brick, "Calculated to Alarm," *Newsweek*, October 11, 2013, https://www.newsweek.com/2013/10/11/calculated-alarm-238082.html.

297 *Sandy Hook parents called*: Chris Boyette, "Newtown Group, Others Call for Starbucks to Ban Guns in Stores," CNN, August 23, 2013, https://www.cnn.com/2013/08/23/us/starbucks-guns.

297 *Starbucks chief executive Howard Schultz*: Pooppy Harlow and James O'Toole, "Starbucks to Customers: Please Don't Bring Your Guns!" CNN, September 18, 2013, https://money.cnn.com/2013/09/18/news/companies/starbucks-guns/index.html.

26. TRUMP SLUMP

299 *Stephen Feinberg and other high-finance*: Alexandra Stevenson, "Financiers to Attend Fund-Raiser for Trump," *The New York Times*, June 17, 2016, A20.

299 *Ruger chief executive Michael Fifer*: Q2 2016 Sturm Ruger & Co. Inc. Earnings Call, Thomson Reuters Street Events, edited transcript, August 3, 2016, https://ruger.com/corporate/PDF/8K-2016-03.pdf.

299 *On the campaign trail*: Bradford Richardson, "Hillary: Australia-Style Gun Control 'Worth Looking At,'" *The Hill*, October 16, 2015, https://thehill.com/blogs/ballot-box/dem-primaries/257172-hillary-australia-style-gun-control-worth-looking-at?rl=1.

300 *ARs generated $780 million*: Nick Clossman and Chris Long, "A Business Case Analysis of the M4/AR-15 Market," Naval Postgraduate School, Monterey, CA, September 2015.

300 *By 2013, at least seventy-six companies*: Clossman and Long, "A Business Case Analysis of the M4/AR-15 Market," 44.

300 *They represented the largest pool*: "First Time Buyers Segmentation," produced by Southwick and Associates for the National Shooting Sports Foundation, 2017.

301 *The massacre was the deadliest*: Several mass shootings hit Southern California in the first half of the 2010s. In November 2013, an unemployed man furious at TSA entered Los Angeles International Airport with a Smith & Wesson M&P 15 to kill one person and injure seven others before police killed him. See Tamara Audi, Jack Nicas, Erica

Phillips, and Andy Pasztor, "TSA Worker Killed in LAX Shooting; Suspect in Custody," *The Wall Street Journal*, November 1, 2013, https://www.wsj.com/articles/SB100 01424052702304073204579171761349872206.

301 *From 2000 through 2007*: "FBI Data: 2000 to 2018 Active Shooter Incidents," https:// www.fbi.gov/file-repository/active-shooter-incidents-2000–2018.pdf/view. In 2012, 90 people were killed and 118 were wounded in active shooter incidents. That same year, the FBI tallied 14,856 homicides in the United States. The FBI defined an active shooter as "an individual actively engaged in killing or attempting to kill people in a populated area." It didn't set a threshold for the number killed as some academics and news organizations did at the time. The FBI also eliminated shootings tied to gang warfare, domestic violence, and robberies as they sought to capture the attacks in public spaces such as schools, movie theaters, and other places where people gathered.

301 *"You walk into class"*: See "Clinton Takes Trump, Bush, and NRA to Task on Guns," Bloomberg Politics, October 5, 2015, https://www.bloomberg.com/news/videos /2015–10–05/clinton-takes-trump-bush-and-nra-to-task-on-guns.

302 *A Gallup poll found*: Art Swift, "Americans' Desire for Stricter Gun Laws Up Sharply," Gallup, October 19, 2015, https://news.gallup.com/poll/186236/americans-desire -stricter-gun-laws-sharply.aspx.

302 *Trump had written a book*: Donald J. Trump and Dave Shiflett, *The America We Deserve* (New York: Renaissance Books, 2000, Kindle edition), 103.

302 *"We oppose ill-conceived laws"*: *Republican Party Platform*, 2016, 13–14, https://prod-cdn -static.gop.com/media/documents/DRAFT_12_FINAL%5B1%5D-ben_1468872234 .pdf.

302 *Weeks before the election*: Author interview with Ryan Busse; his recollections. Debney did not respond to calls seeking comment. See also https://www.sec.gov/Archives /edgar/data/0001092796/000156459016029728/swhc-10q_20161031.htm.

302 *Two months later, Smith & Wesson*: Q3 2017 American Outdoor Brands Corp. Earnings Call-Q3, 2017, March 2, 2017, https://seekingalpha.com/article/4051756-american -outdoor-brands-aobc-james-debney-on-q3–2017-results-earnings-call-transcript.

303 *"There is no fear-based buying right now"*: American Outdoor Brands Corporation, Q2 2018 Earnings Call, Dec 7, 2017, https://www.marketscreener.com/quote/stock /SMITH-WESSON-BRANDS-IN-32683198/news/Transcript-American-Outdoor -Brands-Corporation-Q2–2018-Earnings-Call-Dec-07–2017–37972541.

303 *"We were maxed out"*: Author interview with Michael Cargill.

303 *"When it starts to slow down"*: Zusha Elinson and Cameron McWhirter, "The 'Trump Slump': With a Friend in the White House, Gun Sales Sag," *The Wall Street Journal*, August 30, 2018, 1.

303 *Smith & Wesson came up with more colors*: "Smith & Wesson M&P 15-22—Now in More Colors!" *Guns & Gear* Season 6, https://www.youtube.com/watch?v =NR9U3eMoKPc.

304 *The NRA promoted Smith & Wesson's little .22 caliber gun*: Drema Mann, "4 Things You Need to Know When Picking a Kid's First Rifle," NRA Family, May 22, 2017, https://www.nrafamily.org/articles/2017/5/22/4-things-you-need-to-know-when -picking-a-kids-first-rifle.

304 *But sales stalled*: The Wall Street measure of profitability, EBITDA, fell from $119.8 million to $33.6 million.

304 *Remington struggled to pay off*: See Jesse Barron, "How America's Oldest Gun Maker Went Bankrupt: A Financial Engineering Mystery," *The New York Times Magazine*, May 1, 2019, https://www.nytimes.com/interactive/2019/05/01/magazine/remington-guns -jobs-huntsville.html?mtrref=www.nytimes.com&assetType=REGIWALL.

304 *"The shine is coming off the nickel"*: Zusha Elinson and Cameron McWhirter, "The 'Trump Slump': With a Friend in the White House, Gun Sales Sag," *The Wall Street Journal*, August 30, 2018, 1.

27. BURNING BOOTS

308 *But then Aldean suddenly stopped and ran offstage*: Paddock had fired a few test shots before this moment, but the crowd hadn't heard them.

309 *The Las Vegas massacre was the deadliest*: According to LVMPD's final report: "Fifty-eight people were confirmed deceased; 31 victims were confirmed deceased at the venue and the remaining 27 victims were pronounced deceased at area hospitals. (Four victims were pronounced at Desert Springs Hospital Medical Center; 3 victims were pronounced at Spring Valley Hospital Medical Center; 16 victims were pronounced at Sunrise Hospital & Medical Center; 3 victims were pronounced at University Medical Center; and 1 victim was pronounced at Valley Hospital Medical Center.) Approximately 869 people sustained documented physical injuries. Of those who sustained injuries, FIT was able to confirm approximately 413 gunshot or shrapnel injury victims. Approximately 360 victims sustained injuries other than gunshot or shrapnel injuries. Approximately 96 people were identified as having sustained an injury, but the type of injury sustained was unable to be confirmed."

309 *Using AR-15s*: In the years that followed, two more people died from complications from their injuries that night.

309 *"Are Americans becoming 'numb' to mass shootings?"*: Jim Axelrod, "Are Americans Becoming 'Numb' to Mass Shootings?," CBS News, November 6, 2017, https://www.cbsnews.com/news/are-americans-becoming-numb-to-mass-shootings.

310 *Sheriff Joseph Lombardo, head of the Las Vegas police*: Zusha Elinson, "Police Report on Las Vegas Gunman Finds No Motive for Attack," *The Wall Street Journal*, August 3, 2018, https://www.wsj.com/articles/police-report-on-las-vegas-gunman-finds-no-motive-for-attack-1533326273.

310 *"definitively answer the why"*: Zusha Elinson, "Mass Shootings Raise Questions About Security and Training," *The Wall Street Journal*, November 13, 2019, https://www.wsj.com/articles/mass-shootings-raise-questions-about-security-and-training-11573646404. See also James Silver, Andre Simons, and Sarah Welchans Craun, "A Study of the Pre-Attack Behaviors of Active Shooters in the United States Between 2000–2013," Washington, DC: Federal Bureau of Investigation, U.S. Department of Justice, June 2018.

311 *Numerous gun salesmen who assisted*: Las Vegas Metropolitan Police Department Investigative Files obtained through public records request, "1-Oct-Officers Report," 20.

311 *Paddock always wore white gloves*: Las Vegas Metropolitan Police Department Investigative Files obtained through public records request, "1-Oct-Officers Report," 8.

311 *Dealers in states bordering Mexico*: Corbin Hiar, "Justice Department Enacts Rule for Reporting of Rifle Sales Along the Southwest Border," Center for Public Integrity, July 11, 2011, https://publicintegrity.org/national-security/justice-department-enacts-rule-for-reporting-of-rifle-sales-along-the-southwest-border.

312 *Dianne Feinstein told CBS's* Face the Nation: Kathryn Watson, "Sen. Feinstein Says No Law Could Have Stopped Las Vegas Gunman," CBS News, *Face the Nation*, October 8, 2017, https://www.cbsnews.com/news/dianne-feinstein-talks-to-face-the-nation-after-las-vegas-shooting.

312 *Kelley had a history of mental problems*: Inspector General, U.S. Department of

Defense, "Report of Investigation into the United States Air Force's Failure to Submit Devin Kelley's Criminal History Information to the Federal Bureau of Investigation," December 6, 2018, https://media.defense.gov/2018/Dec/07/2002070069/-1/-1/1/DODIG-2019–030_REDACTED.PDF.

312 *At the time of the shooting*: "Gunman Kills 26 in Rural Texas Church During Sunday Service," Reuters, November 6, 2017, https://www.cnbc.com/2017/11/06/gunman-kills-26-in-rural-texas-church-during-sunday-service.html.

312 *On the day of the shooting*: Michael James, "The Man Who Took Down the Texas Church Gunman," *USA Today*, November 6, 2017, https://www.usatoday.com/story/news/2017/11/06/man-who-put-end-carnage-texas/838700001.

313 *After he heard gunfire, Willeford reached*: Stephen Willeford, Statement for Senate Judiciary Hearing, https://www.judiciary.senate.gov/imo/media/doc/Stephen%20Willeford%20Statement.pdf.

313 *Gun groups exalted Willeford*: An FBI study of 160 active-shooter incidents found that only five of them ended when armed citizens who weren't law-enforcement personnel exchanged gunfire with the suspect. J. Pete Blair and Katherine W. Schweit, "A Study of Active Shooter Incidents, 2000–2013," Texas State University and Federal Bureau of Investigation, Washington, DC: U.S. Department of Justice, 2014.

313 *"He had an AR-15, but so did I"*: Jennifer Brett, "'He Had an AR-15, but So Did I,' Sutherland Springs Hero Hailed by NRA," *Atlanta Journal-Constitution*, May 6, 2018, https://www.ajc.com/blog/buzz/had-but-did-sutherland-springs-hero-hailed-nra/QAO2FwB8GcBBNdrax24lGO.

313 *Their impact on American discourse*: Little occurred on the legislative front. Texas senator John Cornyn, a Republican, introduced the Fix NICs (National Instant Criminal Background Check System) Act of 2017 to encourage federal agencies and departments such as the air force to submit disqualifying records to the background-check system. It would pass the following year.

315 *Studies found high rates*: Holly Orcutt, Lynsey Miron, and Antonia Seligowski, "Impact of Mass Shootings on Individual Adjustment," *PTSD Research Quarterly* vol. 25 (2014), 1–9.

28. LOCKDOWN NATION

317 *On February 14, 2018*: Quotes from Murdock in this chapter are drawn from an author interview.

319 *"I want to show these people"*: Dakin Andone, "Student Journalist Interviewed Classmates as Shooter Walked Parkland School Halls," CNN, February 18, 2018, https://www.cnn.com/2018/02/17/us/david-hogg-profile-florida-shooting/index.html.

319 *In a brief speech broadcast*: See https://www.youtube.com/watch?v=ZxD3o-9H1lY.

320 *Days after the shooting*: See Stephanie Ebbs, "Students Hold 'Lie-In' at White House to Protest Gun Laws," ABC News, February 19, 2018, https://abcnews.go.com/Politics/students-hold-lie-white-house-protest-gun-laws/story?id=53200248; and Cameron McWhirter, "Students Ratcheting Up Anti-Gun Protests After School Shooting," *The Wall Street Journal*, February 19, 2018.

320 *Mina Mazeikis, seventeen, helped organize*: Vikki Ortiz Healy, "Chicago-Area High School Students Chanting 'Save Our Kids' Stage Walkouts to Demand Action on Gun Violence," *Chicago Tribune*, February 21, 2018, https://www.chicagotribune.com/suburbs/ct-met-high-school-students-gun-control-20180221-story.html.

320 *"What really made the difference"*: Author interview with Mina Mazeikis.

321 *"Six minutes and 20 seconds"*: "Why Emma Gonzalez Stood on Stage Silent," CNN, https://www.cnn.com/videos/us/2018/03/24/emma-gonzalez-stood-silent-orig-tc.cnn.

321 *At a meeting with the massacre's survivors*: Catherine Lucey and Ken Thomas, "'We Must Move Past Cliches': Trump Urges Ban on Gun Devices Like Rapid-Fire Bump Stocks," Associated Press, February 20, 2018.

321 *In a meeting with members of Congress*: "Remarks by President Trump, Vice President Pence, and Bipartisan Members of Congress in Meeting on School and Community Safety," Trumpwhitehouse.archives.gov, February 28, 2018, https://trumpwhitehouse .archives.gov/briefings-statements/remarks-president-trump-vice-president-pence-bip artisan-members-congress-meeting-school-community-safety/.

322 *FBI behavioral analysts in 2018 produced*: James Silver, Andre Simons, and Sarah Craun, "A Study of the Pre-Attack Behaviors of Active Shooters in the United States Between 2000 and 2013," U.S. Department of Justice, Federal Bureau of Investigation, June 2018.

322 *Mass shooters were getting younger*: A. Lankford and J. Silver, "Why Have Public Mass Shootings Become More Deadly? Assessing How Perpetrators' Motives and Methods Have Changed over Time," *Criminology and Public Policy* 19, no. 1 (2020): 37–60.

323 *"There's a utility part to this"*: Author interview with James Densley.

323 *"I hate everyone and everything"*: David Ovalle and Nicholas Nehamas, "'You're All Going to Die.' Nikolas Cruz Made Cellphone Videos Plotting Parkland Attack," *Miami Herald*, May 31, 2018, https://www.miamiherald.com/news/local/community /broward/article212199899.html.

323 *"Hello. My name is Nik"*: Marjory Stoneman Douglas High School Public Safety Commission Initial Report, 256.

323 *He wore a Donald Trump "Make America Great Again" hat*: Case Supplemental Report by Detective John Curcio, Broward County Sheriff's Office, August 9, 2018, 234, 240, 256, 313, 337.

324 *One of Cruz's favorite songs*: Megan O'Matz, "On Parkland Shooter's Playlist: 'Pumped Up Kicks,' a Chart-Topping Song About School Slayings," *South Florida Sun Sentinel*, August 31, 2018, https://www.sun-sentinel.com/local/broward/parkland/florida -school-shooting/fl-florida-school-shooting-pumped-up-kicks-20180828-story.html.

324 *After he turned eighteen*: Case Supplemental Report by Detective John Curcio, Broward County Sheriff's Office, August 9, 2018, 159, 168, 238.

324 *Cruz owned other guns*: Case Supplemental Report by Detective John Curcio, Broward County Sheriff's Office, August 9, 2018, 169, 182.

324 *He spent much of his free time*: Case Supplemental Report by Detective John Curcio, Broward County Sheriff's Office, August 9, 2018, 232.

324 *After his mother died*: Unclassified FBI files, https://s3.documentcloud.org/documents /4387059/FBI-Florida-Transcript.pdf.

324 *On Valentine's Day, shortly after 2:00 p.m.*: Case Supplemental Report by Detective John Curcio, Broward County Sheriff's Office, August 9, 2018, 317.

324 *Inside Building 12, where freshmen had*: Case Supplemental Report by Detective John Curcio, Broward County Sheriff's Office, August 9, 2018, 25, 169.

324 *He shot at fleeing students and staff*: Patricia Mazzei, "Gunman Carried Out His Rampage at School Without Ever Entering a Classroom," *The New York Times*, April 25, 2018, 16.

324 *Windows shattered as students cowered*: Case Supplemental Report by Detective John Curcio, Broward County Sheriff's Office, August 9, 2018, 244–87.

324 *Eden Hebron, a fourteen-year-old*: Eden Hebron, "Flashback: Here's What It Was Like to Watch My Friends Die in Room 1216," *USA Today*, April 5, 2018, updated May 18, 2018, https://www.usatoday.com/story/opinion/2018/04/05/parkland-school -shooting-survivor-watched-friends-die-column/487169002/

325 *"Bullets, Alyssa?"*: Eden Hebron, "A Parkland Survivor Remembers: 'I Saw My Friends,'" Gannett News Service, April 10, 2018, https://www.northjersey.com/story/opinion /contributors/2018/04/10/parkland-survivor-remembers-saw-my-friends/502855002.

325 *In six minutes, he fired 140 rounds*: Case Supplemental Report by Detective John Curcio, Broward County Sheriff's Office, August 9, 2018, 241.

325 *He dropped the gun*: Case Supplemental Report by Detective John Curcio, Broward County Sheriff's Office, August 9, 2018, 162.

325 *Police across the country responded*: Julie Bosman, "After Parkland, a Flood of New Threats, Tips and False Alarms," *The New York Times*, February 26, 2018, A13.

325 *"A Formula One race car is for a racer"*: "Interview with the Waffle House Shooting Hero; Kanye West Sparkles a Ton of Debate About Free Speech; One-On-One with Tracee Ellis Ross; 2018 National Teacher of the Year," *The Van Jones Show*, CNN, May 5, 2018, https://transcripts.cnn.com/show/vjs/date/2018-05-05/segment/01.

326 *The father was later convicted*: Paige Blanzy and Jason Howell. "GUILTY: Father of Convicted Waffle House Shooter Convicted of Returning Confiscated Weapons to His Son," WSMV4–Nashville, May 13, 2022. https://www.wsmv.com/2022/05/13/guilty-father -convicted-waffle-house-shooter-convicted-returning-confiscated-weapons-his-son.

326 *"You're going to keep those rights"*: Zusha Elinson, "Trump Exalts Gun Rights at NRA Conference," *The Wall Street Journal*, May 4, 2018, https://www.wsj.com/articles /trump-exalts-gun-rights-at-nra-conference-1525466378.

326 *"AR-15 is a WMD"*: Rick Jervis, "Father of Parkland Victim Heckled by Gun Rights Group as He Speaks at Rally Near NRA Meeting," *USA Today*, May 5, 2018, https: //www.kvue.com/article/news/nation-now/father-of-parkland-victim-heckled-by-gun -rights-group-as-he-speaks-at-rally-near-nra-meeting/465-cd1b198e-266e-4704-9dbc -e320b86041ff.

327 *After police wounded Bowers*: In June 2023, Bowers was on trial in federal court and facing the death penalty.

328 *At a televised Democratic presidential*: ABC News, "Beto O'Rourke: 'Hell Yes, We Are Going to Take Your AR-15,'" https://www.youtube.com/watch?v=lMVhL6OOuR0.

328 *"Democrats will ban the manufacture"*: *2020 Democratic Party Platform*, adopted by the Democratic National Convention, August 18, 2020, 47.

329 *There had been fifty-six mass shootings*: The Violence Project, Mass Shooter Database, https://www.theviolenceproject.org/mass-shooter-database.

329 *"Considering that mass shootings"*: Christopher S. Koper, "Assessing the Potential to Reduce Deaths and Injuries from Mass Shootings Through Restrictions on Assault Weapons and Other High-Capacity Semiautomatic Firearms," *Criminology and Public Policy* 19, no. 1 (2020): 147–70.

329 *On the last day of Passover*: Details from complaint in *U.S.A. v. John Timothy Earnest*, U.S. District Court, Southern California, May 9, 2019, 10.

330 *In the five months after Parkland*: Matt Vasilogambros, "After Parkland, States Pass 50 New Gun-Control Laws," *Stateline*, Pew Charitable Trusts, August 2, 2018, https://www .pewtrusts.org/en/research-and-analysis/blogs/stateline/2018/08/02/after-parkland-states -pass-50-new-gun-control-laws.

330 *Eden Hebron, who saw:* Quotes and discussion of Hebron in this section are drawn from an author interview.

29. COME AND TAKE IT NATION

332 *Some gun owners joked*: Conservatives embraced the couple as heroes, and the two spoke in a taped interview played for the Republican National Convention. They described the "out of control mob" in front of their house and praised Trump. Missouri

Republican governor Mike Parson pardoned the couple. Mark McCloskey, the St. Louis lawyer who had waved an AR-15 at protesters, had been widely mocked by BLM supporters and gun-control advocates, but McCloskey did not shrink from the spotlight. He ran for U.S. Senate from Missouri, having never held public office before. The center photo on his campaign was the infamous photo of him gripping his rifle—and wearing his pink polo shirt. McCloskey won only 3 percent of the vote in the 2022 GOP primary, but he remained a celebrity among gun groups and conservatives across the country.

333 *One car dealership offered*: Simone Jasper, "Dealership Offers AR-15 Vouchers and a Bible to Buyers in SC, Business Says," *The State*, October 1, 2019, https://www.thestate.com/news/state/south-carolina/article235903077.html.

333 *The founder, Evan Hafer*: Author interviews with Evan Hafer.

333 *Gun-rights groups trumpeted*: Bob D'Angelo, "Florida Woman, 8 Months Pregnant, Uses AR-15 to Fatally Shoot Armed Intruder," Cox Media Group National Content Desk via Fox 23 News, https://www.fox23.com/news/trending-now/florida-woman-8-months-pregnant-uses-ar-15-to-fatally-shoot-armed-intruder/1005010679.

334 *Winston was familiar with the weapon*: Author interview with Taylor Winston.

334 *American civilians owned about*: Jim Curcuruto's assessment of manufactured AR-platform rifles from 1990 to 2021. Curcuruto provided this estimate to the authors in April 2022. For years, Curcuruto worked for the National Shooting Sports Foundation, where he tallied the number of ARs and similar guns that were manufactured each year in the United States. He used both publicly available manufacturing data published by the federal government as well as confidential numbers provided by gunmakers.

335 *"It looked cool"*: Paige Williams, "The Complex Task Facing the Kyle Rittenhouse Jury," *The New Yorker*, November 15, 2021, https://www.newyorker.com/news/news-desk/the-complex-task-facing-the-kyle-rittenhouse-jury.

335 *at a highly publicized trial*: Anthony DeRosa, "Kyle Rittenhouse Verdict: Teen Found Not Guilty of All Charges in Killing of Two," *The Wall Street Journal*, November 19, 2021, https://www.wsj.com/articles/kyle-rittenhouse-verdict-not-guilty-11637347243.

336 *The rally in Richmond*: Scott Calvert and Jon Kamp, "Thousands of Pro-Gun Advocates Rally in Virginia," *The Wall Street Journal*, January 20, 2020, https://www.wsj.com/articles/virginia-officials-on-guard-for-pro-gun-rally-in-richmond-11579516202.

337 *A Northern California man*: Zusha Elinson, "The Rise of Untraceable 'Ghost Guns,'" *The Wall Street Journal*, January 4, 2018, https://www.wsj.com/articles/the-rise-of-untraceable-ghost-guns-1515061800.

337 *By 2020, American law enforcement*: Joint Counterterrorism Assessment Team (JCAT), "First Responders Toolkit," June 22, 2021, https://www.dni.gov/index.php/nctc-how-we-work/joint-ct-assessment-team/first-responder-toolbox.

337 *Many who came that day*: See Tom Jackman, Rachel Weiner, and Spencer S. Hsu, "Evidence of Firearms in Jan. 6 Crowd Grows as Arrests and Trials Mount," *The Washington Post*, July 8, 2022, https://www.washingtonpost.com/dc-md-va/2022/07/08/jan6-defendants-guns.

338 *Police arrested him for attacking officers at the Capitol*: See https://www.justice.gov/usao-dc/defendants/quaglin-christopher-joseph.

338 *"We aren't getting through this without a civil war"*: From federal indictments. See also Aruna Viswanatha, "Oath Keepers Cached Weapons for Jan. 6 Capitol Attack, Prosecutors Say," *The Wall Street Journal*, January 20, 2022, https://www.wsj.com/articles/oath-keepers-cached-weapons-for-jan-6-capitol-attack-prosecutors-say-11642693058.

338 *"We are at WAR"*: See court filings in *U.S. vs. Elmer Stewart Rhodes III et al.*, 22-cr-15, especially Government's Memorandum in Support of Motion for Detention, regarding U.S. vs. Edward Vallejo, filed in the U.S. District Court for the District of Arizona, January 18, 2022.

30. BEYOND THE TALKING POINTS

339 *In March 2021, a twenty-one-year-old*: Zusha Elinson and Dan Frosch, "Boulder Grocery Store Shooting Leaves 10 Dead, Including Police Officer," *The Wall Street Journal*, March 23, 2022, https://www.wsj.com/articles/police-respond-to-active-shooter-at-colorado-supermarket-11616454128.

339 *In late April, a former FedEx*: Cameron McWhirter, Jeffrey Horwitz, and Nora Naughton, "Indianapolis Mass Shooting: At Least Eight Dead at FedEx Facility," *The Wall Street Journal*, April 17, 2022, https://www.wsj.com/articles/multiple-people-shot-at-fedex-facility-in-indianapolis-11618551906.

340 *The head of the House caucus on gun safety*: Author interview with Mike Thompson.

341 *During legal proceedings, LaPierre*: Jonathan Randles and Mark Maremont, "NRA CEO LaPierre Acknowledges Failing to Disclose Free Stays on Yacht," *The Wall Street Journal*, April 7, 2021, https://www.wsj.com/articles/nra-ceo-lapierre-acknowledges-failing-to-disclose-free-stays-on-yacht-11617844246?mod=article_inline.

341 *Grady Judd, the conservative sheriff*: Dan Frosch and Zusha Elinson, "Police Have a Tool to Take Guns from Potential Shooters, but Many Aren't Using It," *The Wall Street Journal*, November 15, 2021, https://www.wsj.com/articles/gun-law-allowing-police-to-seize-weapons-from-potential-shooters-often-isnt-used-11636984981.

342 *Authorities in California seized*: Garen J. Wintemute, Veronica A. Pear, Julia P. Schleimer, et al., "Extreme Risk Protection Orders Intended to Prevent Mass Shootings," *Annals of Internal Medicine*, November 5, 2019, https://www.acpjournals.org/doi/10.7326/M19-2162

342 *In one of the most glaring lapses*: Author interviews with Sheila Hole.

343 *Soon after Indianapolis, violence researchers*: Michael Rocque, Grant Duwe, Michael Siegel, James Alan Fox, Max Goder-Reiser, and Emma Fridel, "Policy Solutions to Address Mass Shootings," Rockefeller Institute of Government, Regional Gun Violence Consortium, August 2021, https://rockinst.org/wp-content/uploads/2021/08/policy-solutions-public-mass-shootings.pdf.

343 *"Maybe it's throwing up"*: Author interview with Rocque.

344 *One Stanford study found*: John Donohue and Theodora Boulouta, "That Assault Weapons Ban? It Really Did Work," *The New York Times*, September 4, 2019, https://www.nytimes.com/2019/09/04/opinion/assault-weapon-ban.html.

345 *"The overwhelming majority of citizens"*: See *James Miller et al. v. Rob Bonta in his official capacity as Attorney General of the State of California et al.*, U.S. District Court, Southern California, June 4, 2021.

345 *In 2017, the United States Court of Appeals*: See *Stephen Kolbe et al. v. Lawrence Hogan, Jr. et al.*, United States Court of Appeals for the Fourth Circuit, February 21, 2017.

347 *Judgments and large settlements*: In a related case, a jury and a judge in 2022 ordered Alex Jones, a popular conspiracy theorist who spread lies about the Sandy Hook massacre, to pay $1.44 billion in a defamation suit brought by the Wheelers and other Sandy Hook families.

31. "ARE ANY RESIDENTS SAFE IN THIS COUNTRY ANYWHERE?"

348 *In August 2019, Connor Betts*: Another major mass shooting occurred in August 2019. On August 3, Patrick Crusius, a twenty-one-year-old white nationalist, drove from his

home in a Dallas suburb to attack a Walmart store in El Paso. He used an AK-47 style rifle to kill twenty-two people and wound twenty-six others, most of them Hispanic people. After surrendering to police, he told them he went to the store to target Hispanics. In a rambling manifesto that he posted before the shooting, he wrote that he would primarily use an AK-47 but wanted to bring along an AR-15 if he could get one. "The ar15 is probably the best gun for military applications but this isn't a military application," he wrote. "This will be a test of which is more lethal, either it's fragmentation or tumbling." In the end, he didn't bring along an AR-15.

349 *"Thirty seconds," said Dayton police chief*: Talal Ansari, "Thirty Seconds That Haunt Dayton's Police Chief," *The Wall Street Journal*, August 11, 2019, https://www.wsj.com/articles/thirty-seconds-that-haunt-daytons-police-chief-11565533829.

349 *But an FBI study of 160 active-shooter incidents*: J. Pete Blair and Katherine W. Schweit, "A Study of Active Shooter Incidents, 2000–2013," Texas State University and Federal Bureau of Investigation, Washington, DC: U.S. Department of Justice, 2014.

349 *In 2021, armed citizens killed two*: *Active Shooter Incidents in the United States in 2021*, Washington, DC: Federal Bureau of Investigation and the Advanced Law Enforcement Rapid Response Training (ALERRT) Center at Texas State University, 2022.

349 *John McDonald, the security chief*: Zusha Elinson, "In Columbine's School District, Former Students Are Tracked to Prevent Attacks," *The Wall Street Journal*, February 28, 2018, https://www.wsj.com/articles/in-columbines-school-district-former-students-are-tracked-to-prevent-attacks-1519830001.

350 *"So many of the weapons"*: Author interview with James Densley.

351 *"We've got a problem, a societal problem"*: Quotes from Gerry Dinkel drawn from author interviews.

352 *Almost half of 147 mass shootings*: Michael Rocque, Madison Gerdes, James Alan Fox, Grant Duwe, and Madeline Clark, "Averting Tragedy: An Exploration of Thwarted Mass Public Shootings Relative to Completed Attacks," *Criminal Justice Review*, July 28, 2022, 1–23.

353 *"The AR-15 and its variants"*: Payton S. Gendron, "You Wait for a Signal While Your People Wait for You," 58.

354 *He discussed every part*: Quotes by Payton Gendron in this section drawn from his document "You Wait for a Signal While Your People Wait for You" and his Discord diary.

355 *At the Tops supermarket*: "Who Are the Victims of the Mass Shooting in Buffalo?" WGRZ, May 21, 2022, https://www.wgrz.com/article/news/crime/what-we-know-tops-shooting-victims-buffalo-mass-shooting/71-30ad7b83-6732-4780-8f0d-ce6d5f656752#:~:text=for%20this%20video-,Injured,were%20all%20taken%20to%20ECMC.

355 *Gendron chose the store's location*: In February 2023, Gendron was sentenced to life in prison after he had pleaded guilty in November 2022 to multiple counts of murder.

355 *"I think the question"*: Transcript, Buffalo Mayor Byron Brown on *Face the Nation*, CBS News, May 15, 2022, https://www.cbsnews.com/news/byron-brown-buffalo-mayor-face-the-nation-transcript-05-15-2022.

355 *Armed officers waited in hallways*: Texas House Investigative Committee on the Robb Elementary Shooting, Interim Report 2022, 7.

355 *"I don't want to die"*: J. David Goodman, Serge F. Kovaleski, Eduardo Medina, and Mike Baker, "No Radio, Old Tactics: How the Police Response in Uvalde Broke Down," *The New York Times*, June 4, 2022, A1.

355 *An eleven-year-old smeared herself*: Nora Neus, Melissa Alonso, and Claire Colbert, "She Smeared Blood on Herself and Played Dead: 11-Year-Old Reveals Chilling Details of the Massacre," CNN, June 8, 2022, https://www.cnn.com/2022/05/27/us/robb-shooting-survivor-miah-cerrillo/index.html.

355 *Over an hour after the first officers*: Texas House of Representatives Investigative Committee on the Robb Elementary Shooting, Interim Report 2022, 52.

355 *Before that day, Ramos*: Information from Texas House of Representatives Investigative Committee on the Robb Elementary Shooting, Interim Report 2022.

356 *The owner of the gun store*: Bernard Condon, "Texas School Shooter Left Trail of Ominous Warning Signs," Associated Press, July 19, 2022, https://apnews.com/article/uvalde-school-shooting-warning-signs-f18a8d365aa5edf0d3754df721144cf1.

356 *Dr. Roy Guerrero, Uvalde's only pediatrician*: House Committee on Oversight and Reform, "Testimony of Dr. Roy Guerrero at Hearing on Gun Violence Crisis," June 8, 2022, see https://www.youtube.com/watch?v=RCwwoHRTIMk.

357 *Nearly three-quarters of Americans*: Quinnipiac University Poll, "Nearly 3 out of 4 Support Raising the Legal Age to Buy Any Gun, Quinnipiac University Poll Finds; Support for Assault Weapons Ban Hits New Low," June 8, 2022, https://poll.qu.edu/poll-release?releaseid=3848.

357 *the aged Dianne Feinstein*: In February 2023, Feinstein, eighty-nine, announced she would not seek reelection.

32. VALERIE'S ROAD HOME

362 *These days she found herself thinking*: Most of this chapter is based on extensive interviews with Valerie Kallis-Weber, her doctors, surgeons, therapists, and friends. The account of the attack is based on media and official government reports.

Bibliography

We interviewed hundreds of people for this book and read many books, academic papers, government reports, government and private correspondence and files, newspaper and magazine articles, and other material. We reviewed television and radio programs and other source material as well. Material directly referenced in the book is cited in the endnotes. Below is a selected list of libraries and archives consulted as well as a portion of the material used in *American Gun*.

SELECTED LIBRARIES AND ARCHIVES

Dwight D. Eisenhower Presidential Library, Abilene, Kansas
Robert Woodruff Library, Emory University, Atlanta, Georgia
James Baldwin Memorial Library, MacDowell, Peterborough, New Hampshire
Harry S. Truman Presidential Library, Independence, Missouri
Library of Congress, Manuscript Division, Washington, DC
Smithsonian Institution Archives, Washington, DC
Smithsonian Institution, National Air and Space Museum Archives, Chantilly, Virginia
Columbus State University Archives, Columbus, Georgia
Maneuver Center for Excellence Donovan Research Library, Fort Benning, Georgia
Richard Nixon Presidential Library and Museum, Yorba Linda, California
Pulse Tragedy Public Records, City of Orlando, Florida

Parkland Shooting Records, Broward County Sheriff's Office, Florida
National Archives, College Park, Maryland
Richard B. Russell Library for Political Research and Studies, University of Georgia, Athens, Georgia
Springfield Armory, Springfield, Massachusetts
U.S. Army Heritage and Education Center, Carlisle Barracks, Pennsylvania
LBJ Presidential Library, Austin, Texas
George H. W. Bush Library, College Station, Texas
Center for Missouri Studies, the State Historical Society of Missouri, Columbia, Missouri
Private collection and Eugene Stoner materials, Knight's Armament Co., Vero Beach, Florida
Private papers of Susan Kleinpell

SELECTED BOOKS, PAMPHLETS, MANUALS

Adams, John A. *General Jacob Devers: World War II's Forgotten Four Star General.* Bloomington: Indiana University Press, 2015.
Ambrose, Stephen E. *Eisenhower—Soldier and President.* New York: Simon and Schuster, 1990.
Anonymous. News Media Guide to Firearms. Washington, DC: Treasury Department, Bureau of Alcohol, Tobacco, and Firearms, 1978. http://hdl.handle.net /2027/uiug.30112105190026.
Applin, Capt. R. V. K. *Machine-Gun Tactics.* London: Hugh Rees, 1910.
Archer, Amy. *If I Don't Make It, I Love You: Survivors in the Aftermath of School Shootings.* New York: Skyhorse Publishing, 2019.
ArmaLite Inc. *Operator's Manual for all AR10B and M15 Series Rifles.* Geneseo, IL: ArmaLite Inc., December 1997.
Ayres, Leonard P. *The War with Germany: A Statistical Summary.* Washington, DC: Government Printing Office, 1919.
Bacevich, A. J. *The Pentomic Era: The U.S. Army Between Korea and Vietnam.* Washington, DC: National Defense University Press, 1986.
Bennett, Matt. *The Promise.* Washington, DC: Brookings Institution Press, 2013.
Biggs, Jeffrey R., and Tom Foley. *Honor in the House.* Pullman: Washington State University Press, 1999.
Bond, A. Russell. *Inventions of the Great War.* New York: Century Company, 1920.
Briggs, William. *How America Got Its Guns: A History of the Gun Violence Crisis.* Albuquerque: University of New Mexico Press, 2016.
Carter, Donald A. *The U.S. Army Before Vietnam, 1953–1965.* Washington, DC: Center of Military History, United States Army, 2015.
Chase, Kenneth. *Firearms: A Global History to 1700.* New York: Cambridge University Press, 2003.
Chinn, George M. *The Machine Gun.* Vols. 1 and 2, *History, Evolution, and Development of Manual, Automatic, and Airborne Repeating Weapons.* Prepared for the Bureau of Ordnance, Department of the Navy. Washington, DC: U.S. Government Printing Office, 1952.

Chivers, C. J. *The Gun*. New York: Simon and Schuster, 2010.

Claiborne, Shane, and Michael Martin. *Beating Guns: Hope for People Who Are Weary of Violence*. Grand Rapids, MI: Brazos Press, 2019.

Converse III, Elliott Vanveltner. *History of Acquisition in the Department of Defense*. Vol. 1, *Rearming for the Cold War, 1945–1960*. Washington, DC: Historical Office, Office of the Secretary of Defense, 2012.

Cook, Philip J., and Kristin A. Goss. *The Gun Debate: What Everyone Needs to Know*. New York: Oxford University Press, 2014.

Cox, John Woodward. *Children Under Fire*. New York: Ecco, 2021.

Davidson, Osha Gray. *Under Fire: The NRA and the Battle for Gun Control*. New York: Holt, 1993.

Department of the Army. *Field Manual, No. 23–8—U.S. Rifle, 7.62MM, M14 and M14E2*. Washington, DC: Department of the Army, May 7, 1966.

———. *Field Manual, No. 3–22.9 Rifle Marksmanship: M16A1, M16A2/3. M16A4 and M4 Carbine*. Washington, DC: Department of the Army, April 2003.

———. *The M16A1 Rifle: Operation and Preventive Maintenance*. Illustrated by Will Eisner. Washington, DC: U.S. Government Printing Office, 1968.

Department of Defense. *U.S. Army Operator's Manual for M16, M16A1 Rifle*. Lexington, KY: Pentagon Publishing, 2018. Reprint of 1990 manual.

Diaz, Tom. *The Last Gun: How Changes in the Gun Industry Are Killing Americans and What It Will Take to Stop It*. New York: New Press, 2013.

———. *Tragedy in Aurora: The Culture of Mass Shootings in America*. Lanham, MD: Rowman and Littlefield, 2019.

Dizard, Jan E., Robert Merrill Muth, and Stephen P. Andrews Jr., eds. *Guns in America: A Reader*. New York: New York University Press, 1999.

Eisenhower, Dwight D. *Mandate for Change, 1953–1956*. Garden City, NY: Doubleday, 1963.

———. *Waging Peace, 1956–1961*. Garden City, NY: Doubleday, 1965.

Ellis, John. *The Social History of the Machine Gun*. Baltimore: Johns Hopkins University Press, 1975.

Enthoven, Alain C., and K. Wayne Smith. *How Much Is Enough? Shaping the Defense Program, 1961–1969*. New York: Harper and Row, 1971.

Ezell, Edward. *The Great Rifle Controversy*. Mechanicsburg, PA: Stackpole Books, 1984.

Fallows, James. *National Defense*. New York: Random House, 1981.

Feldman, Richard. *Ricochet: Confessions of a Gun Lobbyist*. Hoboken, NJ: John Wiley and Sons, 2008.

Ferrell, Robert H., ed. *The Diary of James C. Hagerty, Eisenhower in Mid-Course, 1954–1955*. Bloomington: Indiana University Press, 1983.

Ford, Roger. *The Grim Reaper: The Machine-Gun and Machine-Gunners*. London: Sidgwick and Jackson, 1996.

Franklin, William B. *The Gatling Gun for Service Ashore and Afloat*. Hartford, CT: Case, Lockwood and Brainard, 1874.

Fuller, Major General J. F. C. *Armament and History: A Study of the Influence of Armaments on History from the Dawn of Classical Warfare to the Second World War*. New York: Charles Scribner's Sons, 1945.

Gates, Daryl. *Chief: My Life in the LAPD.* New York: Bantam Books, 1993.

Hallahan, William H. *Misfire.* New York: Charles Scribner's Sons, 1994.

Harris, George L., et al. *U.S. Army Area Handbook for Vietnam. Foreign Areas Studies Division, Special Operations Research Office.* Washington, DC: U.S. Government Printing Office, September 1962.

Hatcher, Julian S. *The Book of the Garand.* Washington, DC: Infantry Journal, 1948.

Herr, Michael. *Dispatches.* New York: Knopf, 1977.

Hitchcock, William T. *The Age of Eisenhower: America and the World in the 1950s.* New York: Simon and Schuster, 2018.

Hoffman, Jon T., gen. ed. *A History of Innovation: U.S. Army Adaptation in War and Peace.* Washington, DC: Center of Military History, United States Army, 2009.

———. *Once a Legend: "Red Mike" Edson and the Marine Raiders.* Novato, CA: Presidio Press, 1994.

Howlett, Doug. *Shooter's Bible Guide to AR-15s.* New York: Skyhorse Publishing, 2011.

Ichord, Richard H., with Boyd Upchurch. *Behind Every Bush.* Los Angeles: Seville Publishing, 1979.

Jacobsen, Annie. *The Pentagon's Brain: An Uncensored History of DARPA, America's Top Secret Military Research Agency.* Boston: Little, Brown, 2015.

Kaplan, Lawrence S., Donald D. Landa, and Edward J. Drea. *History of the Office of the Secretary of Defense.* Vol. V, *The McNamara Ascendancy, 1961–1965.* Washington, DC: Historical Office, Office of the Secretary of Defense, 2006.

Kelly, Jack. *Gunpowder: Alchemy, Bombards, and Pyrotechnics: The History of the Explosive That Changed the World.* New York: Basic Books, 2004.

Kopel, David B., ed. *Guns: Who Should Have Them?* Amherst, NY: Prometheus Books, 1995.

Kyle, Chris. *American Gun: A History of the U.S. in Ten Firearms.* New York: William Morrow, 2013.

LaPierre, Wayne, and James Jay Baker. *Shooting Straight: Telling the Truth About Guns in America.* Washington, DC: Regnery Publishing, 2002.

Lassman, Thomas C. *Sources of Weapon System Innovation in the Department of Defense: The Role of In-House Research and Development, 1945–2000.* Washington, DC: United States Army Center of Military History, 2008.

Leckie, Robert. *Warfare.* New York: Harper and Row, 1970.

Leighton, Richard M. *History of the Office of the Secretary of Defense.* Vol. 3, *Strategy, Money, and the New Look, 1953–1956.* Washington, DC: Historical Office, Office of the Secretary of Defense, 2001.

LeMay, Curtis E., with MacKinlay Kantor. *Mission with LeMay.* New York: Doubleday, 1965.

Long, Duncan. *Assault Pistols, Rifles and Submachine Guns.* Boulder, CO: Paladin Press, 1986.

Longstaff, Major F. V., and A. Hilliard Atteridge. *The Book of the Machine Gun.* London: Hugh Rees, 1917.

Lott Jr., John R. *The Bias Against Guns: Why Almost Everything You've Heard About Gun Control Is Wrong.* Washington, DC: Regnery Publishing, 2003.

McNaugher, Tom L. *The M16 Controversies: Military Organizations and Weapons Acquisitions.* New York: Praeger, 1983.

Meacham, John. *Destiny and Power: The America Odyssey of George H. W. Bush.* New York: Random House, 2015.

Miller Jr., John, Owen J. Curroll, and Margaret E. Tackley. *Korea, 1951–1953.* Washington, DC: Center for Military History, Department of the Army, 1989. Reprint, 1997.

Moore, Harold G., and Joseph L. Galloway. *We Were Soldiers Once . . . and Young—Ia Drang: The Battle That Changed the War in Vietnam.* New York: Random House, 1992.

Murphy, Edward F. *The Hill Fights: The First Battle of Khe Sanh.* New York: Ballantine Books, 2003.

Nguyen, Duy Hinh. *Vietnamization and the Cease-fire.* Washington, DC: U.S. Army Center of Military History, 1980.

Orkland, Bob, and Lyman Duryea. *Misfire: The Tragic Failure of the M16 in Vietnam.* Mechanicsburg, PA: Stackpole Books, 2019.

Pauly, Roger. *Firearms: The Life Story of a Technology.* Westport, CT: Greenwood Technographies, 2004.

Poole, Walter S. *Adapting to Flexible Response, 1960–1968.* Vols 1 and 2. Washington, DC: Department of Defense, History of Acquisition in the Department of Defense Series, 2013.

Pollack, Andrew, and Max Eden. *Why Meadow Died.* New York: Post Hill Press, 2019.

Ponting, Clive. *Gunpowder.* London: Chatto and Windus, 2005.

Popenker, Maxim, and Anthony G. Williams. *Assault Rifle.* Ramsbury, UK: Crowood Press, 2004.

Rayle, Roy E. *Random Shots: Episodes in the Life of a Weapons Developer.* Bennington, VT: Merriam Press, 2012.

Reid, William H. *A Dark Night in Aurora: Inside James Holmes and the Colorado Mass Shootings.* New York: Skyhorse Publishing, 2018.

Ridgway, Matthew B., with Harold H. Martin. *Soldier: The Memoirs of Matthew B. Ridgway.* New York: Harper and Brothers, 1956.

Rose, Alexander. *American Rifle: A Biography.* New York: Delacorte Press, 2008.

Rottman, Gordon L. *The M16.* Long Island City, NY: Osprey Publishing, 2011.

Satia, Priya. *Empire of Guns: The Violent Making of the Industrial Revolution.* New York: Penguin, 2018.

Sharpe, Philip B. *The Rifle in America.* New York: Funk and Wagnalls, 1953.

Sheller, Mimi. *Aluminum Dreams: The Making of Light Modernity.* Cambridge, MA: MIT Press, 2014.

Shrader, Charles R. *History of Operations Research in the United States Army.* Vol. 2, *1942–62.* Washington, DC: Office of the Deputy Under Secretary of the Army for Operations Research, 2006.

Skennerton, Ian D. *5.56mm AR15 & M16 series (U.S. M16, M16A1, M16A2).* Philadelphia: Ray Riling Arms Books, 2005.

Smith, Anthony. *Machine Gun: The Story of the Men and the Weapon That Changed the Face of War.* New York: St. Martin's Press, 2002.

Smith, Rick. *The End of Killing: How Our Newest Technologies Can Solve Humanity's Oldest Problem.* Vancouver: Self-published, 2019.

Smith, W. H. B., and Joseph E. Smith. *The Book of Rifles*. Harrisburg, PA: Stackpole, 1963.

Sorley, Lewis. *Honorable Warrior: General Harold K. Johnson and the Ethics of Command*. Lawrence: University of Kansas Press, 1998.

———. *Westmoreland: The General Who Lost Vietnam*. New York: Houghton Mifflin Harcourt, 2011.

Stevens, R. Blake, and Edward Ezell. *The Black Rifle: M16 Retrospective*. Cobourg, Ontario: Collector Grade Publications, 1994.

Tapper, Jake. *The Outpost: An Untold Story of American Valor*. New York: Little, Brown, 2012.

Taylor, John M. *An American Soldier: The Wars of General Maxwell Taylor*. New York: Presidio Press, 1989.

Telfer, Major Gary L., Lieutenant Colonel Lane Rogers, and V. Keith Fleming Jr. *Marines in Vietnam: Fighting the North Vietnamese, 1967*. Washington, DC: History and Museums Division Headquarters, U.S. Marine Corps, 1984.

Tenner, Edward. *Why Things Bite Back: Technology and the Revenge of Unintended Consequences*. New York: Knopf, 1996.

Thibodeau, David, and Leon Whiteson. *A Place Called Waco: A Survivor's Story*. New York: PublicAffairs, 1999.

Thompson, Harry C., and Lida Mayo. *United States Army in World War II: The Technical Services—The Ordnance Department: Procurement and Supply*. Washington, DC: Office of the Chief of Military History, Department of the Army, 1960.

Tregaskis, Richard. *Vietnam Diary*. New York: Holt, Rinehart and Winston, 1963.

Vizzard, William J. *Shots in the Dark: The Policy, Politics, and Symbolism of Gun Control*. New York: Rowman and Littlefield, 2000.

Waldman, Michael. *The Second Amendment: A Biography*. New York: Simon and Schuster, 2014.

Walter, John. *The Rifle Story: An Illustrated History from 1756 to the Present Day*. London: Greenhill Books, 2006.

Watson, Robert J. *History of the Office of the Secretary of Defense*. Vol. 4, *The Missile Age, 1956–1960*. Washington, DC: Historical Office, Office of the Secretary of Defense, 1997.

Weeks, John. *Infantry Weapons*. New York: Ballantine Books, 1971.

Weinberger, Sharon. *The Imagineers of War: The Untold Story of DARPA, the Pentagon Agency That Changed the World*. New York: Knopf, 2017.

Weiner, Tim. *Legacy of Ashes: The History of the CIA*. New York: Anchor Books, 2007.

Wested, Odd Arne. *The Cold War: A World History*. New York: Basic Books, 2017.

Wheeler, James Scott. *Jacob L. Devers: A General's Life*. Lexington: University of Kentucky Press, 2015.

Whitney, Craig R. *Living with Guns: A Liberal's Case for the Second Amendment*. New York: PublicAffairs, 2012.

Wilson, Robert L. *Ruger and His Guns: A History of the Man, the Company and Their Firearms*. New York: Simon and Schuster, 1996.

Winkler, Adam. *Gunfight: The Battle over the Right to Bear Arms in America*. New York: W. W. Norton, 2011.

SELECTED FILMS, VIDEOS, AND AUDIO RECORDINGS

ABC Television Network. *The Vietnam War*. Part 106, "The M16: What Went Wrong?" January 6, 1968. Transcript via *Small Arms Review*.

ArmaLite/Fairchild Industries. *AR-10 Rifle* promotional film. https://archive.org /details/AR10_Promotion.

Smithsonian Institution Archives. "Oral History Program, Video Collection, Twentieth Century Small Arms, Collection Division 1: (Eugene Morrison) Stoner, Sessions 1, 2, 3." http://siarchives.si.edu/research/videohistory_catalog9532 .html.

U.S. Department of Defense. "M16A1 Rifle-PART II-FIELD EXPEDIENTS, July 1, 1968." https://archive.org/details/gov.dod.dimoc.28805.

U.S. War Department. "U.S. Army Cal. .30 M1: Principles of Operation." Army Services Forces, Signal Corps Production, 1943. https://www.youtube.com /watch?v=iKVZmgjEdrU.

SELECTED PAPERS, JOURNAL ARTICLES, EARLY ARTICLES, AND THESES

Abrams, Daniel. "Ending the Other Arms Race: An Argument for a Ban on Assault Weapons." *Yale Law and Policy Review* 10, no. 2 (1992): 488–519.

"Aircraft Company Rifle As Basic Weapon." *Science News-Letter* 71, no. 8 (Feb. 23, 1957): 114.

"The Aluminum Rifle." *Time*, December 3, 1956, 21–22.

Andrieu, Guillaume. "L'Évolution des armes d'infanterie du ST 44 Allemand à l'AK 47 Soviétique de 1942 à 1960." *Guerres mondiales et conflits contemporains* 2010/2 (no. 238): 19–41.

Avakame, Elorm F. "The Problem with 'Common Sense' Gun Control." *Harvard Kennedy School Review* XVII (2017): 15–16.

Baldwin, Hanson W. "Slow-down in the Pentagon." *Foreign Affairs* 43, no. 2 (January 1965): 262–80.

Brezenski, T. F. "Inside the 23rd Congressional District (FL) Gun Violence Task Force: Real-Time Crisis Policymaking in the Wake of the Marjory Stoneman Douglas School Shootings." *Journal of Multidisciplinary Research* 10, no. 1–2 (Spring–Summer 2018): 35–49.

Calfee, Dewey E. "Limited Range Test of the M16 Rifle with Eight Types of Rifles and Hand Grenades." Directorate of Armament Development, Det 4, Research and Technology Division, Air Force Systems Command, Eglin Air Force Base, Florida, January 1965.

Carten, Fred. "Blue Ribbon Defense Panel, Case History: The M16 Rifle; One Point of View." Staff Report B-3, Appendix B, March 9, 1970.

Chu, Vivian S. "Federal Assault Weapons Ban: Legal Issues." *Current Politics and Economics of the United States*. Congressional Research Service Report, February 14, 2013.

Clossman, Nick, and Chris Long. "A Business Case Analysis of the M4/AR-15 Market." Joint Applied Project, Naval Postgraduate School, Monterey, CA, September 2015.

Cook, Philip J., Bruce A. Lawrence, Jens Ludwig, and Ted R. Miller. "The Medical

Costs of Gunshot Injuries in the United States." *JAMA* 281, no. 4 (August 4, 1999): 447–54.

de Jager, Elzerie, Eric Goralnick, Justin McCarty, et al. "Research: Lethality of Civilian Active Shooter Incidents with and Without Semiautomatic Rifles in the United States." *JAMA* 320, no. 10 (September 11, 2018): 1034–35.

Donahue, Capt. Patrick J. "The Danger of Poor Training Management: The U.S. Army in Korea—July 1950." Maneuver Center of Excellence Libraries, MCoE HQ Donovan Research Library, Korean War Student Paper Collection. https: //mcoepublic.blob.core.usgovcloudapi.net/library/DonovanPapers/korea /STUP3/A-F/DonahuePatrickJ%20CPT.pdf.

Downs, Steven L. "Exploring Police Preparedness for Active Shooter Attacks." Dissertation manuscript for Northcentral University, School of Business and Technology Management, San Diego, February 2019.

Dreier, Peter. "Roots of Rebellion: Massacres and Movements: Challenging the Gun Industrial Complex." *New Labor Forum* 22, no. 2 (Spring 2013): 92–95.

Ehrhart, Maj. Thomas P. "Increasing Small Arms Lethality in Afghanistan: Taking Back the Infantry Half-Kilometer." Monograph for School of Advanced Military Studies, United States Army Command and General Staff College, Fort Leavenworth, Texas, 2009.

Eisenhower, Dwight. "Military-Industrial Complex Speech, 1961." The Avalon Project, Yale Law School, Lillian Goldman Law Library. http://avalon.law.yale .edu/20th_century/eisenhower001.asp.

Ezell, Edward Clinton. "Cracks in the Post-War Anglo-American Alliance: The Great Rifle Controversy, 1947–1957." *Military Affairs* 38, no. 4 (December 1974): 138–41.

———. "The Search for a Lightweight Rifle: The M14 and M16 Rifles." PhD thesis for Case Western Reserve University, June 1969.

FBI. "RESMURS Case (Reservation Murders)." Official FBI history website. https: //www.fbi.gov/history/famous-cases/resmurs-case-reservation-murders.

Fleegler, Eric. "Firearm Violence: Mass Shootings and the Numbing of America." *JAMA Internal Medicine* 179, no. 5 (May 2019): 610–11.

Fox, James Alan, and Monica J. DeLateur. "Mass Shootings in America: Moving Beyond Newtown." *Homicide Studies* 18 (2014): 125–45.

Gorman, Paul F. "The Secret of Future Victories." Defense Advanced Research Projects Agency, Institute for Defense Analyses, February 1992.

Hallock, Richard R. "M16 Rifle Case Study." Prepared for the Chairman of the President's Blue Ribbon Defense Panel, March 16, 1970.

Hinrichs, Robert Dale. "Rifle Development, Standardization, and Procurement in the United States Military 1950–1967." MA thesis for Iowa State University, 2009.

Hobart, Major F. W. A. "Small Arms Profile 22: Armalite Weapons." In *Small Arms in Profile*, ed. A. J. R. Cormack. New York: Doubleday, 1973, 179–200.

Jacobs, James B., and Kimberly A. Potter. "Keeping Guns out of the 'Wrong' Hands: The Brady Law and the Limits of Regulation." *Journal of Criminal Law and Criminology* 86, no. 1 (Autumn 1995): 93–120.

Kern, Maj. Danford Allan. "The Influence of Organizational Culture on the Acquisition of the M16 Rifle." Master's thesis for the University of Wisconsin, Madison, 1994.

Kinnard, Douglas. "President Eisenhower and the Defense Budget." *Journal of Politics* 39, no. 3 (August 1977): 596–623.

Klein, Yoram, David Shatz, and Pablo A. Bejarano. "Case Study: Blast-Induced Colon Perforation Secondary to Civilian Gunshot Wound." *European Journal of Trauma and Emergency Surgery* 33, no. 3 (June 2007): 298–300.

Knox, Michael A. "Crime Scene Behaviors of Rampage School Shooters: Developing Strategies for Planning, Response, and Investigation of Multiple-Victim Shooting Incidents on School Campuses." Dissertation for the Department of Justice and Human Services, Nova Southeastern University, Ft. Lauderdale, FL, 2018.

Koper, Christopher S., and Jeffrey A. Roth. "The Impact of the 1994 Federal Assault Weapons Ban on Gun Violence Outcomes: An Assessment of Multiple Outcome Measures and Some Lessons for Policy Evaluation." *Journal of Quantitative Criminology* 17, no. 1 (March 2001): 33–74.

LeFave, Donald George. "The Will to Arm: The National Rifle Association in American Society, 1871–1970." PhD thesis for the University of Colorado, August 11, 1970.

Ling, Wang. "On the Invention and Use of Gunpowder and Firearms in China." *Isis* 37, no. 3/4 (July 1947): 160–78.

McNaugher, Thomas L. "Marksmanship, McNamara and the M16 Rifle: Organizations, Analysis and Weapons Acquisition." RAND Corporation, March 1979.

Miner, Zachary W. "A Kind of Peace: The Real World of Firearms Owners." Dissertation for University at Albany, Department of Sociology, 2016.

Moulton, MaryLee G. "Power Play: The Rhetoric of the NRA After Newtown." Thesis presented to the School of Communication, University of Nebraska at Omaha, August 2017.

"New and Lighter Rifles Signal Fairchild's Entry into Arms Field." *The Washington Post*, November 27, 1956, A14.

Strichman, George A. "Excerpt from a Report by George A. Strichman, Chairman of the Board and President of Colt Industries, Inc., Before the New York Society of Security Analysts on January 26, 1966."

Studdert, David M., John J. Donohue, and Michelle M. Melllo. "Testing the Immunity of the Firearm Industry to Tort Litigation." *JAMA Internal Medicine* 177, no. 1 (January 2017): 102–105.

Vizzard, William James. "The Evolution of Gun Control Policy in the United States: Accessing the Public Agenda." A dissertation for a doctor of public administration at the University of Southern California, December 1993.

Wozniak, Kevin H. "Public Opinion About Gun Control Post–Sandy Hook." *Criminal Justice Policy Review* 28 (2017): 255–78.

SELECTED REPORTS AND PRESENTATIONS

Advanced Research Projects Agency, Office of the Secretary of Defense. "Field Test Report, AR-15 Armalite Rifle, Final Report." OSD/ARPA Research and Development Field Unit—Vietnam, August 20, 1962.

Advanced Research Projects Agency, Project AGILE Remote Area Conflict Research and Engineering. Semiannual Report, July 1–December 31, 1963. Issued

February 1, 1964 (Unclassified 1975). Remote Area Conflict Information Center, Battelle Memorial Institute.

Broward County Sheriff's Office. "Marjory Stoneman Douglas Shooting Overview." No date. https://www.broward.org/Documents/MSD%20Overview%20 Public%204–24–18.pdf.

Ellis, Paul H. "Technical Note 1–85: An Evaluation of the Hitting Performance of the M16A1 Rifle with and Without a Sight Rib." U.S. Army Human Engineering Laboratory, Aberdeen Proving Ground, Maryland, January 1985.

Everytown for Gun Safety. "Mass Shootings in the United States: 2009–2017." https://everytownresearch.org/reports/mass-shootings-analysis.

Godel, William. Transcript of 1975 interview for a DARPA oral history of the agency. Provided by Sharon Weinberger.

Hall, Donald L. "An Effectiveness Study of the Infantry Rifle." Ballistic Research Laboratories Memorandum Report No. 593, Aberdeen Proving Ground, March 1952.

Hitchman, Norman. "Operational Requirements for an Infantry Hand Weapon." Operations Research Office, Johns Hopkins, June 19, 1952.

House Armed Services Committee. *Hearings Before the Special Subcommittee on the M16 Rifle Program, May 15, 16, 31, June 21, July 25, 26, 27, August 8, 9, and 22, 1967.* 90th Cong., 1st Sess. Washington, DC: U.S. Government Printing Office, 1967.

———. *Report of the Special Subcommittee on the M16 Rifle Program, October 19, 1967.* 90th Cong., 1st Sess. Washington, DC: U.S. Government Printing Office, 1967.

House Joint Report by Government Reform and Oversight and Judiciary Committees. *Investigation into the Activities of Federal Law Enforcement Agencies Toward the Branch Davidians.* Washington, DC: U.S. Government Printing Office, 1996.

House Judiciary Committee. *Hearings Before the Subcommittee on Crime. The Semiautomatic Assault Weapons Act of 1989, April 5 and 6, 1989.* 101st Cong., 1st Sess. Washington, DC: U.S. Government Printing Office, 1989.

Hutchings, Thomas D., and Albert E. Rahe. "Study of Man-Weapon Reaction Forces Applicable to the Fabrication of a Standard Rifle Firing Fixture." U.S. Army Armament Command—Research Directorate, October 1, 1975.

Kelly, Joseph J., and John Masengarb. "Technical Report 68–4: M14 Cost Analysis Report." Washington: Systems and Cost Analysis Division, Comptroller and Director of Programs, U.S. Army Materiel Command, October 1968.

Kent, R.H. "Report No. X-65: The Theory of the Motion of a Bullet About Its Center of Gravity in Dense Media, with Applications to Bullet Design." Ballistic Research Laboratories, Aberdeen Proving Ground, January 14, 1930. Reprinted January 1957.

Krouse, William J. "Congressional Research Office Report for Congress: Semiautomatic Assault Weapons Ban." December 16, 2004.

Senate Judiciary Committee. *Hearing on the Assault Weapons Ban of 2013.* 103rd Cong. (February 27, 2013). Washington, DC: U.S. Government Printing Office, 2017.

———. *Hearings Before the Subcommittee on the Constitution. Assault Weapons, Feb.*

10 and May 5, 1989. 101st Cong. Washington, DC: U.S. Government Printing Office, 1990.

Tschappat, Colonel William H., Colonel Ephraim G. Peyton, Commander Ernest W. McKee, et al. "Report of the Board Appointed to Recommend a Specific Caliber for Future Development of the Semiautomatic Shoulder Rifle," produced by order of the Secretary of War, and presented Sept 21, 1926. This board become widely known as "the Pig Board."

U.S. Air Force Marksmanship School, Lackland Military Training Center. Evaluation of the Colt-Armalite AR-15 Automatic Rifle, Caliber .223, August 1960.

U.S. Army, Office Chief of Staff, Office Director of Weapon Systems Analysis. Report of the M16 Rifle Review Panel. History of the M16 Weapon System. June 1, 1968.

U.S. Army Combat Developments Command, "Rifle Evaluation Study (U)." Evaluation of M14, M14 (USAIB), AR-15, AK-47, and SPIW. December 20, 1962.

Wyman, General Willard G. "Army Rifle Marksmanship Today." *Infantry.* Fort Benning, GA: United States Army Infantry School, July–September 1958, 6–14.

———. "The United States Army: Its Doctrine and Influence on U.S. Military Strategy." *Military Review*, March 1958, 3–13.

Acknowledgments

Conceiving, researching, and writing *American Gun* took years, and so many helped in its creation that to catalog them all would be a book in itself.

We spoke and corresponded with hundreds of people. Many, such as Valerie Kallis-Weber, Nadine Lusmoeller, David Wheeler, Fred Monahan, Al White, Marcus Weaver, and Tom Sullivan, spent time with us reliving the worst experiences of their lives, whether in battle or at a concert, movie theater, or school. Thank you so much for doing so. It took courage to speak frankly. We are grateful to Susan Kleinpell for spending many hours telling us stories and providing documents about her father, the inventor Eugene Stoner. Others who helped us with historical and technical aspects of the AR-15 include Jim Sullivan, Mark Westrom, Patrick Sweeney, and C. Reed Knight Jr.

Thanks to our publisher, Farrar, Straus and Giroux, and to our editor, Alex Star. Alex helped shape and improve this text you have just read in myriad ways. Thanks to many others at FSG, including assistant editor Ian Van Wye, Jane Elias, Vivian Kirklin, and Michael Goldstein. Thanks to Colin Dickerman for bringing it to FSG. Thanks to Mac-

Dowell in Peterborough, New Hampshire, for granting us a residency as we finished our manuscript. The time to write and edit was invaluable. The work of our fellow residents—Moriah Evans, Jaime Lowe, Serena Chopra, Mashuq Mushtaq Deen, Diana Guerrero-Maciá, Richard Scott Larson, Linda Geary, and others—was inspiring.

Thanks to close and careful readers of early drafts, including Ramsay McWhirter, the indefatigable Bill Rankin, Andrew McWhirter, Andrew Smith, Jefferson Clark, and Elaine Elinson. Thanks to the precise Julie Tate for her hard work fact-checking this manuscript. Other authors who provided assistance include Richard Rhodes and Sharon Weinberger.

Many current and former colleagues at *The Wall Street Journal* were supportive and helpful, including Dan Frosch, Sadie Gurman, Aruna Viswanatha, Siobhan Hughes, Louise Radnofsky, Justin Scheck, John McCormick, Ariel Zambelich, Lindsay Ellis, Lisa Donovan, Tedra Meyer, Tammy Audi, Kate Linebaugh, Ben Fritz, Steve Yoder, Josh Jamerson, Miguel Bustillo, Emily Nelson, and former editor in chief Matt Murray. A shout-out to the many current and former *WSJ*ers who have also produced or are in the process of producing great books. A partial list: Erich Schwartzel, Kris Maher, Tripp Mickle, Ben Kesling, Valerie Bauerlein, Eliot Brown, Jennifer Levitz, and Melissa Korn.

Thanks to Bret Witter, who patiently listened to Cameron McWhirter talk about the history of the AR-15 one day over lunch, and then suggested strongly that what he had heard was a book. Thanks to our agent, Peter McGuigan, who helped us form our idea and get it before publishers.

Thanks to the many librarians and research assistants who helped us across the country, from the Library of Congress and the Smithsonian Institution to presidential libraries to local and university libraries.

Cameron McWhirter thanks his family, of course—his supportive wife, Ramsay, and his two kind and intelligent children, Blythe and Finn. You three are amazing people and I am forever grateful you are in my life. Friends who aided writing and research include Tia Cudahy, John and Heather Lucas, Mike and Tara Koski, Gur Melamede and Amie Macdonald, Pamela Ferdinand and Mark Thomas, Ben Ferdinand, David Albertson, Tom Rielly, William Dentzer, and James

Schneider. He thanks Julie Johnson, his high school English teacher who showed him the power of words long ago. Thanks, of course, to Zusha. I couldn't have asked for a better coauthor. He is the epitome of a great journalist: relentless in the pursuit of facts, habitually curious, and transparently compassionate.

Zusha Elinson thanks his brilliant and beautiful wife, Annika, for her constant love, and for bringing so much joy to our lives during this long project. He is grateful for the love and support of his parents, Bob and Cecelia, who gave him a strong will and a good heart. He thanks his sister, Sarah, her husband, Rob, and their daughters for all their love and laughter. He thanks his West Coast family, Elaine, Rene, and Matt, for their loyalty and love. He is thankful for his friends Andrew, Jefferson, Ariel, Doyle, and many others who were always there and willingly talked for endless hours about the book. He thanks the people who played important roles on his path to becoming a writer, including his high school English teacher Peter Elliston, the publisher Paul Cobb, and the editor Steve Fainaru. He wishes to thank Dr. Jon Platania for his guidance. He is grateful to those who loved and inspired him and have passed on, including his friend Kirsten, Uncle Richard, his grandparents, and all his little angels. He wishes to thank his coauthor, Cam, whose brilliant writing and hard work made this book possible.

Index

Page numbers in *italics* refer to illustrations

ATF contacted for certain, 311–12; Bushmaster 2008, 249; Bushmaster profit model for, 214–15; criminal record and, 166; crisis impact on, 213, 229, 298; Freedom Group, 250, 294; gun control legislation relation to, 213–14, 300; mainstream market growth for, 239–40; mass shooters and, 166, 350; 9/11 and, 229, 238; in 1999, 213–14, 215; numbers by end of 2021, 334; political motivation behind, 293–94; private, 328; profits for gunmakers, 23, 147, 152, 158, 191, 205, 206, 213, 214–15, 217, 300; Reagan legislation restricting, 351; receivers and, 295, 336; after Sandy Hook massacre, 276–77, 278, 294; Stoner, E., royalties from, 81, 106, 217–18, 221; survivalists and, 164–65; Trump election impact on, 302–304; 2008 presidential election and, 248–49; 2022 gun legislation on, 358; *see also* background checks

gun shows: AR-15s at, 207–208, 213, 239, 379; Stoner, E., reputation at, 220, 379–80

gun testing: ammunition propellant and, 116–17; AR-10 failures in, 51–52; AR-15, 70–77, 79, 95–96, 102; ball-powder ammunition and, 118–19, 141, 146; bullets and, 64–68, 78; combat simulations in, 402n; M14, M16, and AK-47 comparisons in, 111–12; M16, 111–12, 119, 126, 402n; M16 malfunctions in, 119, 126; press on, 112–13; for semiautomatic gun ban, 188–89; weather and temperature, 72, 75–77, 79

Hallock, Richard, 76, 147, 399n, 409n; M16 study and testing under, 119, 402n; M16 support consequences, 113; retirement from military, 130, 404n

handguns: murders and suicides predominate use of, 6; owners on gun control legislation, 293; "Saturday Night Special" ban, 187, 234; Stoner, E., design for, 221–22

Harris, Eric, 212–13

Harvard Park Brims (Brims), 166–70

Henry, DeWitt, 161–62

Heston, Charlton, 201, 231

heterotopic ossification, 369–71

Hickey, George W., Jr., 114

Hill Fights battle, Vietnam, 120–23, 129–30, 402n

Hitch, Charles, 102–103

Hitler, Adolf, 27, 385n

Hoffman, Abbie, 124–25

Hole, Brandon, 342–43

Holmes, James Eagan: arrest, 262; Aurora 2012 theater shooting by, 259–67, 350; background and mental health of, 257–58; guns purchased by, 258, 265–66

Howard, James J., 130–31, 404n

Huber, Anthony, 335

hunters, 195; AR-5 for, 58; "assault rifle" for, 42, 51, 209, 243–44; big game, 88, 94, 209; decline in, 253, 255, 419n; Mini-14 popularity with, 191; rapid-fire rifle for, 152–53; rifle ownership percentage of, 174; shooting range gun usage compared with, 254; Sporter design for, 152–53; Zumbo criticism of AR-15 for, 243–44

Ichord, Richard, Jr.: M16 investigation report from, 140–42, 144; M16 in Vietnam subcommittee investigation under, 124–26, 130–40, 146, 147–48, 403n, 404n, 405n, 406n

Indianapolis mass shooting (2021), 339, 340, 342–43, 350

internet: AR-15 Gun Owners of America group on, 290–92, 294–95, 303; gun education for mass shooters on, 337, 354, 355–56; mass shooters' isolation and, 352–53